ADVANCES IN SPECIAL EDUCATION

Volume 1 • 1980

BASIC CONSTRUCTS AND
THEORETICAL ORIENTATIONS

ADVANCES IN SPECIAL EDUCATION

A Research Annual

BASIC CONSTRUCTS AND
THEORETICAL ORIENTATIONS

Editor: BARBARA K. KEOGH
*Graduate School of Education
University of California,
Los Angeles*

VOLUME 1 • 1980

JAI PRESS INC.
Greenwich, Connecticut

*Copyright © 1980 JAI PRESS INC.
165 West Putnam Avenue
Greenwich, Connecticut 06830
All rights reserved. No part of this publication may be reproduced, stored on a retrieval system, or transmitted in any form or by any means, electronic, mechanical, photocopying, filming or recording or otherwise without prior permission in writing from the publisher.*

*ISBN: 0-89232-077-X
Manufactured in the United States of America*

CONTENTS

PREFACE	vii
INTRODUCTION *Barbara K. Keogh*	ix
COGNITIVE CONSTRUCTING: LEVELS OF PROCESSING AND DEVELOPMENTAL CHANGE *Margaret S. Faust and William L. Faust*	1
MEMORY PROCESSES IN EXCEPTIONAL CHILDREN *Joseph Torgesen and Robert V. Kail, Jr.*	55
ATTENTION PROCESSES: RESEARCH, THEORY AND IMPLICATIONS FOR SPECIAL EDUCATION *Antoinette Krupski*	101
SELECTIVE ATTENTION AND DISTRACTIBILITY *Daniel P. Hallahan and Ronald E. Reeve*	141
OPTIMIZING MOTIVATION IN AN ACHIEVEMENT CONTEXT *Diane N. Ruble and Ann K. Boggiano*	183
TEMPERAMENT INFLUENCES ON THE DEVELOPMENT OF EXCEPTIONAL CHILDREN *Barbara K. Keogh and Michael E. Pullis*	239
OVERVIEW *Barbara K. Keogh*	277
AUTHOR INDEX	281
SUBJECT INDEX	291

PREFACE

This is the first in a series of volumes directed at advanced study in Special Education. While there are already a number of useful and comprehensive texts for beginning students in this field, content appropriate for advanced or graduate level students tends to be found in diverse, even fragmented sources. One purpose in this series of volumes is to organize and synthesize the content of the field at a level useful for graduate study. A second purpose derived from the belief that practice and theory are inextricably tied together. While many descriptive papers document the "state of the art" in the field and provide insight into where we are and where we have been, such description does not provide direction for the development of the field. Improved and refined practice depends upon the power of the theoretical constructs brought to bear on the applied problems. Thus, it is essential that theory and evidence be related at a level which will stimulate advances in research and application. The series as a whole was conceptualized with this goal.

Although contained in separate covers, Volumes 1 and 2 complement each other. Volume 1 is focused on the theoretical constructs which provide the basis for Special Education practices; it contains chapters on Perception-Cognition, Memory, Attention, Selective Attention, Motivation, and Temperament. Volume 2 deals with varying perspectives on applications, and is composed of chapters in which Special Education is discussed from Piagetian, psychodynamic, behaviorist, and information-processing points of view. It also contains chapters identifying possible physiological contributions to individual differences, as well as a discussion of various models of language intervention. A final chapter views Special Education from a cross-cultural perspective, putting into context a number of issues of practical concern, e.g., identification, assessment, and the like. Contributing authors in both volumes represent a variety of disciplinary fields: developmental, experimental, cognitive, social, and clinical Psychology, as well as those from cross-cultural Psychology, Anthropology, and Special Education. Despite their differing disciplinary bases, contributing authors have all been involved with research or educational/clinical practice with children, and many have had extensive experience with a variety of exceptional children.

I wish to thank all the authors for their effort and expertise, and for their willingness to take on this task. Each chapter contains information and insight of real value to the field. I also wish to thank faculty and graduate students in the UCLA Special Education program for their continuing influence on my own thinking; their critical yet supportive discussions have been invaluable. Finally, I thank those who helped put this volume together, particularly Mrs. Kay Carr, whose enthusiasm and skills are greatly appreciated.

Barbara K. Keogh
Series Editor

INTRODUCTION

Barbara K. Keogh, UNIVERSITY OF CALIFORNIA, LOS ANGELES

It is difficult to predict the long-term implications of particular events or historical periods, yet it seems fair to suggest that the past twenty years have been particularly important ones for handicapped individuals. Attitudes toward a variety of minority groups have changed dramatically, and the minority group made of handicapped or exceptional children is no exception. Formerly ignored or rejected, even actively discriminated against, the legal, social, and personal rights of handicapped individuals are now recognized. A number of accommodations and changes by the larger society have already taken place. Such change comes slowly, and is not without pain. In 1976, the Bicentenial year, the National Advisory Committee on the Handicapped titled its annual status report "The Unfinished Revolution," and certainly there has been a revolutionary air to many of the advances made by exceptional individuals and their families.

While many of the changes and opportunities sought by the handicapped minority have been accomplished through litigatory or legislative activities, a major role in the change process has fallen to the formal education system. The responsibilities have been clearly laid out in PL 94-142, the Education for All Handicapped Children Act of 1975. This major piece of legislation made formal and explicit the rights of handicapped children to a free and appropriate public education, and delineated the responsibilities of educational systems in providing services. In the process of implementing educational programs for exceptional children as specified under 94-142, a number of problems have been apparent. For the most part there is laudable intention and good will, but limited understanding and expertise. The rather narrow training base for preparing special education personnel is no longer adequate. More powerful and precise theoretical underpinnings, and more refined instructional and evaluation techniques are required. Yet, the very diversity of the field and the highly applied flavor mitigate against cohesiveness.

Special educators, like professionals in many applied fields, are borrowers. It is difficult to think of a "theory" of special education, and even cursory examination of introductory textbooks reveals the descriptive and atheoretical orientation of the field. For the most part the concepts, theories, and models which are utilized to develop programs and practices come from other disciplines. When we refer to "models" in special education we usually refer to psychological, sociological, or medical models applied to exceptional populations. To date, the majority of the theoretical constructs utilized by special educators have been taken from psychology, and from an historical perspective this is a proper source; the development of handicapped children is usually viewed as involving the same processes proposed to explain the development of nonhandicapped children. It is interesting to note, however, that both special and regular educators have begun to broaden the base of theoretical influence, incorporating concepts and ideas from a number of other disciplines, e.g., anthropology, linguistics, systems organization, and computer models. The appropriateness and applicability of these concepts await empirical test, but it is already clear that they hold promise for improved practices with exceptional children.

It is often true that as theory is translated into practice, the defining concepts become diluted, even distorted. After years of application, concepts and ideas may have been so radically transformed that they no longer maintain theoretical integrity. Practices may be justified by involving theory, but all too often the links are obscure or even nonexistent. At the same time, the critical importance of theory in advancing a field is to be emphasized. Despite its applied orienta-

Introduction

tion, special education is guided by theoretical constructs from related disciplines. It is important, therefore, that these concepts are identified, and that their relevance to special education be delineated. This volume was developed with this goal in mind. In the following chapters contributing authors address topics in Cognition-Perception, Memory, Attention, Motivation, and Temperament, as these areas are viewed as providing basic underpinnings for special education practice.

COGNITIVE CONSTRUCTING: LEVELS OF PROCESSING AND DEVELOPMENTAL CHANGE

Margaret S. Faust, SCRIPPS COLLEGE

William L. Faust, POMONA COLLEGE

All knowledge of reality starts from experience and ends in it. (Einstein, 1934, p. 14)

In light of the upsurge of interest in exceptional children and the cognitive difficulties which many of these children exhibit, the time seems ripe for examining certain developmental aspects of cognition. This paper is neither a prescription for teaching nor a review of literature in cognitive psychology. Rather, from within the broad domain of cognitive development we have selected a limited set of methodological, theoretical, and empirical issues that may explicate individual differences among children in cognitive functioning. Our emphasis upon individual differences is not in the mainstream of cognitive psychology, which has tended to assume that the cognitive processes and systems of the American adult are prototypical. However, a few theorists are "breaking ground" in a refreshing effort to perceive as figure the individual differences that once were considered ground. We shall presently take up the issues of theories which ignore and theories which attend to individual differences in some detail. To anticipate, we will first consider the meaning of the terms "development," "exceptional children," and "cognition." Once the present usage of these terms has been described, the ongoing stream of cognitive processing will be considered from a developmental point of view.

THE CONCEPT OF DEVELOPMENT

In psychology, the term "development" encompasses many kinds of changes which occur during the life span of individuals. Because these changes are usually described as a function of increases in chronological age, the impression is given that increasing age is the cause of the cognitive, emotional, or social changes. Of course, chronological age tells us only how long the individual has lived *ex utero*. Chronological age says nothing about the changes in biological and psychological structure and function that both influence and are subject to the influence of experiential factors which have occurred during the interim since conception (see discussions by Kessen, 1960; Wohlwill, 1970; Zigler, 1963). Although most developmental psychologists agree that age is not a causal variable, age is used almost universally as a convenient marker variable; it is easily measured and it is relatively unambiguous in its referent. Despite the ubiquity of its use, however, the most fruitful theories will be those which explicate significant parameters of development and their interaction throughout the life cycle, without reference to age. A developmental approach is a way of looking at stability and change in various systems; it requires a longitudinal perspective which considers how things have become as they are, and what they may become under diverse conditions.

Wherever we "cut" into the ongoing life cycle to begin an analysis, we find that any organism already has a structure with a definite set of functions and certain predisposing capacities to "become" and to adapt. The general term, "structure," may refer to patterns which are concrete, tangible things such as buildings, trees, and the central nervous system of man. Structure may also refer to more abstract patterns which must be inferred by noting a regularity or a family resemblance. The term "structure," as in cognitive structure, refers to an abstract pattern in the way thought is organized. It is discernible only by recognizing an organization in a fairly large segment of thought. If one stands too close to a large painting, one can see only spots of color and line while the pattern or structure of the picture is not apparent. Analogously, if one attends to the moment-by-moment behavior of the child the pattern or structure of thought is virtually impossible to identify.

Cognitive structures are the "common properties of the intelligent acts of a given stage of mental growth'' (Brainerd, 1978, p. 19). Unlike architectural structures, cognitive structures change from one developmental stage to another. Each stage of mental development is presumed to have its own structure and that structure is inferred by noting the regularities among behaviors that reflect thought (see section on *Operations and Structures*, p. 24). "Perhaps the most important thing to say about structure is that, as we see it, one cannot really have a detailed theory of intellectual development without it" (Flavell, 1963, p. 409). The cognitive structure existing at any moment is the outcome of immediately preceding interactions between the developing structure and ongoing experience. Developmental changes emerge in an orderly and sequential fashion, yielding novel operations, cognitive structures, and capacities to adapt. At every developmental phase, "This orderly and sequential set of changes eventuate in modes of organization not previously manifested in the history of the developing system, such that the system acquires an increased capacity for self-regulation, a larger measure of relative independence from environmental fluctuations" (Nagel, 1957, p. 16).

It should be emphasized that change is not an outcome of maturation alone, if the term "maturation" implies an unfolding of latent, preformed structures independent of the environment. Nor is change simply the result of the impact of the environment. Some theorists have been attracted by the appealing simplicity, conceptually and quantitatively, of a dichotomy between hereditary and environmental influence. They conceptualize change as either a result of biological factors (e.g.,Gesell), in which case one waits for maturation to "cure all ills," or as a result of environmental stimuli (e.g., learning theorists), in which case one uses behavior influence techniques to effect changes. The dichotomy of biological vs. environmental determinants of change is conceptually misleading because both hereditarians and environmentalists choose to ignore the complementary set of interacting determinants that influence developmental change. Each position thereupon claims that the other set has little influence on the changes observed. Although most psychologists today give lip service to the idea of an interaction between biological and environmental factors, some too easily lose sight of one or the other set of factors, treating each independently, and ignoring their interaction. Reasoning by analogy, it is as fruitless to try to parcel out biological versus environmental factors as it is to try to claim that the area of a rectangle is due more to its height than to its width. Persons who consider separately either biological or environmental factors and not their interaction are similar to young children working on conservation problems; they concentrate either on height or width, overlooking interaction, and thereby reach erroneous conclusions. (For further discussion, see Sameroff, 1975.)

The so-called "general" principles of learning cannot be generalized across individual differences among human beings nor across species (Breland & Breland, 1961). To the surprise of some, research investigations have shown, among other things, that performance can improve, and learning can occur, without reinforcement or knowledge of results; delayed knowledge of results may be more effective than immediate feedback; and rewards do not necessarily improve learning. "In fact, each one of the principles confidently enunciated by Skinner in *The Science of Learning and The Art of Teaching* now turns out to be untrue—at least in as general a sense as he believed at that time" (McKeachie & Kulik, 1974, p. 186).

Change requires a constant interplay between the phylogenetic and ontogenetic patterning of the organism and the continually changing properties of the events encountered in the environment. Such ongoing transactions account for continuity as well as orderly and sequential change. The thought, behavior, and personality of the child at any moment is the outcome of prior interactions of biological and environmental factors, and change results from the interaction between presently existing characteristics of the child and the present experiences. Thus, the most effective environment for development will not be the same for all children and certainly not so for "exceptional" children.

One difficulty in designing and implementing the most effective educational methods for different children has arisen from the penchant to conceive of the aptitudes and traits of a person as fixed (Glaser, 1972). If, instead, we view aptitudes as changing as the result of a continuous interaction between organism and environment, then it is evident that the optimum experiences and methods of instruction must progress concomitantly for each child.

IDENTIFYING EXCEPTIONAL CHILDREN

In recent years the definition of the term "exceptional" has been the focus of many articles and books, and the criteria of inclusion are a subject of intense dispute. Among the various issues, only one seems clear. The term is difficult to define because the class to which it refers is heterogeneous; it includes such subclasses as slow learners, visually handicapped, exceptionally low and high IQ, emotionally disturbed, etc. By application of the "law of the excluded middle" a dichotomy has been developed: the class of "exceptional children" is composed of all those who are not members of the "nonexceptional" class!

Differences among children are matters of degree; individual differences among human beings form an uninterrupted continuity, not two disjunctive poles of exceptional and nonexceptional. Moreover, there are a multitude of dimensions on which human beings may be compared or evaluated. We have therefore opted to leave the term "exceptional children" undefined and to use it as an umbrella term that one might deem suitable for a title of a book, chapter, or a course. Our justification for this is that any presumed "class," composed of all the variety of exceptional children, is so diverse and multifaceted that there is not a single defining characteristic which differentiates all exceptional children from all nonexceptional children. There is certainly no educational program which is optimal for all. On the other hand, certain subclasses of exceptional children, such as hearing impaired or visually handicapped, which are somewhat more homogeneous in their "exceptionality" and in their educational needs, can and should be identified. Such empirical identifications are required for research purposes and for planning and evaluating educational programs.

Even within a particular subclass, such as hyperactivity, the defining characteristics extend continuously so that there is only an arbitrary break or separation between those who have the "essential characteristic" and those who do not. Moreover, methods of identification may not serve different kinds of purposes equally well. For example, an identification of "visual handicap" that is useful for optometrists may not be useful for classroom teachers. If a child cannot see the blackboard or cannot read the size of print in the books used in the classroom, the child has a visual problem insofar as that class is concerned. It is also possible that the identification "visual handicap" might vary across groups of optometrists and researchers on visual perception as well as among teachers who teach in different classrooms. Not only should methods of identification be viewed relatively, that is, in relation to a particular goal in a given context, but they should be viewed as *tentative* formulations rather than as representations of reality about the nature of children.

One should not be a nominal realist, believing that because there is a term there must be an essence to which it refers. A scientific definition should be read from right to left (Popper, 1971, p. 14): the important information is contained in the definiens on the right side of the definition while the definiendum on the left is just the label (see also Wittgenstein, 1953, p. 3). Definitions are constructs which take their significance from the theory in which they are established; they are evaluated in light of their construct validity (Cronbach & Meehl, 1955), that is, by the pattern of empirically established relationships with other constructs. Thus, the definition of "learning impairment" is a mental construction or hypothesis temporarily "tried on for size," and not a statement about "reality." Children may be "impaired" with respect to one curriculum and not another, or in one cultural situation and not another. Moreover, a teaching strategy that may remediate one kind of cognitive difficulty may be ineffective or even detrimental for another. For example, Cromer (1970) has distinguished between poor readers whose "deficit" involved inability to identify many common words, and other children whose "deficit" involved the inability to integrate the meanings of separate words to form a meaningful sentence. Children whose difficulty was integrating meanings were helped by segmenting the sentences into phrases. Those children whose deficits involved word identification were helped by printing the words in a vertical column as a list. Identifications and definitions cannot be justified *a priori*, but, properly, may be viewed as emergent, expendable, continually refined, extended, and replaced in light of empirical and theoretical knowledge. In any case, "Nothing has so far been done, when a thing has been named" (Wittgenstein, 1953, p. 24). However much we may wish to believe otherwise, all definitions, identifications, and interpretations of their meaning are in part, at least, a function of the empirical-philosophical-theoretical orientation of the researcher.

LAWFULNESS AND INDIVIDUAL DIFFERENCES

In defining scientific terms and concepts, conducting research, and developing theories, two contrasting strategies can be identified. In this discussion we are indebted to Lewin(1935).

One strategy of theory and research, let us label it "A", begins with a class (e.g., dyslexia, minimal brain damage, hyperactivity, or aggression) and tries to identify the characteristics of the members of that class. Type "A" scientists search for characteristics which all members of the class exhibit and which distinguish members of that class from nonmembers. This type "A" strategy emphasizes differences between groups but neglects differences in degree or amount of a characteristic within a group. A scientist of the "A" persuasion might identify a class of hyperactive children and then attempt to demonstrate that hyperactive children are more easily distracted than other children. According to this "A" strategy of science, if hyperactive children are found to be more easily distracted, it is concluded that distractibility is an intrinsic characteristic of hyperactive children. Moreover, according to this logic, if distractibility is a defining characteristic that is intrinsic to the class, hyperactive children would be expected to be distractible in any ordinary situation: in school, at home, and in research settings. The research paradigm designed to test the hypothesis that hyperactive children are more distractible than other children typically involves measuring the amount of distractibility in a group of hyperactive and a group of nonhyperactive children, and testing the significance of the difference in mean scores for the two groups. Individual differences among children within either group would be described by the within-group variance, often referred to as "error variance"; such variability would be regarded as a nuisance to be minimized in order to sharpen the focus on between-group differences (Cronbach, 1957).

A type "A" theorist might argue that there are varying degrees of hyperactivity and that the more hyperactive children are more distractible and the less hyperactive are less so. If differences in distractibility among hyperactive children are a function of differences in degree of hyperactivity, then are differences in degree of distractibility among nonhyperactive children a function of differences in degree of nonhyperactivity? Such an analysis is self-annulling because the logical outcome leads to a rejection of the notion of distinct classes, each with important properties of its own.

A second group of theorists and researchers, label them "Z", propose a dimension (trait) which all persons have to a greater or lesser degree, and these theorists attempt to explain and predict the relative magnitude of that dimension, the dependent variable, as a function of various independent variables. For example, differences in activity, the dependent variable, might be considered a function of such independent variables as degrees of task demands and relevant skills, delay of gratification, expectations for appropriate personal behavior, fatigue, interest in and familiarity with task, etc.

Type "Z" theorists reason that each individual can be characterized by a different pattern of values on the relevant independent variables, and therefore each individual will have a different magnitude of the dependent variable. This "Z" strategy, then, affirms individual differences and has as a central concern the explanation and prediction of those individual differences.

Theories of the "Z" type frequently involve two kinds of propositions; some very general laws which apply to all people equally, irrespective of their individual charactieristics (an example from physics would be the proposition that all objects fall at the same rate in a perfect vacuum, irrespective of their shape, weight, size, etc.); other propositions take into account the particular, individual characteristics, since these propositions adapt the general law to differences among people and circumstances. The type "Z" researcher does not expect "laws" to be readily demonstrated either in everyday experience or in research settings because many lawful outcomes can be observed only under special conditions; often such conditions are so special that they cannot be produced even in research (e.g., the perfect vacuum in which all objects fall at a constant rate).

In the "Z" strategy, a complex prediction equation must be developed because the purpose is to predict both between-person differences under constant conditions and within-person variability from one circumstance to another. The prediction equations must consider situation, task, and person variables in predicting the magnitude of the dependent variable for each individual. Any discrepancies between the predicted and observed magnitude are considered errors, and they represent inadequacies in the theory (Meehl, 1967).

The difference between "A"- and "Z"-type theorists may be exemplifed by a cognitive problem: One of the tasks which Piagetians pose for children concerns the floating and sinking of objects. For example, a three-inch-long bottle cork might be placed on the water in a vessel where it floats. Next, a one-inch-round steel washer might be placed on the water and it sinks. To the question, "Why does this one float and that one sink?" a four-year-old child might respond, "Large things float and small ones sink." As a consequence of that answer, a very large six-inch-round metal washer is placed on the water and it sinks. The child revises the theory: "Wood floats and metal sinks." The child has been using the type "A" strategy in identifying two classes, one with the property of floating and the other with the property of sinking.

The experimenter, next, takes a small saucer-shaped metal pan and places it flat on the water where it floats. Then the pan is picked up and it is slid edge first into the water, and it sinks. Because the same metal object both sinks and floats, the child's typology is disconfirmed. The researcher will not further confuse the child, but could demonstrate that among objects which float, some float high with only a small portion below the water line, and others float low in the water; among objects that sink, some suspend part way down and others fall more or less rapidly to the bottom. There are not just two classes, floaters and sinkers, but there are gradations along a continuum from high floating to fast sinking.

Of course, we type "Z" theorists know that the principle involved depends upon the weight of the object relative to the weight of the volume of water displaced. When this principle is applied, one must take into account which part of the object enters the water first, because different volumes of water are displaced, initially, by different entry forms. Therefore, the procedure of placing the object on the water and the form of the object are important variables which must be taken into account.

In the study of the cognitive growth of children, we recognize the inadequacy of children's use of the typology of Strategy "A", Unfortunately, in research and theorizing about exceptional children, type "A" thinking is prevalent. The research literature in psychology and education is replete with type "A" hypotheses that are "confirmed" or "proven" in one study and "disconfirmed" in a later study. Articles that review the research literature sometimes seem to tally votes and weigh evidence, as if all the fundamental laws of human nature were open to ready observation under most conditions. To illustrate, some persons persist in classifying children as mixed (or not mixed) dominance. They claim that mixed dominance causes reading disability, and they ignore the research showing that children with mixed dominance differ markedly one from another in reading ability; there are good and poor readers among so-called left, right, and mixed dominant "types." Having constructed a category of mixed dominance has not helped us to predict, explain, or remediate reading problems. Often children are classified according to the "dominant" sensory channel as either visual or auditory; they are separated into those who can seriate versus those who cannot; or they are labeled hyperactive or dyslexic. Children quite literally are classified into sinkers and floaters without illuminating the relevant determinants of individual differences among them.

To be sure, in our typological analysis, we have taken a type "A" strategy in identifying two classes and describing their characteristics. We have done so because it seems to highlight the issues. Classification into kinds or types is frequently the initial strategy used in thinking about a problem and it is the beginning stage of most sciences. Moreover, at any time there are different levels of discourse in any science; analysis of behavior (and misbehavior) at one level of abstraction may be most productive when considering a number of dimensions separately, while inquiry at another level may be more effective when the components are treated as organized or related structures or classes. Sometimes, a research problem seems most amenable to a type "A" approach: e.g., Piaget's analyses of the stages of development of intelligence have been productive in the discovery of new phenomena. However, the type "A" strategy is much overused, and it often obstructs the advancement of knowledge, especially when we cling to discrete types in spite of evidence that human qualities are distributed along a continuum. The hazard of a type "A" approach is that individual differences are not taken seriously as an object of study; instead they are conceived as a nuisance or in statistical terms "error variance." The type "Z" approach, by contrast, attempts to formulate a system of interrelated propositions or laws which, taken together, can predict the ways and the extent to which individuals will differ from each other. Therefore, we propose that, whenever possible, a type "Z" strategy be used because it is based on a more differentiated theory of individual differences.

We all recognize that no group of children is homogeneous; this being the case, an appreciation of individual differences is likely to help both theorists and practitioners. If researchers could get away from using averages for describing the characteristics of groups and turn toward an analysis of individual differences, there might be greater communication among the many professionals who work on behalf of exceptional children. With such children especially, the within-group differences are particularly important, both in terms of scientific inquiry and clinical practice.

THE CONCEPT OF COGNITION

Historically, from the time of the Enlightenment and Kant's *Critique of Pure Reason,* 1781 (1929) to the beginning of the twentieth century, cognition was conceived as one of three mental faculties. In this triskelion, cognition referred to the act of knowing or to the processes (such as perceiving and reasoning) whereby knowledge was obtained; the other two faculties were affection (which referred to feelings and emotions) and conation (which referred to striving, intentions, volition, and conscious tendencies to act). This triskelion was abandoned as the analysis of mental faculties was found to be an unproductive venture. Moreover, evidence accumulated which demonstrated the interdependence between emotion and perception, and between motivation and thought, giving rise to increasingly blurred distinctions among cognition, conation, and affection. Whereas the terms conation and affection are not often used today, the term cognition has become an important label which has been transformed in meaning and incorporated into more recent conceptions of human nature. Although the term "cognitive psychology" implies different things to different people, we shall use the term cognitive to distinguish theories which postulate complex intervening processes of perceiving, reasoning, thinking, and knowing from theories that do not.

The terms perceiving, reasoning, thinking, and knowing carry surplus meanings which present some difficulties at this point. Perception may be conceived as qualitatively different from and independent of remembering. While these constructs are certainly not identical, differences between them are more in the eyes of the beholder than in the processes involved. If one of the present authors holds up her martini and asks her partner in this adventure "What is this?" the answer is presumed to involve perception. If she holds up a peanut and then puts it behind her back and asks "What was it?", the answer is presumed to involve memory. If the next day she asks "What were the two objects which I used in yesterday's demonstration?", both the martini and peanut will be named. Incoming information was received and processed for both objects. The amount and kind of processing for these two experiences seems the same, and the perception-memory distinction has not helped to clarify the cognitive fate of those experiences, that is, whether or not they were processed further, elaborated, and/or integrated with other, transformed, sensory experiences. The only difference has been that the name was requested while the martini was in sight and after the peanut had been removed. In this latter case of the peanut, the person answering attributes his experience to the past. However, both experiences were processed further and could be recalled readily the next day. Sensory experience is progressively transformed by an active, constructive process of selecting, scanning, attending, and categorizing, all of which utilize already developed cognitive structures. Processing may be fleeting and transitory, or it may continue through many different levels. As Jenkins has said,

> What is remembered in a given situation depends on the physical and psychological context in which the event was experienced, the knowledge and skills that the subject brings to the context, the situation in which we ask for evidence for remembering, and the relation of what the subject remembers to what the experimenter demands.
>
> This calls us back to considering what the subject believes and knows, when we talk of memory. It simultaneously suggests that we look to the sources of this belief and to the subject's ways of constructing and reconstructing his experience. William James pointed out that the only thing that distinguishes memory from the other higher mental processes is just that belief. He argued that there is nothing unique in the object of memory and no special faculty evident in its manifestations. Apart from the belief that the construction of the mind is attributed to the past, he saw nothing to set memory apart from perception, imagination, comparison and reasoning (Jenkins, 1974, pp. 793–94).

The distinctions among perception, learning, memory, and cognition are useful for certain purposes, but the interrelated nature of these processes is equally worthy of consideration. The processes of conation and affection need not be excluded from a cognitive theory, but *the primary emphasis should be on processes which reconstruct incoming sensory information while transforming it successively from the level of sense receptors through levels in which recognition is appraised, meaning is extracted, task-specific operations are performed, and overt acts may be planned, directed, and executed.* An act may mark a completion, or it may elicit more information, in which case the process continues.

A sequential processing model seems to be the most useful for our present purpose because a sequential processing model helps to avoid the discreteness of a multistore model of independent "boxes" [such as that proposed by Atkinson & Shiffrin, (1968)]. Our sequential processing model is somewhat similar to levels of processing as described by Craik and Lockhart (1972). However, we use levels of processing for a different purpose; Craik and Lockhart's main purpose was to explain the difference between short and long term memory. We use the model of sequential levels of processing to emphasize continuity from sensation to thought to action, as well as to highlight differences among them. In our view, the differences between short and long term memory seem more related to those structures which provide meaning in sense experience or to the strategies of metamemory (Flavell & Wellman, 1977).

A sequential processing model seems more adaptable than other models to differences among tasks and among persons. We expect that the sequence of steps used by different persons to solve the same problems need not (and often will not) be the same. Indeed, the same person sometimes may use alternative sequences of steps to solve similar or identical problems at different times. The processes required for any complex task involve a sequence of mental events, each of which takes time. However, the sequence need not be linear; earlier steps may be repeated and sequences may be reordered when used later.

The process is directed by the perceived demands of the task and especially by the criteria established by the person for successful completion of the task. The TOTE (Test-Operate-Test-Exit) process described by Miller, Galanter, and Pribram (1960) suggests one organizational structure of such a cognitive process. That is, TOTE processes determine the sequence of mental events. The extent and the steps or strategies of processing are undoubtedly determined by conative and affective as well as cognitive processes. We shall not consider the problem of sequencing in this paper; rather, we shall examine some of the general processes which may occur in the succession of cognitive structures that progressively transform incoming sensory information. Purely for the purpose of exposition, these continuously proceeding, integrated operations that characterize human cognitive processing will be considered in three discrete levels:

Level 1. The transformation of sensory information into an internal representation; "the first stage in the chain of events initiated by the stimulus situation ... is the construction of a cognitive representation of the distal environment" (Baldwin, 1969, p. 326).

Level 2. Operations on these internal representations.

Level 3. Transformation of the outcome of these operations into action.

Each of these three general levels will be considered in some detail in the following sections. Processing which takes place at only one of the three levels is undoubtedly very uncommon. Moreover, such a case would be debatable since we lack the converging operations (Garner, Hake & Eriksen, 1959) necessary to distinguish one level from another.

COGNITIVE PROCESSING: LEVEL 1

Level 1 has to do with the process of (a) receiving sensory information from a variety of receptors, each tuned to accept a specific quality of sense data, and (b) transforming these data into representations of the sensory world in a form that makes them suitable for continued processing.

Attention and Stimulus Change

The first processes at Level 1 involve establishing attention. Piaget points out that an infant in Stage 5 of the sensorimotor period (Tertiary Circular Reactions) seeks novelty and varies events in order to examine all of their possibilities. This search for novelty is more apparent at 12 to 18 months than it was earlier. "It is a remarkable thing that the younger the child, the less novelties seem new to him" (Piaget, 1963, p. 196). The very young child may not have deposited an appropriate number of savings in the memory bank so that a "new" experience can be distinguished from an "old" experience.

Numerous theorists (among them Dember & Earl, 1957; Fiske & Maddi, 1961; Haber, 1958; Hebb, 1949; Hunt, 1963; McCall & McGhee, 1977; McClelland, Atkinson, Clark, & Lowell, 1953; Piaget, 1963; Walker, 1964) have proposed that perception of change is one of the bases of attention: a moderate amount of change in stimulation is attractive whereas a sizeable change is unattractive. (The principles related to holding attention are probably different than those for attracting attention.) McCall and McGhee (1977) have reviewed considerable evidence in support of the captivating nature of moderate stimulus change. (See also Cantor & Cantor, 1964; Jensen, 1932; Munsinger & Kessen, 1964; Wachs, 1977.)

The amount of attention aroused clearly depends upon a number of situational factors in addition to extent of discrepancy. Moreover, there are individual differences in the amount of attraction aroused by any particular magnitude of discrepancy (Wachs, 1977). Clearly, by itself, magnitude of discrepancy does not fully explain all of the individual differences observed. A recent paper by McCall (McCall, Kennedy, & Appelbaum, 1977) is especially interesting because it provides a method for distinguishing (a) the decrement in attraction due to repetition of a stimulus, and (b) the increment in attraction due to the salience of the stimulus, from (c) the increase in attraction due to the discrepancy of a "new" stimulus from the previous stimulus. A stimulus-change theory of attention fits well with a levels of processing model of cognitive functioning because the arousal of attention depends upon the perception of similarity and degrees of difference, which must be based on processing of present stimulation in relation to former constructions.

Images

Only within the last century have empirically-testable models begun to supplant earlier *a priori* approaches to the basic question: How do we gain knowledge of our world? We think it is worthwhile to trace historically some of the changes in paradigms which psychologists have proposed. Before the turn of this century the accepted categories of thought were presumed to involve "images" as basic elements. These mental images were presumably developed in perception, and they were the "content" of thought. However, research in the early 1900s did not provide unambiguous support for such a position. When persons were asked to solve a simple problem mentally and to describe the process, they reported thinking of things, persons, and events. However, when they were asked what mental images they had of these things, persons, and events, their reports showed much disagreement.

> Some reported visual images, some auditory, some kinesthetic, some verbal. Some reported vivid images, some mostly vague and scrappy ones. Some insisted that at the moment of a clear flash of thought they had no true images at all (Woodworth & Schlosberg, 1954, pp. 815-816).

John B. Watson (1924) argued that images did not exist; images, "those ghostlike 'memory' pictures of objects not present to the senses" (p. 213) were illusions, not memorial illustrations. Watson maintained that thinking was behavior, namely, kinesthetic, verbal, and emotional acts; most fundamental were the motor acts of subvocal speech. Subsequent research purporting to show a relation between "thinking" and the motor movements of speech has convinced few people that thinking consists only of speech movements and nothing more. Moreover, research conducted during the 1940s and 1950s was not consistent with the hypothesis that habits were stored as tendencies to perform certain muscle movements. Therefore, Watson's assertion that thinking was simply incipient muscle movements of speech was untenable, and other models of thought were devised which were based neither on images nor on the movements of speech. One proposal, verbal mediation, posits a "language" model which presumes that when a person receives sensory information, he "translates the input-information into words, stores these words, and then uses them as the basis for his final response" (Glanzer & Clark, 1964, p. 62). While considerable evidence was accumulated which was consistent with the verbal mediation hypothesis, a growing body of evidence is dissonant with it. This later evidence indicates that other components of information besides its verbal aspects are processed. Among these, visual components re-emerge to prominence.

In an excellent series of articles, Kolers and Perkins (Kolers, 1968; Kolers & Perkins, 1969a, 1969b) examined the problems of errors which arise in recognizing lower case letters of the alphabet when they are presented in various spatial orientations. They conclude that

> while bee-dee-pee have similar-sounding names, the letter kew, which was confused with them, does not sound like them; and tee, whose name does sound like theirs, was never confused with them. The errors are clearly due not to phonetic or memorial confusion of their names but to confusions in visual processing (Kolers & Perkins, 1969a, p. 266).

In the early 1960s the visual image was endowed with nothing more than a fleeting existence. Sperling (1963) argued that "the visual image of the stimulus persists for a short time after the stimulus has been turned off, and that the subjects can utilize this rapidly fading image" (p. 21) during this fleeting moment. After that very short life the visual input was presumed to be transformed into verbal representation for storage. However, as researchers have developed techniques for distinguishing "visual" from "verbal" and for following the fate of the "visual" image, they have extended the life of the visual image (Kroll et al., 1970; Parks et al., 1972; Salthouse, 1974). What can be recalled by a subject is now thought to be based not only upon verbal categories but also upon the difficult, perhaps impossible to name visual qualities of stimuli as well (Hintzman, Block, & Inskeep, 1972; Kirsner, 1973; Klatzky & Stoy, 1974; Posner, 1969; Sheerer-Neumann, 1974).

Further, a variety of studies support the more recent position that no matter what the sense modality through which new information arrives, multiple attributes of the stimulus will be processed. Wickens (1972) has argued that, when presented with a word, persons code a variety of attributes among which are the physical properties of words, the connotative and denotative meanings, and the ways in which the word is presented and pronounced. Such multiple encoding is found not only for words but also for pictures (Goldstein & Chance, 1970) and and other stimulus information.

Constructive Nature of Perception

Some theorists (Shaw & Bransford, 1977) propose that our knowledge of the physical world is immediate and direct, that is, we see the world as it "really" is. In contrast, we maintain that our knowledge of the physical world is constructed from sensory data. Such constructions are not hallucinations—they are interpretations of more or less ambiguous sensory data. Such interpretations provide optimally predictable and meaningful experiences of the environment for an individual. The kinds and degrees of predictability and the meaningfulness of experiences (the semantic bases of cognition) are a function of developing cognitive operations and structures and of developing motivational and emotional patterns.

The external world, brought to receptors by physical energy and transformed into neural impulses, is *not* subsequently reconstructed as an isomorphic, pictorial representation of the real world. Some 50 years ago Kohler (1929) noted,

> Indeed, the waves of light entering the eye do not contain the slightest indication of any organization or any "belonging together" which may exist among the parts of the object by which they are reflected. Each element of the physical surface reflects light independently ... [As the light strikes the retina], therefore, no trace is left of those units which exist in the physical world (p. 175).

In essence, the waves of light reflected from the lines of a geometric design are independent of and indifferent to each other. They are discrete events. Kohler proposed that, in the perception of objects, there is an optimal organization of the relations between and among the isolated "bits" of energy impinging upon sense receptors, and that this organization of the physical stimulus is accomplished by constructive processing. Optimal organization does not depend solely upon the characteristics of the stimulus but it also depends upon characteristics of the person such as the "rules" for construction, memory for prior experiences with the pattern, and present feelings and motives.

The Constructive Nature of Cognitive Representation

As a very elegant demonstration of the constructive nature of the cognitive representation of designs, Kolers (1964) studied the perceived reversal of the Necker Cube design. The Necker Cube is a two-dimensional line drawing which has been constructed so that the pattern can be perceived as two different, three-dimensional cubes. Kolers placed two identical Necker Cube line drawing designs in front of the subject, one on the left and one on the right, in an apparent-motion apparatus. The cube design on the left was exposed and then it was concealed (made invisible). After a very short interval during which no cube was shown, the cube on the right was exposed. Then it disappeared, and after the same short interval, the cube on the left was re-exposed. The two designs continuously alternated exposure, with a blank period between. If the distance between the two cubes, the duration of exposure, and the blank interval are appropriate, the observer sees a single cube design oscillating back and forth, even though nothing moves. This is called perception of apparent movement. The Necker Cube design is a reversible figure because either one of the two "squares" in the line design can be seen as the front face of the three-dimensional cube. (See Figure 1, a and b.) Kolers (1964) reports that the cube sometimes reverses perspective (perceived organization switches from "a" to "b") during apparent movement. Obviously, perceived reversal during the interval in which no cube is presented must be a cognitive construction.

Perception of a continuous black line or a complex design is a cognitive construction, and changes in such construction follow a developmental course. Spielman (1976) points out that initially young children perceive lines as paths rather than as boundaries (edges enclosing objects) and that only later do they perceive those lines which are the outline of a figure as enclosing a space which is the figure. As further illustration, Braine (1978) found that young children identify one particular orientation of a nonrepresentational design as "upright" and other orientations (sideways or upside down) as "not upright" and they do not distinguish one of these non-upright orientations of a figure from another. That is, their construction system develops representations for upright versus any other orientation. Somewhat older children can distinguish between two variants of a non-upright figure, upside down versus sideways, yet they typically fail to distinguish left facing from right facing among "sideways" figures. Here the child (and adult) carry the processing further and distinguish between upside down and upright figures as well as right and left orientations. (See page 21 for further discussion of perception of the orientation of a figure.) This developmen-

Figure 1. Perceptual constructions of the Necker Cube.

THE NECKER CUBE

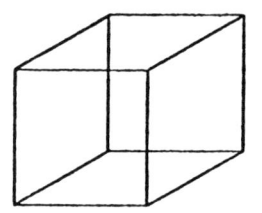

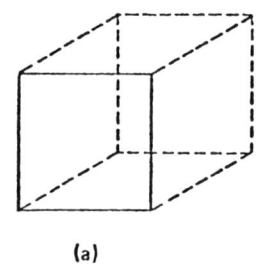

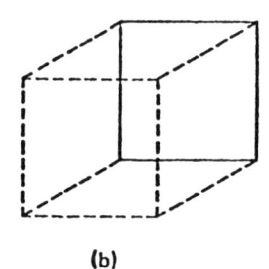

(a) (b)

tal progression is an example of levels of information processing and of developmental sequences in those levels.

Einstein (1934) noted that, in physics, "to speak of the simultaneity of two events has no meaning except in relation to a given co-ordinate system" (p. 56). Spatial coordinate systems are also required in cognitive processing. In Level 1, coordinate systems are required to maintain a stable orientation of objects in space as one tilts one's head or moves about. People, telephone poles, or other objects appear upright as we incline our heads. More specifically, Kolers and Perkins (1969a) have shown that, when letters of the alphabet are presented in various orientations (normal, rotated, inverted), or in mirror reflection, the confusions among the letters are specific to the orientation. "It is entirely conceivable that there are specific constructive strategies for building percepts of objects in the more common misorientations" (Kolers & Perkins, 1969a, p. 269). Coordinate systems can be adapted to task demands and, within a given coordinate system, one can rotate or revise relationships in order to evaluate new experiences or to consider other possible interrelationships and outcomes.

Of course, the internal cognitive representation involves much more complex processes than simply transforming a two-dimensional array of lines into a perceived three-dimensional cube which moves and reverses (as in Kolers' demonstration) or than simply perceiving the upright. The process of cognitive construction must represent space, time, sound, taste and other sensations as well as abstract ideas and relations.

One of the very important cognitive processes transforms sensory stimulation into a model of physical space—the representation which guides action, locomotion, gross and fine motor activities such as throwing, drawing, pointing, as well as complex activities such as reading. Using sensory stimulation from the real three-dimensional world around us, internal cognitive processes develop a tridimensional representation of that real world (see Attneave, 1974). In Level 1 processing, more or less ambiguous data from the senses are processed to develop a "meaningful" organization of those data.

Thus, for example, operations that separately process line, angle, and relative position must become integrated by cognitive structures which, in turn, process shape, "upright" orientation, three dimensional space, and organize a meaningful, sometimes idiomatically meaningful, world. Level 1 processing services incoming sensory information and constructs a "meaningful" organization from relatively ambiguous sensory data. The agenda of Level 1 is ordered by the sequence of sensory stimulation.

Some psychologists account for the organization of perception on the basis of the qualities of sensory stimulation. The "distinctive feature" theory (Gibson, 1969) of recognition proposes that there are essential, salient features of the physical object which distinguish that object from other similar objects and which remain invariant when the object is observed under different circumstances; according to this theory, perception of objects depends upon identifying and extracting the features of the object itself. While retinal fields certainly have feature-specific receptors, "distinctive features" do not seem to be a sufficient basis for cognitive constructions because the stimulus context and the cognitive, conative, and affective capacities of the perceiver tend to be undervalued.

There may be distinctive features which distinguish each letter of the alphabet from others when the letters are "standard" school models. However, there are certainly no invariant, distinctive features in the geometry of letters of cursive writing which would unambiguously identify each letter out of context. Nor are there distinctive features of printed letters which are invariant across the variety of standard fonts. We agree with Kolers' conclusions:

> Any letter of the English alphabet can be printed in an infinite number of ways. Any set of rules established to define a letter in terms of its geometry of hooks, bars, arches, loops, and the like can be violated easily and the letter still be recognized.... The rules can be drawn so as to minimize (or maximize) false positives and negatives, but never so as to make any imaginable instance of a letter recognizable. Thus, its specific geometry—the collocation of

marks—cannot by itself provide a sufficient basis for a letter's recognition; hence, lists of "distinctive features" based on geometry cannot by themselves account for performance (Kolers & Perkins, 1969b, p. 279).

[For a criticism of the distinctive feature theory from a linguistic position see Wittgenstein (1953), pp. 32 ff™.]

The inadequacies of a distinctive feature approach seem obvious, considering the handwriting of one of the authors. Seldom is a letter produced in the same way twice, but his typist can read his scrawl.[1] Her coordinate system is adapted to the general "style" of the letters, but more importantly, she considers the particular alternatives which develop from knowledge of the total context, from the vocabulary which the author uses, from the meaning of the piece as a whole, the meaning of the paragraph, the meaning of the sentence, and possibilities given by the shape, length and identifiable "letters" in a word. Distinctive features seem to be required in order to obtain consensus in the definition of a class, and therefore specification of distinctive features may be appropriate for communication, lexicography, or definitions. Distinctive features are presented to justify or defend, to self or others, the basis for a construction. Rather than being a principle of perceptual organization, distinctive features seem to be the result of analysis and a basis for justification of a perceptual judgment.

COGNITIVE PROCESSING: LEVEL 2

Level 1 refers to processes that transform information about the multiple attributes of objects present to the senses; these cognitive processes develop representations which are particular to the objects and events of the senses. Level 2 involves cognitive representations for objects and events which need not be present to the senses, and thus, for qualities which are abstractions. With development these symbolic abstractions become differentiated from those significates (objects or events) to which the symbols refer. The more fully a child has developed internal representations of objects and their qualities the more will the "meaning" of any event be provided by Level 2 structures and the less by momentary perceptual features. Some Level 2 representations are quite concrete and action-oriented, while others are much more abstract, symbolic. "What is a hole?" Compare the concrete answer that one child gave, "A hole is to dig" (Krauss, 1952), with the more abstract comments of six-year-old Stuart to his teacher as he was digging in the school yard:

> What is a hole? It is a thing, but it is nothing . . . I mean, there is just really not anything there—just an emptiness so you can say there is something; you can say it is a hole. . . . It is funny to have a name for something that is not. What do you call the part of a thing when it is taken away so there is a hole there? . . . A hole (whole) means something that is all right—not broken, not with any part taken away. (Teacher says, "That is another word"). But how do

you tell? (Teacher says, "The spelling is different"). But it is mixing to have words that mean the opposite and sound just the same.[2]

While Level 1 processes form mental constructions of concrete incoming sensory data, the operations of Level 2 may refer to absent events or things, and may even involve imagining novel past, future, or spatially distant events. In Level 1, sensory information is processed in such a way as to provide the best, most meaningful, organization. But Level 2 processes must be used to resolve ambiguous cases. Young children often accept sensory information "as given," whereas older children are more likely to recognize when information is inadequate and attempt to clarify it.

Cosgrove and Patterson (1977) provide an excellent developmental example of what children do when they are given inadequate information to make a decision. Their task required that the child select, from among four visually present alternatives, that one which the experimenter described. The child was told he could ask any questions which would help make a correct decision. On some trials, the description was fully adequate for the children to pick the correct alternative. On other trials, the message contained too little information to identify the correct item. When the information was inadequate, preschool, kindergarten, and second-grade children did not spontaneously request more information (and they made "unnecessary" mistakes), whereas fourth-grade children asked appropriate questions to seek more information. Level 2 processes are not at the mercy of the immediately given sensory information; as processing proceeds, if the information is inadequate to the task, a search for relevant information may be instituted.

Not only does the child with more developed structures seek information in order to resolve ambiguities, but he devises plans for remembering and for recalling. These strategies for organizing cognitions are metacognitions; they are procedural operations employed to form a plan. Young children are less likely than older children to form a strategy to remember. Young children, if asked how they could remember to take their costume for a special classroom party the next day, would most often indicate they "will remember." Older children suggest that they might put it next to the front door the night before so that they will see it as they leave for school or they might place it on top of their lunch box. Level 2 processes develop not only knowledge about the world, e.g., the content of thought, but knowledge about how to see, to learn, to remember, to solve problems—how to think. [For a detailed discussion on metamemory, see Flavell and Wellman (1977).]

The recognition of perceptual identity is carried out largely at Level 1, but the matching of a present object with an abstracted "class" of objects depends upon Level 2 processes, as does any recognition of qualitative similarities that comprise a class. For young children, the basis for inclusion of items in a class depends heavily upon perception and upon motor involvement, as implied by the phrase "a hole is to dig." For some children almost all meanings seem dependent upon motor activity or upon concrete sensorimotor experience. Such children may classify as "the same" those objects that are perceptually similar, but classify as "different" those which appear dissimilar in some conspicuous way. For example, Jacqueline, at about 2 years of age,

> used the term "*the slug*" for the slugs we went to see every morning along a certain road... she cried: "*There it is!*" on seeing one, and when we saw another ten yards further on she said: "*There's that slug again.*" I answered: "But isn't it another one?" J. then went back to see the first one. "Is it the same one?"—"*Yes*"—"Another slug?"—"*Yes*"—"Another or the same?"... The question obviously had no meaning for J. (Piaget, 1962, p. 225).

Piaget describes another episode in which Jacqueline saw her sister, Lucienne,

> in a new bathing suit, with a cap; J. asked: "*What's the baby's name?*" Her mother explained that it was a bathing costume, but J. pointed to L. herself and said: "*But what's the name of that?*" (indicating L.'s face) and repeated the question several times. But as soon as L. had her dress on again, J. exclaimed very seriously: "*It's Lucienne again,*" as if her sister had changed her identity in changing her clothes (Piaget, 1962, p. 224).

It is very difficult for some children to recognize identity when clothes, hair style, and other visible characteristics change, and it is difficult to recognize uniqueness when certain things look so much alike.

Classification is an essential activity of cognitive operations, and many difficulties arise in their application. For example:

> Arl (5:0) was shown ten little blue cones ("roofs") and three blue beads. Look. Are there more blue things or more roofs?—*More roofs*—What colour are the beads?—*Blue*—And the roofs?—*They're blue too.*—Then are there more roofs or more blue things?—*More roofs*—Why?—*Because there are a lot*—And what about the blue things?—*Everything's blue*—Are there more blue things, then, or more roofs?—*More roofs* (Piaget, 1965, p. 168).

The example illustrates the difficulty which children have when including one class within another. The child does not seem to have an operation in which blue cones and blue beads each can be subsumed within the class of blue things, and still be treated as a subgroup of a smaller quantity than the whole. For a detailed discussion of classification from the viewpoint of Piaget, see Flavell (1963).

At Level 2, operations must be developed which compose classification hierarchies and decompose and recompose constituent classes. Young children and some exceptional children often employ transductive thinking. Such transductive thinking is neither induction nor deduction based upon characteristics of a class. Rather, transductive thinking proceeds from one particular to another; it focuses on one attribute common to different instances or on the contiguity of the instances and draws conclusions from those. In transductive thinking, events which are fortuitously juxtaposed are interpreted as causally related. For example:

> Jacqueline wanted for her doll a dress that was upstairs. She said "*dress*" and when her mother refused it, "*Daddy get dress.*" As I also refused, she wanted to go herself "*to mummy's room.*" After several repetitions of this she was told it was too cold there. There was a long silence, and then: "*Not too cold.*"—Where?—"*In the room.*"—Why isn't it too cold?—"*Get dress.*" Thus, the judgment "not too cold," made to meet the need of the situation, was subordinated to the practical end in view. (Piaget, 1962, pp. 230-231).

In this transductive argument, "warm room" and "getting dress" are particulars which Jacqueline had experienced together in the past so she considered that "When the room is warm we can get the dress" is equivalent to "When we get the dress the room will be warm."

In all of its development, Level 2 depends upon the emergence of operations and structures which become relatively less dependent on perceptual impressions. That is, the older child gives more weight to cognitive inference and less to the immediate perceptual qualities. This point is elaborated in our subsequent section, *Operations and Structures* (p. 24).

In this regard, it is important to note the role of language in the development of Level 2 processing. Although thought is not limited to verbal representation, language, both spoken and written, does provide a complex means of communicating with others; also, talking to ourselves and writing down our thoughts frequently helps to clarify them. Language provides certain dimensions of meaning, and therefore it focuses attention on salient aspects of perceptual experience and affects Level 1 processes. This in turn is likely to lead to further processing and therefore to additional learning and the development of new operations. Language also provides a structure for the control of action, affecting Level 3 processes. Such structures result in more adaptable, intelligent behavior and more efficient problem solving.

Mental Rotations

For all of the importance of language, thought requires more than simply verbal mediation. Shepard has provided a demonstration of the adaptability of mental images in a series of studies on mental rotations of simple geometric figures (i.e., letters and numbers) (Shepard & Metzler, 1971; Cooper & Shepard, 1973). If subjects are asked to report whether two line drawings (of either letters or numbers) are of the same shape, the time to make a decision increases in proportion to the degree that the test figure (e.g., E) is rotated relative to the examplar (E). However, if subjects are told in advance how much the test figure will be rotated, "They can prepare for the presentation of the tilted test stimulus by carrying out a purely mental rotation of a mental image" (Cooper & Shepard, 1973, p. 250), and the time to make a decision of identity is independent of degree of rotation. This ability to rotate a mental image is clearly an important process; for example, it is instrumental in recognizing faces tilted this way or turned that way, recognizing objects in a multiplicity of orientations, or recognizing handwritten, cursive letters when a constant slant is maintained.

Contextual-Categorical Processing

The processes of Level 2 may be organized in ways represented by a dimension from contextual at one extreme to categorical at the other. The contextual strategy is based upon the concrete experiences of objects, places, and events. The organization is a kind of personal and chronological narrative in which each sensory experience is imbedded in a rich set of contiguous sensory experiences. These multiple interrelations provide both coherence for the narrative and cues for recall.

The question "What did you do today in school?" evokes anecdotal answers where all experiences support recall; the child's narrative is likely to be expressed in a context-bound language (Bernstein, 1961) which assumes that the listeners know the person, places, and things mentioned. "You know" is a common phrase in such conversations. Most of our everyday conversations and social interactions are conducted using such contextual processing.

By contrast, at the other end of the dimension representing the organization of Level 2 processes, an item is separated from the context, and nonessential experience is ignored as irrelevant and distracting. For example, if the teacher explains that "George Washington was the first President of the United States," this item of experience is not to be processed in association with other contiguous experiences such as "the teacher is wearing a red dress," "the room is hot," or "who is making that noise in the playground?" That fact is to be remembered as related to abstract categories involving presidents, governments, fathers of their country, etc., which may have been learned earlier or perhaps will be learned later. In categorical processing, an experience must be divorced or alienated from its present context and allied with other items which are logically similar.

Some exceptional children appear to be concrete in their thinking, seemingly limited to contextual processing. One child, when asked to tell how much a car cost which had just been advertised in a TV commercial, would accurately repeat the entire commercial from beginning to end. Although he was unable to select the particular information from the context, the price was always reported as part of the total commercial. Few children are as context-bound as he. On the other end of the continuum, some children seem to categorize excessively and to miss the meaning and joy of the immediate experience.

Still other children (and adults) avoid categorical processing and rely upon sequential, contextual cues in learning. For example, one third-grade boy was learning his 3-times multiplication tables using flash cards. The cards were shuffled for the first run-through but thereafter they were kept in the same order. After a few trials the lad gave the correct answer for each card. However, it was apparent that he had memorized the order of answers since he did not look at the cards, and he gave consistently wrong answers when a card was skipped. When told that he should have paid attention to the numbers being multiplied, he described some of the multipliers and multiplicands, but he also described a pencil mark and other blemishes on some of the cards.

Level 1 Recognition and Level 2 Copying

As Maccoby and Bee (1965) have pointed out, production or copying lags behind recognition of similarities and differences. A 12-month-old child can correctly place a round block into the round hole in a form board and a 21-month-old child can correctly place a square block in a form board; about one-half of the children at 2½ years of age can place three different-shaped blocks (triangle, circle, and square) into the correct holes in a form board. However, not until three years of age can half the children draw a copy of a circle, and not until five years of age can half of the children copy a square (Terman & Merrill, 1937). The greater difficulty of drawing compared with matching or placing in a form board is not due to motor incoordination (except in a very small number of cases). A triangle can be copied by age six but not until seven years of age can half of the children copy a diamond $\diamondsuit$, even when the diamond is a square rotated 45° and contains the oblique lines of the triangle.

Olson (1968, 1970) analyses the gap between recognition and copying a geometric design, reasoning that it is not filled by developing a steady hand or "by more and better perception but by the development of a way of 'representing' the perceptual event in terms of a system relating parts to the whole" (Olson, 1968, p. 178). When children copy simple geometric designs they look at the model and then look at their paper, guiding their hand movements by memorial representations. When "the reproductions of kindergarten children are compared with those of older children, several kinds of differences are apparent. In comparison with kindergarten drawings, the reproductions of an older group of children consistently show: "(1) More indications of planning ahead, resulting in improved organization and integration of the details of the design; (2) better spatial and directional orientations of the design; (3) greater critical capacity in recognition of errors and in attempts to correct them" (Faust & Faust, 1966, p. 101). Copying is more complex than matching because it involves Level 1 and Level 2 representations of the design and requires a more comprehensive coordination with motor plans (see Level 3).

Piaget maintains that the difference in difficulty between recognition and drawing originates in the difference between perceptual space and conceptual space. Perceptual space develops first in the presence of objects; it is a "complex product, resulting both from direct perception and from sensorimotor activity applied to the control and direction of the various movements" (Piaget & Inhelder, 1967, p. 451). The construction of perceptual space follows a developmental course during the sensorimotor stages of the first two years of life during which time cognitive structures are successively developed to represent the spatial relations of proximity, separation of neighboring elements, spatial succession, enclosures, and lastly, continuity. Conceptual space provides memorial representations for those occasions when the object is absent. It involves a symbolic function in which mental representations are recognized as being different from that to which they refer. Conceptual space begins to develop with the commencement of representation of events which are not present to the senses, and it evolves with the development of the structures of intelligence during the preoperational and concrete operational stages.

Perceptual space develops more rapidly than conceptual space, and each evolves its own kind of cognitive structures. The sensorimotor component employed in the construction of perceptual space is an essential foundation for conceptual space.

> In this way one can understand why there should be both continuity of perceptual and representational space, and at the same time, a gap separating the two types of structures. This gap is of such a nature that although representational space benefits from and has its imagery enriched by forms already developed by perception, it has nevertheless to reconstruct on its own plane and in the same order of succession the elementary spatial relationships (Piaget & Inhelder, 1967, p. 42).

The distinction that perceptual space develops in the presence of the object while conceptual space develops in the absence of the object may provide a way to specify the differential courses of development. Undoubtedly, different cognitive programs are required for processing information in the presence and in the absence of the object. The gap or décalage we have been discussing is implied in our distinction between Level 1 and Level 2. Developmentally, Level 2 follows and evolves from Level 1; and, in contemporaneous processing, Level 2 depends upon the products of Level 1 but conducts additional and more complex steps.

Operations and Structures

Of particular relevance to Level 2 transformations are such Piagetian structures as seriation and grouping. Piaget's primary abridgement of his works (Piaget & Inhelder, 1969) and the many excellent secondary sources describing Piaget's theory (Flavell, 1963; Furth, 1969; Ginsburg & Opper, 1969) make it superfluous to summarize this material here.

Piaget's distinction between perception and cognition is much the same as our distinction between Level 1 and Level 2. The relative utilization of Level 1 or Level 2 processing has developmental parameters. As children mature during the period of concrete operations, they tend to rely more on inference than on immediate perceptions per se, in attempting to solve problems. Consider the following children's answers to a conservation of number task in which an equal number of objects have been placed into a taller-narrower glass and into a shorter-wider glass. A four-year-old child might say that there are "more" objects in the tall jar "Because the pile is higher." That child is using a single perceptual dimension of height as the basis for judgment of number and is not considering the compensating factor of width.

Older children analyze more aspects of the problem and do not depend as exclusively upon immediate perceptual features of it, as suggested in the following examples: A five-year-old child who closes her eyes while deliberating her answer to the conservation of number task; a six-year-old child who says "That one looks like it has more, but they both have the same amount"; another six-year-old child who says "Let's count"; and a seven-year-old who concludes, "You put the same number in the tall jar and the fat jar, so they have the same." These examples, in sequence, illustrate a progression from relatively greater reliance on perceptual information toward relatively greater reliance on cognitive operations in solving the same conservation problem.

The overt behavior of problem solving can be observed, but cognitive processes cannot. Consistencies across tasks in style, strategy, and plans of cognition, however, can be inferred at various levels of abstraction. Patterns, similarities, and resemblances across tasks reflect a structure in cognitive processes but that concept of cognitive structure does not refer to an observable entity (Piaget, 1972, p. 16). Analogously, Einstein (1934) has argued that the fundamental concepts and postulates of science cannot be extracted from experience but must be constructed. In his criticism of the natural philosophers of Newton's day, Einstein wrote, they were

> possessed with the idea that the fundamental concepts and postulates of physics [were] not in the logical sense free inventions of the human mind but [could] be deduced from experience by "abstraction"—that is to say, by logical means [p. 16]. The fictitious character of fundamental principles is perfectly evident from the fact that we can point to two essentially different principles, both of which correspond with experience to a large extent; this proves... that every attempt at logical deduction of the basic concepts and postulates... from elementary experience is doomed to failure (Einstein, 1934, p. 17).

All of the concepts used to describe Level 2 events are unobservable; they are constructions, "free inventions" of the mind. Although they are not deduced from past experience, scientific utility requires that they must *imply* testable statements which are amenable to evaluation in terms of their correspondence with future observations. The concept of structure is such a "free invention" of the mind.

In this paper we use the term "cognitive structures" to refer to the lawful processes which transform physical energy into meaningful experience during perception, which comprise thought, or which transform the result of thought processes into motor instructions for behavior. On the other hand, cognitive operations refer to a particular class of internalized processes, that is, processes which can be conducted in thought. The internal characteristic of these processes becomes apparent when a person closes his eyes or tries to block out sounds in order to "think." Children who have just developed conservation of number may close their eyes while deciding lest they be distracted by the immediate visual display which may still "look" as it did in the pre-conservation period.

Consider the four-year-old child described above engaging in the conservation of number task. Although the two glasses contained the same number of objects, the young child said that the tall glass contained more. Suppose that a conservation of volume task is given next. Two equal-shaped glasses, A and A^1 are presented, and the child pours juice into the two glasses until satisfied that there is an equal amount in each. Then a taller-narrower glass and a shorter-wider glass are brought out. The child pours the juice from A into the taller-narrower glass, and from A^1 into the shorter-wider glass, and decides that there is more juice in the taller-narrower glass "because the juice is high." This pre-operational conclusion, that there is more juice in the tall glass, involves cognitive processing which emphasizes direct perceptual comparison. The same child next participates in another conservation of quantity demonstration. Two rows with seven objects in each are lined up matched in one-to-one correspondence. The child says that the two rows have the same number of objects. Then the objects in one row are spread out so that the row is now longer but less dense. The child studies the two rows and says "The long row has more." Subsequently, other conservation demonstrations are conducted in a similar fashion, and each time the child decides that one of the two equal displays has "more" than the other. The dimensions, taller-narrower, longer-less dense, etc. would be different for each task, and the content of the reason given would be different. Yet the child's answers consistently indicate that changes in spatial arrangement can influence number, volume, etc. Thus, certain consistencies in strategy can be inferred: The young child responds to only one of the relevant dimensions; to the final state or condition rather than the transformations; and to the absolute qualities of objects, tall-short, rather than their scalar attributes, taller-shorter. Each of these consistencies in approach to such problems will be termed an operation.

When a congruence in strategy of problem-solution is evident, as in the foregoing example, it encourages us to construe these similarities as cognitive structures. However, in research and everyday experience, one is likely to observe greater inconsistencies than presented in our example. The basis upon which children evaluate and give up less efficient strategies, how they develop new structures, and how they learn to apply them to different kinds of tasks is an important area for further research. In each of the foregoing demonstrations of conservation the two choices were, in fact, equal in number or in volume. Would our young child use the same strategies on tasks where the choices were actually unequal? Could these strategies be called a structure if they were used only on equal-choice tasks and not on unequal-choice tasks? Or in this latter case, would the strategies be too task-specific to be termed structures?

It is obvious that inferences implying structure need to be evaluated in many circumstances, and the breadth of problems to which each cognitive structure applies needs to be precisely stated. At present, the results of research are equivocal and challenging. In some cases presumed cognitive structures seem more task specific than previously thought and, in others, cognitive structures seem to be evident much earlier than some theories predict. Analyses of component processes have provided the basis for "discovering" structures at earlier ages. Despite these problems, it is our view that the analysis of cognitive development will be more fruitful if one starts by postulating cognitive operations and cognitive structures and then limits their domain, than if one starts with task specific elements. Thus, our view leans toward a preference for holism over what Kelly (1970) calls "accumulative fragmentalism" (p. 2).

An Application. What difference does it make if we theorize that children, as they develop more complex structures, frequently trust and depend more on cognitions than perceptions, especially since we can't see these versatile cognitions which seem to account for everything. One difference such a theory makes is in teaching. Suppose that a teacher at the end of the first week in a second-grade class asks, "How many children are present in class today?" James immediately shouts, "Twenty-three." Teacher asks, "How did you figure that out?", James replies, "We are all here except Jo." Peter says, "There are twenty-two. I counted." Unfortunately for James, two children are absent and the correct answer is twenty-two. This example raises important pedagogical issues. Is it more important for the teacher to emphasize the correct answer or the more mature strategy for deriving an answer? That is, should the teacher encourage Peter and advocate a tried and true method of counting whereby children can get the correct answer almost every time? Or should the teacher support James's method while encouraging greater care in noting absences? Will the children understand if the teacher tries to communicate the idea that there are alternative operations and that more competent persons can use a variety of them?

Invention
In our view, the most important quality of Level 2 processing is not parroting (or should it be pigeoning?) correct answers; rather "The problem we must solve, in order to explain cognitive development, is that of invention and not of mere copying" (Piaget, 1970, p. 714). The reverse is equally true: the problem we must solve in order to explain invention requires a theory of cognitive development. To construct meaning requires that structures, once acquired, can be rearranged, such as finding new relationships in representations of one's experience, looking for novel means of achieving desired ends, discovering new goals that may be sought by familiar means, or creating new models of the world. At all stages of cognition there are inventions, and at the highest stages these may culminate in a poem, a theory, a gourmet meal, or a symphony.

The most powerful thought involves invention (Piaget, 1973) which comprises both divergent and convergent thought processes. Thus, invention requires flexible constructing of both old and new meanings. Immediate sensory experience is made up of particulars, but subsequent cognitive processing constructs integrative meaning; the particulars are subordinated to this meaning of the whole, with the consequence that details are often distorted or forgotten, whereas meaning is likely to be processed further. "In general, memory is for systems, not for instances" (Jenkins, 1974, p. 792). Invention is the utilization of such semantic systems on incoming sensory information. When the semantic systems are simple, egocentric, nonreversible, etc., and the new problems are routine, the outcomes of thought are novel to that individual although not to others. But, the toddler discovering how to open the latch to get into a cupboard is inventing by the same type of process as is the individual who constructs a novel, creative product. In the latter case, though, the semantic systems are more complex, mobile, and less stimulus determined, i.e., relatively more dependent upon already developed cognitive structures.

Mentally retarded persons have difficulty in constructing multiple contexts of meaning and in reorganizing what has been learned in one context and applying it to another. Each experience seems "new" and unrelated to previous meanings. Young children, also, have difficulty in constructing meaning in novel contexts.

The mobility, flexibility, integration, and differentiation of operations required for invention seem to develop under certain conditions and not others. [See Easterbrook, (1978), *The Determinants of Free Will* for discussion of some of these conditions]. Further, some of the principles of cognitive development that explain succession of stages may provide some valuable clues to the process of invention.

COGNITIVE PROCESSING: LEVEL 3

Once the processes of Levels 1 and 2 have resulted in an internal representation of the perceptual stimuli, these must be coordinated with the demands of motor output. As noted earlier, Level 3 processes involve the transformation of Level 1 and 2 outcomes into action. Keogh[3] has given an excellent description of the difficulty children may have in transforming a memorial representation into motor instructions. Mentally retarded children were asked to copy simple geometric figures (e.g., ⊗), by walking the pattern in a "sandbox" (Keogh & Keogh, 1967). In order to understand the example, recall that almost all children perceive a triangle to be right side up when it is standing on its base, △ (Ghent, 1961). Most children, in drawing a copy, start at the top apex. However, older children can start at other places if asked. When children were copying the ○ for Keogh, they would step in the sand "at the bottom of the circle" and walk the circle and then step out of the sandbox. To make the triangle inside the circle, the child would walk around the sandbox to the "top" of it, jump backwards onto the circle, and proceed to make the side of the triangle by walking backwards from the apex to the base. These children could walk the pattern; they had adequate operations to process the design in perceptual space, but many of them seemed unable to rotate the memorial representation of the design or to start at any corner and walk forward, indicating that operations constructing conceptual space were limited.

Level 3 involves not only the transformation of visually represented forms into motor actions, but also it involves the coordination of appropriate motor patterns with intentions to execute them. An interesting and revealing illustration of this Level 3 problem may be seen in efforts to learn to wiggle one's ears, a stunt that relatively few adults have mastered.

You may believe that ear wiggling is the kind of task that is basically controlled by involuntary muscles and that there is not much to be learned about voluntary motor activities by studying involuntary acts. We suggest that the voluntary versus involuntary distinction is poorly phrased and even confusing; when one can't wiggle one's ears, the act is deemed involuntary, but once one can wiggle one's ears, an involuntary activity becomes a voluntary one! Some time ago, Bair (cited in Kimble & Perlmuter, 1970) conducted a study of ear wiggling in which many of his subjects acquired this skill. Persons were selected who could not wiggle their ears, and Bair taught at least some of his subjects to do it successfully. Subjects reported that the task seemed almost impossible because they had no idea of what they should "do" in order to wiggle their ears. The following quotation from Kimble and Perlmuter (1970) describes problems which Bair's successful learners encountered:

1. The first successful voluntary movements of the ears occurred as part of a much larger facial contortion involving a lifting of brows and vigorous grimacing. Once this occurred and the subject detected the movement even in a minimal way, the ear movement began to be differentiated from the general response.
2. Matters of attention were essential to the process in two ways: The subjects reported that it was extremely important (A) to focus attention on the response to be performed, but at the same time (B) to ignore the unwanted elements of the response. In connection with the second of these aspects, the subjects specifically stated that this did *not* mean trying to inhibit these other responses and that when they did try to do so it only made the wrong responses occur more vigorously (Kimble & Perlmuter, 1970, p. 375).

This analysis of how to learn to transform an intention into effective action reminds us of the distinction between learning to perform a new act, one which has never been accomplished before, and learning to employ an old act, at which one is proficient, in new circumstances; that is, the distinction between discovering how to wiggle your ears initially compared with later, after becoming skillful at ear wiggling, learning to wiggle them in time to the tune of "Yankee Doodle Dandy." The distinction is not as clear as the example suggests. A child who can draw a straight line may be able to do so in the vertical but not in the oblique. These are not the same act under different circumstances but different acts.

When one intends to learn a new act, one must attend to the act and the sensory experience of the act while ignoring accompanying, uninvited movements. When learning to produce an accomplished act in a new circumstance, the person will attend to the circumstantial clues while eliminating unwanted movements.

Clearly the non-ear-wiggler can recognize other people's ear wiggling. The non-ear-wiggler can intend or "try" to wiggle his ears, yet, if he can't send the appropriate motor signals the ears don't wiggle. He may grimace, blink, and/or frown, but those acts are a result of "not-knowing-what-to-do." The cognitive representations, while satisfactory for recognition of ear wiggling in others, may not be adequate for wiggling one's own ears. Serviceable cognitive representations, intentions to transform those cognitions to actions, and requisite motor skills are all necessary for proficient performance. Inferences drawn from inadequate performance or from a child's failure to perform the requisite motor acts are problematical, because it is not always clear wherein lies the problem. Some children who lack proficiency in a motor task, such as design copying, may be deficient in an appropriate cognitive representation of the design, but others may simply lack a means for producing that which they have represented mentally. For some children (e.g., cerebral palsied youngsters) the child's cognitions seem locked into a body whose motor system does not "obey" intentions or self-instructions to act. In such cases, training in motor movement is arduous and sometimes frustrating, but certainly it is gratifying when successful. In some cases, alternative motor patterns may be learned as effective substitutes. When an orthopedically handicapped child learns a new, alternative mode of behavior response, he may be able to express more complex thoughts than had seemed possible previously. The cognitive ability of some children may be underestimated unless they learn suitable modes or forms of expression (e.g., sign language or computer languages) to communicate existing cognitions.

Unless a child can transform his cognitions into an appropriate expression (communication) in overt behavior, his level of intentionality may be misjudged as well. Indeed, until a child develops ways to express his thoughts and thereby produce effects upon the outside world, he may have few intentions to express. Intentions develop in relation to sensorimotor activities that produce interesting outcomes or spectacles; only after a child recognizes a relationship between his behavior and a novel event that is assimilable, can he begin to develop a construct of intention. Subsequently the intention can be utilized to produce the desired effect. Thenceforth, what formerly had been an involuntary act (e.g., ear wiggling) may become volitionally controlled and executed intentionally.

To return to more traditional research examples, considerable work demonstrates that different coordinate systems are needed to meet the requirements of various rotations, reversals, and confusions between right and left obliques. Behavioral and neurophysiological evidence indicates that in both humans and lower animals the oblique is more difficult to process than either vertical or horizontal orientations (Appelle, 1972).

Goldstein and Wicklund (1973) report that there is a very low probability that three, four, and five-year-old children will "spontaneously" make a diagonal pattern when they are encouraged to place five checkers in a 5× 5 checkerboard matrix to create any pattern they wish. Not only are such oblique lines less likely to be produced spontaneously but lines in oblique orientation are more difficult for young children to recognize, remember, and draw than are lines which are either horizontal or vertical (Rudel & Teuber, 1963; Jeffrey, 1966; Over & Over, 1967). One oblique is often confused with another oblique.

Is the oblique orientation more difficult under all conditions? Probably not. Over and Over (1967) and Olson (1968) report that when three- and four-year-old children are given a standard line and asked to choose from among a set of lines the one that *matches* the standard, they can choose a line of identical orientation to the standard as long as they can view and compare all of the instances simultaneously (a Level 1 task). The difficulty children have in recognizing or reproducing the oblique arises under two conditions: (a) When the child must remember the orientation for a period of time in the absence of the stimulus, i.e., in successive discrimination rather than a simultaneous discrimination (requiring Levels 1 and 2); and (b) When the child must produce an oblique line, that is, place checkers, orient a stick, or draw one (requiring Levels 1, 2, and 3).

There is some evidence that the relative difficulty in copying horizontal, vertical, and oblique lines depends upon the coordinate frame in which the decision is made. When lines are presented in a circular frame (e.g., lines on circular cards, a rod rotated on a circular table, or checkers placed in circular checkerboards), the line in vertical orientation is copied as accurately as if the frame were rectangular, but lines in the horizontal orientation are less accurately copied. Lines in the oblique orientation are copied as accurately as those that are horizontal but less accurately than the vertical ones (Berman et al., 1974).

INTERRELATIONS AMONG LEVELS 1, 2, AND 3: AN EXAMPLE

The cognitive processes of these three levels certainly interact with each other, and one source of interaction is the simultaneous use of the same processing system for two purposes. Woodworth and Schlosberg (1954) describe a person who had excellent visual imagery. Her memory span for digits presented serially was greater when the digits were given auditorily than when they were presented visually. "The reason for this paradox turned out to be simple: she visualized the digits as she heard them, but the visually presented digits obliterated her images" (p. 721). The example raises the question of facilitating or interfering interactive patterns.

Brooks (1967, 1968) has proposed that the development of a visual image of an object or situation is hindered by concurrently engaging in an activity which requires visual guidance (as in writing or reading); however, if the concurrent experience were auditory, it would not interfere with the development of a visual image because auditory input does not compete with visual operations. According to Brooks' hypothesis, it should take a longer time to develop a "visual image" of a floor plan of a house if you read about the plan than it would if the plan were read to you. As the words were read, you might even close your eyes to limit visual experiences while you were developing the appropriate visual image.

Brooks (1967) also proposes that there is interference if one tries to make decisions from (perform operations on) a visual image and at the same time use vision for some spatial orientation purpose. Suppose that a person had learned the aforementioned house plan as a visual image and he were asked to appraise, from memory, certain features of the design. He could more easily describe the conclusions of his analysis in words than draw a diagram to represent it. In order to draw a diagram, vision would be required of the person in guiding the spatial movements of his pencil, and such spatial use of vision would interfere with his analyses of the visual image. Several investigators (Atwood, 1971; Bower, 1970; Brooks, 1967, 1968) have provided data from adult subjects that are consistent with these hypotheses, and the phenomenon does seem robust since it is replicable by students in psychology laboratories.

A study of Fitzgerald (1977) with children as subjects is relevant to the "Brooks hypothesis." Children were identified as those who used verbal mediation in learning and those who did not. In a learning task, those children who were nonverbal mediators were helped more by naming the stimuli than were those who were verbal mediators—it may be the case that naming interfered with the development of verbal representation. Further, Atwood (1971) has elaborated the hypothesis by showing that interference may occur even when the two processing operations are not concurrent. Subjects who were given instructions to "visualize" (use visual representation) when learning word phrases heard from a tape recording were more disrupted by a visual than by an auditory activity which followed one second after hearing each phrase. On the other hand, subjects who were given instructions to "contemplate the meaning" (use semantic representation) when learning phrases heard from a tape recording were more disrupted by auditory than by visual activities which followed each phrase by one second.

LEVELS OF COGNITIVE PROCESSING RELATED TO METHODS OF TEACHING

Earlier in this paper we took the position that a comprehensive cognitive theory must attempt to explain (rather than ignore) individual differences. Since cognitive processes are functional mental events, theories of cognitive processes must take into account the characteristics of the task as well as the qualities of the child. The outcome of a situation will depend upon the skills, knowledge, and the strategies of cognitive processing which the child brings to the task, the characteristics of the task, as well as "... what is explicitly or implicitly expected of him in a given situation, what is important to him, and what he perceives to be the probable consequences of alternative behaviors'' (Hobbs, 1975, p. 119).

Until recently, there has been an overweening tendency to construe cognitive characteristics as stable, constant traits throughout the course of the life of the individual; this approach has been most common when children are identified as exceptional. When we ask, "How can we make an early identification of children who are likely to have learning problems?" the onus of being a learning problem is placed on the child (Faust, 1970). Presumably, precursors of those personal characteristics which make the child a learning problem today could have been identified in the child years earlier. If we take seriously the idea that development depends on the successive transactions between the characteristics of the present situation and the child, the fallacy of any presumed "constant trait" is evident. We suggest that aptitude, cognitive processes, and traits should be considered variable (Glaser, 1972); they change as a result of a continuous interaction between organism and environment. Optimal development is a function of the match between characteristics of the person and the qualities of experience; specifically, an optimal discrepancy between the individual's cognitive processing and present experience (the pacer) (Dember & Earl, 1957) leads to optimal development (Wachs, 1977). Therefore, optimal experiences and methods of instruction must change apace for every child if teaching methods are to match a child's readiness for them (Cronbach, 1967; Cronbach & Snow, 1976). To what should the method of teaching be matched? The child's general aptitude (IQ)? The relevant preparation to learn the particular material (amount of prior experience)? Or the cognitive structure of the child?

There are two contrasting theories of what constitutes aptitude. The first proposes that aptitude is an index of a child's "ceiling of achievement," that is, the highest level that a person could possibly attain if the circumstances were most favorable. It is often phrased as an individual's "potential" in a supporting environment. The second theory proposes that aptitude denotes the amount of time which an individual needs to reach a criterion level of achievement (Carroll, 1963). In the latter theory, differences in aptitude are construed as differences in time required to accomplish a task to an equal standard of excellence. This second view makes no assumption of a ceiling which limits the child; learning to a specified equal standard is possible for all children who persist, although the view implies that it will take different amounts of study time to reach that standard. The proposition that aptitude equals time to learn to a criterion is easily assimilated into a cognitive processing point of view such as the one elaborated in this article; the ceiling notion not only has significant evidence against it (Bloom, 1974), but is discordant with current cognitive-developmental theories.

Optimal Learning and Optimal Match

That children differ from one another in rate and quality of material learned in school cannot be doubted. We suggest that this difference is not simply a function of present characteristics of the child nor solely a function of methods of instruction. Differences in learning are the derivative of the match among the methods of instruction, the requirements of the task, and the task-relevant cognitive processes of the learner. [For a sophisticated analysis of the methodology required to study this proposition, see Golding (1975).] We hope that our levels of processing analysis will provide some additional stimulation and help in this direction.

Not only do children differ from each other in level of complexity in cognitive structures and in type of information-processing strategy preferred, but teachers differ from each other in their methods of teaching, including their relative reliance on visual, auditory, or other modes of presenting material. One method or style of teaching may not in any absolute sense be superior or inferior to another method or style, but the effectiveness of each may depend specifically upon the way in which any given approach interacts with individual differences among children in cognitive structures and in strategies for learning the particular task at hand.

Despite years of research and practical experience in special education, differential methods of teaching have not yet been identified which are optimally effective for children of different levels of general intelligence. However, there is evidence to indicate that methods of teaching are differentially effective for children with various amounts of initial skill and/or information (Egan & Greeno, 1973; Mayer, Stiehl, & Greeno, 1975; Tobias & Ingber, 1976). The rate at which a student learns depends on what he already knows (that is, the information or skills he brings to the learning situation). If time is fixed, a student who is prepared starts higher, learns faster during the given time, and ends up proportionately further ahead of students who began with less preparation (Anderson, 1976; Bloom, 1968, 1974; Carroll, 1963).

Recent evidence indicates that methods of teaching are differentially effective for different task-relevant cognitive operations. Egan and Greeno (1973) taught propositions in binomial probability using two methods: (1) a discovery method in which the learner proceeded by solving problems and generalizing the rules; and (2) a rule method which required the learner to interpret the rule and apply it to problems. Students were assessed on a prelearning measure of cognitive operations requisite for binomial probability derived from Piaget's theory. Egan and Greeno examined the hypothesis that the relative effectiveness of the two methods of teaching would vary with the extent of relevant cognitive structure with which the learner started. Rule-learning subjects were better than discovery learners in solving familiar problems and problems involving a direct use of rules. However, individual differences in the prelearning measures of relevant cognitive operations were not correlated with differences in performance for subjects who learned by this method. The advantage which the rule learners had on familiar problems was lost when the problems required more interpretation. This suggests that for rule learners the new rules were not well integrated into existing cognitive structures. On the other hand, for discovery learners, individual differences in the prelearning measures of relevant cognitive operations were correlated with differences in performance after learning. It is likely that cognitive operations were relevant for discovery learning because the method of learning by discovery requires conceptualizing the learning material, generating relationships between known and unknown elements, systematizing, and other operations, and consequently, new knowledge was developed out of the preexisting operations.

LEVELS OF PROCESSING AND THE MATCH

In determining the appropriate match between present cognitive characteristics of the child and teaching strategies, we should consider multiple determinants of performance. The competency-based model outlined by Hobbs (1975) is consistent with our position and suggests clearly some of the aspects of performance that are important to consider:

> ... behavior is the result of the interaction between those skills and competencies that an individual already has and the demands or expectations of others in a given situation ... If the discrepancy between what he knows or can do and what he is asked to do is too great, he will be forced to choose between responding inappropriately or not responding at all ... If, however, the discrepancy between what the child already knows or can do and what he is asked to do is optimal, then behavior that cannot be tolerated in the setting is less likely to occur ... Maintaining this optimal discrepancy requires a detailed knowledge of the behaviors that the child has already mastered (Hobbs, 1975, pp. 118-119).

At this point it will be profitable to consider the usefulness of the three levels of processing suggested in this paper by analysing a few examples in which teaching methods might be matched to individual differences among pupils with respect to their processing of information at Levels 1, 2, and 3.

Level 1: Matched to Student Differences in Level 1 Constructions

Many young children make errors in matching forms which are similar except for differences in orientation of an oblique line. A child who writes her name DONИA and does not recognize the discrepancy between her two N's may be said to have a Level 1 difficulty; she does not notice the error of the oblique. This may involve a problem in maintaining a stable coordinate system for letters in which different slants of line must be discriminated. The development of a stable coordinate system for geometric forms and letters probably depends as much upon general orientation and coordination of bodily space as it does on perceptual experience with letters, particularly since the former occurs prior to the latter. Therefore, it might be more effective to work on bodily space coordinate systems in general than on letters, such as N's in particular. Thus, if a problem is diagnosed as arising in Level 1, treatment might focus upon processes that aid perceptual construction of sensory data or the development of perceptual space. Kephart's *The Slow Learner in the Classroom* (1960) provides many interesting suggestions for such remedial programs.

Level 2: Matched to Student Differences in Level 2 Operations and Structures

Different teaching methods may be differentially effective for pupils of the same age. Consider two children, one of whom compares pairs of objects on one dimension alone—i.e., "that one is big and this one is little," and one who spontaneously compares objects on two dimensions such as height and width or who uses "vectors" (as Piaget and Inhelder, 1969, p. 89, call them) to compare objects on two dimensions, i.e., "This is taller and narrower than this one." The difference between the children is in a Level 2 operation. Sometimes, however, determining the level in which the difficulty arises is not easy.

As example, some children seem to lack shape constancy so that R and *R* and **R** are treated as different unintelligible configurations; other children reverse letters and words. Level 1 difficulties are evident when such errors are made in simultaneous judgments, that is, when the child compares different forms all visible at the same time. More frequently, however, the difficulty will be discovered in successive discrimination. In the latter case, the deficit in shape constancy would be treated as a Level 2 problem in the development of conceptual space and in the construction of meaning. Conceptual space develops in the structures of intelligence, e.g., conservation and centering. Therefore, in this latter instance, the remedial program might be focused on attempts to preclude transductive thought which emphasizes the dissimilarity: this specific shape is R; this other shape (*R*) is not congruent with the first, so it is not R.

The use of discrepancy from expectation (novelty) is also a powerful procedure at Level 2 as it confronts the child with a practical experience which is not consistent with a prediction that the child would make. In the example of Rs where the child could match correctly but not recognize "identity" in successive discrimination, disconfirmation of predictions might be used to emphasize the difficulties in concrete (transductive) reasoning based upon specific individual characteristics and not upon class concepts. While some teaching efforts might be directed to the development of a conception of the letter R as a class, much more time might well be devoted to the development of more abstract, symbolic mental operations. Constancy of letters, for school children, must be mastered on the plane of symbolic operations just as constancy of objects, in infants, must be mastered on the plane of actions and as shape constancy for simultaneous discriminations must be solved in perceptual discriminations. Eventually, identification of letters becomes embedded within integrated, flexible cognitive structures.

The most common difficulties in Level 2 involve insufficient differentiation and integration of structures to provide "meaning" or context for present experience. Inadequate connotations for words so that communication is distorted, inappropriate categories within which to integrate the present facts, inability to recognize that every event belongs to many different classes, are some examples of these difficulties. The more fully developed the cognitive structures become, the more likely is the child to recognize discrepancies in his experience, and to seek further information when initial information is ambiguous. Information seeking not only clarifies present experience but it provides a basis for increasing the complexity of cognitive processes.

Level 3: Matched to Student Differences in Level 3 Transformation of Cognitions into Action

A striking example of a difficulty in inferring the locus of a cognitive deficit (problem) comes from recent breakthroughs in teaching apes to communicate with humans. Apes were once thought to be unable to use language, because early efforts at instruction met with limited success in the production of vocal language. However, when apes were given a different form of expression, such as sign language, it was discovered that they could communicate much more complex idea-sequences than had been expected. Notwithstanding some disagreement over whether apes use "true" language, we now know that we had underestimated their cognitive ability. Specifically, we had incorrectly inferred from Level 3 difficulties in vocal functioning that the apes had Level 2 disabilities in cognition. We need to be equally creative in arranging means for children with Level 3 deficits to communicate, to solve problems, to express intentions—in general, to translate cognitions into action. We urgently need now some very specific theories of cognition and complementary methods of instruction so that psychoeducational research can become better focused on this central problem. Task-relevant cognitive processes of children must be taken into account in evaluating the effectiveness of different teaching strategies.

ASSESSMENT OF OUTCOMES

A persisting issue underlying empirical research on educational questions involves the criterion: What do we value and thereby deem to be "effective" outcomes of schooling? Some theorists and researchers tend to select behavioral outcome measures which share stimulus elements and specific response patterns in common with the original learning task. A developmental-cognitive approach would require us to select a variety of outcome measures, some of which would be simply new examples of the problems taught, others of which might require extensive adaptation of either the principles learned or the operations developed. Methods of teaching necessarily must be evaluated in terms of whether or not the student learned the skills taught; the methods should also be judged by whether the student learned cognitive strategies (structures) which are applicable to a very wide variety of problems. This implies, of course, that an appropriate test of the effectiveness of a method of teaching will be possible only after some time interval during which the operations learned have a chance to develop supporting structures and to instigate new operations. A developmental-cognitive approach clearly enriches, yet complicates the assessment of educational outcomes.

OTHER IMPLICATIONS

Different children use different "citizen band" channels to process information. When asked to spell a word orally without resort to paper or pen, some children close their eyes and seem to visualize the letters, others pronounce the letters and seem to hear the correct sequence, and some write in the air and read the sky-written motor patterns. The significance of these differences in favored processing channels is often underestimated. A pertinent example comes from the different cues which children use to recognize a word when hearing it than when visually perceiving it. In visual identification of pseudo-words (trigrams) kindergarten and first-grade children tend to use a single letter, usually the first letter, which is particularly salient, rather than the configuration of the whole word (Marchbanks & Levin, 1965; Williams et al., 1970). However, fifth- and sixth-graders use both the first letter and shape of word to recognize a three-letter pseudo-word, but they depend somewhat more on shape. College students rely much more on shape than first letter in identifying pseudo-words visually (Rayner, 1976). By contrast, in auditory identification of pseudo-words, kindergarten and first- and second-grade children tend to rely on sequences of letters, usually the final two letters, particularly when the final segment rhymes with the examplar to be identified (Kuenne & Williams, 1973). It should be noted that different features of a word are used to identify it when it is presented visually than when it is presented auditorily; in addition, there is a developmental change in the feature(s) of a word attended to when recognition is visual versus auditory. Finally, there may be a sex difference in the course of development for auditory word recognition (Kuenne & Williams, 1973).

The processing of sensory information constructs not only spatial representation but representations of other sensory qualities as well, e.g., audition, touch, taste, smell, kinesthesis, equilibrium, etc. Some methods of teaching, for example Montessori, have emphasized the importance of variation and diversity in sensory experience. Objects of different texture, hardness, shape, etc., are identified by touch without seeing them in order to develop these other discriminations. Although these other modalities will be mentioned only briefly, they should not be considered unimportant in the education of children. A beginning step in learning to read involves some coordination between new visual symbols and known auditory speech patterns. Because reading disabilities are often associated with difficulties in auditory discrimination or articulation (Harris, 1968; Wepman, 1960), an analysis of cognitive processes that focuses only on visual discrimination of letters and words as a basis for reading is certainly much too limited.

Consider the possible interactions between teachers' preferred styles of teaching and children's preferred modality of processing new information. A number of possible matches and mismatches can be imagined. In beginning stages of reading, as we have mentioned above, children tend to rely on the initial letter of a word to recognize or identify it. If a first-grade child misreads a word, should the teacher help by pronouncing the first letter of the word? Based on Brooks' (1967, 1968) work, we are inclined to expect that a teacher's pronunciation of the first letter of a troublesome word might be beneficial for children who use visual imagery to process words, but disruptive for children who use auditory processing. In the latter case the auditory channel would be overloaded with competing, same-modality information.

In extracting meaning from printed words and sentences, some children rely more heavily on auditory or acoustical properties of the words, in representing them internally. Other children rely more upon a visual means of processing the verbal material. There will be a continuous spectrum of children between these extremes. Reading aloud might be more disruptive for children whose customary channel of processing is auditory than for children who use visual imagery. Verbal correction by the teacher for errors made in reading might cause similar interference, and it would affect particularly children who rely on acoustical concepts of words.

We expect that such "channels of processing" will be related to prior experience and the structures developed from those experiences. These channel preferences will be more or less situation and task specific. We are referring above to the specific task of processing written material in learning to read. We would not expect the modality preferences to be transsituational. That is, we explicitly reject the class conception of "visual" or "auditory" learners which has been a focus of much controversy in special education.

Further extrapolation from a "channels of processing" model might provide a different way of explaining why recognition of speech patterns and of geometric designs is easier than reproducing them. It could be argued that the auditory representation of a word or idea becomes disrupted by the very act of producing the speech sounds, especially in the beginning stages of language learning. Similarly, among kindergarten children, the actual process of drawing designs may seriously disrupt the cognitive operations on the visual representations of them; such interference by competing use of the visual channel would result in copies which are rotated, fragmented, or otherwise distorted reproductions of the child's cognitive representation of the design. These difficulties in reproducing auditory and visual patterns may disappear after children develop more complex cognitive operations for matching and processing incoming information, as for instance, by time-sharing a common visual channel while perceiving, analyzing, and reproducing a geometric design.

BOUNDARIES OF COGNITION

In this section we will take up some of the issues and concepts at the interface between cognition and other domains that are usually treated as motivation and emotion. Although cognitive psychologists do not often concern themselves with such issues, cognitive processes do not function independently from emotional or motivational ones. While it may be possible to identify contrasting behavioral outcomes of certain cognitive, motivational, or emotional processes, it can also reasonably be presumed that information coming from any sensory modality or from memory becomes processed through common channels; it becomes transformed through common levels, whether this information is concerned with "cognition, conation, or affection." It is almost certainly the case that further illumination of the variegated problems of disabled learners will depend upon models which incorporate rather than exclude motivational and emotional parameters. Particularly with exceptional children, measures of IQ and other cognitive assessments have been found to be inadequate predictors of success on many learning and problem-solving tasks. Stevenson and his co-workers have speculated that "such factors as differences in motivation and attention may be more important in determining individual differences for atypical groups of Ss than they are for an average group" (Stevenson et al., 1968, pp. 31-32).

Cognitive psychologists have developed some powerful laboratory techniques in which noncognitive variables are randomized across conditions while a limited type of cognitive processing is investigated, e.g., reaction times to carefully selected stimuli. (*Editor's note:* See chapter by Krupski in this book.) Although it is possible to select laboratory tasks that are relatively purified and free of emotional and motivational content, the generalizations derived from such materials may contribute only a limited understanding of children's basic (fundamental) processes of learning and problem-solving in real-life situations. Variables that have been experimentally controlled so that their influence is constant across conditions cannot be presumed to be unimportant. Rather than stress presumed points of demarcation among cognition, motivation, and emotion, we will illustrate ways in which information processing and cognitive operations are united and common to the three. In emphasizing the essential wholeness of the same ongoing process, we are elaborating a Piagetian position, although similar views have been taken by others (Hebb, 1949; Hunt, 1961, 1965; Kelly, 1955; Leeper, 1965; White, 1959). So as not to stray too far afield in this rich and challenging interface, we will limit our discussions to a few examples.

Intentionality

Let us take up the concept of intentionality first. Intentions, in our triskelion model fall under the rubric of conation, that is, volitional striving. The notion that striving is essential for successful performance is as much a part of our American heritage as is the "myth" of Horatio Alger and the prescriptions in *McGuffey's Readers*. American teachers and parents for generations have admonished children to "try." Beliefs about the importance of "trying" are implicit when lack of effort is attributed to children who fail to learn. To label a child "lazy" implies that the onus is on the child and if he only "tried" he could succeed in learning. Cases of "laziness" tend to be easily dismissed with the familiar but empty phrase, "He could if he would." Such pseudo-explanations of children's learning problems are not very useful because they do not illuminate the determinants of "trying" or "willing." Indeed, the concept of laziness is a class conception (type "A" reasoning) which is based on an implicit assumption that willing is "free" of constraints, determinants, and influences (Easterbrook, 1978).

Watson's behaviorism in the early part of this century repudiated such explanations and proclaimed that any analysis of "will" was futile; indeed, Watson rejected all unobservable causes of behavior such as "will" or "volition," just as Skinner (1962) does today. Adherents of behaviorism as well as nativists of the Gesellian school both are inclined to reject the proposition "He could if he would." For different reasons, they argue that ability determines performance and therefore they propose that "A child would if he could." The behaviorist position assumes that if a child were taught to make appropriate responses through proper reinforcement contingencies, he would perform them. For the nativist, maturational readiness, acquired over time, presumably explains the quality of a child's performance. Similar views characterize those who believe that "intelligence" or "lack of intelligence" determines a child's level of achievement in school.

None of these viewpoints is adequate, because each considers only one aspect of the multitude of factors that enter into achievement outcomes. Each view attributes to the child a different problem: not trying, not giving the correct response, not being "ready," or not being intelligent enough. If we take a cognitive-developmental view, we are more likely to hunt for the component processes and sequential stages through which intentions, mature cognitive structures, and behavioral alternatives develop and become integrated, as well as the ways in which teaching strategies or learning opportunities might be matched to them. The latter approach is obviously more complicated and difficult, but in the long run it is likely to produce better theories and more effective teachers and learners.

If we take a cognitive-developmental approach to intentionality, we see that several components of "can" and "try" are inextricably interwoven. At the initial step of information processing, incoming information is transformed by existing structures; that is, construction of an event by an individual is the first stage of the process (Baldwin, 1969). Level 1, as we have described it, does not "purify" information into colorless, affect-free data, nor do the stimulus features of the situation determine what will be selected in either the initial stages or later ones. Quite the contrary. Anticipations and affect-laden expectations are an integral part of the data that become transformed.

Piaget proposes that intentional behavior first emerges during the sensorimotor period, around the latter half of the first year of life. "The sensory-motor period shows a remarkable evolution from non-intentional habits to experimental and exploratory activity which is obviously intentional or goal-oriented" (Flavell,

1963, p. 107). Thus, intentionality presupposes the ability to distinguish between means and ends, a capacity to create new means, and a sufficient mobility of schemas to adapt means flexibly to ends. In Piaget's theory, unlike some others, intentional striving is not given innately nor as part of the instinctual apparatus, but it is developed or constructed by the child from his own experience in the world of objects and persons. Intentional, voluntary action stems from and develops out of an infant's efforts to make interesting sights last, to repeat interesting spectacles, and to create, in due course, new combinations of action-schemas that produce novel occurrences. In addition, the infant may try to discover "what will happen if I do this" and to test his voluntary action by noting changes in subsequent events. A consistent relationship between one's own action and a subsequent event may lead to the construction that one's action caused the event. If, after a series of tests, certain effects are presumed to depend upon one's behavior, a sense of efficacy (White, 1959), a feeling of personal causation (de Charmes, 1968), a belief in internal locus of control (Rotter, 1966) are likely consequences. (*Editor's note*: See the chapter by Ruble and Boggiano in this book for detailed discussion of motivational constructs.)

In the course of development, as a result of active, continuous processing of successive events, more mature, complex, differentiated and mobile structures emerge. Among other things, these structures culminate in more efficient strategies for attending, for gaining further information, for learning to learn, and for intending to produce increasingly novel events. Hence, cognition, intentionality, and sustained interest develop concomitantly, hand in hand (Sroufe, 1972).

From the child's continuing experience he develops beliefs about the extent to which the application of personal effort and ability counts or makes a difference. Uniquely constructed out of individual experiences in dealing with the world, expectations of ability or inability to control events differ markedly across people. Whether we believe we can influence events makes a great difference in what we do in relation to particular situations.

A psychological state of "helplessness" (Seligman, 1975) may develop when one finds little or no correspondence between one's efforts to control or to produce changes in the world and the actual happenings in the world, that is, when outcomes appear to be independent of one's voluntary effort, when events occur with the same likelihood, whether or not one tries to influence them. The belief that certain events lie outside the realm of our causal influence is an important component of our construction of reality. Were it not for such beliefs in the futility of our efforts against certain intractable objects or inevitable events, we might consume and waste inordinate amounts of energy and time attempting to change that which is resistive and unchangeable, beating our heads against a stone wall, as it were. Of course, our beliefs about the relationship of our efforts to outcomes need not be "true." We may believe that we can have no effect on a situation when, in fact, we could influence it if we tried, or we may believe that we did have an effect when we did not. Personal beliefs and expectations about the relevance of one's effort to changes in the world may be called "cognitions," but they are also pregnant with motivational and affective implications and meanings: feelings of joy, disappointment, delight, frustration, and anxiety. A child who is more successful in effecting changes in his world by his intentional efforts will be more likely to extend the domain of his intentional effort and to enjoy it than is a child who perceives that his efforts matter not to success or failure of the outcome.

Most people believe that what they intend to teach is what the child learns (or does not learn, as the case may be). The father who helps his daughter solve a math problem undoubtedly believes that the child will feel achievement at getting the correct answer and will learn how to solve such problems; the father does not imagine that the daughter might learn that she can't do math problems without help. Similarly, the mother who pays her son for carrying out the trash is probably acting on the belief that the boy will learn responsibility, not avarice.

What will be inferred by the child, from a given series of encounters, is the relation between personal intentions, actions, and outcomes. This inference does not necessarily correspond with the consequences that are hoped for or intended by the adult. When the child's goals in a situation differ from the adult's goals, then the same outcome may be interpreted as success by one and failure by the other. Thus, the informational meaning of the situation depends upon the learner's personal goals, and it changes with successive experiences; the salient dimensions of the experiential event will be construed and coded by the child according to his evaluation of his own efficacy in achieving his intended goals.

Information Versus Reward

What difference does it make whether we apply cognitive-developmental concepts or the concepts of reinforcement to the issues of teaching and learning? This question involves (a) ethical issues concerned with the nature of valuable and desirable goals as well as the justification of means to achieve those goals, and (b) empirical issues. The empirical side asks: When is reward more effective and when is it less effective for learning? What are some of the consequences of extrinsic reinforcement on a child's conception of himself and his world? How do external reinforcements affect self-motivation, the learning of attitudes, and future interest in achieving competence and efficacy?

Cognitive theories focus upon the relevance, to the learner, of information about the relation of outcomes to intentions and about the relation of personal estimations of success and failure to aspirations. In this context, extrinsic rewards are often disruptive and detrimental. One writer (Levine & Fasnacht, 1974) reports that he "had the rare experience of watching his five-year-old son keep his room tidy for several days." In the best of operant traditions, the author gave his son a toy as a reward for tidiness. Not only was the room never voluntarily cleaned again, but a reward was demanded for many other once-routine responses: "Will I get a reward if I give you a hug?", etc. (p. 817). One conclusion in the article just mentioned is: "Based both on theoretical considerations and on practical experience, we feel that token (reward) approaches will do more harm than good when applied in what is an increasingly promiscuous manner" (Levine & Fasnacht, 1974, p. 816). Not only may extrinsic rewards do harm by producing an acquisitive attitude but they may interfere with the efficacy of learning by distracting attention from the task at hand. Surprising as this may seem, under many conditions "the use of material reinforcers produces poorer performance than purely symbolic ones" (Spence, 1970, p. 109). A great deal of evidence has accumulated recently to show that children's self-motivation and interest in a task *decrease* when extrinsic rewards are expected for engaging in the task. The phenomenon is known as the negative effect of extrinsic rewards on intrinsic motivation (Condry, 1977; Deci, 1971; Lepper, Greene & Nisbett, 1973; Levine & Fasnacht, 1974; Notz, 1975).

Many studies and outcomes of practical programs are consistent with the notion that reinforcement influences behavior. When reinforcement is contingent upon a particular act, that act is likely to increase in frequency under circumstances in which the reward seems likely to be forthcoming. When the reward becomes a goal, satisfaction in doing the task diminishes. Control of behavior is readily demonstrable but the cost to cognitive development may be very high. Maximum development of intelligence requires an elaboration of cognitive structures commensurate to task structures. Cognitive structures develop most satisfactorily not by repetition but through elaboration in which "... the conclusions reached through experience are likely to be in the form of new questions which set the stage for new ventures" (Kelly, 1970, p.21).

An individual who is interested in learning, who seeks to expand his understanding and competence, will continue learning and developing new strategies and cognitive processes later on. Furthermore, engaging in activities for their own sake is important for cognitive development because changes in cognitive structures are more likely when a child's experience matches well with his existing conceptions and structures (Hunt, 1965). Moderate discrepancies from expectation are interesting and facilitate growth; greater intrinsic pleasure is derived from mastering problems that are challenging than from those that are easy (Harter, 1974). In summarizing the recent evidence on the effects of task-extrinsic rewards on the cognitive-motivational-affective decisions about which we are concerned, Condry says:

> ... in general, compared to non-rewarded subjects, subjects offered a task-extrinsic incentive choose easier tasks, are less efficient in using the information available to solve novel problems, and tend to be answer oriented and more illogical in their problem-solving strategies. They seem to work harder and produce more activity, but the activity is of a lower quality, contains more errors, and is more stereotyped and less creative than the work of comparable nonrewarded subjects working on the same problems. Finally, to return to the

point of departure, subjects are less likely to return to a task they, at one time, considered interesting after being rewarded to do it. The facts appear true of a wide range of subjects doing a wide range of tasks. Attempting to account for these facts is a formidable challenge (Condry, 1977, pp. 471-472).

The conditions which lead to a decrease in interest and in intrinsic motivation should be specified carefully and precisely because the phenomenon has important educational implications.

Anxiety

There are many ways to conceptualize the term anxiety; most personality and motivational theories include the construct of anxiety and attempt to explain certain aspects of learning and behavior in terms of it. In his theory of personal constructs Kelly (1955) defines anxiety as "recognition that the events with which one is confronted lie outside the range of convenience of one's construct system" (p. 495). This interesting conception of anxiety suggests that the absence of constructs or knowledge may be anxiety-producing because events are uninterpretable and meaningless within that domain of experience. Not only is it impossible to "intend" to produce effects that lie outside one's own construction system, but anticipations of change and confirmation of prediction are not possible without relevant cognitive conceptions. This suggests that a child's failure to learn in one cognitive domain may influence his subsequent perception of that domain as one which is chaotic and unpredictable. A child who has already failed in one school task not only has no effective constructs to succeed in the task, thereby raising anxiety, but whatever predictability he has in this area depends mainly upon his expectation that he will fail. A circular and cumulative process of impoverishment may result, because anxiety also affects perception and hence subsequent processing. Leeper (1965) has expressed it this way: "Whatever perception or cognition gets developed first will tend to obstruct the development of other perceptions or cognitions" (p. 32). Moreover, under anxiety and threat the perceptual field is narrowed; attentional focus is confined to only a limited aspect of the situation. If perceptual "pickup" is limited, further stages of processing have meager data, and adequate learning or appropriate problem solution is unlikely.

Although the results of anxiety are not necessarily detrimental to learning and problem solving (Leeper, 1948; McKeachie & Kulik, 1975) the preponderance of research finds a relationship between measures of anxiety and academic performance (Hill & Sarason, 1966). However, many inconsistencies have been obtained for various subjects, tasks, instructional conditions, and types or degrees of anxiety (Phillips et al., 1972). Many models and hypotheses have been proposed to account for the findings, and we will add to the confusion by suggesting that the diverse consequences of anxiety be analysed in relation to the three levels of information processing described in this chapter. Furthermore, we propose that developmental changes in cognitive structures probably alter the nature of the interaction between conditions that give rise to anxiety, and the consequences of anxiety on information processing.

The debilitating effects of anxiety upon intellectual performance have been attributed to the disruption of a broad spectrum of cognitive processes including attention, perceptual scanning, semantic coding, memory span, memory retrieval, utilization of informational feedback, availability and utilization of "plans" or strategies, and selection of appropriate behavioral alternatives. Yet, the increased arousal that characterizes anxiety states may, under some conditions, facilitate task performance. Coping strategies that are developed to defend against anxiety may be adaptive under special circumstances, but not under all conditions. Because of the complex nature of the consequences of anxiety and the interactions between anxiety and cognitive performance, it would seem fruitful to analyze sequentially the influences of anxiety on the three levels of information processing proposed above. To reiterate, there is no clear delineation or demarcation between the successive levels of information processing; moreover, developmental changes occur within each level.

Cognitive processes of Level 1 (which encompass the reception and transformation of presently impinging stimulation) show significant disruption under anxiety. Narrowing of the perceptual field, reduced attention to "incidental" cues, loss of concentration under conditions of excessive stimulation or understimulation, and whatever mechanisms one wishes to propose to account for "perceptual defense" or "perceptual sensitization" are included here.

Level 2 processing encompasses mental constructions of events which may be temporally and spatially distant, absent, partially remembered, or even imaginary. Among the variety of anxiety-related disruptions on Level 2 processes, we suspect that a rather direct interference with information processing may occur in a particular channel. For instance, verbal material has been shown to be particularly vulnerable to disruption under anxiety. Consistent with this, Stevenson and Odom (1965) found that the most negative effects of anxiety on children's performance of five learning tasks occurred on the two tasks which most directly involved verbal materials, namely, a paired-associates and an anagram task. Following Brooks' (1967, 1968) model discussed earlier, it seems not improbable that anxiety-laden content, such as thinking self-deprecating auditory messages, might preempt the verbal channel and thus intrude upon reading or other kinds of acoustic processing, just as recalling visual images picturing past failure might intrude upon visual processing. This is an alternative view and interpretation for distractibility and absence of attention that is often noted among children who are failing to learn. The child who dwells upon past failure may preempt the preferred learning channel, thereby disrupting learning; as failures multiply, the interference effect increases.

Operations and other "plans" and strategies for accessing, transforming, or processing information are characteristic of Level 2. Typical effects of anxiety upon Level 2 include disruptions in remembering and in sequencing thoughts or plans for action. Such disruptions may be manifested in inflexibility and rigidity in thought.

Level 3 disruptions include stereotyped responding, uncoordinated cognitive and motor output, inability to delay responding, and making motor responses that are incompatible with task demands. Increased stuttering and the slurring of speech under high anxiety are further examples of Level 3 effects.

Epstein (1972) has conceptualized three basic sources of anxiety, or conditions for its arousal. "Primary overstimulation" is the most fundamental of the three sources; its corresponding feeling state is one of being overwhelmed and bombarded by stimulation. The second source is "Cognitive incongruity," and the third is "Response unavailability." These three sources correspond fairly neatly with our three levels of processing, and will be discussed in relation to them.

Primary overstimulation can and does occur even in adulthood, for instance when intense auditory, visual, or tactual stimulation is prolonged to a painful degree. However, primary overstimulation is a more characteristic condition and easier to imagine in relation to infants, who are adapted to relatively narrow ranges of auditory, tactual, kinesthetic, and equilibratory stimulation. Because of individual differences in thresholds for incoming stimulation and differential sensitivity to various sensory modalities, even at birth (Escalona, 1968; Thomas et al., 1963), babies are affected differently by a given degree and type of stimulation. Some babies react strongly to stimulation that others ignore. Yet, one would suspect that all infants who are threatened by sudden changes in stimulation would be overwhelmed by a roller-coaster ride that most older children would enjoy! Primary overstimulation may best be analyzed in relation to processes of Level 1. Epstein notes that it is difficult to separate it entirely from Cognitive incongruity, the second source, for reasons that are similar to our inability to distinguish absolutely Level 1 from Level 2. That is, "overstimulation" may be, in part, produced by the lack of cognitive significance of the stimulation and not by the physical intensity alone. Nevertheless, the limits of tolerance for or adaptation to different kinds of "overstimulation" normally change throughout the course of development. They should not be thought of as biologically or immutably fixed.

Cognitive incongruity involves a mismatch between a cognitive structure or "plan" and the person's experience in the world; experiences that are too discrepant to integrate into existing cognitive structures lead to negative affect, withdrawal, and anxiety (Sroufe, 1977); gross violations of expectations of many sorts give rise to anxiety. Generalizing from a review of studies Epstein says:

> Individuals have a need to organize the data of the world into a consistent and integrative predictive system, and disturbance and a high level of excitation results when the system or its elements, corresponding to hypotheses, are disconfirmed, or seen as inconsistent with each other (Epstein, 1972, p. 304).

Experiences that are meaningless, in the sense that they cannot be assimilated into one's construction system, are a source of anxiety centered upon Level 2. This type of stress and disorganization is likely to occur when rather effective strategies developed earlier in life no longer bring predictable outcomes, for instance, when a child leaves home for the first time to begin kindergarten, or when a traveler experiences "culture shock" in a radically different country. Anxiety may arise when one's strategies and plans are not differentiated enough or sequenced properly and sufficiently in relation to all the demands and expectations of a new environment, whether in school or a different culture.

Cognitive incongruity contributes to Response unavailability, the third source of anxiety, just as Level 2 processing affects the behavioral alternatives characteristically available at Level 3. But Response unavailability may arise for other reasons as well, including the lack of skill in performing the required behavioral sequences, inability to inhibit or to delay responding appropriately, and conflict between competing, antagonistic responses.

A Summary Statement

The cognitive-developmental approach taken here suggests that any human decision for action depends upon a complex series of cognitive processes, each component of which almost invariably follows a developmental course. The meaning of any encounter of a child with a learning environment depends upon both what the child brings by way of structures and the relevant aspects provided by the situation. The effective teacher and the "intelligent" environment (Stone & Church, 1973) match well with these individual, developmental characteristics.

FOOTNOTES

1. V. Cannon, Personal communication, January 1978, confirmed by drafts produced.
2. A mimeographed copy of this comment was given to the authors by L. Joseph Stone, 1969.
3. B. Keogh, Personal communication, November 11, 1977.

REFERENCES

Anderson, L. W. (1976) "An empirical investigation of individual differences in time to learn." *Journal of Educational Psychology* 68: 226-233.

Appelle, S. (1972) "Perception and discrimination as a function of stimulus orientation: The 'oblique effect' in man and animals." *Psychological Bulletin* 78: 266-278.

Atkinson, R. C., & Shiffrin, R. M. (1968) "Human memory: A proposed system and its control processes." In K. W. Spence & J. T. Spence (eds.), *The psychology of learning and motivation*, Vol. 2. New York: Academic Press.

Attneave, F. (1974) "How do you know?" *American Psychologist* 29: 493-499.

Atwood, G. (1971) "An experimental study of visual imagination and memory." *Cognitive Psychology* 2: 290-299.

Baldwin, A. L. (1969) "A cognitive theory of socialization." In D. A. Goslin (ed.) *Handbook of socialization theory and research*. Chicago: Rand McNally.

Berman, P. W., Cunningham, J. G., & Harkulich, J. (1974) "Construction of the horizontal, vertical and oblique by young children: Failure to find the 'oblique effect.'" *Child Development* 45: 474-478.

Bernstein, B. (1961) "Social class and linguistic development: A theory of social learning." In A. H. Halsey, J. Floud, & C. A. Anderson (eds.) *Education, economy, and society*. Glencoe, Ill: The Free Press.

Bloom, B. S. (1968) "Learning for mastery." *Evaluation Comment* 1(2).

———(1974) "Time and learning." *American Psychologist* 29: 682-688.

Bower, G. H. (1970) " Analysis of a mnemonic device." *American Scientist* 58: 496-510.

Braine, L. G. (1978) "A new slant on orientation perception." *American Psychologist* 33: 10-22.

Brainerd, C. J. (1978) *Piaget's theory of intelligence*. New York: Prentice-Hall.

Breland, K., & Breland, M. (1961) "The misbehavior of organisms." *American Psychologist* 16: 681-684.

Brooks, L. R. (1967) "The suppression of visualization by reading." *Quarterly Journal of Experimental Psychology* 19: 289-299.

——— (1968) " Spatial and verbal components of the act of recall." *Canadian Journal of Psychology* 22: 349-368.

Cantor, J. H., & Cantor, G. N. (1964) "Observing behavior in children as a function of stimulus novelty." *Child Development* 35; 119-128.

Carroll, J. B. (1963) "A model of school learning." *Teachers College Record* 64: 723-733.

Condry, J. (1977) "Enemies of exploration: Self-initiated versus other-initiated learning." *Journal of Personality and Social Psychology* 35: 459-477.

Cooper, L. A., & Shepard, R. N. (1973) "The time required to prepare for a rotated stimulus." *Memory and Cognition* 1: 246-250.

Cosgrove, J. M., & Patterson, C. J. (1977) "Plans and the development of listener skills." *Developmental Psychology* 13; 557-564.

Craik, F. I. M., & Lockhart, R. S. (1972) "Levels of processing: A framework for memory research." *Journal of Verbal Learning and Verbal Behavior* 11: 671-684.

Cromer, W. (1970) "The difference model: A new explanation for some reading difficulties." *Journal of Educational Psychology* 61: 471-483.

Cronbach, L. J. (1957) "The two disciplines of scientific psychology." *American Psychologist* 12: 671-84.

———(1967) "How can instruction be adapted to individual differences? In R. M. Gagné (ed.), *Learning and individual differences*. Columbus, Ohio: Charles E. Merrill.

———, & Meehl, P. E. (1955) "Construct validity in psychological tests." *Psychological Bulletin* 52: 281-302.

———, & Snow, R. E. (1976) *Aptitudes and instructional methods: A handbook for research on interactions*. New York: Irvington Press.

de Charms, R. (1968) *Personal causation*. New York: Academic Press.

Deci, E. L. (1971) "Effects of externally mediated rewards on intrinsic motivation." *Journal of Personality and Social Psychology* 18: 105-115.

Dember, W. N., & Earl, R. W. (1957) "Analysis of exploratory, manipulatory, and curiosity behaviors." *Psychological Review* 64: 91-96.

Easterbrook, J. A. (1978) *The determinants of free will*. New York: Academic Press.

Egan, D. E., & Greeno, J. G. (1973) "Acquiring cognitive structure by discovery and rule learning." *Journal of Educational Psychology* 64: 85-97.

Einstein, A. (1934) *Essays in science*. New York: The Philosophical Library.

Epstein, S. (1972) "The nature of anxiety." In C. D. Spielberger (ed.) *Anxiety: Current trends in theory and research*, Vol. 2. New York: Academic Press.

Escalona, S. K. (1968) *The roots of individuality*. Chicago: Aldine.

Faust, M. S. (1970) "Cognitive and language factors." In B. K. Keogh (ed.), "Early identification of children with potential learning problems." *Journal of Special Education* 4; 335-346.

———, & Faust, W. L. (1966) "Pathology or immaturity: An evaluation of changes in form copying." In M. P. Douglass (ed.) *Thirtieth Yearbook of the Claremont Reading Conference.*
Fiske, D. W., & Maddi, S. R. (1961) *Functions of varied experience.* Homewood, Ill.: Dorsey Press.
Fitzgerald, J. M. (1977) "Verbalization effects in young children: Classification abilities and the use of labels." *Child Development* 48: 604-611.
Flavell, J. H. (1963) *The developmental psychology of Jean Piaget.* Princeton, N.J.: D. Von Nostrand.
———, & Wellman, H. M. (1977) "Metamemory." In R. V. Kail, Jr., & J. W. Hagen (eds.) *Perspectives on the development of memory and cognition.* Hillsdale, N.J.: Lawrence Erlbaum Associates.
Furth, H. G. (1969) *Piaget and knowledge: Theoretical foundations.* Englewood Cliffs, N.J.: Prentice-Hall.
Garner, W. R., Hake, H. W., & Eriksen, C. W. (1956) "Operationism and the concept of perception." *Psychological Review* 63: 149-159.
Ghent, L. (1961) "Form and its orientation: A child's eye view." *American Journal of Psychology* 74: 177-190.
Gibson, E. J. (1969) *Principles of perceptual learning and development.* New York: Appleton-Century-Crofts.
Ginsburg, H., & Opper, S. (1969) *Piaget's theory of intellectual development.* Englewood Cliffs, N.J.: Prentice-Hall.
Glanzer, M., & Clark, W. H. (1964) "The verbal-loop hypothesis: Conventional figures." *American Journal of Psychology* 77: 621-626.
Glaser, R. (1972) "Individuals and learning: the new aptitude." *Educational Research* 1(6): 5-13.
Golding, S. L. (1975) "Flies in the ointment: Methodological problems in the analysis of the percentage of variance due to persons and situations." *Psychological Bulletin* 82(2): 278-288.
Goldstein, A. B., & Chance, J. E. (1970) "Visual recognition memory for complex configurations." *Perception and Psychophysics* 9(2b): 237-241.
Goldstein, D. M., & Wicklund, D. A. (1973) "The acquisition of the diagonal concept." *Child Development* 44: 210-213.
Haber, R. N. (1958) "Discrepancy from adaptation level as a source of affect." *Journal of Experimental Psychology* 56: 370-375.
Harris, A. J. (1968) "Diagnosis and remedial instruction in reading." In H. M. Robinson (ed.) *Innovation and change in reading instruction.* Sixty-seventh Yearbook of the National Society for the Study of Education. Chicago: University of Chicago Press, pp. 159-194.
Harter, S. (1974) "Pleasure derived by children from cognitive challenge and mastery." *Child Development* 45: 661-669.
Hebb, D. O. (1949) *Organization of behavior.* New York: John Wiley.
Hill, K., & Sarason, S. B. (1966) "The relation of test anxiety and defensiveness to test and school performance over the elementary school years: A further longitudinal study." *Monographs of the Society for Research in Child Development* 31(Serial No. 104).
Hintzman, D. I., Block, R. A., & Inskeep, N. R. (1972) "Memory for mode of input." *Journal of Verbal Learning and Verbal Behavior* 11: 741-749.
Hobbs, N. (1975) *The futures of children.* San Francisco: Jossey-Bass.
Hunt, J. McV. (1961) *Intelligence and experience.* New York: Ronald.
———,(1963) "Motivation inherent in information processing and action. In O. J. Harvey (ed.) *Motivation and social interaction.* New York: Ronald.
———.(1965) "Intrinsic motivation and its role in psychological development." In D. Levine (ed.) *Nebraska Symposium on Motivation.* Lincoln: University of Nebraska Press.
Jeffrey, W. E. (1966) "Discrimination of oblique lines by children." *Journal of Comparative and Physiological Psychology* 62: 154-156.

Jenkins, J. J. (1974) "Remember that old theory of memory? Well, forget it!" *American Psychologist* 29: 785-795.
Jensen, K. (1932) "Differential reactions to taste and temperature stimuli in newborn infants." *Genetic Psychology Monographs* 12: 361-479.
Kant, I. (1929) *Critique of pure reason.* N. Kemp Smith (trans.). London: Macmillan.
Kelly, G. A. (1955) *The psychology of personal constructs.* Vol. 1 & 2. New York: Norton.
———— (1970) "A brief introduction to personal construct theory." In D. Bannister (ed.) *Perspectives in personal construct theory.* New York: Academic Press.
Keogh, B. K., & Keogh, J. F. (1967) "Pattern copying and pattern walking performance of normal and educationally subnormal boys." *American Journal of Mental Deficiency* 71: 1009-1013.
Kephart, N. C. (1960) *The slow learner in the classroom.* Columbus, Ohio: Charles E. Merrill.
Kessen, W. (1960) "Research design in the study of developmental problems." In P. H. Mussen (ed.) *Handbook of research methods in child development.* New York: John Wiley.
Kimble, G. A., & Perlmuter, L. C. (1970) "The problems of volition." *Psychological Review* 77: 361-384.
Kirsner, K. (1973) "An analysis of the visual component in recognition memory for verbal stimuli." *Memory and Cognition* 1: 449-453.
Klatzky, R. L., & Stoy, A. M. (1974) "Using visual codes for comparisons of pictures." *Memory and Cognition* 2: 727-736.
Kohler, W. (1929) *Gestalt psychology.* New York: Liveright.
Kolers, P. A. (1964) "Apparent movement of a Necker cube." *American Journal of Psychology* 77: 220-230.
————(1968) "The recognition of geometrically transformed text." *Perception and Psychophysics* 3 (1b): 57-63.
————, & Perkins, D. N. (1969a) "Orientation of letters and errors in their recognition." *Perception and Psychophysics* 5: 265-269.
————, ————. (1969b) "Orientation of letters and their speed of recognition." *Perception and Psychophysics* 5: 275-280.
Krauss, R. (1952) *A hole is to dig.* New York: Harper.
Kroll, N. E. A., Parks, T., Parkinson, S. R., Bieber, S. L., & Johnson, A. L. (1970) "Short term memory while shadowing: Recall of visually and aurally presented letters." *Journal of Experimental Psychology* 85: 220-224.
Kuenne, J. B., & Williams, J. (1973) "Auditory recognition cues in the primary grades." *Journal of Educational Psychology* 64: 241-246.
Lepper, M. R., Greene, D., & Nisbett, R. E. (1973) "Undermining children's intrinsic interest with extrinsic rewards: A test of the overjustification hypothesis." *Journal of Personality and Social Psychology* 28: 129-137.
Leeper, R. W. (1948) "A motivational theory of emotion to replace 'emotion as a disorganized response.'" *Psychological Review* 55: 5-21.
———— (1965) "Some needed developments in the motivational theory of emotions." In D. Levine (ed.), *Nebraska Symposium on Motivation.* Lincoln: University of Nebraska Press, pp. 25-122.
Lepper, M. R., Greene, D., & Nisbett, R. E. (1973) "Undermining children's intrinsic interests with extrinsic rewards: A test of the overjustification hypothesis." *Journal of Personality and Social Psychology* 28: 129-137.
Levine, F. M., & Fasnacht, G. (1974) "Token rewards may lead to token learning." *American Psychologist* 29: 816-820.
Lewin, K. (1935) *A dynamic theory of personality: Selected papers.* New York: McGraw-Hill.
Maccoby, E. E., & Bee, H. L. (1965) "Some speculations concerning the lag between perceiving and performing." *Child Development* 36: 367-377.
Marchbanks, G., & Levin, H. (1965) "Cues by which children recognize words." *Journal of Educational Psychology* 56: 57-61.
Mayer, R. E., Stiehl, C. C., & Greeno, J. G. (1975) "Acquisition of understanding and skill in

relation to subjects' preparation and meaningfulness of instructions." *Journal of Educational Psychology* 67: 331-350.

McCall, R. B., Kennedy, C. B., Appelbaum, M. I. (1977) "Magnitude of discrepancy and the distribution of attention in infants." *Child Development* 48: 772-785.

———, & McGhee, P. E. (1977) "The discrepancy hypothesis of attention and affect in human infants." In I. C. Uzgiris & F. Weizmann (eds.) *The structuring of experience.* New York: Plenum.

McClelland, D. C., Atkinson, J. W., Clark, R. A., & Lowell, E. L. (1953) *The achievement motive.* New York: Appleton-Century-Crofts.

McKeachie, W. J. (1974) "Instructional psychology." In M. R. Rosenzweig, & L. W. Porter. *Annual review of psychology* Palo Alto, Calif.: Annual Reviews: 161-194.

———, & Kulik, J. A. (1974) "Effective college teaching." In F. N. Kerlinger (ed.) *Review of research in education* Vol. 3: Itasca, Ill. F. E. Peacock.

Meehl, P. E. (1967) "Theory-testing in psychology and physics: A methodological paradox." *Philosophy of Science* 34: 103-115.

Miller, G. A., Galanter, E., & Pribram, K. H. (1960) *Plans and the structure of behavior.* New York: Holt, Rinehart & Winston.

Munsinger, H., & Kessen, W. (1964) "Uncertainty, structure and preference." *Psychological Monographs* 78 (whole No. 586): 1-24.

Nagel, E. (1957) "Determinism and development." In D. B. Harris (ed.), *The concept of development.* Minneapolis: University of Minnesota Press.

Notz, W. W. (1975) "Work motivation and the negative effects of extrinsic rewards: A review with implications for theory and practice." *American Psychologist* 30: 884-891.

Olson, D. R. (1968) "From perceiving to performing the diagonal." In D. R. Olson, & S. Pagliuso (eds.), "From perceiving to performing: An aspect of cognitive growth." Special issue, *Ontario Journal of Educational Research* 10: 171-180.

——— (1970) *Cognitive development: The child's acquisition of diagonality.* New York: Academic Press.

Over, R., & Over, J. (1967) "Detection and recognition of mirror-image obliques by young children." *Journal of Comparative and Physiological Psychology* 64: 467-470.

Parks, T. E., Kroll, N. E. A., Salzberg, P. M., & Parkinson, S. R. (1972) "Persistence of visual memory as indicated by decision time in a matching task." *Journal of Experimental Psychology* 92: 437-438.

Phillips, B. N., Martin, R. P., & Meyers, J. (1972) "Interventions in relation to anxiety in school. In C. D. Spielberger, *Anxiety: Current trends in theory and research,* Vol. 2. New York: Academic Press.

Piaget, J. (1962) *Play, dreams and imitation in childhood.* New York: W. W. Norton.

——— (1963) *The origins of intelligence in children.* New York: W. W. Norton.

——— (1965) *The child's conception of number.* New York: W. W. Norton.

——— (1972) "Some aspects of operations." In M. W. Piers (ed.), *Play and Development.* New York: W. W. Norton.

——— (1970) "Piaget's theory." In P. H. Mussen (ed.), *Carmichael's manual of child psychology,* 3rd ed., Vol. 1. New York: John Wiley.

——— (1973) *To understand is to invent: The future of education.* New York: Grossman.

———, & Inhelder, B. (1967) *The child's conception of space.* New York: W. W. Norton.

———, & Inhelder, B. (1969) *The psychology of the child.* New York: Basic Books.

Popper, K. R. (1971) *The open society and its enemies,* Vol. 2. Princeton, N.J.: Princeton University Press.

Posner, M. I. (1969) "Abstraction and the process of recognition." In G. H. Bower & J. T. Spence (eds.), *The psychology of learning and motivation: Advances in research and theory,* Vol. 3. New York: Academic Press.

Rayner, K. (1968) "Developmental changes in word recognition strategies." *Journal of Educational Psychology* 68: 323-329.

Rotter, J. B. (1966) "Generalized expectancies for internal versus external control of reinforcement." *Psychological Monographs* 80 (whole No. 609).

Rudel, R. G., & Teuber, H. (1963) "Discrimination of direction of line in children." *Journal of Comparative and Physiological Psychology* 56: 892-898.

Salthouse, T. A. (1974) "Using selective interference to investigate spatial memory representations." *Memory and Cognition* 2: 749-757.

Sameroff, A. J. (1975) "Early influences on development: Fact or fancy?" *Merrill-Palmer Quarterly* 21: 267-294.

Scheerer-Neumann, G. (1974) "Formation and utilization of the visual and verbal codes of pictures and words." *Psychological Research* 37: 81-106.

Seligman, M. E. P. (1975) *Helplessness.* San Francisco: Freeman.

Shaw, R., & Bransford, J. (1977) *Perceiving, acting, and knowing: Toward an ecological psychology.* Hillsdale, N.J.: Erlbaum.

Shepard, R. N., & Metzler, J. (1971) "Mental rotation of three-dimensional objects." *Science 171*: 701-703.

Skinner, B. F. (1962) "Behaviorism at fifty." *Science* 140: 951-958.

Spence, J. T. (1970) "The distracting effects of material reinforcers in the discrimination learning of lower- and middle-class children." *Child Development* 41: 104-111.

Sperling, G. (1963) "A model for visual memory tasks." *Human Factors* 5: 19-31.

Spielman, K. S. (1976) "Development of the perception and production of line forms." *Child Development* 47: 787-793.

Sroufe, L. A. (1977) "Wariness of strangers and the study of infant development." *Child Development* 48: 731-746.

———, & Wunsch, J. P. (1972) "The development of laughter in the first year of life." *Child Development* 43: 1326-1344.

Stevenson, H. W., Hale, G. A., Klein, R. E., & Miller, L. K. (1968) "Interrelations and correlates in children's learning and problem solving." *Monographs of the Society for Research in Child Development* 33, (Serial No. 123).

———, & Odom, R. D. (1965) "Interrelationships in children's learning." *Child Development* 36: 7-19.

Stone, L. J., & Church, J. (1973) *Childhood & adolescence: A psychology of the growing person,* 3rd ed. New York: Random House.

Terman, L. M., & Merrill, M. A. (1937) *Measuring intelligence: A guide to the administration of the new revised Stanford-Binet tests of intelligence.* Boston: Houghton Mifflin.

Thomas, A., Birch, H. G., Chess, S., Hertzig, M. E., & Korn, S. (1963) *Behavioral individuality in early childhood.* New York: New York University Press.

Tobias, S., & Ingber, T. (1976) "Achievement-treatment interactions in programmed instruction." *Journal of Educational Psychology* 68: 43-47.

Wachs, T. D. (1977) "The optimal stimulation hypothesis and early development: Anybody got a match?" In I. C. Uzgiris & F. Weizmann (eds.) *The structuring of experience.* New York: Plenum.

Walker, E. L. (1964) "Psychological complexity as a basis for a theory of motivation and choice." In D. Levine (ed.) *Nebraska Symposium on Motivation.* Lincoln: University of Nebraska Press.

Watson, J. B. (1924) *Behaviorism.* New York: The Peoples Institute Publishing Co.

Wepman, J. M. (1960) "Auditory discrimination, speech and reading." *Elementary School Journal* 60: 325-333.

White, R. W. (1959) "Motivation reconsidered: The concept of competence." *Psychological Review* 66: 297-333.

Wickens, D. D. (1972) "Characteristics of word encoding." In A. W. Melton & E. Martin (eds.) *Coding processes in human memory.* Washington, D.C.: Winston & Sons.

Williams, J. P., Blumberg, E. L., & Williams, D. V. (1970) "Cues used in visual word recognition." *Journal of Educational Psychology* 61: 310-315.

Wittgenstein, L. (1953) *Philosophical investigations.* New York: Macmillan.

Wohlwill, J. F. (1970) "The age variable in psychological research." *Psychological Review* 77: 49-64.

Woodworth, R. S., & Schlosberg, H. (1954) *Experimental psychology* (rev. ed.), New York: Holt.

Zigler, E. (1963) "Metatheoretical issues in developmental psychology." In M. H. Marx (ed.) *Theories in contemporary psychology.* New York: Macmillan.

MEMORY PROCESSES IN EXCEPTIONAL CHILDREN

Joseph Torgesen, FLORIDA STATE UNIVERSITY
Robert V. Kail, Jr., PURDUE UNIVERSITY

INTRODUCTION

The last 15 years has been a period of rapid expansion of interest in research on cognitive development in children. Nowhere is this growth more dramatically exemplified than in the study of memory processes. The development of research on memory is largely attributable to the advent of information processing models of cognition that directed attention to many interesting new questions concerning the cognitive activities underlying efficient memory performance. Although many of these questions remain unanswered, those which have been answered provide us with a much greater understanding of how memory skills develop in children than we possessed 15 years ago. The purpose of this chapter is to outline some of the recent advances in our knowledge of memory development and to show how this knowledge may be applied in understanding some of the academic problems of exceptional children.

Memory in an Educational Context

A basic assumption which is made throughout this paper is that memory skills occupy a position of central importance in the growth of general intellectual competence. A corollary of this proposition is that memory skills are essential in the performance of complex academic tasks such as learning to read, write, and spell. We recognize that an emphasis on memory skills may be unpopular in some educational circles. In fact, several recently developed techniques appear to relegate memory skills to a "second class" status, de-emphasizing them because of a feeling that memorization may interfere with more creative and higher-level kinds of learning. While it may be true that long, uninteresting "rote" memory sessions dull a child's appetite and capacity for more meaningful learning experiences, the role of memory skills in educational development is nevertheless an important one. By emphasizing the role of memory in educational contexts, we do not necessarily mean to advocate "rote" memorization activities, but rather seek to clarify how children's cognitive activities may enhance or interfere with their retention of learning experiences in school. We are also interested in identifying a number of different memory skills in order to form a more differentiated picture of the processes that underlie various cognitive abilities.

A major point of this paper is that there are many different kinds of memory processes: memory is not a unitary skill. Whether or not something is remembered depends upon a complex set of activities involving at least encoding, retention, and retrieval processes (Cofer, 1975). In addition, information also appears to be stored in several different ways, perhaps in separate "memory" systems, during different stages of processing. Because of these considerations, the role of memory skills in any given intellectual task is certain to be complex. As an example of the variety of roles that memory may play in a complex intellectual task, it is instructive to consider its central role in skilled reading.

Although the names for several of the memory processes discussed here may vary with different models of reading, most theoretical concepts of how reading takes place would include at least the following mnemonic components:

1. *Sensory visual trace*—a very briefly stored (250 msec) visual image of the input resulting from one eye fixation. This image is typically erased, or masked, by the next visual input.
2. *Iconic image*—this results from matching the visual input to a stored visual image. It lasts from one to two seconds and allows sufficient time for visual information to be coded verbally. This type of storage has the potential to hold several inputs at once and may thus act to help create context effects in deriving meaning from separate and sequentially presented inputs (Geyer, 1970).
3. *Short-term memory*—this is the "working memory for the mechanisms of sentence comprehension" (Gough, 1972, p. 340) in skilled reading. Here,

verbally encoded information is stored briefly (several seconds) while meaning is being extracted from sentences. In less skilled, or beginning reading, short-term memory probably provides a "working area" for assembling smaller units of words such as spelling patterns into whole words (West, 1975).

4. *Long-term memory*—access to long-term memory is necessary at several stages in the reading process. At the level of word recognition, visual input must be matched with some representation stored in long-term memory in order for it to acquire meaning (La Berge & Samuels, 1974). In comprehending written text, the sum total of the reader's experience and previous learning in many areas may be brought to bear in understanding the meaning of a particular passage.

The example just offered underlines the central role of memory skills in an important academic task. It also indicates that several different kinds of memory processes are involved in reading. If the importance of memory skills in academic tasks is accepted, the next logical question for those concerned with education involves the ways in which memory abilities may vary in children who must be taught to perform these tasks. This is the question of individual differences in memory skill. As it happens, the study of individual differences in memory has a long history, but only recently have we begun to study these differences in a way that can have direct impact on educational practices.

MEMORY AND INDIVIDUAL DIFFERENCES

Two of the earliest studies concerned with individual differences in memory performance were conducted by Hawkins (1897) and Galton (1887). While Galton presented evidence of memory deficiencies in retarded individuals, Hawkins was concerned with age-related changes in memory as well as differences associated with educational attainment. He presented sixth- and seventh-grade children from a public school, 15- and 20-year-old students from a "commercial" school, and college students with a serial recall task (ten digits). The "commercial" students recalled the digits least accurately; the college students, most accurately. Hawkins noted that "The power of retaining or recalling the memory-image varies with different persons" (p. 291) and that recall improved regularly with age.

These early, isolated studies provided a background for developments which were to insure that individual differences in memory would be thoroughly investigated over the next half century. The most important development in this regard was the inclusion of various tests of memory in standardized intelligence tests. In developing the first widely used test, Binet (Wolf, 1973) searched for test items that: (1) showed a regular improvement with age; (2) were related to achievement in school; and (3) were reasonably correlated with items measuring other intellectual abilities. One of the tests he selected was called "memory span." In this test, the child was asked to repeat sequences of numbers or words of increasing length. The number of auditorily presented digits recalled correctly increases with age, and performance is moderately related to other measures of ability to perform more complex intellectual tasks.

The role of memory items in the measurement of individual differences in intellectual ability has recently been reaffirmed by their inclusion in the McCarthy Scales of Children's Abilities (McCarthy, 1972). This test, which was developed as a measure of both general and specific cognitive abilities in young children, includes four different memory tests: a standard auditory digit span task; a pictorial memory test in which the child must remember the names of pictures; a measure of ability to duplicate sequences of notes; and a test of verbal memory requiring recall of sequences of words, sentences, and major elements of a story. The average correlation between the "memory index" (derived by combining the scores on the four memory subtests) and other measures of cognitive skill on the McCarthy scales is .71.

The inclusion of memory tests in tests of intelligence has made it convenient to study the memory skills of various classes of exceptional children. Over the years, deficiencies in memory performance have been consistently associated with the general range of intellectual deficiencies which define mental retardation. Research has shown that mentally retarded children perform deficiently on most measures of memory (Anastasi, 1968; Brown, 1974). There has also been a substantial amount of research on memory skills of children who are not deficient in general intelligence but who experience various kinds of learning difficulty in school. With this group, whom we shall label "learning disabled," the evidence of memory deficits is less consistent than it is for mentally retarded children (Rizzo, 1939). However, two recent reviews (Huelsman, 1970; Rugel, 1974) of profile studies using the Wechsler Intelligence Scale for Children (Wechsler, 1974) suggest that the digit span test is one of the most reliable of all subtests in differentiating between children with special reading problems and those who learn to read normally. Thus, a substantial amount of research indicates that memory problems may be an important correlate of academic difficulties in some exceptional children.

Until about ten years ago, almost all of the information available concerning individual differences in memory was derived from studies using psychometric instruments. This resulted in the description of individual differences in terms of memory products. That is, it was known that some children could remember more than others on a variety of memory tests, but information about the reasons for these differences was almost nonexistent. It is still true that psychometric instruments, by themselves, do not provide the kind of information necessary for the formation of remedial plans. This is so because there is really no way of telling, from scores on these instruments alone, which of a number of potentially relevant processes are responsible for the deficiencies observed. Without an understanding of the reasons *why* some children experience difficulties on memory tasks, there is little that can be done directly to remediate the difficulties (Glanzer, 1967).

More than 40 years ago, Heinz Werner (1937), one of the pioneers in the assessment of intellectual deficiency, pointed out the utility of describing abilities in terms of processes rather than products (test scores). The distinction between products and processes is the distinction between *what* an individual does and *how* he does it. A description of performance on memory tasks in terms of psychological processes involves a specification of the cognitive activities that are required to accomplish the task. It is in the area of providing process-oriented descriptions of memory skills that recent developmental research has made its greatest contribution. In fact, as Flavell (1977) has pointed out, the very life and vitality of memory research as an area of interest has depended upon the "redirection of attention from overt memory products to the cognitive activities that generate them" (p. 184). (*Editor's Note*: See chapter by Faust and Faust, in this volume, for discussion of cognitive processing.)

Chapter Overview

Research on memory development conducted in the last 15 years enables us to provide a fairly complete description of many of the psychological processes involved in performance on memory tasks. This information has served as an impetus to research on the memory skills of several populations of exceptional children, with resulting increases in our knowledge concerning some of the reasons why they exhibit poor memory in various situations. The rest of this chapter is organized in three sections. We will first provide a selective review of research concerning the cognitive attainments that underlie age-related improvement in performance on memory tasks. Following this, we will present research on the memory skills of two major groups of exceptional children: those classified as mildly mentally retarded and those who qualify for the general label of "learning disabled." Finally, we will conclude with a brief statement about the educational implications of our newly acquired knowledge of memory processes.

PRINCIPLES OF MEMORY DEVELOPMENT

As was pointed out earlier, memory does not refer to a single process or structure, but instead is a convenient shorthand for an array of processes. Elaboration, encoding, retrieval, search, chunking, and rehearsal—these are just a few of the memory operations that have been studied by cognitive psychologists. Given this proliferation of memory processes, it is clear that we cannot speak of memory development as if it consisted of a single system that changes with age. Instead, the developmental course of each component of memory must be considered separately.

In the present section, we will consider developmental changes in three major components of memory. First, there are certain basic processes that are necessary for any organism—rat, child, or adult—to possess what we call memory. Included here would be, for example, the processes whereby we recognize that an object is familiar. We shall see that these basic processes show little developmental change. The second and third components of memory to be considered here are of greater interest, because of the marked developmental change that they exhibit. In the second part of this section, we will consider developmental changes in the use of mnemonic strategies. Perhaps the most well-documented finding in the literature of memory development is that developmental changes in memory reflect, in large part, changes in the degree to which children use mnemonic strategies to aid retention. The third component of memory that we will examine is the relation between semantic knowledge and memory. Specifically, we know that a child's knowledge base increases with age and that memory processes ordinarily interact extensively with this knowledge base. Thus, we will conclude with a consideration of how developmental changes in the knowledge base may underlie developmental change in memory.

Basic Processes of Memory

What we have called basic processes are analoguous to the systems programs of a computer. These are the programs that, for instance, allow the the computer to recognize a sequence of symbols from a card, or allow it to search memory for information. These are, in other words, the programs that allow the computer to follow the instructions contained in the programs that are read into it. Similar processes function in the operation of human memory. That is, there are "mental programs" that allow us to recognize stimuli if they are familiar and that allow us to find information in memory when we need it. In this section we will consider developmental changes in two of these processes: the process of recognition and the search of memory. As will become apparent, both of these processes show little change with age.

Recognition Memory

Recognition appears to be a necessary component of a memory system, for without recognition every event would be experienced as novel, regardless of the extent to which it had actually been encountered previously. Given this position of importance as a foundation for memory, it is perhaps not so surprising that (a) impressive recognition memory is seen early in the first year of life, and (b) recognition memory seems to change very little with age. Let us consider each of these phenomena in turn.

Many facets of infant development—imitation, object performance, and attachment, to name a few—require the presence of some mnemonic skill. Yet it is only recently that developmental psychologists have begun to study infant memory directly. In this research, an infant is shown a stimulus (such as a picture) several times, until s/he habituates, or no longer responds to it as a novel stimulus. Next, the habituated (and hence, presumably familiar) picture is interspersed with novel pictures to determine if the infant responds differently to the novel and familiar stimuli. Reviewing research in which these procedures have been used, Cohen and Gelber (1975) concluded:

> As early as 6 or 8 weeks of age, a long-term exposure [to a picture] will produce recognition 24 hours later, and as early as 4 or 5 months of age, exposure as short as 1 or 2 minutes will lead to recognition 2 weeks later (p. 368).

Thus, there can be little doubt that the foundations of recognition memory are present in the first few months of life.

We know relatively little about the development of memory in the later stages of infancy. Beyond infancy, however, the results of numerous studies of recognition memory fit a consistent pattern. An experiment by Nelson (1971) is a case in point. Children from Grades 1, 4, and 7 were shown 60 pictures, depicting realistic paintings, abstract paintings, or puzzle pieces. Immediately thereafter, 18 pictures were shown again, each paired with a picture that had not been presented. Children were asked to indicate which picture from the pair had been presented initially. Two weeks later, another recognition test was given in which a different set of 18 pictures was selected and paired with new items. The results were straightforward: no age differences were found, either in immediate recognition performance or following the two-week delay.

This pattern of results is quite robust, for very accurate recognition memory has been reported for preschoolers in studies by Brown & Scott (1971), and Corsini et al. (1969), among others. Of course, it is possible to create developmental change in recognition accuracy by establishing conditions in which, for example, recognition is enhanced by verbal labeling (e.g., Mandler & Day, 1975). This, however, seems to be telling us more about the developmental effects of verbal coding rather than about the development of recognition processes. That is, it is important to distinguish between recognition memory as a *process* and as a *task* (Brown & DeLoache, 1978). Developmental differences may be found in performance on recognition tasks, but most frequently this seems to be attributable to factors other than the recognition process.

Memory Search

We argued earlier that a second basic process of memory would be the ability to search memory for information. The experimental analog to this process is the memory search task originally devised by Sternberg (1966). In this task, a small set of digits is shown, which is followed by the presentation of a single digit. The subject's task is to indicate if the single digit belonged to the set immediately preceding it. Of particular interest is the function relating response time to the number of digits in the presented set. The function is typically linear, both for

Yes and No responses, which suggests an *exhaustive, serial* search of memory. That is, the single digit would appear to be compared with each of the members of the set. After all comparisons have been made, the subject checks to see if a match has occurred.

The speed with which these search and comparison processes are executed is relatively invariant developmentally. For each additional digit that is to be remembered, reaction times increase by approximately 40 to 50 msec. Of course, overall response time in this task drops dramatically with age, but the slope of the function relating reaction time to set size does not change with age (e.g., Hoving, Morin, & Konick, 1970).

In summary, the basic processes of recognition and memory search show little developmental change. This should not be surprising, for it would be maladaptive for either process to have a lengthy ontogeny. As will become clear in later sections, the developmental invariance of this first component of memory contrasts sharply with the large developmental change that is seen in the remaining two components of memory.

DEVELOPMENTAL CHANGES IN USE OF MNEMONIC STRATEGIES

We now turn to the second component of memory development: the increased use of mnemonic strategies with age. It has been widely demonstrated that as children grow older, their approach to memory tasks becomes increasingly planful, strategic, purposive, and otherwise generally more mnemonically intelligent. In this section, we will first examine some of the results that exemplify these developmental differences; then we will critique some of the explanations that have been proposed for developmental differences in use of mnemonics.

Development of Rehearsal Skills

Much of our evidence concerning age changes in use of mnemonics comes from studies of children's rehearsal skills. Rehearsal usually refers to the repetitive, often cyclical, naming of stimuli to be remembered. One of the initial experiments concerning children's rehearsal, a study by Flavell et al. (1966), remains one of the most instructive studies in the area. In this experiment, kindergarten, second-, and fifth-grade children were shown seven pictures; then the experimenter pointed to a subset of two to five pictures that the child was to remember. Recall of this subset of pictures was tested after a delay of 15 seconds. During the delay, the child wore a space helmet with a visor that covered the eyes but left the lips visible. The experimenter was trained as a lip reader, and thus could determine if children were overtly rehearsing the stimuli. At each grade level, an increasing number of children showed evidence of rehearsal or related verbal activity. Furthermore, at each grade those children who rehearsed recalled more accurately than children who did not.

A similar pattern of results emerges from a large literature (see review by Hagen & Stanovich, 1977) in which developmental changes in rehearsal were assessed through the use of a *serial position recall* task. In this task, the child is shown several pictures of familiar objects, one at a time. Each picture is shown briefly, then is turned face down. After several pictures have been shown, a duplicate of one of the pictures is presented, and the child is asked to select the matching picture from the array of face-down pictures. Children as young as age three years, like adults, accurately recall items presented at the end of an array (Atkinson et al., 1964). Recall of items from the middle of the list, which is presumed to represent recall from long-term memory (Atkinson & Shiffrin, 1968) is lower, and also changes little with age. A large age difference in recall *is* found, however, for items presented at the beginning of a list (i.e., "primacy recall"), with accuracy improving developmentally (e.g., Hagen & Kail, 1973). Two lines of evidence suggest that this age difference in performance reflects the development of rehearsal. First, when children are required to rehearse aloud, large developmental differences in rehearsal are found, which are related directly to developmental differences in primacy recall (Ornstein et al., 1975). Second, when younger "non-rehearsing" children are taught to rehearse, recency recall is unaffected, but primacy recall increased (Kingsley & Hagen, 1969).

In both of the studies described thus far, rehearsal has apparently increased with age. What is left unspecified is the manner in which rehearsal has changed. Several studies by Ornstein and his colleagues have further clarified the development of rehearsal. First, older children rehearse more items at one time than do younger children (Ornstein et al., 1977). Second, older children are more likely to adjust their rehearsal to take advantage of relations that exist among the stimuli to be remembered. For example, if several words from a common category are scattered throughout a list, adolescents will rehearse the category members together, but younger children typically will not (Ornstein et al., 1975).

Ornstein's (1975, 1977) results should remind us that the emergence of proficiency in the use of a strategy is not an all-or-none phenomenon whereby children go from incompetence to competence in a single developmental leap. Rather, children gradually acquire competence in a strategy. As children grow older, they become able to use strategies in ways that are less stereotypic and task-evoked, and instead use them in ways that are more flexible and goal-determined. Furthermore, it should be emphasized that while the youngest children in the studies considered here did not spontaneously use mnemonics, we are not suggesting that young children are incapable of such strategic behaviors. Indeed, very young children can and do use simple mnemonics (Wellman et al., 1975).

Metamemory

The question that remains, then, is why children of a particular age often fail to use a given strategy, or why they use it ineffectively. One explanation of these developmental changes has to do with a child's knowledge of memory—what has been called "metamemory" (Flavell & Wellman, 1977). The core of this idea is that an individual's mnemonic behavior is often guided by that person's (implicit) knowledge of memory. Consider, for example, these two simple facts about memory: (1) Items that are well learned that are not currently retrievable (for unspecified reasons) may well be retrieved on subsequent attempts; (2) information that can be organized in a meaningful way is more readily remembered than information that lacks such organization. Adults quite probably know both of these facts. The first is seen in the tendency on multiple-choice exams to skip over those items for which the answer is not immediately apparent, returning to them when all other questions have been answered. As for the second fact, witness the extensive emphasis on outlining chapters of a textbook as a skill used in preparing for exams. In each of these instances, it seems likely that adults' behavior in preparation for memory tests is directed by intuitive knowledge of some simple characteristics of human memory.

The developmental question then becomes, *what could a child learn about memory that would influence his behavior when he is confronted with memory problems?* Several varieties of such metamnemonic knowledge have been distinguished by Flavell & Wellman (1977). They suggest that there are two broad domains of metamnemonic knowledge. The first concerns knowledge that "... some situations call for planful memory-related exertions and some do not" (p. 5). The second domain deals with knowledge of the factors that could potentially contribute to the difficulty or ease of a memory problem. Three of the factors identified by Flavell & Wellman (1977) are:

1. A person's knowledge of the characteristics of his memory (e.g., I remember faces well, but am considerably less accurate with names).
2. Knowledge of different facets of a memory task that relate to its ease (e.g., multiple choice exams are typically much easier than short-answer tests).
3. Knowledge of the assets and liabilities of a particular strategy that may determine how well suited it is for a given memory problem (e.g., rehearsal is fine for telephone numbers but is hardly the strategy choice in memorizing the plot of *Othello*).

What is known of developmental changes in each of these domains of metamemory? A thorough discussion of this literature is given by Flavell and Wellman (1977); we will provide some conclusions that are derived from their review.

First, even preschoolers are sensitive to the fact that an explicit instruction to remember is really an implicit instruction to engage in some type of mnemonic preparation. Preschoolers are, for example, more likely to touch or look at stimuli following instructions to remember than following non-mnemonic instructions. However, younger children often seem to be at a loss as to *the type of processing*—beyond simple looking or pointing—that is appropriate. In other words, it may often be the case that younger children "... grasp the general meaning and implications of the memorization instructions but typically do not command the study techniques that would behaviorally testify to the presence of that understanding'' (Flavell & Wellman, 1977, p. 8).

Second, younger children seem particularly insensitive to the limitations of their memory and are not terribly accurate at predicting the status of information in memory. Young children's ignorance of memory limitations has been documented in many studies in which children are asked to predict how much information they will be able to recall. In one typical study (Yussen & Levy, 1975), cards that depicted varying numbers of pictures were shown to children, who were asked to predict how many pictures they would be able to recall. Most four-year-olds felt they would easily be able to remember the maximum number of pictures, which in their case, was ten! An actual memory task followed, in which the limited span of memory was made readily apparent to the children, as most recalled only three-four pictures. Perhaps the most interesting finding concerns what happened when the prediction task was repeated immediately after the memory task. Again, many four-year-olds predicted that they would be able to recall all ten pictures easily. When asked to reconcile the difference between predicted and actual recall, most children attributed their limited recall to idiosyncratic aspects of the stimuli rather than to a permanent feature of their own memories.

Developmental differences in children's ability to assess their "state of mnemonic preparedness" is well illustrated in a study by Flavell, Friedrichs, and Hoyt (1970). Children were given an unlimited amount of time to memorize a set of pictures; it was emphasized that children continue to study until they were absolutely sure they would be able to recall all the pictures. For each child, the number of pictures to be remembered was 1.5 times his measured memory span—thus the difficulty of the task was equated across ages. Children older than ten years were able to interpret their readiness for recall, as most children recalled all of the pictures perfectly. Younger children were not nearly as proficient in their estimates of readiness, nor did they improve over a series of trials.

Third, younger children know some of the simple characteristics of stimuli that contribute to their memorability, but are less knowledgeable concerning how relations among items may influence memorability. Children as young as age six years know that familiarity of an item—especially whether it can be labeled—is an important determinant of memorability. When the focus is shifted from one item to sets of items, children of this age seem to know principally that the number of items is a critical variable. They apparently do not appreciate the fact that given certain relationships among stimuli, memorizing even a lengthy list may be trivial. This point is well illustrated in a finding from a study by Kreutzer et al. (1975). Children first practiced learning a list of paired associates. Then they were shown two lists and were asked to predict which would be easier to learn and remember. Pairs in one list consisted of names and actions (Mary-walk, Anne-sit); pairs in the second list consisted of highly associated antonyms (cry-laugh, black-white). While nine-and eleven-year-olds were confident that the latter of the two lists was less formidable, six- and seven-year-olds saw no compelling reason why they should differ in difficulty, even though the semantic relations in the second list had been described explicitly.

The importance that six- and seven-year-olds attach to quantity of information as a factor underlying memory difficulty was also demonstrated in this study. After children had indicated which of the two lists would be easier to learn, the experimenter added one more pair to this "preferred" list and asked the child to reevaluate his or her decision. Nearly all six- and seven-year-olds immediately changed their minds, deciding that the previously more difficult but currently shorter list would be less difficult. The older children, however, were confident in their original selection of the list of antonyms. Most were certain that a list of seven pairs of antonyms would still be easier than a list of four pairs of unrelated words. One child—obviously the budding mnemonist of the group—felt that a list of 50 antonyms would still be preferable to four unrelated pairs!

Younger children's apparent ignorance of the benefits of semantic relations between items is also seen in a study by Moynahan (1973). Children were asked to evaluate the relative difficulties of memorizing conceptually related versus conceptually unrelated lists of words. The nine- and ten-year-olds, like those in the Kreutzer et al. (1975) study, were confident of the mnemonic benefits of the presence of conceptual categories; younger children were less likely to be aware of these benefits.

Fourth, the relationship between metamemory and memory behavior seems to change developmentally. Evidence concerning the influence of metamnemonic knowledge on memory behavior is surprisingly scarce. In summarizing the relevant literature, Flavell & Wellman (1977) suggest that

> ... the casual chain may be more clearly and exclusively metamemory→memory behavior later in development than it is earlier. At the same time, and paradoxically, metamemory in the sense of present, conscious monitoring of mnemonic means, goals, and variables may actually diminish, as effective storage and retrieval behaviors become progressively automatized and quasi-reflexive through repeated use and overlearning. The metamemory-memory behavior link of the older child is not thereby extinguished, of course. However, the need for it to become clearly conscious may well diminish as the behaviors once mediated become more self-starting (pp. 28-29).

Ritter (1975), for example, has shown that many three-year-olds who understand the purpose of a retrieval cue fail to use it when appropriate. By age five, most children understand *and* use the cue, while by age nine all do so.

In summary, it seems clear that children grow to learn more about their own memories and about memory problems generally. The relation between metamnemonic knowledge and use of strategies appears relatively straightforward, yet there is a paucity of relevant data. In particular, our understanding of the proposed causal link between metamemory and memory development is meager.

Schooling and Memory Development

A second, more general, explanation of developmental changes in use of strategies is one that has been evoked to explain developmental changes in many cognitive processes. Several psychologists have argued that schooling is the essential condition for the development of strategies like those used in so many memory problems. Cole & Scribner (1977) argue the point in the following way:

> Schools represent the major cultural institution in technological societies where remembering as a distinct activity, occuring apart from the application of anything remembered, is engaged in repeatedly with a great variety of stimulus material.... It is difficult to think of any other generally experienced setting in which members of technological societies engage in deliberate memorizing.... When we turn to societies that lack formal educational institutions, where can we find such activities? The answer we believe, is rarely (p. 269).

That is, according to Cole & Scribner (1977), schools are unique in their emphasis on memorization per se as a goal. Children apparently acquire "general purpose" mnemonic strategies in response to this emphasis.

Evidence supporting these conclusions comes from studies in which children and adults who have not attended formal schools are tested on strategic memory tasks like those described in earlier parts of this section. The consistent finding is that uneducated individuals behave in ways akin to young Western children. That is, such persons typically fail to use mnemonics when it would be appropriate to do so. For example, Wagner (1974) found little developmental change in use of rehearsal between age six years and adulthood in a group of uneducated persons from the Yucatan peninsula.

Before linking schooling specifically to use of strategy, several alternative explanations must be eliminated. First, perhaps unschooled individuals fail to use strategies because they are intimidated by or unfamiliar with the laboratory setting. A second explanation would be that the failure to use strategies actually reflects a more general mnemonic deficiency. That is, inefficient use of strategy would be just one instance of poor memory skills in illiterate people. If either of these suggestions is accurate, then we would expect uneducated individuals to perform poorly on all memory tasks, not just those that require the use of strategies. Wagner (1978) examined these various explanations by testing literate and illiterate Moroccan children and adults on two different memory tasks. In a serial position task like the one described earlier in this chapter, developmental changes in rehearsal were found for groups of subjects who had been to school, while rehearsal was developmentally invariant and uniformly infrequent in the unschooled groups. In contrast, when the subjects were tested on a recognition memory task that minimized the need for strategies, a completely different pattern of results emerged: differences in recall were virtually eliminated between literate and illiterate subjects.

The studies by Wagner (1974, 1978) are just a small part of the growing literature (reviewed by Cole & Scribner, 1977) implicating schooling in the development of strategic behavior. Yet, as was the case with metamemory, our understanding of *how* schooling fosters a child's acquisition of strategies is far from complete.

Summary

In this section we have outlined developmental changes in the use of one strategy, rehearsal, which are prototypic for changes in many other storage and retrieval strategies (Hagen et al., 1975). Furthermore, we have considered evidence which suggests that metamemory development and schooling may underlie these age changes in strategic behavior. Our description of age-related changes in memory is not yet complete, however, for we must examine a third component of memory development—influence of semantic and conceptual development—which, like the use of strategies, shows considerable ontogenic change.

KNOWLEDGE, CONCEPTUAL DEVELOPMENT, AND MEMORY

Heretofore we have spoken of memory as if it were an independent skill, isolated from other cognitive activities. This was done only to facilitate exposition, for as we discussed in the introduction, memory is an inseparable component of all cognition. Given that these other components of cognition are changing with age, it is important to examine how these changes influence the course of memory development. As Flavell & Wellman (1977) put it:

> Older individuals presumably store, retain and retrieve a great many inputs better or differently than younger ones. They will do so simply because developmental advances in the content and structure of their semantic or conceptual systems render these inputs more familiar, meaningful, conceptually interrelated, subject to inference and gap-filling, or otherwise more memorable for them (p. 4).

These developmental changes are the focus of the present section. Three ways in which conceptual and semantic development influence memory development will be considered. First we will examine general changes in the child's level of cognitive functioning. Of course, such changes are implicated in the research on strategies discussed in the previous section. However, as Piaget & Inhelder (1973) point out, the development of memory involves "... not only quantitative changes in the acquisition, retention, and loss of [specific] data ... but also the fundamental qualitative factor, namely [changes in] the organization of the memory" (p. 379). Thus, our attention will first be drawn to studies which suggest that the "trace," once established in memory, changes over time in step with more general cognitive changes. The second and third cases of semantic influence on memory concern the manner in which information is initially encoded in memory. We shall see that changes in semantic and conceptual knowledge result in a memory trace that is increasingly more elaborate with age.

The Piagetian Approach to Memory

According to Piaget (1970), operative schemes—generalized, repeated actions—are the processes through which the child constructs his knowledge of the world. These schemes develop in accordance with Piaget's familiar sequence of stages. Piaget & Inhelder (1973) emphasize that memory is intimately linked to these developing operative schemes. Two implications of this view have stimulated a great deal of research. The first is that the manner in which an event is remembered should reflect the child's level of cognitive development. That is, preoperational and concrete operational children should remember the same stimulus differently, consistent with the operative schemes appropriate to each stage. The second implication is that, as a child grows, there should be longitudinal change in the way in which an event is remembered. In other words, the mnemonic representation of an event experienced during the preoperational stage will change as the child moves into the concrete-operational stage.

Both predictions were upheld in experiments described by Piaget & Inhelder (1973), in which children of various ages were shown and later asked to remember a seriated array of sticks. Either a few days or several months later children were asked to draw the array from memory. Preoperational children typically drew lines of equal or irregular length. Only advanced concrete operational children drew the sticks in the appropriate seriated manner. The longitudinal data also were in accord with the predictions made by Piaget & Inhelder (1973). Nearly three-quarters of the children tested showed "memory improvement" in that their drawings were more seriated several months after seeing an array than after only a few days.

Of course, a finding as unusual as *improvements* in long-term memory would be expected to provoke controversy, and Piaget & Inhelder's (1973) findings certainly have. Repeated testing, developmental changes in drawing skill, and children's response strategies have all been suggested as non-mnemonic explanations of these memory improvements. Yet, experimental attempts to reduce the memory improvement to these factors have failed for the most part (Liben, 1977). It should also be clear, however, that although memory and conceptual level typically are found to correspond in replications of Piaget & Inhelder's (1973) original experiments, the *magnitude* of the relationship is not great.

Semantic Knowledge and Encoding

The close tie between conceptual development and memory development can also be seen in developmental changes in encoding. Specifically, the changes in age that are found in encoding seem to parallel the child's acquisition of semantic knowledge. Let us first examine the ways in which encoding changes with age, then see how this developmental progression corresponds to the acquisition of semantic knowledge.

The Development of Encoding When we use the term "encoding" we are referring to an internal, mental description of a stimulus. Typically, such descriptions are given in terms of a set of attributes or features (Bower, 1967). For example, the act of encoding the word "teacher" might consist of generating an internal description that includes features such as "adult," "intelligent," "helpful." Encoding of this type is thought to occur automatically, such that an individual is not aware or conscious of the process (Wickens, 1972). Using this model of encoding, it has been possible to identify three (nonindependent) ways in which encoding changes with age. Each will be considered here.

First, there is a developmental shift from encoding of words based primarily on acoustic features to encoding based on semantic features. Evidence for such a developmental shift in features of encoding has come from the study of the errors children make on recognition memory tasks. Several words are first presented to the child. Then a recognition test is given which includes the words presented originally, new words that rhyme with the original words, and new words that are related semantically to the original words (e.g., from the same taxonomic category). Of particular interest is the frequency with which children mistakenly say one of the related words that was presented previously. It is assumed that after a child has encoded a word, he will be more likely to confuse that word with subsequent words if they are encoded similarly. Consequently, if "hat" were presented originally, and a child mistakenly recognized "fat," we would infer acoustic encoding. If he falsely recognized "cap," we would infer semantic encoding. In several studies of this type (reviewed by Hagen et al., 1975), it has been found that younger children typically are more likely to falsely recognize acoustically related words than semantically related words, while the pattern of errors is reversed for older children.

Second, the number of encoded semantic features increases with age. Evidence for this increase comes principally from studies in which a release from proactive interference (PI) procedure was used. (This literature is reviewed in detail by Kail & Siegel, 1977.) Each of several trials in this procedure involves, first, presentation of two words to be remembered; second, a distracting task (e.g., naming colors or digits) for 10 to 15 seconds in order to prevent rehearsal, and finally, a period for recall of the words. Words that share a common feature are presented on successive trials. For example, in a study by Kail & Levine (1976), the words presented on trials 1 to 4 all referred to toys or activities with masculine sex-role connotations (e.g., football, cowboy). Recall was quite accurate on trial 1, but declined on trials 2 to 4. On Trial 5, for children in the control group, the two words presented again referred to toys and activities with masculine sex-role connotations; for children in the experimental group, they referred to toys and activities with *feminine* sex-role connotations. If recall is greater in the experimental condition than in the control condition, we would infer that children encoded the particular feature manipulated in the experiment. Kail & Levine found such a difference in recall, suggesting that children did encode the sex-role connotations of the word presented.

From the results of several studies like the one just described, it has become clear that the *denotative* characteristics of words—those that form the kernel of a word's meaning—are encoded by very young children. For example, Esrov et al. (1974) found that three-and four-year-olds encoded several taxonomic categories. In contrast, *connotative* aspects of meaning are often encoded only by older children, and in some cases only by adolescents and adults. The three dimensions of semantic space—evaluation, activity, and potency (Osgood et al., 1957)—are encoded by adults (Wickens & Clark, 1968), but typically not by children younger than age ten (e.g., Cermak et al., 1972; Kail & Schroll, 1974). Similar results are found for the encoding of the "sense impression" evoked by a stimulus. That is, adults seem to encode connotations such as roundness for words like "barrel," "head," "balloon" (Wickens et al., 1972), while children typically do not. The single dimension of connotative meaning which children are more likely than adults to encode seems to be the sex-role connotations mentioned earlier (Kail & Levine, 1976), a finding that is not surprising given the importance of sex-role related issues during childhood.

Third, the speed with which semantic features are encoded increases with age. The evidence for this conclusion is more tentative than for the preceding two conclusions, and comes principally from studies in which children are asked to answer questions about different attributes of words. An experiment by Bisanz et al. (1977) is illustrative. Third-graders, sixth-graders, and college students were asked to judge whether a word presented rhymed with a given word, *or* was a member of a specified taxonomic category. Acoustic processing—as inferred from questions of the first type—was more rapid than semantic processing, as inferred from questions of the second type, at all age levels. The important finding was that the magnitude of the difference decreased with age: The difference between acoustic and semantic processing times was 130 msec for third-graders, 60 msec for sixth-graders, and 49 msec for adults. Thus, using acoustic processing as a baseline, it would seem that semantic information is processed with increasing speed developmentally.

Encoding as "applied semantics." We have presented three ways in which the nature of mnemonic encoding changes with age. How do these changes relate to changes in semantic knowledge? First, it is important to note that the description given here of developmental changes in encoding corresponds to changes noted by developmental psycholinguists in their studies of children's acquisition of semantic knowledge. Clark (1973) has argued that the meaning of a word for a child corresponds to an incomplete list of the same features that are used to describe that word in the adult's lexicon. For example, a child's initial definition of "dog" may be functionally equivalent to the adult's definition of "animal." It is only with development that such other discriminating features as "four-legged," "barks," and "man's best friend" are added to the list of features that constitute the child's knowledge of "dog." More specifically, "... the acquisition of semantic knowledge ... will consist of adding more features of meaning to the lexical entry of the word until the child's combination of features in the entry for that word corresponds to the adult's" (Clark, 1973, p. 72). Viewed in this way, semantic development can be seen as both a prerequisite for developmental changes in encoding, and as determining the possible level of a child's competence in encoding.

Furthermore, the findings of a developmental shift in likelihood of acoustic and semantic encoding, as well as developmental changes in the speed with which these types of encoding occur, may reflect the fact that knowledge of the acoustic and semantic features of language develop at different rates. Phonological development occurs rapidly during the preschool years (Menyuk, 1971). In contrast, the development of semantic knowledge occurs much more slowly, continuing throughout childhood and adolescence (Anglin, 1970). The increase with age in speed of encoding of semantic features, and the increased likelihood of such encodings may well reflect this relatively slow rate of development. That is, as semantic knowledge becomes more organized during childhood and adolescence, this knowledge would presumably be accessed more rapidly and would provide a more extensive code for stimuli.

Recall of Sentences and Stories

From reading the contemporary psychological literature, one might conclude that research on the relation between semantic knowledge and memory is a product of the 1970s. Nothing could be further from the truth, as more than 40 years ago Bartlett (1932) provided clear documentation of the way in which adult's knowledge typically influences the way in which information is remembered. He demonstrated that adults rarely recall meaningful material, such as stories, verbatim, but instead transform that information according to some general rules. Adults tended to *delete* irrelevant and unnecessary information in their attempts to remember stories. What is particularly interesting is that the deletion of information was inevitably accompanied by extensive *elaboration* of the meaningful parts of the story. Adults seem to incorporate the meaningful portions of stories into their existing knowledge, in a manner akin to Piaget's process of assimilation.

Since the child's knowledge base increases with age, we would expect that the nature and frequency of these elaborations might also change. In fact, Paris and his colleagues (Paris, 1975; Paris & Lindauer, 1977) have shown in several studies that, with age, children are increasingly likely to elaborate, embellish, and extend the information contained in sentences or stories.

A study by Paris & Lindauer (1976, Expt. 1) provides a good illustration of the way in which older children are more likely to "go beyond the information given" when they remember sentences and stories. Sentences were created in which certain information that was highly associated with the action in the sentence could be deleted without affecting the meaning or sense of the sentence as a whole. Two of the sentences—with the material to be deleted in parentheses—were the following:

> Our neighbor unlocked the door (with a key). Her friend swept the kitchen floor (with a broom).

Paris & Lindauer were interested in whether children would spontaneously infer the instruments (i.e., key, broom) used to complete the action. They argued that if the instrument was inferred spontaneously, then it should be an effective cue for recall of the entire sentence. Thus, children were read several sentences. In half of the sentences, the instruments were presented; in half, they were deleted. Later, recall of the sentences was tested, with the experimenter providing the instrument for each sentence as a cue.

The results were quite straightforward. For eleven-year-olds, the instrument cues were as effective when the instrument had been presented as when it was absent. For seven-and nine-year-olds, however, the instrument cue was much more effective when the instrument had been presented than when it had to be inferred. In other words, the older children "... apparently generated implicit information during encoding of the sentences, incorporated these relationships in their memory representations, and subsequently utilized them to access the entire sentence's meaning" (Paris & Lindauer, 1976).

From these results we can clearly see an increase with age in the tendency to elaborate meaningful material. These effects were examined in greater detail in a complementary study by Paris & Upton (1976, Expt. 2). Brief stories were read to five-, eight-, and ten-year-old children. Immediately following presentation of each story, children were asked questions that assessed their memory for information that had been presented in the story, as well as for information that could be inferred from material presented in the story. Finally, children were asked to recall as much of the story as possible.

We will first consider children's answers to the two types of questions. Older children answered all questions more accurately than did the younger children. But, as we might expect from the results of the previous study (Paris & Lindauer, 1976), the age changes were particularly marked for questions that required the child to make inferences based on information from several phrases in a sentence (as in the examples given above) or from several sentences.

What is more provocative was the relationship between children's answers to the questions and their ability to recall the stories. At each age level, multiple regression analyses were performed to determine which type of questions were the most effective predictors of free recall. Two aspects of these results are of particular interest. First, at each age level, the best predictor of recall was the accuracy with which the child answered inferential questions. In other words, the ease with which a child recalled the story was highly related to the extent of his/her understanding of the various inferential relationships that existed in the story. Second, the relationship between free recall and comprehension of inferences increased with age. The percentage of variance accounted for by the relationship between free recall and comprehension of inferences doubled between ages five and ten years. From these results, Paris & Upton (1976) argue that:

> Whether deliberate or automatic, attempts to infer additional information appear to enhance comprehension of the original information,... If a person constructs implied relationships and integrates them with original information, the derived memory representation may permit a temporally ordered, logical, sequential unit that can be stored parsimoniously and accessed readily (p. 667).

A different approach to the study of the effects of conceptual knowledge on story recall was used by Bisanz (1977), who measured children's understanding of the structure of a story, then compared that to the structure of their recall of the story. Her findings with first- and fourth-graders and college students were consistent with Paris' work.

The theme that is common to the work of Paris and colleagues (e.g., Paris & Lindauer, 1977) and the work of Bisanz (1977) is the continuity of comprehension and memory. Older children are better able to detect subtle relationships that exist in a story and are more likely to infer additional relationships that are not stated explicitly in prose. In other words, as children grow older they seem to represent meaningful stimuli in an increasingly elaborated network of semantic relations, with the mnemonic consequence that they are better able to remember what they have heard or read.

Summary

We have attempted to show the correspondence between memory development and conceptual development by examining three areas of research that would, at least initially, seem to be totally unrelated. Yet in each case a common principle can be detected, namely, that changes in a child's knowledge and changes in the organization of that knowledge have profound effects on the way in which events are stored and remembered. Thus, this third component of memory is akin to the second component—use of strategies—in showing considerable ontogenetic change.

Concluding Remarks on Memory Development

In the present section we have outlined developmental changes in several components of memory. First we considered the development of two basic features of memory—recognition and memory search. This component is marked by developmental invariance rather than developmental change. Then we examined developmental changes in the use of strategies, focusing on the development of rehearsal strategies. Two factors that are probably related to a child's tendency to use strategies were discussed. One factor was the extent of the child's knowledge of memory—what was termed "metamemory." The second was the extent of the child's education, for it was shown that there are enormous cross-cultural differences in memory, but only when the memory tasks require the use of strategies. The final component of memory that we addressed in this section was the relation between memory and knowledge. It was demonstrated that older children often remember more effectively than younger children because their larger base of knowledge allows them to more effectively encode and elaborate information that is to be remembered.

MEMORY IN EXCEPTIONAL CHILDREN

Research on the development of memory in normal children suggests several different kinds of memory processes. To aid in the exposition of research on memory in exceptional children, it may be helpful to provide additional clarification concerning one kind of distinction that is often made among memory processes. This is the distinction between the *structural* and *control* features of memory. Structural features are analagous to the basic processes discussed in the previous section, and include "... both the physical system and the built-in processes that are unvarying and fixed from one situation to another" (Atkinson & Shiffrin, 1968, p. 90). Although these processes may develop with long-term maturation, they are not modifiable through short-term training, nor are they subject to the conscious control of the individual. Control processes, in contrast, are optional activities that an individual may engage in to maximize the performance of a limited capacity system. There are strategies like rehearsal which help to organize and maintain information to be remembered. As we will see, both of these major types of memory processes have been invoked as potential explanations for the memory problems of exceptional children.

Research With the Mentally Retarded

Like all major categories of exceptionality, the classification "mentally retarded" is applied to a heterogeneous group of individuals. The classification includes people with a broad range of IQ whose retardation is the result of many different organic and environmental factors. The information presented in this section was derived from research with mildly retarded children (IQ = 50-70) who had no known organic impairment—children typically classified in educational terms as the "educable mentally retarded."

From the early research of Galton (1887) through the proliferation of studies comparing the performance of retarded and nonretarded children in intelligence tests, retardation has been consistently associated with poor performance on memory tests. A major aim of psychological research on memory in retardates has been to identify the specific mental processes that are responsible for their deficient memory performance. Our answers to this question have changed dramatically in the past 10 to 15 years.

Early speculation about memory deficits in retarded individuals focused on structural limitations. These theories identified a variety of basic processes that were thought to be unmodifiable by experience and which constituted a basic and stable difference in mental capacity between retarded and nonretarded individuals. An example of such a theory is the one proposed by Ellis (1963). Briefly, the *stimulus trace theory* suggests that memory traces decay more rapidly in retardates that in people of normal intelligence. This formulation stimulated much research that ultimately led to the rejection of the theory. If rate of decay is more rapid in retardates, then memory differences between retarded and nonretarded children should increase as the retention interval increases. This pattern of results was not found often, and when it did emerge, it seemed to reflect differences in the extent to which children used effective strategies to learn material initially, rather than differences in rate of decay per se (Belmont & Butterfield, 1969).

This latter finding prompted a new series of studies designed to investigate the possibility that retarded and nonretarded children differ in the likelihood and success with which they use mnemonic strategies. These investigations were fruitful, and it is now accepted that one basis for the memory deficits found in retardates is their failure to use strategies appropriately (Belmont & Butterfield, 1971; Brown, 1974). The mentally retarded child, like the preschool and young school-aged child, does not engage in the sort of planful behavior typical of adults and older children.

Although deficiencies in the use of mnemonic strategies are clearly implicated in the memory problems of retardates, several new approaches have begun to emphasize a complementary role for structural deficits on some kinds of memory tasks. Thus, a complete statement about the memory problems of retarded children derived from present theory and research will have to consider the possibility that both structural and control features are involved.

Our description of the research on retardate memory will be selective. Several recent reviews (Brown, 1974; Campione & Brown, 1977; Belmont & Butterfield, 1977) provide excellent secondary sources for those interested in a more detailed treatment of the research. Another good source of research on retardate memory is the annual series *International Review of Research on Mental Retardation*. The discussion that follows is organized around two issues. We will first consider several different aspects of memory in order to illustrate the ways in which retarded and nonretarded children differ in their memory skills. Since we know that retardates do suffer a memory deficit, it is important for both theoretical and practical reasons to determine if we can limit or reduce that deficit. Consequently, we will also examine several training programs that have been designed to improve retardates' memory.

Retardates' Use of Strategies

Instances in which retarded children fail to use mnemonic strategies or use them inappropriately are numerous. We will describe research that has focused on two different types of strategies. Retardates' use of rehearsal was studied by Belmont & Butterfield (1971). Retarded and nonretarded adolescents were tested on a serial position recall task that was modified to allow the subjects to control the rate of presentation of the stimuli. After the children have viewed a sequence of letters, a duplicate of one of the letters appeared and subjects indicated where the letter had appeared in the series. This task provides two different kinds of data that are relevant to inferences about the use of rehearsal. A fairly direct measure of rehearsal is provided by the pattern of pauses when subjects view the stimuli one after another. Nonretarded subjects typically paused for a long period of time between items early in the list, but paused only briefly between the last few items. Such a pattern was thought to indicate a "cumulative rehearsal, fast finish strategy." In contrast, the retarded children paused for about the same amount of time between all items, suggesting that they did not use the same acquisition strategy as the nonretarded children.

As would be expected from research on rehearsal described previously, non-retarded adolescents recalled items from the beginning of the list quite accurately, performance which presumably reflects their skilled use of rehearsal. The retarded subjects, in contrast, had uniformly low recall of items from the beginning of the list. This finding is consistent with their flat pause patterns in suggesting that the retarded subjects did not rehearse the letters as they were shown. Another important feature of the results is that retardates recalled items from the final positions as accurately as nonretarded adolescents, a finding to which we will return shortly.

Rehearsal is a particularly useful mnemonic when the amount of information to be remembered is small. As the amount of information increases, mnemonics that serve to organize the information to be remembered become more appropriate. Such organizational strategies have been studied most frequently with a free recall paradigm in which several words are presented from each of a few different categories. We might, for example, ask a child to remember "pants, orange, car, shirt, plane, shoes, blue, boat, green." The child might recall "pants, shoes, orange, green, blue, car, boat, plane." Even though retention was not perfect, the child used the categories—clothing, colors, vehicles—to simplify the task. Retardates use this kind of organizing scheme less frequently than nonretarded persons, just as preschool and young school-aged children are less likely to do so than older children. The finding has been documented in a series of studies by Spitz (1966). In one study, for example, retarded and nonretarded adolescents were to remember 20 words, five words from each of four categories. The words were presented in a random order. Only rarely did retardates recall words in a way that would suggest they had used the categories to aid in recall.

Training Retardates to Use Strategies

The studies by Belmont and Butterfield (1971) and Spitz (1966) that we have just described are representative of many studies in which it has been found that retarded children are unlikely to use mnemonic strategies in standard laboratory memory tasks. Having identifed one source of a retardate memory deficit, the obvious next issue to be addressed is whether we can improve retardates' memory, perhaps even to the level of their nonretarded peers, through the use of appropriate training procedures. This turns out to be a more complex problem than it might first appear to be, because we can define the success of a training program in many ways. No one doubts that retardates can be taught, for example, to rehearse. In fact, in the study by Belmont & Butterfield (1971) that we have just described, at one point retardates were instructed in the use of rehearsal. The resulting change in performance was dramatic: retardates taught to rehearse recalled twice as much as they had previously.

Demonstrating that retardates can be taught to rehearse and that their recall improves as a consequence is a necessary step in a program of memory remediation for retardates, but this finding should be evaluated in the perspective of several other relevant criteria. First, the durability of training must be considered. If these retarded children were tested a week later, and no effects of training were apparent, then the finding of enhanced rehearsal is much less interesting. Assuming a training program meets the criterion of durability, the extent to which the trained retardates could *generalize* their newly acquired skills to situations different from those in which they were learned must also be considered. If the skill is limited to a particular set of stimuli presented by a particular experimenter in a particular context, then the value of the training program is questionable. If, instead, we find that retardates are using rehearsal to remember the events planned for a day, or what should be bought at the supermarket, then the program would appear to be worth pursuing. A final point that should be considered in evaluating training programs is the extent to which they eliminate differences in recall between retarded and nonretarded individuals. As programs fall further from this goal, their success becomes more open to question.

With these three criteria—durability, generalizability, and minimization of retardate-nonretardate differences—we are in a better position to evaluate studies in which the goal was to improve retardates' memory. Let us now consider these studies in terms of each criterion.

Judging from the results of a study by Brown et al. (1974), there is little doubt that the goal of durability can be achieved. These investigators taught retardates to rehearse. Six months later, the subjects were retested without further instruction or reference to the training they had received previously. The effects of the rehearsal training were just as evident in this delayed recall period as they had been immediately following instruction. However, not all training programs demonstrate the durability of effect shown by Brown et al. One aspect of training which appears to be associated with durability is length of the training period. Not surprisingly, greater amounts of training produce more durable effects. Other factors relating to the specific behaviors required by different mnemonics may also affect long-term retention of strategies. Unfortunately, the evidence presently available is insufficient to indicate the kinds of variables that might make some strategies easier to retain than others.

Although training programs have frequently been able to demonstrate durable effects, they have not fared as well against the criterion of generalization. After reviewing studies which tested for generalization, Campione & Brown (1977) concluded that "... there is almost no evidence showing impressive generalization effects" (p. 281). The fragility of training effects can be seen by returning briefly to the study by Brown et al. which showed impressive durability of training. In addition to being tested on a task for which they were originally trained, the retarded children were also asked to perform a different task which also required the use of rehearsal in order to obtain good scores. Their performance in this case was indistinguishable from a control group of retardates who had received no training in rehearsal. In other words, for retardates who had received training, rehearsal seemed to be linked specifically to the context in which it had been instructed.

Apparently, it is not sufficient merely to instruct retardates in a specific strategy. Additional training is necessary to achieve generalization. What should be the nature of this additional training? Belmont & Butterfield (1977) have suggested that, for generalization to occur, retardates need training in general skills that are not related to a specific strategy but instead are common to the successful application of all strategies. Their reasoning covers the following points: (1) successful response to training in the use of a strategy implies that the capacity for executing the strategy was always present, but simply was not applied to the task; (2) failure to apply a strategy spontaneously was the probable result of a failure to analyze or understand the cognitive requirements of the task, skills Belmont & Butterfield call "executive functions"; and (3) failure to generalize results from the same deficiencies that produced the original lack of spontaneous application of a strategy. Without training in "executive functions," one would not expect retarded individuals to be able to apply their newly acquired mnemonic skills in a variety of contexts because they still have difficulty assessing the need for the use of strategies on specific tasks.

What are some of the components of successful decision making about whether or not to use a mnemonic strategy? One might involve an awareness of how difficult a given task is going to be. Campione & Brown (1977) argue that retardates tend to underestimate the difficulty of many memory tasks. Retardates see little need to resort to mnemonics because, like the preschoolers described in the previous section, they perceive the task to be quite easy. For example, Brown et al. (1974) found that when retarded adolescents were asked to predict the number of pictures they could recall from a set of ten, more than two-thirds of the subjects overestimated by at least three items. Equally important, Brown et al. also demonstrated that these children could be trained to estimate more accurately. For the older children in their sample, the effects of this training persisted for a year, but there was no evidence that the ability to estimate task difficulty generalized to tasks only slightly different from those used in training.

Thus, estimating the difficulty of a task—a prerequisite to the successful use of strategy—appears to be a nontask-specific skill in which retardates are deficient. Other general areas in which retardates may also experience special difficulties involve selecting an appropriate strategy and monitoring the effectiveness of the strategy once selected (Campione & Brown, 1977). We would argue that training in these nonspecific skills is likely to assume increasing importance in those training programs in which generalization of training is the goal.

Let us now return to the final criterion against which memory programs for retardates should be evaluated: the extent to which retardate-nonretardate differences in memory are reduced or eliminated. A consistent finding in training studies of the type we have described is that even though the increases in retardates' memory performance are enormous, their performance rarely reaches the level of the nonretarded subjects with whom they are being compared (e.g., Belmont & Butterfield, 1971). What processes are responsible for this residual memory deficit? This is a more difficult question to answer than we might first suspect. The difficulty arises because the memory differences between retarded and nonretarded persons may reflect a failure to train the retardates adequately rather than a specific retardate memory deficit. In other words, it is conceivable that after months—or perhaps years—of training, all memory differences between retarded and nonretarded persons could be eliminated. It is also possible that motivational factors may be involved in the residual memory deficit (e.g., Zigler, 1969).

Deficiencies in Basic Processing Capacity

Still another possibility is that the residual differences found following training in strategies may reflect differences in the basic processes or structural components of memory. We can test this hypothesis by examining the performance of retarded persons using tasks on which strategies typically are not used. If differences are found here, then we would infer that perhaps retardates' memory deficit is more than a simple failure to use mnemonic strategies. From studies of this type, it appears that many of the encoding and recognition aspects of retardates' memory function with the same degree of automaticity found in nonretarded children. For example, in recognition memory experiments, retardates are generally as accurate as nonretarded adolescents (Brown, 1972). Furthermore, in serial position tasks, retarded and nonretarded children remember items occuring at the end of the list with equal accuracy (e.g., the data from Belmont & Butterfield, 1971, discussed earlier). This "recency effect" seems to indicate that the basic capacity of short-term memory may be similar for retarded and nonretarded children.

A quite different picture emerges when we consider another structural component of memory, the speed of memory search and recognition. Evidence from the Sternberg (1966) memory search paradigm indicates that retardates are consistently slower in their memory search than nonretarded persons. Differences between retarded and nonretarded children in speed of memory search have been found in two studies in which the Sternberg paradigm was used. Dugas & Kellas (1974) compared the performance of retarded adolescents with a group of fifth and sixth-graders. Memory search times of the normal children increased 45 msec for every additional item that was remembered; retardates' search times were much slower, approximately 90 msec.

Similar findings were reported in a more elaborate experiment by Harris & Fleer (1974). Four groups were tested. Two groups of retardates, both with average IQs of approximately 56, differed according to etiology. One consisted of children whose retardation could be traced directly to brain damage (e.g., prenatal injury, anoxia at birth). Children in the second group were "cultural-familial" retardates who were classified as retarded solely on the basis of intelligence test scores and who had no apparent organic damage. Two groups of nonretarded eight-year-olds and high school students were also tested. The former group matched the retardates in mental age, the latter in chronological age.

For both eight-year-olds and high school students, the increase in memory search was approximately 40 msec. for every additional digit that was to be recalled. For the two groups of retardates, the values were larger. The increase was 66 msec for the cultural-familial group and 111 msec for the brain damaged group. Thus, both Dugas & Kellas (1974) and Harris & Fleer (1974) found that memory search time was slower in retardates. The estimate of retardates' memory search time differs between the two studies, but this is quite probably due to the fact that Dugas & Kellas selected subjects without regard to etiology. Consistent with this explanation, if the search times for Harris & Fleer's two classes of retardates are averaged, the value obtained, 88 msec, is almost exactly the value obtained by Dugas & Kellas from retardates of mixed etiology.

The findings from these investigations of speed of memory search are intriguing; however, more research needs to be done before we can conclude with Harris & Fleer (1974) that they reflect "some kind of permanent deficiency in central processing"(p. 458) in mentally retarded individuals. For example, Silverman (1974) also compared the performance of retarded and nonretarded children within a memory search paradigm, but instead of using digits as stimuli, he used unfamiliar, letterlike forms. Although he obtained results which were in many respects comparable to those obtained when digits were used as stimuli, he also found no differences in scanning rate between the retarded children and his normal control group. Other research has shown that scanning rate decreases with increasing familiarity of stimuli (Briggs & Blaha, 1969; Lyons & Briggs, 1971). Thus, it may be possible to explain some of the variation in scanning rate obtained between retarded and nonretarded groups in terms of the greater familiarity of children in the control groups with the digits which were used as stimuli.

Although studies using the memory scanning paradigm have produced inconclusive results, they are only one example of the increasing interest in research which focuses on structural differences between individuals of different general intelligence. The emphasis in most of the recent research is on studying speed, rather than accuracy, of processing. Hunt and his colleagues (Hunt, Frost, & Lunneborg, 1973; Hunt, Lunneborg, & Lewis, 1975), for example, provided evidence which suggests that verbal intelligence is related to speed of access to material stored in long-term memory. Other researchers (Fisher & Zeaman, 1973; Sperber et al., 1973) are developing theoretical descriptions of retardate memory which note possible deficiencies in both structural and control processes. These theoretical frameworks may be of use in suggesting ways to determine the relative importance of different kinds of memory processes in accounting for a variety of deficiencies in retardate memory performance.

Summary and Conclusions

In the previous several pages, we have seen how a simple theory of retardate memory trace (trace decay) was replaced by a more elaborate description based on deficits in the use of strategies. At the same time, we have seen that simple training programs directed toward the instruction of a single strategy are insufficient to completely eliminate this deficit. Perhaps the most important conclusion to be drawn from this research is that the memory deficit in retardates is *multifaceted*. Some aspects of retardates' memory differ greatly from that of the nonretarded population, while others differ hardly at all. It will be worthwhile to keep this conclusion in mind as we examine research on memory in learning disabled children, where the theoretical and empirical efforts have not reached this level of refinement.

Research with Children Who Have Special Learning Problems

General Methodological and Conceptual Issues. One of the most striking developments of recent years within the field of special education has been the phenomenal growth of interest and concern for children of normal intelligence who do not learn normally in the classroom. These children, most frequently labeled "learning disabled," have come to represent a population of special interest to many educators and researchers interested in the relationship between individual differences in cognitive functioning and learning. Unfortunately, much of the research in this area has been plagued by several thorny methodological problems which limit the usefulness of most of the data that it has produced. Two of the most important problems facing researchers in this area involve the selection of research samples and interpretation of experimental results. Although these issues have been presented in detail elsewhere (Senf, 1976; Torgesen, 1975), they will be discussed briefly here in order to provide a background for the review of research which follows. We will also consider briefly some historical and conceptual issues which have had a particularly unfortunate influence on the study of memory processes in learning disabled children.

Problem of Sample Definition. Probably the most basic problem interfering with the efforts of researchers to establish a coherent body of knowledge and theory relating to the cognitive functioning of learning disabled children involves difficulties in defining the population of interest. There are two aspects to this problem. First, "learning disabilities" as a classification for children is unreliable because its operational definition varies among different regions of the country and among different researchers. Second, the classification is almost invariably so broad that children with a variety of different problems are included within any given sample. The first problem makes it difficult to compare the results of one study with another and to resolve inconsistent findings. Because of the second difficulty, it is almost impossible to generate conclusions that will be helpful to clinicians and educators in their attempts to develop remedial procedures for these children. The fact that the disabled population is most often heterogeneous with regard to the dependent variable under study leads to low-order relationships among variables and produces research conclusions which apply only to learning disabled children "on the average." In other words, the researcher is most often not able to describe to educators the defining characteristics of the subpopulation of learning-disabled children to which his/her research conclusions may apply.

What is greatly needed at present are ways to classify children with learning problems that will insure the formation of more homogeneous groups for study. The classification principles that we use need to be made more reliable (consistent between researchers) and more specific if future research is to contribute to increasingly sophisticated and coherent theoretical formulations about the nature of the cognitive problems experienced by children with learning problem. Beginning efforts in this direction have been reported by Senf (1974) and by Doehring (1976).

Problems of Interpretation. One research design that has often been used to investigate the cognitive deficiencies of learning-disabled children involves a comparison of disabled and normal control children on one or more tasks which are purported to measure specific intellectual abilities. Quite frequently, measures are specially developed to test the hypotheses in question. When new measures are used, this approach has been described by one critic as the "simple sample difference approach utilizing an unvalidated, meaningless instrument" (Senf, 1976, p. 256). The results of studies using this approach are particularly hard to interpret because there is little evidence that the tests being used are valid measures of any particular cognitive process or ability. Thus, unless a measure has been used systematically in previous research or has been validated through formal procedures (cf. Campbell & Fiske, 1959), studies which use it to measure specific cognitive functions are essentially meaningless.

The second problem with the "simple sample difference" approach is related to the first but is even more basic. Simply stated, it is never possible to provide an adequate measure of a psychological process in a single operation. As Flavell (1977) has pointed out, "every task demands from the child knowledge and skills other than, and in addition to, the target concept or ability it was designed to tap" (p. 224). Thus, if a child fails a particular task, one cannot be sure that the problem was due to deficiencies in the particular psychological processes the task was designed to measure, other processing skills which are also required for good performance on the task, or to a variety of nonspecific factors such as motivation or attention.

Since research which compares disabled and normal children on a single task does not provide an adequate basis for inferences regarding specific cognitive deficiencies, better experimental paradigms must be used in research involving learning-disabled children. Two paradigms currently used by experimental psychologists to study psychological processes appear to have immediate relevance to research on exceptional children. One of these methods involves comparisons of the performance of learning-disabled and normal children as various experimental factors are manipulated within a given task. The basic question raised in this design is whether a given experimental manipulation will produce the same behavioral adjustment among children within the different groups. Experimenters should search for theoretically meaningful variables which produce variability in group differences. This design helps to control the influence of nonspecific factors which may lead to group differences on a single task (Chapman & Chapman, 1973) and, if task variations are carried out systematically, it is also possible to verify the validity of one's interpretation of the results. More complete presentations of the advantages of studying interactions between subject and experimental variables in investigations of deficient cognitive functioning may be found in articles by Baumeister (1967), Labouvie-Vief (1976), and Milgram (1973).

A second method of studying the psychological processes underlying poor performance on a task involves providing training designed to affect the psychological processes which are thought to be deficient in the group with performance problems. This method is frequently used to test hypotheses about the nature of cognitive acquisitions which underlie age-related improvements on intellectual tasks (Belmont & Butterfield, 1977). In the case of developmental research, the technique assumes that if training in certain subskills successfully eliminates differences in performance between older and younger children, then deficiencies in those subskills were probably responsible for the original performance problems. As we discussed in the previous section, this technique has been used extensively to study memory skills in mentally retarded children.

Historical and Conceptual Issues. The field of learning disabilities has been powerfully influenced by a relatively small group of dominant personalities (Hallahan & Cruickshank, 1973). Two of the most influential of these figures were Heinz Werner and Alfred Strauss, whose work on the perceptual and attentional problems of "brain damaged" retarded children has been very important in the development of theory and research concerning the intellectual deficiencies of learning-disabled children. Their emphasis on the perceptual and attentional problems of their subjects has served to limit the range of cognitive functions studied in subsequent research. Areas like memory, problem solving, and language skills have not been studied as extensively as they might have been because of a "premature foreclosure" of opinion about which kinds of cognitive deficiencies are most important in accounting for the difficulties of learning-disabled children.

A second, and perhaps more subtle, influence of the work by Werner and Strauss has been the association between learning disabilities and brain damage. This influence has been subtle in the sense that the emphasis on brain damage as the underlying cause of learning disabilities has diverted attention from the development of sophisticated *psychological* models of the cognitive deficiencies of these children. Rather than attempting to understand the performance problems of learning-disabled children in terms of cognitive activities which are required for performance on a given task, many researchers have been content to describe the difficulty as a "specific disability" resulting from brain damage (Torgesen, 1977a). The availability of such explanations has supported the retention of relatively simple conceptions of cognitive abilities and disabilities. Memory, for example, has often been treated as though it were a unitary "capacity" rather than as a multifaceted skill dependent on a variety of subskills and processing activities.

Memory Performance and Reading Skill

Because of the problems outlined in the previous section, it is difficult to arrive at any reliable conclusions from research on the memory skills of learning-disabled children. The most reliable finding, and one that provides no real increase in our understanding of the problems of these children, is that learning-disabled children do poorly on memory tasks when compared with children who learn normally in the classroom (Torgesen, 1975). In the last several years, however, this finding has begun to be elaborated by research which has been based on more sophisticated models of memory processes. Although this research is in its infancy, it is possible to provide some tentative conclusions and to indicate areas which need to be pursued further. In addition to limiting ourselves to very recent research, we have also decided to restrict the scope of this review to research which has been conducted using a particular subsample of children with learning problems. These are children of essentially average intelligence but who were experiencing moderate to severe difficulties in learning to read. Although these children are still bound to be heterogeneous with regard to the causes of their reading problems (Applebee, 1971), they are at least more homogeneous than the sample of all children who might be considered learning-disabled.

The research to be considered here has been derived from two different conceptualizations of the relationship between performance on memory tasks and reading proficiency. The first set of studies has focused on the possibility that "memory" differences between good and poor readers may reflect differences between the groups in general learning strategies that affect both performance on experimental tasks and the attainment of beginning reading skills. The second set of studies has been conducted from the perspective that poor readers may be deficient in certain specific processing skills such as the linguistic skills involved in encoding verbal stimuli which affects their performance on both memory tasks and during reading.

The Use of Memory Strategies by Poor Readers. From two similar studies (Kastner & Rickards, 1974; Torgesen & Goldman, 1977), we know that young children who are experiencing difficulty in learning to read do not label stimuli as readily or rehearse them as much as do good readers of the same age and general intelligence. In both studies, the experimenters pointed to pictures of objects in sequence and, after a 15-second delay, children were required to point to the pictures in the same sequence. During the delay, the children were carefully observed for evidence of the use of rehearsal such as lip movements or whispered words. Following the memory task, the children were also asked to describe any procedures they had used to remember the order of the pictures. Kastner & Rickards (1974) tested third-grade children using two kinds of stimuli. In one condition, the children recalled sequences of familiar stimuli (e.g., pictures of a flag, moon, apple, etc.), while in the other they were exposed to novel stimuli (line patterns which were difficult to label). Although equal numbers of children from both groups rehearsed the familiar stimuli, differences between groups were found with the novel stimuli, in that only the good readers continued to rehearse when the stimuli were novel and hard to label. Subsequent testing of these children indicated that the poor readers took a much longer time to generate labels for the novel stimuli than the good readers.

In order to provide a fair test of the hypothesis that poor readers are slower than children who read well to develop in their use of efficient task strategies, the age of the children used as subjects must be carefully matched with the particular strategy being studied. This matching is necessary because certain strategies appear to undergo periods of maximum development at particular age levels (Hagen, et al., 1975). Since developmental research has shown that rehearsal of familiar objects develops relatively early (Flavell et al., 1966), it is possible that Kastner & Rickards' (1974) failure to find rehearsal differences between good and poor readers when familiar stimuli were used was due to the age of the children in their study. Consistent with this hypothesis are the results from a study by Torgesen & Goldman (1977), who found that, among second-grade children, good readers recalled sequences of familiar stimuli better and rehearsed them more than did children with reading problems. They also found that when children were told to name the stimuli aloud as they were presented, differences between groups in both recall and rehearsal were eliminated.

Taken together, these studies provide support for at least two major hypotheses about the reasons for memory deficiencies in children with reading problems. First, children who read well appear to be more proficient at supplying verbal labels for certain kinds of stimuli. This finding will appear again in the next section, and suggests a possible linguistic base for the memory problems of poor readers. It is, however, also apparent that children who are poor readers may be deficient in the use of active strategies like rehearsal even when the appropriate labels are easily available to them. This conclusion is supported by the fact that all the poor readers in the Torgesen & Goldman (1977) study could name the stimuli they were asked to remember, and only minimal prompting was required to raise their performance to the level of the good readers.

In addition to differences between skilled and less-skilled readers in the use of relatively simple strategies such as stimulus labeling and rehearsal, there is also evidence to suggest that poor readers may be inefficient in the application of more complex strategies such as making use of categorical structure to aid recall. For example, Torgesen (1977b) asked fourth-grade children of different reading levels to study 24 pictures of common objects, which could be grouped into four categories. The children were encouraged to move the pictures around or to do anything else during a two-minute study period which they felt would help them remember the pictures better. In addition to recalling more pictures, the good readers were more likely to sort the material into categories during the study period. However, brief training in the use of categorization as a mnemonic strategy eliminated differences in recall between children in the two reading groups.

The finding that poor readers are less likely than good readers to take advantage of categorical relationships among stimuli in their preparation for recall has been replicated with another sample of poor readers from a different region of the United States (Torgesen, et al., 1978). Again, recall differences were eliminated when the good and poor readers were induced to process the stimuli in the same manner. In this second study, however, instead of providing explicit training in the use of categorization as a mnemonic strategy, the children were simply asked to sort the stimuli into categories as rapidly as they could. Under these conditions, the poor readers recalled more pictures than when they were simply told to study the stimuli, while the recall of the good readers remained the same.

The research reviewed here, as well as other studies that might be mentioned (Parker et al., 1975; Tarver et al., 1976; Torgesen et al., 1978), support the hypothesis that children with reading problems engage in less efficient study plans or strategies when asked to memorize nonmeaningful material. (*Editor's Note:* See the chapter by Hallahan and Reeve in this volume for discussion of this point.) However, there are a variety of competing hypotheses which might explain the observed differences. Since all of these studies have investigated the use of strategies which require verbal skills, it is possible that the differences in strategy use may be accounted for in terms of differences in the basic linguistic knowledge or verbal skills required for the strategies to be implemented. If this is the only explanation, however, it is difficult to account for the rapid improvement of poor readers' recall when they are provided with brief training and support in the use of the strategies. In other words, if the differences between reading groups are due solely to relatively stable differences between groups in basic linguistic skills, it would seem that minimal training would not have such a powerful effect in reducing the differences in performance between groups. Thus, the studies reviewed here also provide support for the idea that some reading disabled children do poorly on memory tasks because they fail to adopt an active, planful, and organized approach to the task (Torgesen, 1977a). The use of these kinds of variables to explain the differences in memory performance would imply that poor readers experience difficulties in the "management" of their capacities rather than limitations of capacities per se.

Linguistic Subskills of Memory Performance. We saw in a previous section of this paper how semantic and conceptual development produces striking changes in the ways in which children remember. The converse seems also to be true: deficiencies in the linguistic knowledge or skills required to encode material in memory can lead to serious performance problems on many kinds of memory tasks. Recent research has begun to identify a variety of deficiencies in the verbal skills of poor readers which appear to influence their performance on memory tasks as well as to limit their reading proficiency. Perfetti & Goldman (1976), for example, tested good and poor readers from grades three and five on two memory tasks. These investigators were interested to see if poor readers had a general deficit in short-term memory, or if their memory problems were specific to reading-like, verbal tasks. The first task administered was a probe digit task. The children were asked to listen to strings of 13 digits and then to indicate which digit followed a probe digit. Both groups of readers remembered the digits equally well, and the conclusion was drawn that good and poor readers did not differ in short-term memory capacity.

In a prose analog to the digit task, the children *listened* to stories. Periodically a word from the story was repeated and the child was to recall the word that had followed the repeated word in the story. On this task, the poor readers were much less accurate than the good readers. This was true even when the answers were scored as correct if a semantically appropriate word was recalled instead of the exact word. From these results, Perfetti & Goldman (1976) concluded that good and poor readers may differ in the way in which they encode linguistic information in working memory. Perhaps the most important conclusion from this study, and one which is consistent with research using quite different types of memory tasks (Vellutino, Steger, Harding, & Phillips, 1975), is the suggestion of a specific rather than general memory deficit in poor readers.

If, indeed, poor readers have language-specific memory problems, it remains necessary to isolate the particular processes that are involved. One possible source of the differences between good and poor readers may involve skills in naming and labeling required for rapid encoding of material presented for memory. For example, Spring & Capps (1974) present evidence that good readers are able to name a variety of different kinds of stimuli more rapidly than poor readers. Furthermore, speed of naming was correlated in their study with performance on a task involving memory for sequences of numbers. One of the major conclusions from this study was that the slow naming speed of the poor readers interfered with their ability to process the material efficiently through the use of a strategy like verbal rehearsal. Other work by Denckla & Rudel (1976a, 1976b) confirms that poor readers have difficulties on "rapid automatic naming" tasks. Thus, poor readers may experience problems on tasks requiring the rapid manipulation of verbal materials because they encode, and perhaps access, these materials more slowly than do children with normal reading skills.

The fact that children with reading problems may have less efficient access to stored verbal materials than children who read well is confirmed in a study by Kail et al. (1977). These investigators asked sixth-graders to read a three-statement paragraph, then read and answer a simple yes-no question concerning the information presented in the paragraph. Scores on a reading comprehension test were found to be highly related to the speed with which questions were answered, with higher reading scores associated with faster answers. This was not surprising, since it was necessary to read the questions prior to answering them, and the measure of question answering speed reflected both reading and answering times. However, when reading time was held constant statistically, reading ability and answering speed were still highly correlated (.64). Kail et al. (1977) argued that with reading time held constant, answering time presumably reflects the time required to complete two processes. The first is search of memory for information relevant to the question; the second is the comparison of the retrieved information with the question and the determination of the appropriate answer. Thus, higher scores on reading comprehension tests seem to be associated with faster mnemonic search, comparison, and decision times. These results were replicated in a subsequent study (Kail & Marshall, 1978) in which it was found that good readers complete these different processes more rapidly in silent as well as oral reading.

Why should less-skilled readers search memory more slowly than skilled readers? Kail & Marshall (1978) suggested, as had Perfetti & Goldman (1976), that a likely source of the difference in rate of memory search is the manner in which information is encoded originally in working memory. Perhaps less-skilled readers tend to encode sentences verbatim, while skilled readers typically encode a "syntactically bare" version of a sentence that preserved important semantic relations. Alternatively, Perfetti & Goldman suggested that poor readers may be less likely to use various syntactic and semantic cues to aid the encoding of sentences. This latter hypothesis is supported in a study by Waller (1976) in which poor readers remembered the general meaning of sentences as well as good readers, but were deficient in their memory of grammatical markers and specific word strings. From the existing data it is not possible to eliminate either of these alternatives. What is perhaps more important, however, is the conclusion reached by Perfetti & Goldman. Specifically, memory deficits in poor readers may "be a question of how a limited capacity system is used rather than what its capacity is" (p. 41).

Summary and Conclusions. Both of the areas of research reviewed in this section support the idea that poor readers fail to take advantage of their "normal" memory capacities because of various inefficiencies in the way they process the information to be remembered. This inefficiency may take the form of a failure to apply consciously organized mnemonic strategies when they are appropriate, or it may involve language-based problems in rapid and accurate encoding which are less susceptible to conscious control.

Even within the narrow range of research considered here, several important problems remain for further investigation. What, for example, might be the relationship between the two different kinds of processing problems identified in this research? Spring & Capps (1974) suggest that deficiencies in the use of appropriate mnemonic strategies may be secondary to a lack of development of the linguistic subskills on which they are based. However, it is also possible that consistent and long-standing differences between good and poor readers in the level of activity and planfulness with which they approach school learning tasks may contribute to different degrees of "automaticity" of certain basic information processing skills (La Berge & Samuels, 1974). A final possibility is that these different kinds of processing problems are characteristic of different populations of poor readers. However these problems are resolved, future research in this area promises to make significant contributions both to our understanding of individual differences in memory processes and to our knowledge of the variables which influence the attainment of reading proficiency.

CONCLUSIONS AND IMPLICATIONS

In this chapter, we have provided an overview of research on memory skills that emphasizes certain basic theoretical concepts and distinctions. Taken together, the research reported here provides a fairly comprehensive view of the factors which lead to more or less efficient performance on memory tasks. We have seen that performance on most memory tasks improves with age, and we have obtained some understanding of the developmental attainments which underlie improvement in memory performance. We have also seen that many of the same concepts which can be used to account for developmental change are useful in describing the problems which exceptional children face on memory tasks.

Although recent research has provided a substantial increase in our scientific understanding of memory processes in children, the maximum benefit of this research will not be felt until the results are translated into improvements in educational practice. Because most of the studies reviewed in this chapter were conducted in the laboratory using tasks which are not part of the normal school curriculum, they do not yield techniques which have immediate application in the classroom. Yet, the conceptual analysis of memory skills made possible by laboratory research has the potential to make important contributions to educational technique. In fact, as Rohwer & Dempster (1977) have pointed out, the general principles and major distinctions which are derived from basic research on memory can provide a useful framework from which to evaluate current practices and to develop new approaches to instruction. We turn now to a consideration of some of the implications of memory research for education. This will also serve as a chapter summary, as the principles outlined here are, in our view, among the most basic and well demonstrated findings from laboratory research on memory development

1. *Most memory tasks require active memorization activities or strategies.* One of the clearest conclusions from research on the development of memory is that children who deal with memory tasks actively through the use of efficient memorization strategies remember best. Thus, it is important for educators to pay attention to the ways in which children process information that is to be remembered. For example, Chalfant (1977) has suggested that many children become poor spellers because they do not know how to prepare effectively for a spelling test through the use of systematic rehearsal and self-testing. It would be incorrect to say that these children have "poor memories"; rather, they are deficient in certain study, or memorization, skills which are necessary to gain maximum benefit from the basic capacities which they possess. Educators who become convinced of the importance of initial processing activities on subsequent memory performance may change their educational practices in several ways. They may, for example, begin to observe more closely and systematically the individual study or information processing habits of their students. They may also

begin to teach explicitly such simple strategies as rehearsal (perhaps even practice it in class) or the use of organization to aid memory. Finally, they may begin to observe their own teaching procedures for ways to build in the requirement that children actively process or manipulate the material which they present to their classes.

2. *Many exceptional children approach memory tasks differently than children who learn normally in the classroom.* Certain classes of exceptional children, particularly the mildly mentally retarded, consistently fail to approach memory tasks in an efficient manner. Not only do they fail to use appropriate mnemonic strategies in most instances, but retarded children also appear to be much less sensitive than children of normal intelligence to the need to modify strategies in response to the particular requirements of a task. In attempts to see if retarded children's use of strategies can be modified by training, laboratory research has addressed educational concerns directly. The results of training studies indicate that the memory performance of retarded children can be dramatically increased when they are induced to use appropriate mnemonic strategies. At present, however, the educational implications of this finding are uncertain because of the frequent failure of training in the use of specific strategies to generalize to situations other than the one in which the training was conducted. At present, there appear to be three alternative approaches to the enhancement of memory skills in retarded children that need to be tested for their utility in educational settings.

The first approach involves direct training and practice in the use of specific mnemonic strategies. Although previous research indicates that such training would not lead to a *general* improvement in memory skills, it may be possible to improve performance on certain crucial academic tasks by providing training on strategies which are specifically relevant to them. To have a positive effect, such training would not have to lead to enhancement of learning in many different areas, but could be justified because of its salutory effect on specific, isolated areas of academic performance.

A second way in which memory might be enhanced would be through training and instruction in the "executive skills" that appear to underlie the spontaneous application of appropriate strategies across different tasks. The knowledge and awareness associated with the "executive functions" appear to be acquired by most normal children as a natural result of their attempts to meet the demands of various academic tasks. If this knowledge can be acquired experientially without formal instruction, then formal instruction, or structured experience, may enhance the development of these skills in retarded children.

A final approach to the enhancement of memory performance in retarded children might involve the development of certain simple tasks which explicitly require the children to process information in ways which enhance retention. Such tasks, often referred to as orienting tasks (Jenkins, 1974), require children to process, or manipulate, information in a certain way in order to comply with the basic goal of the task. These tasks are designed so that children acquire knowledge "incidentally" as they interact with the material. This is not a totally new procedure and is often applied in various workbook types of assignments. However, as educators become more aware of the specific kinds of processing activities which are most beneficial to long-term retention, these "orienting activities" may assume greater importance in the instruction of exceptional children.

3. *Memory is not a unitary process and it reflects overall cognitive development.* The idea that memory is not a unitary process, but instead is dependent on a complex array of subskills, may help educators to differentiate among a variety of different kinds of memory problems. For example, instead of simply saying that a child who has problems remembering things has a "specific memory deficit," knowledge of the basic processes which underlie memory performance directs our attention to specific aspects of the child's behavior which may produce a memory problem. This idea has powerful implications for the diagnosis of educational problems and points diagnosticians toward the kind of information that can suggest appropriate remedial procedures. Rather than giving a child general practice on memory tasks to remediate a "memory problem," for example, s/he may be given much more focused training on the particular subskills that are most central to the overall difficulty.

An awareness of the close relationship between memory and other cognitive attainments provides potentially important information to educators about the interdependence of intellectual skills. Research which demonstrates the relationship between memory performance and linguistic development, general knowledge, and information processing skills suggests the impact which training in many different areas may have on memory skills.

4. *There are large individual differences in the functional capacity of short-term memory.* Young children and many exceptional children are able to retain less information on a short-term basis than older and normal children. Short-term memory is often referred to as "working memory" because of its role in storing information relevant to ongoing cognitive activities. For example, all of the numbers and relationships necessary to the solution of a verbally administered word problem in arithmetic must be stored together briefly while the problem is being solved. Awareness of the fact that many children are severely limited in the amount of information they can retain in short-term memory should sensitize educators to the memory demands of various academic tasks. A child may appear to be deficient in the ability to solve certain kinds of complex problems because of an inability to retain all the information required for solution. Thus, educators of exceptional children, in particular, need to carefully evaluate the memory demands of classroom activities to insure that they do not exceed the functional memory capacities of the children who are expected to profit from them. It should be emphasized that we are referring to the functional rather than absolute capacity of short-term memory. As we have seen throughout this chapter, the

absolute capacity of short-term or working memory changes little as children grow older, and there is no compelling evidence that exceptional children have abnormally small short-term memory capacity. Exceptional and normal children differ in the use of, rather than the absolute size of, short-term memory.

In this summary, we have not attempted to provide specific educational suggestions which might be derived from basic research on memory. Rather, we have indicated various ways in which general, and firmly established, concepts supported by this research may be used to guide educational efforts and concerns. We expect that as more of the specific details of the kinds of research we have reviewed are assimilated by educators, many specific applications to education will become apparent. Both the education of exceptional children and our basic knowledge of memory processes can only be enriched by increased interaction between educators and psychologists interested in the scientific examination of memory development.

REFERENCES

Anastasia, A. (1968) *Psychological testing.* New York: Macmillan.

Anglin, J. M. (1970) *The growth of word meaning.* Cambridge, Mass.: MIT Press.

Applebee, A. N. (1971) "Research in reading retardation: Two critical problems." *Journal of Child Psychology and Psychiatry* 12: 91-113.

Atkinson, R. C., Hansen, D. C., and Bernbach, H. (1964) "Short-term memory with young children." *Psychonomic Science 1964* 1: 255-156.

———, and Shiffrin, R. M. (1968) "Human memory: A proposed system and its control processes." In K. W. Spence and J. T. Spence (eds.), *The psychology of learning and motivation.* Vol. 2. New York: Academic Press.

Bartlett, F. C. (1932) *Remembering.* New York: Cambridge University Press.

Baumeister, A. A. (1967) "Problems in comparative studies of mental retardates and normals." *American Journal of Mental Deficiency, 71:* 869-875.

Belmont, J. M., and Butterfield, E. C. (1969) "The relations of short-term memory to development and intelligence." In L. P. Lipsett and H. W. Reese (eds.), *Advances in child development and behavior,* Vol. 4. New York: Academic Press.

———, and ——— Learning strategies as determinants of memory deficiencies. (1971) *Cognitive Psychology,* 2: 411-420.

———, and ——— (1977) "The instructional approach to developmental cognitive research." In R. V. Kail and J. W. Hagen (eds.), *Perspectives on the development of memory and cognition.* Hillsdale, N.J.: Erlbaum Associates.

Bisanz, G. L. (1977) "A framework for developmental investigations of story comprehension: Thematic structure and author-reader communication." Unpublished master's thesis, University of Pittsburgh.

Bisanz, J. H., Kail, R. V., Pellegrino, J. W., and Siegel, A. W. (1977) "The locus of developmental changes in encoding." Presented at the annual meeting of the Midwestern Psychological Association, Chicago.

Bower, G. H. (1967) "A multicompetent theory of the memory trace." In K. W. Spence and J. T. Spence (eds.), *The psychology of learning and motivation,* Vol. 1. New York: Academic Press.

Briggs, G. E., and Blaha, J. (1969) "Memory retrieval and central comparison times in information processing." *Journal of Experimental Psychology* 79: 395-402.

Brown, A. L., (1972) "Context and recency cues in the recognition memory of retarded children and adolescents." *American Journal of Mental Deficiency* 77: 54-58.

———— (1974) "The role of strategic behavior in retardate memory." In N. R. Ellis (ed.), *International review of research in mental retardation,* Vol. 7. New York: Academic Press.

————, Campione, J. C., and Murphy, M. D. (1974) "Keeping track of changing variables: Long-term retention of a trained rehearsal strategy by retarded adolescents." *American Journal of Mental Deficiency.* 78: 446-453.

————, and DeLoache, J. S. (1978) "Skills, plans, and self-regulation." In R. Siegler (ed.), *Children's thinking: What Develops?* Hillsdale, N.J. LEA (in press).

————, and Scott, M.S. (1971) "Recognition memory for pictures in preschool children." *Journal of Experimental Child Psychology* 11: 401-412.

Campbell, D. T., and Fiske, D. W. (1959) "Convergent and discriminant validation by the multitrait-multimethod matrix." *Psychological Bulletin* 56: 81-105.

Campione, J. C., and Brown, A. L. (1977) "Memory and metamemory development in educable mentally retarded children." In Kail, R. V. and Hagen, J. W. (eds.), *Perspectives on the development of memory and cognition.* Hillsdale, N.J.: Erlbaum Associates.

Cermak, L. S., Sagotsky, G., and Moshier, C. (1972) "Development of the ability to encode within evaluative dimensions." *Journal of Experimental Child Psychology* 13: 210-219.

Chalfant, J. C. (1977) "Improving the memory process." Paper presented at the annual meetings of the Association for Children with Learning Disabilities.

Chapman, L. J., and Chapman, J. P. (1973) "Problems in the measurement of cognitive deficit. *Psychological Bulletin* 79: 380-385.

Clark, E. V. (1973) "What's in a word? On the child's acquisition of semantics in his first language." In T. E. Moore (ed.), *Cognitive development and the acquisition of language.* New York: Academic Press.

Cofer, C. N. 1975) "An historical perspective." In C. N. Cofer (ed.), *The structure of human memory.* San Francisco: W. H. Freeman.

Cohen, L. B., and Gelber, E. R. (1975) "Infant visual memory." In L. B. Cohen and P. Salapatek (eds.), *Infant perception: From sensation to cognition,* Vol. 1. New York: Academic Press.

Cole, M., and Scribner, S. (1977) "Cross-cultural studies of memory and cognition." In R. V. Kail and J. W. Hagen (eds.), *Perspectives on the development of memory and cognition.* Hillsdale, N.J.: Erlbaum Associates.

Corsini, D. A., Jacobus, K. A., and Leonard, S. D. (1969) "Recognition memory of preschool children for pictures and words." *Psychonomic Science* 16: 192-193.

Denckla, M., and Rudel, R. (1976a) "Naming of object drawings by dyslexic and other learning disabled children." *Brain and Language,* 3: 1-16.

————, and Rudel, R. (1976b) "Rapid 'automatized' naming (R.A.N.): Dyslexia differentiated from other learning disabilities." *Neurophychologia* 14: 471-479.

Doehring, D. G. (1976) "The evaluation of two models of reading disability." In R. M. Knights and D. J. Baker (eds.), *Neuropsychology of learning disorders: Theoretical approaches.* Baltimore, Md.: University Park Press.

Dugas, J. L., and Kellas, G. (1974) "Encoding and retrieval processes in normal children and retarded adolescents." *Journal of Experimental Child Psychology* 17: 177-185.

Ellis, N. R. (1963) "The stimulus trace and behavioral inadequacy." In N. R. Ellis (ed.), *Handbook of mental deficiency.* New York: McGraw-Hill.

Esrov, L. V., Hall, J. W., and LaFaver, D. K. (1974) "Preschooler's conceptual and acoustic encoding as evidenced by release from PI." *Bulletin of the Psychonomic Society* 4: 89-90.

Fisher, M. A., and Zeaman, D. (1973) "An attention-retention theory of retardate discrimination learning." In N. R. Ellis (ed.), *International review of research in mental retardation,* Vol 6, New York: Academic Press.

Flavell, J. H. (1977) *Cognitive Development.* Englewood Cliffs, N.J.: Prentice-Hall.
———, Beach, D. R., and Chinsky, J. M. (1966) "Spontaneous verbal rehearsal in a memory task as a function age." *Child Development* 37; 283-299.
———Friederichs, A. G., and Hoyt, J. D. Developmental changes in memorization processes. *Cognitive Psychology,* 1970, *1*, 324-40.
———, and Wellman, H. (1977) "Metamemory." In R. V. Kail and J. W. Hagen (eds.), *Perspectives on the development of memory and cognition.* Hillsdale, : Erlbaum.
Galton, F. (1887) "Supplementary notes on "prehension" in idiots. *Mind* 12; 79-82.
Geyer, J. J. (1970) "Models of perceptual processing in reading." In H. Singer and R. B. Ruddell (eds.), *Theoretical models and processes of reading.* Newark, Del.: International Reading Association, pp. 47-94.
Glanzer, M. (1967) "Individual performance, R-R theory, and perception." In R. M. Gagne (ed.), *Learning and individual differences.* Columbus, Ohio: Merrill.
Gough, P. B. (1972) "One second of reading." In J. F. Kavanaugh, and I. G. Mattingly (eds.), *Language by ear and by eye.* Cambridge, Mass.: PIT Press.
Hagen, J. W., Jongeward, R. H., and Kail, R. V. (1975) "Cognitive perspectives on the development of memory." In H. W. Reese (ed.), *Advances in child development and behavior,* Vol. 10. New York: Academic Press.
———, and Kail, R. V. (1973) "Facilitation and distraction in short-term memory." *Child Development* 44; 831-836.
———, and Stanovich, K. E. (1973) " Memory: Strategies of acquisition." In R. V. Kail and J. W. Hagen (eds.), *Perspectives on the development of memory and cognition.* Hillsdale, N.J.: LEA.
Hallahan, D. P., and Cruickshank, W. M. (1973) *Psycho-educational foundations of learning disabilities.* Englewood Cliffs, N.J.: Prentice-Hall.
Harris, G. J., and Fleer, R. E. (1974) "High speed memory scanning in mental retardates: Evidence for a central processing deficit." *Journal of Experimental Child Psychology* 17: 452-459.
Hawkins, C. J. (1897) "Experiments on memory types." *Psychological Review,* 4: 289-294.
Huelsman, C. B. (1970) "The WISC subtest syndrome for disabled readers." *Perceptual and Motor Skills* 30: 535-550.
Hoving, K. L., Morin, R. E., and Konick, D. S. (1970) "Recognition reaction time and size of the memory set: A developmental study." *Psychonomic Science* 21: 247-248.
Hunt, E., Frost, N., and Lunneborg, C. (1973) "Individual differences in cognition: A new approach to intelligence." In C. Bower (ed.), *The psychology of learning and motivation,* Vol.8.
———, Lunneborg, C., and Lewis, J. (1975) "What does it mean to be high verbal?" *Cognitive Psychology* 7: 194-227.
Jenkins, J. J. (1974) "Remember that old theory of memory? Well, forget it!" *American Psychologist* 29: 785-795.
Kail, R. V., Chi, M. T. H., Ingram, A. L., and Danner, F. W. (1977) "Constructive Aspects of children's reading comprehension." *Child Development* 48: 684-688.
———, and Levine, L. E. (1976) "Encoding processes and sex-role preferences." *Journal of Experimental Child Psychology* 21: 256-263.
———, and Marshall, C. V. (1978) "Reading skill and memory scanning." Unpublished manuscript, University of Pittsburgh, 1978.
———, and Schroll, J. T. (1974) "Evaluative and taxonomic encoding in children's memory." *Journal of Experimental Child Psychology* 18: 426-37.
———, and Siegel, A. W. (1977) "The development of mnemonic encoding in children: From perception to abstraction." In R. V. Kail and J. W. Hagen (eds.), *Perspectives on the development of memory and cognition.* Hillsdale, N.J.: LEA, 1977.
Kastner, S. B., and Rickards, C. (1974) "Mediated memory with novel and familiar stimuli in good and poor readers." *Journal of Genetic Psychology* 124: 105-113.

Kingsley, P. R., and Hagen, J. W. (1969) "Induced versus spontaneous rehearsal in short-term memory in nursery school children." *Developmental Psychology* 1: 40–46.

Kreutzer, M. A., Leonard, C., and Flavell, J. H. (1975) "An interview study of children's knowledge about memory." *Monographs of the Society for Research in Child Development* 40 (1): 1–58.

LaBerge, D., and Samuels, S. J. (1974) "Toward a theory of automatic information processing in reading." *Cognitive Psychology,* 6: 293–323.

Labouvie-Vief, G. (1976) "Intellectual abilities and learning: Retrospect and Prospect." In J. R. Levin and V. L. Allen (eds.), *Cognitive learning in children: Theories and strategies.* New York: Academic Press.

Liben, L. S. (1977) "Memory in the context of cognitive development: The Piagetian approach." In R. V. Kail and J. W. Hagen (eds.), *Perspectives on the development of memory and cognition.* Hillsdale, N.J.: Erlbaum.

Lyons, J. J., and Briggs, G. E. (1971) "Speed-accuracy tradeoff with different types of stimuli." *Journal of Experimental Psychology* 91: 115–119.

Mandler, J. M., and Day, J. (1975) "Memory for orientation of forms as a function of their meaningfulness and complexity." *Journal of Experimental Child Psychology* 20: 430–443.

McCarthy, D. (1972) *McCarthy's scales of children's abilities.* New York: The Psychological Corporation.

Menyuk, P. (1971) *The acquisition and development of language.* Englewood Cliffs, N.J.: Prentice-Hall.

Milgram, N. A. (1973) "Cognition and language in mental retardation: Distinctions and implications." In D. K. Routh (ed.), *The experimental psychology of mental retardation.* Chicago: Aldine.

Moynahan, E. D. (1973) "The development of knowledge concerning the effect of categorization upon free recall." *Child Development* 44: 238–246.

Nelson, K. E. (1971) "Memory development in children: Evidence from nonverbal tasks." *Psychonomic Science* 25: 346–348.

Ornstein, P. A., Naus, M. J., and Liberty, C. (1975) "Rehearsal and organizational processes in children's memory." *Child Development* 46: 818–830.

———, ———, and Stone, B. P. (1977) "Rehearsal training and developmental differences in memory." *Developmental Psychology* 13: 15–24.

Osgood, C. E., Suci, G. J., and Tannenbaum, P. H. (1957) *The measurement of meaning.* Urbana, Ill.: University of Illinois Press.

Paris, S. G. (1975) "Integration and inference in children's comprehension and memory." In F. Restle et al. (eds.), *Cognitive theory,* Vol. 1. Hillsdale, N.J.: LEA.

———, and Lindauer, B. K. (1977) "Constructive aspects of children's comprehension and memory." In R. V. Kail and J. W. Hagen (eds.), *Perspectives on the development of memory and cognition.* Hillsdale, N. J.: Erlbaum.

———, and Lindauer, B. K. (1976) "The role of inference in children's comprehension and memory for sentences." *Cognitive Psychology* 8: 217–227.

———, and Upton, L. R. (1976) "Children's memory for inferential relationships in prose." *Child Development* 47: 660–668.

Parker, T. B., Freston, C. W., and Drew, C. J. (1975) "Comparison of verbal performance of normal and learning disabled children as a function of input organization." *Journal of Learning Disabilities* 8: 53–60.

Perfetti, C. A., and Goldman, S. R. (1976) "Discourse memory and reading comprehension skill." *Journal of Verbal Learning and Verbal Behavior* 14: 33–42.

Piaget, J. (1970) "Piaget's theory." In P. Mussen (ed.), *Carmichael's manual of child psychology.* New York: Wiley,

———— and Inhelder, B. (1973) *Memory and intelligence.* New York: Basic Books.

Ritter, K. (1975) "Development of production and maintenance of a retrieval cue strategy." Unpublished doctoral dissertation, University of Minnesota.

Rizzo, N. D. (1939) "Studies in visual and auditory memory span with special references to reading disability." *Journal of Experimental Education* 8: 208-244.

Rohwer, W. D., and Dempster, F. N. (1977) "Memory development and educational processes." In R. V. Kail and J. W. Hagen (eds.), *Perspectives on the development of memory and cognition.* Hillsdale, N.J.: Erlbaum.

Rugel, R. P. (1974) "Wisc subtest scores of disabled readings. A review with respect to Dannatyne's recategorization," *Journal of Learning Disabilities* 7: 57-64.

Senf, G. M. (1976) "Future research needs in learning disabilities." In R. P. Anderson and C. G. Halcomb (eds.), *Learning disability minimal brain dysfunction syndrome.* Springfield, Ill.: Charles C Thomas.,

———— (1974) "Issues surrounding classification in learning disabilities." Paper presented at Annual National Convention, Association for Children with Learning Disabilities.

Silverman, W. P. (1974) "High speed scanning of nonalphanumeric symbols in cultural-familially retarded and nonretarded children." *American Journal of Mental Deficiency* 79: 44-51.

Sperber, R. D., Greenfield, D. B., and House, B. J. (1973) "A nonmonotonic effect of distribution of trials in retardate learning and memory." *Journal of Experimental Psychology* 99: 186-198.

Spitz, H. H. (1966) "The role of input organization in the learning and memory of mental retardates." In N. H. Ellis (ed.), *International review in mental retardation,* Vol. 2. New York: Academic Press.

Spring, C., and Capps, C. (1974) "Encoding speed, rehearsal, and probed recall of dyslexic boys." *Journal of Educational Psychology* 66: 780-786.

Sternberg, S. (1966) "High speed scanning in human memory." *Science* 153: 652-654.

Tarver, S. G., Hallahan, D. P., and Kauffman, J. M. (1976) "Verbal rehearsal and selective attention in children with learning disabilities: A developmental lag." *Journal of Experimental Child Psychology* 22: 375-385.

Torgesen, J. K. (1975) "Problems and prospects in the study of learning disabilities." In M. Hetherington and J. Hagen (eds.), *Review of child development research,* Vol. 5. New York: Russell Sage Foundation.

————, (1977a) "The role of non-specific factors in the task performance of learning disabled children: A theoretical assessment." *Journal of Learning Disabilities* 10: 127-34.

————, (1977b) "Memorization processes in reading disabled children." *Journal of Educational Psychology* 69: 571-578.

————, Bowen, C., and Ivey, C. (1978) "Task structure vs. modality of presentation: a study of the construct validity of the visual-aural digit span test." *Journal of Educational Psychology* (in press).

————, and Goldman, T. (1977) "Rehearsal and short-term memory in reading disabled children." *Child Development,* 48: 56-60.

————, Murphy, H. A., and Ivey, C. (1979) "The influence of an orienting task on the memory performance of children with reading problems." *Journal of Learning Disabilities,* 12: 396-401.

Vellutino, F., Steger, J., Harding, C., and Phillips, F. (1975) "Verbal vs. non-verbal paired-associates learning in poor and normal readers." *Neuropsychologia* 13: 75-82.

Wagner, D. A. (1974) "The development of short-term and incidental memory: A cross-cultural study." *Child Development* 45: 389-396.

———— (1978) "Memories of Morocco: The influence of age, schooling, and environment on memory." *Cognitive Psychology* 10: 1-28.

Waller, G. T. (1976) "Children's recognition memory for written sentences: A comparison of good and poor readers." *Child Development,* 47: 90-95.

Wechsler, D. (1974) *Wechsler intelligence scale for children-revised*. New York: The Psychological Corporation.
Wellman, H. M., Ritter, K., and Flavell, J. H. (1975) "Deliberate memory behavior in the delayed reactions of very young children." *Developmental Psychology* 11; 780-787.
Werner, H. (1937) "Process and achievement—a basic problem of education and developmental psychology." *Harvard Educational Review*, 7: 353-368.
West, R. F. (1975) *Cognitive development and reading processes* (Developmental Report Number 76). Department of Psychology, University of Michigan.
Wickens, D. D. (1972) "Characteristics of word encoding." In A. W. Melton and E. Martin (eds.), *Coding processes in human memory*. Washington, D.C.: Winston,
———, and Clark, S. E. (1968) "Osgood dimensions as an encoding category in short-term memory." *Journal of Experimental Psychology* 78: 580-584.
———, Reutener, D. B., and Eggemeier, F. T. (1972) "Sense impression as an encoding dimension of words." *Journal of Experimental Psychology* 96: 301-306.
Wolf, T. H. (1973) *Alfred Binet*, Chicago, Ill. University of Chicago Press.
Yussen, S. R., and Levy, V. M. (1975) "Developmental change in predicting one's own span of short-term memory." *Journal of Experimental Child Psychology* 19: 502-508.
Zigler, E. (1969) "Developmental versus difference theories of mental retardation and the problem of motivation." *American Journal of Mental Deficiency* 73: 536-556.

ATTENTION PROCESSES: RESEARCH, THEORY, AND IMPLICATIONS FOR SPECIAL EDUCATION*

Antoinette Krupski,** UNIVERSITY OF CALIFORNIA, LOS ANGELES

INTRODUCTION

Attention problems are associated with almost every type of handicapping condition. For example, mentally retarded (Crosby & Blatt, 1968; Denny, 1964; Krupski, 1975, 1976, 1977), learning-disabled/hyperactive (Alabiso, 1972; Douglas, 1972; Dykman et al., 1971; Harris, 1976; Keogh & Margolis, 1976a; Tarver & Hallahan, 1974; Torgesen, 1975), epileptic (Stores, 1973), autistic (Gold & Gold, 1975), and low achieving normal youngsters (Soli & Devine, 1976) have all been characterized as having serious attentional problems. This characterization has its source in anecdotal reports from teachers and parents, as well as in reports of researchers who interpret performance differences between handicapped and normal youngsters on attention-demanding tasks as being due to the handicapped groups' problems with attention. The frequency with which attention problems are mentioned coupled with the self-evident relationship between attention and learning attest to the central role these processes play in the education of exceptional youngsters.

That problems of attention bear such close association with special education populations is consistent with data reported in the adult psychopathological literature. "Deficits" in attention have been hypothesized as at least one of the primary characteristics of many diverse psychopathological conditions found in adults such as schizophrenia, acute and chronic brain disorders, and the like. This consistent association between diverse expressions of psychopathology and attention problems has led at least one author to argue "... The so-called mental disorders may be comprehensively reconstrued as signs, symptoms, and syndromes of the diseases of attention" (Meldman, 1970, p. 156).

Given the wide agreement regarding prevalence of attention problems in deviant groups including special education populations, it is not surprising that a rather extensive experimental literature focused on problems of attention has accumulated. Since comprehensive reviews of developmental aspects of attention are available (e.g., Alabiso, 1972; Douglas, 1972; Keogh & Margolis, 1976a; Pick, et al., 1975; Tarver & Hallahan, 1974), these data will not be discussed in detail here. Rather, the purpose of this chapter will be to review select aspects of research and theory focused on attention processes with the aim of identifying those areas that appear to present most frequent and serious problems to handicapped children. Before reviewing specific data, it is instructive to examine the history of attention research as well as various proposed definitions of attention. Such examination will provide a context in which to discuss the research related to handicapped children.

History of Attention Research

Historically, attention was regarded as a central construct in early psychological study (e.g., James, 1890, Ribot, 1903; Titchner, 1908) and was studied through introspection. With the advent of the Behavioristic and Gestalt movements early in the twentieth century, however, the concept of attention fell into disuse and, to some extent, disrepute. During this time, the predominant schools of thought sought simple and straightforward laws of behavior relating input to output. Attention was viewed as an internal mechanism that contributed little to an understanding of these laws (Kahneman, 1973). Further, the introspectionist methodology, which played such a predominant role in the early study of attention, was the object of critical attack by the Behaviorists. Questions were raised regarding experimental control, the feasibility of replication, and interpretation of introspection-based attention studies. Such questions, coupled with a changing emphasis in psychological theory, led to an abandonment of the study of attention until the 1950s (Moray, 1969).

Resurgence of interest in attention processes since the 1950s has been attributed to several sources. First, the use of operational definitions, in stimulus-response terms, of "objects" of attention served to restore a sense of respectability to the study of attention (Moray, 1969). Second, during the Second World War, applied psychologists were required to deal with important practical problems that were clearly related to attention processes. Among these practical concerns were situations where human operators were required to monitor complex communications systems with a high flow of incoming information. Often these operators were required to do more than one thing at once. Thus, questions regarding how many things a person could attend to at one time, or the division of attention, became a problem of serious study (Moray, 1969). Sustained attention was also highlighted in studies of radar operators. The appearance of enemy submarines in recently searched waters led to initial studies on the effects of fatigue on radar detection of such targets (J. F. Mackworth, 1969), thus commencing the voluminous literature on vigilance performance. These investigations were originally designed to solve practical problems, which they did. But they also led to major theoretical formulations which had wide-reaching implications for understanding psychological processes. The impact of this early work is still very much in evidence in current theorizing about attention processes.

A third force which has been acknowledged as supporting increased research activity in attention has been the advance of technological knowledge. The invention of the tape recorder (Moray, 1969) as well as the computer (Neisser, 1976) are but two examples of technological contributions that have had an incalculable impact on the development of psychological theory, including theories of attention. Finally, the emergence of cognitive psychology cannot be ignored as a significant influence in the resurgence of attention research (Kahneman, 1973). The difficulty of predicting behavior by stimulus characteristics alone led the early cognitive psychologists to place a renewed emphasis on attention and other presumed internal mechanisms.

In summary, the resurgence of interest in attention processes over the last 30 years has been attributed to a number of converging forces: The introduction of operational definitions of attention-related processes, the highly productive attention-related research during World War II, technological advances, as well as the emergence of cognitive psychology. The result of this increased activity is a voluminous and unwieldy literature in which multiple approaches and paradigms, all designed to illuminate some aspect of attention processes, are represented.

Definitions of Attention

Given the history of attention research, it is not surprising that many definitions of attention exist. Often these definitions are nonoverlapping and make reference to specific properties that encompass related processes such as memory and learning. Moray (1969), for example, suggested that the concept of attention consisted of at least seven subdivisions including: mental concentration, vigilance, selective attention, search, activation, set, and "analysis by synthesis." The diversity among these components led Moray to conclude that there may be a need for as many different theories as there are subdivisions. In a similar vein, Meldman (1970) states, "The word 'attention' has had more varied usages than perhaps any other in psychology" (p. 2). On the basis of these descriptions, it is probably fair to conclude that the term "attention" is so encompassing that it may be impossible to know what it means unless substantial contextual information is provided.

The existence of multiple idiosyncratic definitions of attention is particularly problematic in the study of handicapped children. Here, it is not unusual for attention problems to be employed as a post hoc explanation for anomolous results in studies of other psychological functions (Torgesen, 1975). As noted by Keogh and Margolis (1976a), it is also not unusual for educators to view "attention problems" as a single or unitary characteristic or trait. Such practices reflect imprecision in use of the term which make it difficult to draw general conclusions about the specific nature of "attention problems" that are so frequently reported for handicapped youngsters.

The practical implications of this situation are serious. First, it is impossible to identify relevant treatment approaches (not to mention the impossibility of evaluating the effectiveness of such approaches) on anything other than an individual basis unless the presenting problems can be specifically described. Second, ill-defined characteristics such as "distractibility" or "inattention" are frequently used in conjunction with other assessment information as the basis for diagnosing various types of learning handicaps. One can only wonder about the reliability of clinical judgment in such situations. Thus, on both practical and conceptual levels, it would be useful to have specific descriptions of the attention problems that are so frequently associated with handicapping conditions.

A number of authors interested in attention problems have attempted to bring some order to these definitional problems by providing organizational schemes that incorporate the various definitions of attention. Illustrations of this approach include Alabiso (1972) who suggested that attention include span, focus, and selectivity components. Dykman et al. (1971) similarly suggested that attention consisted of four interrelated functions which included alertness, stimulus selection, focusing, and vigilance. A third illustration is provided by Keogh & Margolis (1976a). Using a clinically based functional approach, these investigators suggested three separate interactive components of attention which included coming to attention, decision-making, and sustaining attention.

Such illustrations demonstrate attempts to organize the rather diverse definitions and properties of attention that have been proposed in the past. All are based on the assumption that attention can be conceptualized as a series of components and, further, all acknowledge that there is probably some interaction among components, although little information is provided as to the specific nature of these interactions. Common components in these illustrations include sustained as well as selective aspects of attention. *(Editor's Note:* See the chapter by Hallahan and Reeves in this volume for detailed review of selective attention.)

A TWO-DIMENSIONAL VIEW OF ATTENTION

Another system of organization of attention processes which extends the previously described frameworks will be proposed here. In this view, attention processes are conceptualized as having two relevant dimensions. The first dimension is based on the traditional distinction between voluntary and involuntary attention, while the second dimension reflects the temporal properties of attention, either sustained or short-term. Each of these dimensions will be described below and will then be related directly to the problems of attention that comprise the focus of this chapter.

Voluntary/Involuntary Dimension

The first dimension includes the distinction that has been traditionally drawn between voluntary and involuntary attention processes. Ribot (1903) and William James (1890) were among the first to discuss this dichotomy, although various forms of it have emerged in more recent writings (Gibson & Rader, 1979; Leontiev, 1932; Kahneman, 1973; Porges, 1976; Yendovitskaya, 1971). This view of attention processes deserves some elaboration, as it appears to provide a parsimonious framework in which to discuss a rather sizable and diverse literature as well as to provide direction for understanding developmental aspects of attention. Let us look first at James's description of these aspects of attention.

Involuntary attention was characterized by James as elicited directly by particular qualities of a stimulus. For example, intense, sudden, or voluminous stimuli were thought to elicit a form of involuntary attention as were stimuli that had "congenital appeal" such as blood, strange things, moving things, etc. Voluntary attention, in contrast, appears to have a strong volitional component. It was described by James as removed from immediate stimuli and as requiring effort for its maintenance. He suggested that one spends effort on stimuli or ideas that, although removed, are associated with some other immediately interesting thing. Sustaining attention to an undesirable task in order to obtain a reward later is an example of voluntary attention taken from James.

James suggested that children express primarily involuntary forms of attention. Take, for example, the following statement, "... this reflexive and passive character... makes the child seem to belong less to himself than to every object which happens to catch his notice..." (p. 417). One indication of maturity, according to James, is the ability to express voluntary forms of attention and, thus, exert more instrumental control over the stimuli in one's life.

An early theorist who expanded upon these notions was Leontiev (1932). He was clearly influenced by the writings of Ribot (1903) and Vygotsky (1962). His work is relevant to the present discussion because of his emphasis on developmental aspects of the voluntary/involuntary attention dichotomy. Like James, he distinguished voluntary attention from the involuntary form by its independence from direct and immediate stimulation as well as by the presence of effort. Initially, Leontiev argued, a child's attention is entirely involuntary; stimulus characteristics determine the length of time that a child will remain attentive. With continued development, the child's span of attention can be increased beyond the direct control of the immediate stimulus by the promise of a reward. Finally, in the most mature stage of development, Leontiev states that the child becomes capable of using external stimuli to organize his/her own behavior. In this final stage, then, the child controls his/her own attention by controlling stimulation. The development of voluntary attention in this framework clearly parallels traditional views of cognitive development.

Yendovitskaya's (1971) discussion of the development of voluntary attention is similar to that of Leontiev (1932). She reported a number of experiments that were interpreted as indicating increases in both voluntary and involuntary attention span with increasing age. In terms of involuntary attention span increases, it is argued that more elements in a situation and the relationships between them directly evoke exploration or orienting reactions as the child matures. The switch to voluntary attention processes is viewed as transformational and closely related to language; once linguistic components come to regulate a child's activity, voluntary forms of attention become more evident. This position is similar to that presented by Luria (1963). Again, the link between voluntary attention and cognition is intimate.

In summary, attention can be classified as voluntary or involuntary depending on the nature of the stimulus situation. Younger children are thought to exhibit primarily involuntary attention, although the number and type of stimuli that elicit involuntary attention are thought to change as a function of development. Unlike children, adults are thought to engage in more voluntary forms of attention. The emergence of voluntary attention appears closely linked to cognition and is viewed as a transformational shift in development.

Temporal Dimensions

Earlier it was suggested that two dimensions of attention were relevant to the present discussion, with the first being the voluntary/involuntary attention dimension. The second dimension meriting discussion is the distinction between sustained and brief episodes of attention. Sustained attention will be defined as the kind that lasts several minutes or hours, whereas short-term attention will be defined as lasting a matter of seconds.

Length of attention, i.e., sustained or short-term, is relevant in that it interacts with the voluntary/involuntary dimension. As such, the nature of these interactions will be overviewed in the sections that follow. The first section will focus on sustained aspects of attention whereas the second section will focus on short-term attention.

Sustained Attention. A variety of tasks and experimental paradigms have been employed to study sustained attention. Although the common feature of these experiments is that participants are expected to maintain attention to a particular task for an extended period of time, the tasks employed to elicit this effect differ considerably in the degree to which voluntary attention is demanded.

Although it appears logical to divide sustained attention into voluntary and involuntary subcomponents, such a division is problematic. Most tasks requiring sustained attention appear to have both voluntary and involuntary components. This is especially true in attempts to identify tasks that reflect involuntary sustained attention. "Pure" illustrations of this process, although conceptually feasible, are difficult to identify within real world experimental paradigms.

Thus, within the dimension of sustained attention, it does not appear possible to make a clean division between voluntary and involuntary processes. At the same time, however, it does appear possible to speak of tasks as having relatively greater or lesser demands for voluntary attention. In this regard, degree of demand for voluntary attention can be viewed as continuous, with tasks requiring high degrees of voluntary attention at one extreme of the continuum and those requiring relatively lesser degrees of voluntary attention at the other extreme.

Two tasks that appear to require high degrees of voluntary sustained attention are vigilance and reaction time. In vigilance, the participant is required to continuously monitor a monotonous stream of stimuli for an extended time. The participant's task is to detect infrequent and unpredictable signals that are usually interspersed among background stimuli (J. P. Mackworth, 1969, 1970, Stroh, 1971). A brief lapse in attention could easily result in a missed signal. Such demands rather easily fit the description of a task that requires a high degree of voluntary sustained attention. There has been a great deal of theoretical work on vigilance which is primarily based on experiments conducted with adult male subjects. The interested reader can find comprehensive reviews of this work in the following sources: Broadbent (1971), J. P. Mackworth (1969, 1970), Stroh (1971).

Reaction-time tasks, like vigilance, also appear to reflect demands for a high degree of voluntary sustained attention. Here, the participant is usually required to respond as quickly as possible to the onset of a stimulus that has been designated as a reaction signal. Even a brief lapse of attention during a trial could result in a significantly depressed reaction-time score. When the task involves an extended series of such trials, the participant is required to sustain attention for a period of minutes. Clearly, such demands characterize reaction time as a task that requires a high degree of voluntary sustained attention.

In summary, relatively high demands for voluntary sustained attention are exemplified in vigilance and reaction-time tasks. It is likely that most challenging school tasks would also fit into this category. In each of these tasks, maintenance of attention is required for an extended period and attention is not directly controlled nor directly elicited by physical properties of the stimuli. These tasks all require participants to bring themselves back to the task when attention drifts. This process calls for a degree of conscious monitoring and effort that is characteristic of voluntary attention.

Demands for voluntary attention appear significantly less in tasks that are inherently interesting or compelling, or in tasks that characteristically "hold" the attention of the participant for an extended period. Fast-moving, colorful, and exciting movies or television programs fit into this category. Also, attentive behaviors that are observed in unstructured or informal free-play situations where children are given a variety of interesting toys from which to choose also appear to reflect lesser demands for voluntary process than are found in vigilance or reaction-time tasks (Barkley, 1977b; Ellis et al., 1974; Routh & Schroeder, 1976). In both of these examples, it is assumed that the stimuli, i. e., movies or toys, are directly eliciting and holding the attention of a child for an extended time and, thus, qualify as examples of tasks with relatively low demand for voluntary attention.

Several investigators have made a distinction between tasks with active and passive demands (e.g., Cohen & Douglas, 1972). This distinction has typically occurred in investigations of particular physiological responses. In general, there appears to be a parallel between the active and passive task distinction and the continuum postulated to reflect degree of voluntary process proposed here. For example, in passive tasks, children are instructed to simply "watch" a light or "listen" to a tone; such stimuli are typically presented at intervals. No overt response is required of participants in the passive situation, although one or more physiological response systems are usually monitored during stimulus presentation.

Active tasks, in contrast, require the child to make an overt response (such as pressing a button) to the light or tone and/or to monitor these stimuli in a continuous fashion. In active tasks, it is assumed that stimuli acquire meaning by virtue of the requirement for overt responding to them. As such, it is likely that any resulting physiological change in relation to ongoing stimulation is likely to be a function of the meaning that the stimulus has acquired over time. Physiological change in relation to ongoing stimulation in the passive task, on the other hand, is more likely to be a function of the physical properties of the stimuli since the participant is not given any reason to attribute meaning to the occurrence of stimuli. Given this reasoning, it appears as though tasks typically designated as active in nature can be considered as requiring relatively greater demands for voluntary attention than can those tasks which have typically been designated as passive.

In summary, it has been suggested that tasks requiring sustained attention vary in the degree of voluntary processing demands. Tasks such as vigilance, reaction time, and challenging school tasks, all appear to require high degrees of voluntary sustained attention. In contrast, tasks which are inherently interesting or compelling or which "hold" the attention of participants appear to require relatively lesser degrees of voluntary processes. Distinctions between active and passive tasks appear to parallel the distinction proposed between greater and lesser demands for voluntary processes.

Short-term Attention. In long-term, or sustained attention, voluntary processes were conceptualized as continuous in nature. This is because it is difficult to draw a clear distinction between voluntary and involuntary processes within the sustained dimension and also because the notion of involuntary sustained attention has few illustrations in real-world tasks. Within the context of short-term attention, however, the distinction between voluntary and involuntary attention processes appears to be clear.

For example, involuntary short-term attention is illustrated in studies employing measures of the orienting response to stimulus onset. As the reader will recall, this designation encompasses attention that is directly elicited by the stimulus for a brief period, i.e., seconds. Orienting responses, or the brief physiological response to a change in ongoing stimulation, appear to reflect this passive and reflexive character.

The orienting response was first described by Russian physiologists (Pavlov, 1960; Sokolov, 1963) and is currently conceptualized as a loosely organized set of physiological and motoric responses to changes in ongoing stimulation. Responses such as changes in brain waves (specifically, alpha desynchronization), pupil dilation, decreased skin resistance (or, palmar sweating), and changes in the blood vessels (dilation of blood vessels in the head and constriction of blood vessels in the limbs) are thought to accompany orienting reactions (Lynn, 1966; Sokolov, 1963). Heart rate deceleration is also thought to reflect orienting activity (Graham & Clifton, 1966) as is momentary inhibition of ongoing motor activity (Obrist et al., 1970).

Recent discussions of the orienting response make a distinction between involuntary reflexive instances of orienting which are brought about by stimulus properties and voluntary, instrumental orienting that occurs in situations where an individual is required to make decisions (Kahneman, 1973) or in situations where an individual selects one stimulus over another on the basis of past experience or factors other than the immediate physical properties of the stimulus (Pick et al., 1975). In the first case, brief responses seem reflexive and passive in nature; the individual appears to respond with little or no instrumental control. This description parallels traditional definitions of involuntary short-term attention. The second case, where volition plays a greater role, calls for decision making or selection processes that are removed from the direct properties of the stimuli in addition to probably requiring some effort. Thus, this latter type of orienting behavior parallels traditional descriptions of voluntary attention.

In summary, it has been proposed that short-term attention processes can be viewed as involuntary or voluntary in nature. Studies of the orienting response appear to illustrate involuntary short-term processes while studies of short-term attention involving decision making or selective attention appear to illustrate voluntary short-term processes.

Summary

Experimental findings related to attention problems in handicapped children have been characterized as voluminous and diverse. A framework based on voluntary/involuntary and temporal dimensions was suggested as a context in which to organize this diverse literature. Although it is acknowledged that this framework has inherent limitations, it appears to be a useful heuristic in which to attempt parsimonious integration and interpretation of research findings related to attention problems in handicapped individuals as well as to explore directions for future research.

EXPERIMENTAL STUDIES OF ATTENTION IN ATYPICAL YOUNGSTERS

In general, traditional study of attention processes in atypical youngsters can be characterized as primarily laboratory-based experiments where groups of handicapped and nonhandicapped children are tested on a single task. Although experimental tasks employed in these studies typically bear little similarity to stimuli children encounter in their daily lives (Pick et al., 1975), they usually require high levels of attention for good performance. In general, then, the tasks used in traditional experimental research can be characterized as novel and as having high face validity.

Vigilance and reaction-time tasks are examples of tasks that fall into this category. Performance scores are the predominant dependent variable used for making inferences about attention processes. Experiments that employ some form of observation in either a laboratory or naturalistic setting have also been prevalent in the attention literature. In this approach, glances off-task or frequency of toy-changing are typical dependent measures used as a basis for making inferences about attentional processes.

In this section, four representative areas of attention research conducted with handicapped youngsters will be reviewed. These areas include vigilance, reaction time, observational research in multiple settings, and classroom observational research. The emphasis is on involuntary short-term and sustained attention. Little discussion is devoted to voluntary short-term attention as comprehensive reviews of this work already exist (e.g., Hallahan & Reeves, in this volume;

Attention Processes: Research, Theory and Implications for Special Education 111

Humphrey & Kleiman, 1978). The purpose of this review is to critically examine select aspects of existing literature in order to identify the nature of attention problems typically exhibited by handicapped youngsters.

Vigilance

As the reader will recall, vigilance tasks require an observer to continuously monitor a monotonous stream of stimuli for an extended time. The observer's task is to detect infrequent and unpredictable signals that are interspersed among background stimuli (J. P. Mackworth, 1969, 1970; Stroh, 1971). Often these stimuli are light flashes or auditory signals such as beeps. Stimuli of this nature are used presumably to simulate the real-life demands of a radar watch or of a communications monitoring task. Detections of the changes in the brightness of a light, loudness of a tone, or two jumps instead of one jump of a clock hand are examples of demands inherent in such tasks.

Vigilance tasks with greater cognitive demands have also been studied. Detecting an odd-even-odd combination of auditorily presented digits at the rate of one digit per second is an example of such a task (Bakan, 1959; Krupski et al., 1971). Another illustration is the Continuous Performance Test which has been adapted for measuring sustained attention in children and handicapped individuals (Sykes et al., 1973). The stimuli for this test are 12 letters which appear on a screen, one at a time. Each remains on the screen for two seconds and there is a 1-to 2-second period between letters when the screen is blank. The observer's task is to press a button each time an X appears on the screen. In a more difficult version of the task, the observer is required to respond to the X signal only after it has been preceded by an A. For a description of other representative vigilance tasks, the interested reader should consult the Appendix in J. R. Mackworth's (1970) book.

Vigilance performance is usually reported as the number of signals missed, or omissions. Sometimes the reciprocal of omissions, percentage of detections, is reported instead. Decrement scores, or the decline in detection performance that occurs over time, usually take the form of omissions plotted against time. Finally, commission errors, or false alarms, are also typically reported. Both total omission scores and decrement data are usually inferred to reflect sustained attention.

Vigilance in Normal-Achieving Youngsters. Children's performance on vigilance and vigilance-like tasks is of particular interest to educators as there appears to be a significant relationship between omission scores and reading achievement which is independent of IQ. For example, Margolis (1972) correlated total omissions on a cognitive vigilance task with both standardized reading achievement test scores and IQ scores. She found significant correlations between omissions and reading test scores ($r = .49$), while finding the correlation between omissions and IQ to be nonsignificant ($r = .19$). It is relevant to note that the correlation between reading and IQ scores was also found to be significant (r

= .42). Thus, Margolis's data indicate that although both vigilance performance and IQ are related to reading achievement, each appears to account for nonoverlapping portions of the variance. In support of Margolis is a report by Gale & Lynn (1972) who also found a nonsignificant relationship between IQ and vigilance performance. Similarly, Noland & Schuldt (1972) tested groups of good and poor readers and found vigilance performance differences favoring the good readers. In summary, data from a variety of experiments converge to suggest vigilance performance is positively related to reading achievement in normal achieving youngsters.

Vigilance in Handicapped Youngsters. Given this relationship in normal-achieving youngsters, one would expect handicapped youngsters, who are also usually low achievers, to perform more poorly on vigilance measures than their normal-achieving peers. With few exceptions (Kirby et al., 1978; Ware et al., 1962), this prediction has been supported. For example, when total omissions are used as a measure of performance, mentally retarded (Crosby, 1972; Mulcahy, 1976; Semmel, 1965), hyperactive (Sykes et al., 1973; Sykes, Douglass et al., 1971), learning-disabled (Doyle et al., 1976; Rugel et al., 1978), educationally handicapped (Keogh & Margolis, 1976b), behaviorally deviant (Kupietz, 1976), brain-damaged (Campanelli, 1970; Grassi, 1970; Rosvold et al., 1956), highly active normals (Kirchner, 1976), low-achieving normals (Brackup & Knopf, 1978; Kirchner & Knopf, 1974), and children rated as low in persistence by their teachers (Dureman & Palshammar, 1970) have all been reported to make more omissions than a nondeviant comparison group.

In a similar vein, deviant groups are frequently reported to exhibit greater decrement in performance over time when compared to controls. Group differences in decrement are not as universal as in omissions (e.g., Kirby et al., 1977; Kirchner, 1976; Kirchner & Knopf, 1974), but have been reported for educationally handicapped (Keogh & Margolis, 1976b), hyperactive (Sykes et al., 1973), institutionalized behaviorally deviant (Kupietz, 1976), mentally retarded (Semmel, 1965), and low-achieving normal youngsters (Brackup & Knopf, 1976).

Commission errors, or false alarms, have also been reported as occurring more frequently in deviant groups. Group differences in commission errors appear related to the task as well as to the deviant group being tested. Mentally retarded (Kirby et al., 1978) educationally handicapped (Keogh & Margolis, 1976b), hyperactive (Sykes et al., 1973), learning disabled (Doyle et al., 1976), and low-achieving normal youngsters (Kirchner, 1976) have all been reported to make more false alarms than their nondeviant counterparts.

In most studies only task performance scores have been reported. However, in the few studies where concurrent behavior was measured, there is converging evidence for inattention in the deviant group. For example, in the Sykes et al. (1971) study, motor restlessness was monitored by having all children sit on a stabilimetric cushion while they completed the vigilance task. Frequency of movement was found to be greater in the hyperactive than in the normal group, suggesting that greater degrees of restlessness were associated with the hyperactive group's poorer vigilance performance. Rugel, et al. (1976) also reported greater levels of body movement in groups of learning-disabled children relative to normal-achieving youngsters during vigilance performance. Similar findings were obtained by Doyle et al. (1976) who measured frequency and duration of eye contact made with a visual distractor that occurred during the vigilance task. Learning-disabled children made more frequent eye contact with the distractor than did children from the normal-achieving control group. Since Doyle et al. employed a visual vigilance task, such off-task glances were incompatible with the primary task demands and, thus, could have interfered with the making of correct detections.

In two studies monitoring physiological changes during vigilance, responses thought to reflect lower levels of attention accompanied lower levels of vigilance performance. For example, Dureman and Palshammar (1970) found that skin conductance and respiratory rates were lower in a group of children rated by their teachers as "low in classroom persistence" while they performed a tracking task relative to a group rated as "high in persistence." Although no group differences were evident in heart rate changes, the conductance and respiratory differences were interpreted to indicate lower levels of alertness in the low persistent children, the group who performed most poorly in the tracking task.

Mulcahy (1976) examined phasic skin conductance responses to discrete vigilance signals in groups of retarded and nonretarded adolescent boys. Skin conductance responses (thought to reflect attention) were found to occur in greater magnitude at the appropriate time among boys who also detected more vigilance signals; large, but inappropriately timed skin conductance responses occurred in those boys who detected fewer signals—primarily mentally retarded boys. Thus, Sykes et al. (1971), Rugel et al. (1976), Doyle et al. (1976), Dureman and Palshammar (1970), and Mulcahy (1976), taken together suggest that concurrent behavioral and physiological measures are consistently related to vigilance performance measures.

In summary, it appears that poor vigilance performance is a remarkably consistent characteristic of handicapped youngsters who represent a variety of diagnostic categories. Such consistency is noteworthy since investigators reporting these differences employed a variety of vigilance tasks with markedly different task characteristics. For example, sensory and cognitive vigilance tasks are represented in the preceding review as well as a tracking task. Further, in those cases where concurrent behavior was monitored, it was found that relative to comparison or control groups, the deviant groups exhibited greater degrees of behaviors thought to reflect inattention (e.g., motor restlessness, eye contact with a distracting stimulus, and select psychophysiological measures) which paralleled their poor vigilance performance. Thus, if one assumes that vigilance performance reflects processes of voluntary sustained attention, these data provide evidence of such difficulties among a heterogeneous group of exceptional youngsters.

A number of investigators have attempted to provide a broader understanding of exceptional children's poor vigilance performance by systematically manipulating task demands and/or studying children's performance on more than one task. These analyses are revealing, as they indicate the conditions under which poor performance is exacerbated. In one such study, Sykes et al. (1973) tested hyperactive and normal children on three tasks: (1) a choice reaction-time task that required children to deploy attention to task stimuli for brief periods, (2) a serial reaction-time task and, (3) a long version of the Continuous Performance Test. The serial reaction-time task and the Continuous Performance Test both required sustained attention for good performance.

Hyperactive youngsters performed poorly relative to the nonhyperactive controls on the latter two measures that required sustained attention; there was no difference between groups in their performance on the choice reaction-time task that required intermittent attention. Since the sustained tasks used in this study appear similar to other tasks that have been interpreted to require high degrees of voluntary sustained attention for good performance, these data are consistent with those presented earlier. That is, hyperactive youngsters appear to exhibit difficulty when demands for voluntary sustained attention are greatest and appear not to be impaired when such demands are not imposed.

In a similar vein, stimulant drug treatment has been consistently reported as having beneficial effects on the vigilance performance of learning-disordered children (Barkley, 1977a; Sroufe, 1975). Both overall detection score improvements and improvements in decrement over time have been reported as a result of stimulant treatments. Such data are interesting in that they suggest that voluntary sustained processes may be altered through drug treatment.

Summary. In summary, vigilance performance is related to academic achievement, especially reading achievement in normal youngsters. Handicapped youngsters, who are also frequently reported to have low academic achievement standings, are almost always found to perform more poorly on vigilance tasks relative to normal-achieving youngsters. Specifically, exceptional children tend to detect fewer signals overall, exhibit more decrement in performance over time, and also make more commission errors when compared to their nonexceptional peers. Concurrent behavioral and physiological measures appear to parallel performance scores and are usually interpreted as providing convergent evidence for more frequent expressions of inattention among exceptional groups.

Vigilance tasks have been defined as requiring voluntary sustained attention for good performance. Thus, it is reasonable to conclude that the reported vigilance data provide evidence suggesting that exceptional youngsters identified as having mild to moderate learning handicaps (e.g., mental retardation, hyperactivity, minimal brain dysfunction, etc.) exhibit serious problems with voluntary sustained attention. It appears that stimulant drugs can have beneficial effects on vigilance performance, and, by inference, on voluntary sustained attention.

Distraction

Given that many learning handicapped children are thought to be less attentive than their normal-achieving peers, a number of authors have speculated that they would also be more distractible. Tests of this hypothesis have, for the most part, not been supported. Neither blasts of white noise (Sykes et al., 1971), task-relevant auditory and/or visual distractors (Crosby, 1972), intermittent doorbell chimes (Kirchner, 1976), nor the introduction of a novel red light (Semmel, 1965) were found to affect the vigilance performance of exceptional groups to a greater extent than normals. This finding is similar to the conclusion drawn in several reviews of distraction in which a wider variety of tasks were surveyed (Doleys, 1976; Tarver & Hallahan, 1974). (*Editor's Note:* See the Hallahan and Reeve chapter in this volume.)

One interesting exception is the Margolis (1972) study where normal children were tested under two sets of naturalistic circumstances. The first setting was a regular classroom where all children completed the vigilance task as a group in enforced silence. The second setting was, again, the regular classroom. However, in this case children were tested in small groups while children who were not being tested carried on their usual activities with (presumably) the typical amount of noise and distraction that exists normally in a classroom. In this study, vigilance performance was significantly better under the condition of nondistracting silence. Although Margolis studied normal-achieving children, it is interesting to speculate that the more familiar forms of distraction inherent in a classroom setting may have different effects on exceptional youngsters as well.

In a recent paper, Humphrey & Kleiman (1978) attempt to reconcile the diverse findings on distractibility with the more general literature on attention problems. They propose a model of distractibility which provides a parsimonious basis for predicting the nature of effective distractors at different levels of development. Although this model has only been applied to normal youngsters of varying ages thus far, it appears to have promise in extending current conceptualizations of distractibility in handicapped youngsters as well as providing greater understanding of the relationship between distractibility and sustained attention. For example, according to this model, only very immature children, e.g., preschool level, would be susceptible to the distracting influence of external stimuli such as bells, lights, and buzzers which are unrelated to the task at hand. Thus, it is not surprising that, for the most part, such distractors have not been demonstrated to affect the performance of learning-handicapped children to a greater extent than normal-control children. Particular types of distractors internal to the task have, however, been demonstrated to differentially affect the performance of children at different developmental levels (Humphrey, 1978). Thus, it is possible that future applications of the Humphrey & Kleiman work to handicapped children will provide a parsimonious explanation for the seemingly discrepant results that characterize the distractibility literature.

Reaction Time

The simple reaction-time task is frequently used in studies of attention, especially with young normal children and handicapped populations. Essentially, the task involves the successive presentation of a warning and a response signal. The participant's job is to respond (by pressing or releasing a telegraph key or some similar device) as quickly as possible to the onset of the reaction signal. A reaction-time score, or latency of the participant's response to reaction signal onset, is usually measured in 1/100 or 1/1000-second units.

The time between warning and reaction signals is referred to as the preparatory interval, or PI. As its name implies, the PI is the time during which the participant can prepare for a fast response. It is generally assumed that a participant must be in an attentive state during the PI in order to execute a fast reaction-time score. When the PI remains the same length from trial to trial, the task is called a fixed reaction-time task. When the PI varies in length, the task is referred to as a variable reaction-time task.

Unlike vigilance, reaction time usually involves a series of discrete trials. For example, a typical trial might involve the following sequence of events: a one-second tone (serving as the warning signal), ten seconds of no apparent stimulation (serving as the PI), followed by a light (serving as the reaction signal) which is extinguished as soon as the participant responds.

In most experiments, an intertrial interval follows the participant's response. This interval can last anywhere from one second to 60 seconds depending on the design of the study. Thus, participants usually receive a brief "break" between discrete trials during a reaction-time task, whereas no such "breaks" are given in vigilance. This feature of reaction-time makes it a somewhat less rigorous test of sustained attention compared to the vigilance procedure. Nonetheless, a number of authors have argued that the requirement for continuous monitoring during the PI as well as over the length of the task (multiple trials) provides the reaction-time task with face validity as a reflection of voluntary sustained attention (Krupski & Boyle, 1978; Wickens, 1974).

Reaction Time in Handicapped Youngsters. In general, most comparative studies of simple reaction-time performance in exceptional and normal youngsters report performance scores that favor the normal controls. Almost every reaction-time study conducted with retarded individuals reveals them to be significantly slower than their nonretarded counterparts (Baumeister & Kellas, 1968; Bower & Tate, 1976; Gosling & Jenness, 1974; Krupski, 1975, 1976, 1977; Runcie & O'Bannon, 1975). Some investigators have also examined consistency of performance over trials as another index of attention processes. In this case, variance (or standard deviation) of an individual's reaction-time scores is the usual dependent variable employed. When such variance analyses are performed, retarded individuals are almost always found to be significantly less consistent (or, more variable) in their trial-to-trial performance when compared to a nonretarded control group of the same chronological age (Baumeister & Kellas, 1968; Berkson & Baumeister, 1967; Bower & Tate, 1976; Krupski, 1976, 1977; Runcie & O'Bannon, 1975).

Studies of hyperactive, minimal brain dysfunction, and/or learning-disabled youngsters have demonstrated similar performance score and/or variability differences when the exceptional group has been compared to a nonexceptional control group (Cohen & Douglas, 1972; Firestone & Douglas, 1975; Rugel & Rosenthal, 1974; Sroufe et al., 1973; Zahn et al., 1975; Zahn, et al., 1978). These data, taken together, have led to the conclusion that youngsters diagnosed as mentally retarded, learning disabled, hyperactive, and with minimal brain dysfunction are less likely to sustain attention during the PI of a reaction-time trial and, further, are less likely to maintain consistent performance over a block of reaction-time trials when compared to a nonexceptional group of control youngsters. Assuming that the reaction-time task taps some aspects of voluntary sustained attention, such data suggest that impairments in reaction time are similar to those uncovered in vigilance. That is, they suggest that handicapped youngsters express greatest performance decrements when they are required to voluntarily sustain attention for extended time periods.

This interpretation is supported by a number of experiments in which performance scores have been supplemented with other measures. Other measures have included observational as well as physiological indices. In the case of concurrent behavioral observations, Krupski (1977) found significantly more glances off-task during a visual reaction-time task in a group of mentally retarded adolescents when they were compared with a nonretarded control group. Similar behavioral differences were obtained in a subsequent study of normal-achieving youngsters who were subdivided into fast and slow reaction time groups (Krupski & Boyle, 1978). In both studies, the group with the slower reaction-time scores glanced away from task during the PI significantly more often than the fast responders. Since glances off-task during the PI were clearly incompatible with making a fast response in both studies, the results were interpreted to indicate that slow children were not attending to the critical stimuli. It is interesting to note that most off-task glances occurred during the middle and/or end of the PI. Thus, attention appeared adequate during initial aspects of the PI and became less evident when demands for sustained attention were greatest.

Krupski's findings are similar to reports of experiments in which heart-rate recordings were made concurrent with reaction time. These studies provide clues as to specifically where in the sequence of events handicapped children exhibit greatest difficulty. In the simple fixed reaction-time task, heart-rate deceleration is usually observed to occur in two places—immediately after the warning signal and concomitantly with the reaction signal. Heart-rate deceleration, as the reader will recall, is assumed to be a component of the orienting response. It has been argued that the orienting which occurs after the warning signal is linked to stimulus onset and, thus, reflects involuntary short-term attention (Porges, 1976). Decelerations occuring at the reaction signal, however, appear to reflect an intent to respond that is at least partially independent of the physical properties of the stimulus and, thus, are interpreted as indices of voluntary attention (Krupski, 1975; van Hover, 1974).

Studies of heart-rate changes during reaction time in retarded individuals generally report that they exhibit significantly smaller heart-rate decelerations concomitant with the reaction signal when compared to normal control groups of the same chronological age (Bower & Tate, 1976; Krupski, 1975). When responses to the warning signal are examined there is evidence suggesting that retarded individuals do not differ from nonretarded controls (Krupski, 1975). Results from a study comparing heart-rate responses between groups given passive instructions (listen to the tones) and active instructions (press button every time you hear the tone) reported similar findings: nonretarded and retarded individuals did not differ in their heart-rate responses to stimuli in the passive condition; both groups demonstrated comparable heart-rate deceleration. Yet, these groups differed significantly in response to stimuli in the active condition; in this case, retarded individuals exhibited heart-rate acceleration rather than the deceleration that typified nonretarded performance (Powazek & Johnson, 1973).

Taken together, these data suggest that retarded youngsters do not differ from their nonretarded counterparts in reflexive orienting, or involuntary short-term attention. Rather, it appears that differences occur under conditions that require greater volition or voluntary attention.

Similar patterns of results have been reported for children diagnosed as hyperactive, learning-disabled, and with minimal brain dysfunction. For example, Zahn, Little, & Wender (1978) found no significant differences in groups of children with minimal brain dysfunction and normal children in heart-rate deceleration responses to a tone or to the warning signal of a fixed reaction-time task. They did find group differences, however, in degree of heart-rate deceleration to the reaction signal with normal youngsters exhibiting greater deceleration. Sroufe et al. (1973) reported attenuated heart-rate decelerations at the reaction signal for a group referred for learning-disabilities relative to a group of nonhandicapped youngsters. These investigators did not examine heart-rate changes at the warning signal, however. Overall, such findings are similar to those reported for retarded individuals where they were interpreted to indicate problems in voluntary aspects of attention but not in involuntary aspects.

Skin conductance responses, another measure of the orienting response, have also been examined in learning-disordered youngsters under passive and active task requirements. Results of these studies indicated that neither hyperactive

(Cohen & Douglas, 1972) nor learning-disabled children (Rugel & Rosenthal, 1974) differed from age-matched controls in skin conductance responsivity during passive task requirements. Significant differences, however, were obtained under active conditions with normal youngsters exhibiting greater responsivity relative to the handicapped group. Such differences were not obtained in a study that employed a group of children with minimal brain dysfunction (Zahn et al., 1975), although in a similar, more recent study Zahn et al. (1978) obtained active/passive heart-rate results that are consistent with other findings.

Thus, performance scores, heart-rate data, and behavioral measures all seem to indicate that slow reaction-time performance observed in exceptional youngsters is due, at least in part, to inadequate voluntary sustained attention. This finding is interesting as it appears relatively consistent for children who represent a variety of etiological categories of exceptionality. Additionally, the similarity of findings from different reaction-time tasks is equally impressive. In general, the reaction-time findings seem to parallel those reported for vigilance. With few exceptions, handicapped youngsters appear to exhibit problems when the demand for voluntary sustained attention is greatest.

Further, the physiological data appear to indicate that there are few group differences when the task requires involuntary short-term or passive attention. Thus, it is not that handicapped groups studied are simply nonresponsive as they appear to respond within normal limits to novel or nonsignal stimuli; it is only when tasks requiring voluntary attention are imposed that we see impaired performance.

As in vigilance, a number of investigators have examined the conditions under which exceptional groups' reaction-time performance can be improved. Some of the most effective manipulations in this respect have been motivational in nature. When mentally retarded (Baumeister & Kellas, 1968) or hyperactive children (Firestone & Douglas, 1975) have been rewarded, their reaction-time scores have been found to decrease significantly, although they do not generally reach the levels attained by the nonexceptional control group. In those cases where children are tested after rewards are withdrawn, reaction-time scores typically return to pre-reinforcement baselines suggesting that the effect of rewards is short-lived.

Another manipulation that has been effective in improving reaction time scores has been to vary the pacing demands of a task. The reaction-time task is typically experimenter-paced. That is, onset of warning and reaction signals is almost always controlled by the experimenter. In a doctoral dissertation, Robertson (1979) predicted that since learning-disabled youngsters, relative to normal-achieving youngsters, are more likely to have difficulty attending, they should benefit more from a self-pacing procedure. In order to test this prediction, Robertson administered a self- and experimenter-paced version of a reaction-time task to groups of normal and learning-disabled youngsters. In the self-paced task, participants were required to initiate each trial, thus assuring attention to task at least during initial aspects of a trial. No such assurance was possible in the experimenter-paced version as the stimuli were programmed to occur at preselected intervals that were independent of the participant's state of attention.

Robertson found that the self-paced condition resulted in superior reaction-time performance for all participants when compared to the experimenter-paced condition. He also found a significant Group x Condition interaction indicating that learning-disabled youngsters benefited from self-pacing procedures to a greater extent than normal-achieving youngsters. Although learning-disabled children's performance in the self-paced condition remained inferior to that of normal-achieving children, this study demonstrates that the learning disabled are capable of faster reaction times than are usually observed.

Another form of treatment that has been found to have consistent beneficial effects on reaction-time scores and/or reaction-time variability of exceptional youngsters is stimulant drug treatment. Recent reviews of literature indicate that virtually every study employing reaction-time measures report that stimulant drugs have beneficial effects (Barkley, 1977a; Sroufe, 1975). These findings are similar to those obtained for vigilance and are supportive of the notion that stimulant medication has consistently beneficial effects on sustained voluntary attention processes.

Summary. Conclusions from reaction-time studies parallel and extend those reported for vigilance. Children identified as having mild to moderate learning handicaps are reported to perform more poorly relative to their nonhandicapped age-mates under circumstances that require voluntary sustained attention. When task demands require passive or reflexive responding, such differences are not apparent. Manipulations such as reinforcement, self-pacing, and treatment with stimulants all appear to have beneficial effects on reaction-time performance, suggesting that voluntary aspects of attention can be modified to some extent.

Observational Research in Multiple Settings

Studies of vigilance and reaction time are similar in that they are both highly structured situations. It is instructive at this point to examine experiments that have been conducted under a wider range of circumstances including the study of children under more informal circumstances. Results from this work both complement and expand upon results from laboratory studies in identifying variables related to expressions of inattention in handicapped youngsters. This section will be devoted to a discussion of studies in which children were observed in more than one setting with particular emphasis on those variables that emerge from independent investigations as relevant to attention.

One variable that has been identified in a number of contexts as relevant to expressions of attention and inattention is the degree of structure in a situation. A number of studies suggest that children diagnosed as hyperactive are more likely to differ from nonhyperactive controls in behaviors reflecting attention when observed under structured conditions (Routh & Schroeder, 1976; Schleifer et al., 1975). Observations of attention-related behaviors in unstructured or free play situations have, for the most part, not been useful in discriminating hyperactive and normal youngsters (Barkley & Ullman, 1975; Jacob et al., 1978; Routh & Schroeder, 1976; Schleifer et al., 1975).

An illustration of this work is provided by Routh & Schroeder (1976). These investigators observed two groups of children. One group had been referred to a clinic for assessment of suspected hyperactivity; half of the referred children were mentally retarded and half were within the normal range on IQ measures. A second group served as a control and consisted of nonreferred children from the community. All children were observed under a free play condition ("stay in the room and play") as well as in a restricted condition. In the restricted condition, children were instructed to stay in only one quadrant of the room, not to cross over any of the black lines that divided the room into quadrants, and to play with only one toy for the entire 15-minute session. Number of room quadrants traversed served as a measure of motor activity while toy-changing score served as a measure of attention span.

Essentially, results indicated that referred children, regardless of IQ, were more active than nonreferred children under both free plan and restricted conditions. Thus, the degree of motor activity was observed to be greater for referred children regardless of situation. The attention measure, however, differed as a function of situation. All children changed toys with the same degree of frequency in the free play condition. In the restricted condition, on the other hand, referred children changed toys more frequently than nonreferred children.

It is likely that limitations inherent in Routh & Schroeder's restricted condition required a child to maintain a greater consistency in on-task behavior than was required in the free play condition. As such, the demands for voluntary sustained attention were probably greater in the restricted condition. Fewer inherent restrictions in the free play condition allowed for frequent breaks from the task at hand and thus were probably not as demanding of voluntary sustained attention. Therefore, as in previous studies, differences observed between hyperactive and normal children in the Routh & Schroeder study appear to occur under those conditions where demand for voluntary sustained attention is greatest.

Jacob et al. (1978), in an unusually well-controlled study, examined a variety of behaviors among hyperactive and normal youngsters in formal and informal classroom settings. These investigators attempted to simulate structured and "open" classroom environments as instances of formal and informal conditions. The behaviors examined included the following: attempts to interact with the teacher, instances of aggression, noncompliance, body movement, not attending to task (e.g., looking out of the window, talking to neighbor), and weird sounds. Results of this study are interesting as they correspond almost exactly to those reported by Routh & Shroeder (1976). For example, when the dependent variable was defined as the total of all measures *excluding* the attention category, hyperactive youngsters scored higher than nonhyperactive controls in both formal and informal settings. This is similar to the results of Routh & Schoeder, who found that hyperactive children were more motorically active than control children regardless of setting.

Group differences in the attention category, however, were found to interact with setting. In the formal, structured setting, hyperactive children exhibited more inattention to task than normal control children while no such group differences were apparent in the informal setting. Thus, as in the Routh & Schroeder work, instances of inattention among hyperactive youngsters appear to be more frequent under formal or structured conditions but not so under informal or unstructured conditions. Other measures thought to be characteristic of hyperactivity, such as motor activity, do not appear to be as sensitive to setting variables.

Another somewhat different illustration of this point comes from an unpublished Master's thesis by Patricia R. Boyle (1976). Boyle studied groups of first-grade youngsters who had been identified as being at high or low educational risk in the previous year (Forness, 1975). Although risk designation was determined by multiple factors, a primary characteristic of the high-risk group was poor classroom attention. Boyle predicted that the high-risk children would do more poorly than low-risk children on a reaction-time task since attention to task is a necessary prerequisite for good reaction-time performance. Results of the reaction-time data, however, indicated no significant difference between groups. In interpreting these results, Boyle suggested that the discrepancy between expression of inattention in classroom and reaction-time settings was due to differences in task demands in these two settings. The reaction-time task was presented as a competitive racing-car game and appeared to be highly motivating to most of Boyle's participants. Classroom tasks, on the other hand, could probably be characterized as more structured than the reaction-time game and as requiring more restraint. Thus, although sustained attention was required in both settings, it is possible that the apparent cross-situational inconsistencies may be due to the degree of structure inherent in each situation and/or to motivational differences between situations.

Several studies focused on hyperactive children's response to drugs report findings consistent with the above data. Beneficial effects of methylphenidate treatment are usually based on reports of children's behavior in formal settings. As the reader will recall, improvements are consistently reported in vigilance and reaction time as well as other tests of voluntary sustained attention (Barkley, 1977a; Sroufe, 1975). Few investigators, however, have studied the effect of such treatment on behaviors exhibited in less formal settings. Two papers (Ellis et al., 1974; Barkley, 1977b) that specifically addressed the effect of methylphenidate on attention in unstructured situations found no significant effects, suggesting that only behavior in structured or formal settings is affected by methylphenidate treatment.

The report of no significant behavioral improvement in informal settings under methylphenidate treatment has been used to account for discrepancies between parent and teacher reports of child behavior (Ellis et al., 1974; Spring et al., 1977). Teachers often report improvement in classroom behaviors after children are given psychotropic drugs, while parents are less likely to report such improvement. Essentially, it is argued that parents and teachers observe children in different settings which are, in turn, correlated with different task demands. Teachers are likely to observe children in formal situations demanding voluntary sustained attention where it is likely that the beneficial effects of drug treatment would be noticeable. Parents, on the other hand, are likely to observe children in less structured situations where drugs are thought to have fewer effects. Thus, it appears unlikely that parents would have the same opportunity to notice any improvement in attention as do teachers.

Although there are exceptions (Pope, 1970; Shaffer, McNamara, & Pincus, 1974), the evidence taken together suggests that child characteristics interact with task demands such that more frequent instances of inattention are observed in structured that in unstructured settings, especially among children identified as hyperactive. Further, it appears that psychotropic drugs have most beneficial effects on performance of hyperactive children in structured situations and that performance in unstructured or informal settings may not be affected by drugs.

These findings are consistent with data presented earlier. For example, restrictions and/or limitations inherent in structured or formal situations require a child to maintain a greater consistency in on-task behavior than is required in informal settings. As such, the child who successfully maintains attention in formal settings probably goes through a process of bringing him or herself back to the task when attention drifts. This process calls for a degree of conscious monitoring and effort that is characteristic of voluntary sustained attention. Fewer inherent restrictions in the less formal situation, on the other hand, allow for frequent breaks from the task at hand and thus are not as demanding of voluntary sustained attention.

Given this reasoning, it is likely that more frequent episodes of inattention among hyperactive and other learning-handicapped children observed in formal but not informal settings reflects, once again, difficulties in tasks with high demands for voluntary sustained attention. Thus, the results of studies conducted in multiple settings are consistent with other data that point to difficulties among children with a variety of learning handicaps in situations requiring a high degree of voluntary attention but not in situations that require relatively lower degrees of voluntary attention.

Further, it seems relevant to note that group differences in behavior appear related to setting only when the measure taps some form of voluntary attention. Measures of motor activity or other variables thought to be characteristic of hyperactivity do not appear to be as sensitive to setting variables as are attention measures. Although the relationship between activity level and attention is known to be complex and is poorly understood (Alabiso, 1972; Rugel et al., 1976), this review clearly suggests that attention and motor variables are at least partially independent.

Classroom Observations

The last group of studies to be reported are those conducted in classrooms. These data are included in this review because they provide a framework for viewing expressions of attention and inattention under naturalistic circumstances. As such, they are the most direct link presented thus far with the real-life concerns of teachers, parents, and clinicians who must deal with children who exhibit attention problems on a day-to-day basis. On one hand, then, it appears that classroom observation work has the potential for expanding and complementing the laboratory-based work toward furthering an understanding of mechanisms underlying poor attention. Unfortunately, this work is characterized by a lack of experimental control relative to laboratory-based studies which precludes drawing unqualified conclusions about expressions of inattention in the classroom. In spite of these limitations, it is instructive to review studies conducted in this setting.

Current studies of classroom attention are most closely associated with the Behavioristic tradition (Werry & Quay, 1969), although this technique has had a visible and controversial educational history that preceded behavior modification by several decades (Jackson, 1968). The convention in most contemporary studies is to consider a child to be "on task" or "attending" when he/she is making eye contact with academic materials or is physically oriented toward the task or some relevant aspect of it.

A serious problem with this convention is that there is no way of knowing whether a child who is making eye contact with appropriate academic materials is, in fact, involved in the task or is engaged in subtle task-irrelevant behaviors such as daydreaming. In the same vein, looking away from task could indicate distraction as well as thoughtful contemplation of a task-related idea. The point to be made here is that conventional operational definitions of classroom attention are probably a gross estimation, at best, of whether a child is actually involved or not with a particular task. Although investigators have devised means intended to overcome this shortcoming (e.g., Hudgins, 1967), all studies to be reviewed here used the conventional definition.

In spite of the global nature of classroom attention measures, a series of studies focused on normal-achieving youngsters report a rather consistent relationship between classroom attention and academic achievement tests (Lahaderne, 1968; Cobb, 1972; McKinney et al., 1975; Samuels & Turnure, 1974). The correlations between classroom attention and achievement measures are reported to be approximately .40.

These data are similar to those reported for vigilance. In both cases, high degrees of sustained attention (inferred from vigilance performance or from on-task classroom behaviors) were reported to be directly correlated with high academic achievement in normal youngsters. The conclusion that attention and achievement are related in a direct way for all children is tempered, however, by a study conducted by Soli and Devine (1976).

Soli and Devine (1976) reasoned that the relationship between classroom behaviors and achievement may vary for different subgroups within the classroom. Unlike their predecessors, then, these investigators looked at the relationship between classroom attention and achievement separately for high and low achievers within a regular classroom. They found that time spent in task-oriented behavior was correlated with achievement only in groups of low achievers; classroom behaviors observed in high-achieving youngsters, for the most part, were not related to achievement. When high and low achievement categories were collapsed and global correlations performed, the resulting relationship between achievement and attention was consistent with that reported in previous investigations. Thus, it appears possible that the relationship between attention and achievement previously thought to hold for all children in the classroom may hold only for low achievers.

Support for this reasoning comes from two observational studies that focused on classroom attention measures in groups of good and poor readers who were enrolled in regular classrooms (Camp & Zimet, 1975; Harper & Graham, 1974). Results of both studies indicated that good readers, relative to poor readers, spent significantly more time on-task when observed in their classrooms. In an attempt to explain these differences, Camp and Zimet did an informal examination of instructional materials used by the various groups of readers in their study. They concluded that task difficulty was not a likely explanation for group differences, as instructional materials were chosen specifically to match students' current functioning levels. Rather, they suggested that children with low reading skill may also have serious attention problems requiring special aids to improve attention or concentration during reading instruction. This conclusion is similar to that drawn by Soli & Devine (1976) in that attention problems appear more prevalent in low-achieving children.

Given the relationship between poor classroom attention and low achievement, one would expect exceptional populations who are low achievers to exhibit more off-task classroom behavior than their nonexceptional counterparts. Surprisingly, few observational studies of this nature have been reported. Even more surprising are the equivocal findings that are reported. First, studies that have reported unqualified differences between behavior of a handicapped group and a normal group will be described, followed by a summary of comparative studies where significant group differences are qualified or nonexistent.

Four comparative studies that reported clear differences between groups share many similarities (Forness & Esveldt, 1975; Nelson, 1971; Werner & Simpson, 1974; Werry & Quay, 1969). All were focused on children who exhibited some form of behavior disorder, e.g., referred for evaluation of school learning/

behavior or conduct problem, scored two standard deviations below the mean on select subscales of the Devereaux Child Behavior Rating Scale, judged by teachers to be "poorly adjusted." Also, all participants were enrolled in regular classes at the time that they were observed. In all four of these studies, the behavior-disordered group demonstrated significantly less on-task behavior when observed in their classrooms than a group of nonbehavior-disordered peers. These consistent findings are noteworthy since the definition of samples and the observational systems used in each study were different.

In two of these studies (Nelson, 1971; Werner & Simpson, 1974), only on-task and off-task behaviors were reported. In the other two (Forness & Esveldt, 1975; Werry & Quay, 1969), a more fine-grained analysis of specific behavior was presented which allowed description of what children were doing when they were not attending. Essentially, the fine-grained analyses indicated that most instances of off-task behavior were not disruptive but were best described as potentially irritating or passive-aggressive type acts such as doodling, fiddling, playing with toys, etc. Data from the four studies are consistent in reporting that behavior-disordered children are significantly less attentive while working on classroom tasks than are their nonhandicapped classmates. Further evidence suggests that off-task episodes primarily involve nondisruptive activities that can be described as potentially irritating or passive aggressive.

Learning-disabled and educably mentally retarded children have also been reported to exhibit less on task behavior in the classroom than their nonhandicapped peers. However, in studies of these groups, the results are qualified to a greater extent than in the studies of behavior-disordered youngsters reviewed above. For example, Bryan (1974) found that learning-disabled youngsters who were integrated in a regular classroom exhibited less task-oriented behavior than did nonhandicapped children enrolled in the same classroom. Overall, learning-disabled youngsters were observed to be oriented to task 60 percent of the time in the regular classroom whereas the control group was observed to be on-task 87.7 percent of the time. A fine-grained analysis of subject area was also reported which indicated that regardless of what subject area students were working on, e.g., arithmetic, language, art, these group differences were maintained.

The learning-disabled students employed in the Bryan experiment were also observed while they worked in a segregated resource room. In this setting, the learning-disabled children worked in small groups with an itinerant specialist for relatively short periods of time. In the special class setting, the learning-disabled students spent significantly more time on-task than they did in the integrated setting (89 percent versus 68 percent, respectively). In fact, their overall on-task score in the special class setting (89 percent) was comparable to the normal-achieving youngsters' score in the regular classroom (87.7 percent). In summary, Bryan's study demonstrates that although learning-disabled children spend less time on-task than their normal-achieving peers when in a regular classroom, their on-task behavior is indistinguishable from their normal-achieving peers when they are working in a special-class setting. These data strongly suggest that educational setting type of instruction, and/or task demands exert powerful effects on attention in learning-disabled children.

The importance of task demands is illustrated in another classroom observation study reported by Krupski (1979), who observed a group of educably mentally retarded children enrolled in self-contained classes as well as a group of normal-achieving youngsters who were enrolled in regular classes. The educably mentally retarded children were found to spend significantly less time on-task (77 percent) than the CA-matched control group (85 percent) when both groups worked on academic tasks. However, when the retarded students were observed while working on art projects, their level of on-task behavior was significantly higher (82 percent) and was comparable to the normal-achieving youngsters on-task score in the academic setting (85 percent). Thus, as with the learning-disabled students described by Bryan (1974), the level of on-task behavior for retarded students varied as a function of task demands.

Two classroom observation studies reported no significant attention differences between groups of educably mentally retarded and CA-matched normal achieving students (Gampel et al., 1974; Gampel, 1972). However, examination of means indicated a trend for retarded students to spend more time engaged in passive withdrawal from task (i.e., looking around, turning in seat, daydreaming, looking at another child, etc.) relative to normal-achieving students. These studies, then, do not provide strong support for the notion that retarded youngsters exhibit more behaviors reflective of inattention in the classroom relative to nonretarded children, yet trends in measures of passive withdrawal are suggestive of some consistency between these and other studies reported in the literature.

In general, classroom observation studies provide qualified evidence for greater attention problems in handicapped youngsters relative to a normal control group. For example, Werry & Quay (1969) reported significant differences in on-task behaviors between behavior-disordered children enrolled in regular classes and their normal classmates. It is relevant to note, however, that these investigators also studied groups of behavior-disordered children enrolled in special classes and reported no differences in on-task behavior in these segregated children relative to the normal sample. Similarly, Bryan (1974) found significant differences between learning-disabled and normal-achieving youngsters, but only in a regular classroom setting. When the learning-handicapped group was observed in a special resource room, their on-task behavior was comparable to the normal-achieving group. Krupski (1979), too, only found on-task differences between average IQ and retarded learners while both groups worked on academics; retarded youngsters were comparable to average IQ children in terms of on-task behaviors when they worked on art projects. These qualified results coupled with the nonsignificant findings reported in the two Gampel et al. (1972, 1974) studies suggest that behavioral expression of inattention in the classroom, as conventionally measured, is intimately related to setting variables, instructional variables, and to task demands. In other words, expression of behaviors reflective of inattention are not consistent, but depend to a great extent upon when and where a given child is observed as well as on what, exactly, that child is doing.

Since such descriptions are rarely provided in classroom observation studies, interpretations of group differences or lack of differences are difficult to make. Variables such as task difficulty or complexity, degree of restraint required both within and between classrooms studied, length of time children are expected to persist on one task, as well as the degree of voluntary attention demanded by a task would be among the relevant factors that could influence on-task or off-task behavior. Without knowledge of these factors, it is simply impossible to reconcile equivocal findings with studies conducted under more controlled circumstances.

ASSUMPTIONS ABOUT ATTENTION PROBLEMS

The bulk of data reviewed to this point demonstrate that handicapped youngsters perform more poorly on a variety of tasks requiring attention when compared to a nonhandicapped group. Interpretations of such group differences are important, as they reveal a great deal about investigators' assumptions regarding the nature and etiology of attention problems. Since such assumptions are critical determinants of how attention processes are studied and dictate, to a great extent, the nature of educational interventions that are attempted to remediate existent problems, it is relevant to devote the next section to a discussion of what appear to be the dominant assumptions underlying interpretation of results of attention studies with atypical youngsters.

Essentially, most interpretations fall into one of three camps. There are those who interpret group differences as due to an attention deficit in the handicapped group (e.g., Doyle et al., 1976). Others interpret such differences as indicating a developmental lag such that handicapped youngsters are considered to be more like younger, normal children (e.g., Kinsbourne, 1973). Finally, there is a group that stresses the importance of the interaction between task demands and child characteristics (e.g., Semmel, 1965; Sykes et al., 1973). Extended discussions of the virtues of deficit or developmental lag positions in mental retardation (Ellis, 1969; Milgram, 1969; Paris & Haywood, 1973; Zigler, 1967), learning disabilities (Rourke, 1976; Satz & van Nostrant, 1973), and hyperkinesis/minimal brain dysfunction (Kinsbourne, 1973) research currently exist. Thus, these arguments will not be presented in detail here. Rather, each position will be overviewed briefly with the intention of clarifying the implications that follow for research and practice.

Interpretations of group differences being due to the handicapped groups' attention deficit is a view that is closely related to the medical model. Here, attention problems are often considered to be one of a number of problems that stem from organic or neurological damage. Such damage is not always required to be demonstrated, as some argue that currently available assessment techniques may be too crude to detect many cases of subtle damage (e.g., Spitz, 1963). Thus, the assumption that attention problems are due to an in-child deficit does not appear to require external validation of a damaged state.

The developmental lag assumption is similar in some respects to the deficit assumption. Both focus on conditions that are presumed to be inherent child characteristics. The developmental lag position differs from the deficit assumption in that the handicapped youngster is presumed to be slower in development although not qualitatively different from other children. Deficit positions, on the other hand, often imply qualitiative as well as quantitative differences between handicapped and nonhandicapped youngsters.

Arguments regarding deficiency versus developmental lag assumptions are complex and inconclusive (e.g., Zigler, 1967; Ellis, 1969). The danger in both of these positions is that they can lead to research efforts and suggestions for educational practice that are limited in scope. For example, interpreting group differences in reaction-time performance as being due to the handicapped groups' "attention deficit" is not very illuminating. Nor is the conclusion that learning-disabled youngsters perform like younger nondisabled children.

Alternatively, if one views expressions of inattention as being due to the interaction of particular child characteristics (such as IQ or diagnostic category) and task demands, it is more likely that research efforts will be focused on the conditions under which expressions of inattention occur and do not occur. Such information is significantly more interesting on a theoretical level and also offers greater promise in specifying direction for remediation efforts.

Assuming an interactionist position could also serve to clarify some of the cross-situational inconsistencies that have been uncovered. The review of cross-situational work demonstrates the importance of task demands and situational variables on expressions of inattention. Once one ventures out of the well-controlled laboratory and into the classroom, it becomes clear that expressions of inattention cannot be simply explained as an inherent characteristic of handicapped youngsters. Why does the mentally retarded child attend to art projects but not reading (Krupski, 1979)? Or, why does the learning-disabled child attend in the resource room but not in the regular classroom (Bryan, 1974)? These questions cannot be answered by assuming that a child has an inherent inability to sustain attention. If for no other than functional reasons, then, it appears productive to adopt an interactionist position in the study of attention problems.

INTERACTIONIST VIEW OF ATTENTION

If one adopts an interactionist viewpoint in the study of attention problems, specific task variables and child characteristics become critical elements to be identified. In the following sections select task and child characteristics that have been identified as potentially relevant to expressions of attention will be discussed.

Task Characteristics

It is important to distinguish between tasks that require different degrees of voluntary attention as a number of studies reviewed here suggest that expressions of inattention among atypical youngsters are likely to be observed when task demands require high degrees of voluntary attention. Illustrations of such tasks, sometimes call tasks with active demands, are prolonged vigils or reaction-time tasks paced by the experimenter that require the child to sustain attention for a prolonged period in order to respond appropriately. When tasks do not have these demands, such as when children are told to simply "Watch the lights" or to monitor a display in a noncontinuous fashion, few differences between exceptional and nonexceptional groups are noted. These latter tasks are sometimes called tasks with passive requirements and appear to make less rigorous demands for voluntary attention.

A second task characteristic, also related to the voluntary/involuntary distinction, is the degree of structure required for task execution. Atypical youngsters representing a variety of etiological categories appear to express inattention more frequently in structured or formal settings than in informal settings (e.g., Routh & Schroeder, 1976). Again, the formal setting requires a degree of restraint that reflects demands for instrumental control, or voluntary attention. Informal settings, on the other hand, appear to make less rigorous demands for voluntary attention.

Other task characteristics that appear to influence expressions of attention/inattention include task difficulty level (Camp & Zimet, 1975), reinforcement or motivational attributes (Firestone & Douglas, 1975), and degree of self-initiation permitted (Robertson, 1979). By virtue of their demonstrated empirical relationship to attention processes, these task characteristics taken together are important to consider in the design of studies aimed at understanding attention problems in atypical youngsters.

Child Characteristics

Potentially relevant child variables that may interact with task variables have been discussed to a lesser extent than have task characteristics. Since it is self-evident that resources which a child brings to a task are likely to influence performance significantly, such variables are important to examine. Thus, specific child-based characteristics and their potential roles in the expression of attention and inattention will be discussed in the pages that follow.

In the review of comparative studies presented earlier in this chapter, the organization was based on task or paradigm rather than diagnostic category. This approach was assumed because etiology simply has not been distinguished as a relevant variable in the study of attention problems. The few studies that examined behavior of more than one diagnostic category of handicapping conditions provide little support for the notion that groups differ to any great extent in either frequency or nature of problems in sustained attention (e.g., Jacoby et al., 1978; Routh & Schroeder, 1976). This observation is similar to that made by Hallahan & Kauffman (1977), who suggest that children with mild learning handicaps such as mental retardation, learning disabilities, and behavior disorders are more similar in behavior than they are different. These authors, among others (e.g., Hewett & Forness, 1977) recommend that functional behavior descriptors are more relevant than are traditional diagnostic classifications in instructional planning and educational placement.

The same argument probably holds true for research in attention problems. In addition to the lack of definitive characteristics based on categorical designations, there is almost always greater variability reported for handicapped groups of subjects than for nonhandicapped control groups (Berkson, 1966; Krupski, 1976; Liebert & Baumeister, 1973). Even within a diagnostic category, wide variability is probably the most distinguishing feature of any exceptional group. What this means is that children who are classified as deviant, for whatever reason, are very different from each other. Because of this, group means on any performance measure can be very misleading in that they often are not representative of most individuals' performance within the group.

A solution to this problem was suggested by Berkson (1966, 1973). He argues that it may be more productive to classify children by processing characteristics than by diagnostic category. This suggestion is similar to the recommendation that children be grouped by functional characteristics for purposes of instruction. To apply this idea to attention research, it may be reasonable to group children on the basis of the specific attention problems they express.

An illustration of this point is provided by Krupski (1976) who found a group of retarded individuals to be significantly more variable on reaction-time performance relative to a group of normal individuals. In an attempt to understand this variability, she divided her groups into equal numbers of fast, middle, and slow reaction-time responders. She found that fast reaction-time performers in the retarded group were similar to normal participants in both reaction-time performance and heart-rate responses. Thus, one-third of her retarded sample demonstrated no impairments in reaction-time and, for all practical purposes, could be considered within normal limits in attention processes reflected in the reaction-time task.

Middle and slow retarded performers, however, were clearly deviant relative to the fast group and could also be distinguished from each other by their heart-rate responses. Fast responders demonstrated heart-rate decelerations that were precisely timed with the reaction signal; the greatest deceleration occurred precisely during the second in which the reaction signal occurred. Middle retarded responders demonstrated heart-rate decelerations that were more variable in relation to the reaction signal. In some cases this response preceded the reaction signal by two or more seconds or did not occur until after the reaction signal. Krupski suggested that the subgroup of middle retarded responders may have simply been misjudging the length of the PI and may have benefited from pacing cues or incentives.

Individuals in the slow retarded responder group, on the other hand, demonstrated markedly deviant heart-rate patterns relative to any of the other subgroups. These patterns could not be interpreted as reflecting particular strategic errors but seemed to distinguish this subgroup as quantitatively and qualitatively different performers relative to either normal or retarded individuals who were observed in this situation. Krupski suggested that remediation of attention problems in this latter group of responders would require a different approach than that taken with individuals who fell into the middle responder category.

The Krupski (1976) study is suggestive of how processing characteristics of deviant children may be used to assess various treatment effects or to predict behavior in other situations. Although atypical processing characteristics appear more frequently in youngsters who have been identified as atypical in other respects, it is important to note that diagnostic category alone is an insufficient basis for inferring that specific problems exist. Porges et al. (1975) demonstrated this with hyperactive youngsters; they reported differential responses to methylphenidate treatment to be associated with pretreatment processing characteristics *within* a group of children identified as hyperactive. Similarly, Krupski (1976) found that one-third of the individuals in her retarded sample were not "retarded" in their reaction-time performance but responded much like individuals of normal intelligence. Thus, even though hyperactive youngsters as a group or retarded individuals as a group are reported to have "attention problems," one cannot assume that such problems exist in all representatives of a particular diagnostic category.

In addition to identifying processing differences among children with attention problems, it also appears potentially productive to incorporate broader definitions of child characteristics than has been done in the past. Suggestions for identifying such broader classes of variables can be found in recent discussions of personality which emphasize the importance of subjective perceptions of tasks and situations (Bem & Allen, 1974; Magnusson & Endler, 1977; Mischel, 1973). The clearest statement of this point is made by Mischel (1973). He points out that the meaning and impact of a stimulus can be dramatically modified by cognitive transformations performed by the subject. The example he presents to illustrate this point is an experiment with preschool children on delay of gratification. When such children are presented with reward objects, such as marshmallows and pretzels, it is difficult for them to resist consuming these foods immediately even though they could obtain a preferred reward by waiting. If, on the other hand, these children are instructed to transform the reward objects (e.g., think of the marshmallows as cotton balls and the pretzels as sticks), they can resist consuming the reward objects for extended periods of time. Mischel argues that this example is one of many showing that what is physically present is less important than what is "in the children's heads."

Common sense as well as empirical evidence (e.g., Dweck, 1977; Magnusson & Endler, 1977; Weiner, 1977) support Mischel's argument that individuals differ widely in their interpretation of situations and that such subjective interpretations substantially affect behavior. These observations have direct relevance for the study of attention problems in exceptional youngsters. They suggest that in order to understand the interaction between child and situational variables one should assess child perceptions of the task/situation in addition to the usual objective physical characterization of the task. Such subjective assessment could potentially allow the investigator to determine the meaning a stimulus or class of stimuli has for a given child; it can potentially provide insight into how a child has "cognitively transformed" or organized the situation in which he/she is engaged.

In summary, it appears likely that a broader view than those represented by traditional approaches may be productive in expanding current understanding of attention problems. One such perspective is represented by the interactionist position. In this view it becomes relevant to examine the situations and task demands that are operative when children express appropriate as well as inappropriate attending behaviors. Thus, the question becomes, Under what conditions do children with varying characteristics express inattention? It appears relevant to describe these situational characteristics from the child's perspective as well as in traditional objective terms.

CONCLUSION

My experience is what I agree to attend to (William James, 1890, p. 402).

James's quote stands alone in describing the importance of attention processes. Yet, this chapter documents the fact that many children have difficulty in sustaining attention under particular circumstances. It is not possible to calculate the primary effects of such problems on the experience of these children nor is it possible to estimate the secondary effects on other processes, such as learning. Undoubtedly, they are significant.

This chapter was an attempt to describe the nature of these problems and also to offer suggestions for future research directions. Data reviewed here demonstrate that learning-handicapped children do not differ from their nonhandicapped peers in tasks requiring involuntary short-term attention nor in tasks with low demand for voluntary sustained attention. Consistent group differences are reported, however, when such children engage in tasks requiring high degrees of voluntary sustained attention. In addition to problems in voluntary sustained attention documented here, other sources are consistent in documenting significant and frequent problems in voluntary short-term attention as well (Hallahan and Reeve, in this volume; Humphrey & Kleiman, 1978; Tarver & Hallahan, 1976; Zeaman & House, 1963). Thus, it seems reasonable to conclude that situations which have high demand for voluntary attention, both sustained and short-term, are the primary areas of difficulty for many handicapped children.

In light of this information, it appears that future research would be most productively directed toward greater understanding of tasks with demands for high degrees of voluntary attention. Since others have documented research on voluntary short-term attention in handicapped youngsters (e.g., Hallahan & Reeve in this volume; Humphrey & Kleiman, 1978; Tarver & Hallahan, 1976; Zeaman & House, 1963), the emphasis here will be on tasks requiring a high degree of voluntary sustained attention. Given this limited focus, the question of interest becomes, Why do handicapped children exhibit frequent problems when they are required to voluntarily sustain attention? Clearly, the intimate relationship between cognition and attention that was alluded to earlier in this chapter is a likely starting point in future attempts to answer this question.

The writings of Leontiev (1932), Yendovitskaya (1971), and Luria (1963) described earlier suggest that the link between cognitive development and voluntary attention is an intimate one. More direct links between sustained attention and cognition have been proposed by Humphrey & Kleiman (1978). These authors propose that specific metacognitive processes serve to regulate sustained attention. Such regulating processes include an awareness of task demands, the ability to monitor performance while working on a task, as well as the knowledge of when a task is complete. Although these functions occur in an automatic fashion in most situations among individuals of normal intelligence, there is evidence that children with serious cognitive limitations may not have such skills readily available to them. For example, studies of memory in retarded youngsters demonstrate that these children typically do not spontaneously adjust their behavior in relation to task demands unless specifically coached to do so (Butterfield et al., 1973; Brown, 1978. *Editor's note:* see the chapter on memory in this volume, by Torgesen and Kail.) Thus, in general, there is good reason to believe that cognitive limitations of learning-handicapped children may account, at least in part, for the frequent reports of poor sustained attention in this group. Future research along these lines appears to be promising.

Another point made in this chapter that merits reiteration concerns the importance of an interactionist approach. Often attention problems are assumed to be a traitlike characteristic in many handicapped children. The research reviewed here, however, suggests that situations and/or task demands are of considerable importance in the expression of attention problems and that traitlike explanations cannot adequately account for cross-situational inconsistencies that have been reported. Thus, it appears that a productive approach for future research would be to conceptualize instances of attention and inattention as the result of an interaction between specific child and task characteristics. The research questions of interest stemming from this perspective involve an exploration of when and where children with a variety of learning handicaps exhibit both attention and inattention. Although suggestions were made regarding which child and task characteristics may be relevant, this is clearly an initial and exploratory list. Much work remains to be done in this respect. At the same time, the existence of a number of potentially productive routes to greater understanding of attention problems suggests an optimistic outlook for future research in this area.

FOOTNOTES

*Preparation of this manuscript was supported in part by a grant from the Spencer Foundation and by Project REACH (funded under Contract #300-77-0306 between the University of California and the Bureau of Education for the Handicapped, U.S. Office of Education).

**The author wishes to acknowledge Nancy Burstein and Joel Hoffman for their assistance in reviewing the literature and Gershon Berkson, Mary Humphrey, and Barbara Keogh for their comments on an earlier draft of this chapter. The author also thanks Mary Humphrey for her suggestion to include short- and long-term aspects of attention.

REFERENCES

Alabiso, F. (1972) "Inhibitory functions of attention in reducing hyperactive behavior." *American Journal of Mental Deficiency* 77: 259-282.

Bakan, P. (1959) "Extraversion—introversion and improvement in an auditory vigilance task. *British Journal of Psychology* 50: 325-332.

Barkley, R. A. (1977a) "A review of stimulant drug research with hyperactive children." *Journal of Child Psychology and Psychiatry* 18: 137-165.

———(1977b) "The effects of methylphenidate on various types of activity level and attention in hyperkinetic children." *Journal of Abnormal Child Psychology* 5: 351-369.

———, & Ullman, D. G. (1975) "A comparison of objective measures of activity and distractibility in hyperactive and nonhyperactive children." *Journal of Abnormal Child Psychology* 3: 231-244.

Baumeister, A. A., & Kellas, G. (1968) "Reaction time and mental retardation." In N. R. Ellis (ed.), *International review of research in mental retardation*, Vol. 3. New York: Academic Press, pp. 163-193.

Bem, D. J., & Allen A. (1974) "On predicting some of the people some of the time: The search for cross-situational consistencies in behavior." *Psychological Review* 81: 506-520.

Berkson, G. (1966) "When exceptions obscure the rule." *Mental Retardation* 4: 24-27.

———(1973) "Behavior." In J. Wortis (ed.), *Mental Retardation*, Vol. 5. New York: Grune & Stratton.

———, & Baumesiter, A. (1967) "Reaction time variability of mental defectives and normals." *American Journal of Mental Deficiency* 72: 262-266.

Berlyne, D. D. (1960) *Conflict, arousal, and curiosity*, New York: McGraw-Hill.

Bower, A. A., & Tate, D. L. (1976) "Cardiovascular and skin conductance correlates of a fixed-foreperiod reaction time task in retarded and nonretarded youth." *Psychophysiology* 13: 1-9.

Boyle, P. R. (1976) "Reaction time performance and off-task glancing activity in educationally high risk and low risk second grade students." Unpublished master's thesis, University of California, Los Angeles.

Brackup, E. S., & Knopf, I. J. (1978) "The effects of extraneous speech on visual vigilance performance of children." *Child Development* 49: 505-508.

Broadbent, D. E. (1971) *Decision and stress.* London and New York: Academic Press.

Brown, A. L. (1978) "Knowing when, where, and how to remember: A problem of metacognition." In R. Glaser (ed.), *Advances in Instructional Psychology*, Hillsdale, N.J.: Erlbaum. (In press.)

Bryan, T. S. (1974) "An observational analysis of classroom behaviors of children with learning disabilities." *Journal of Learning Disabilities* 7: 35-43.

Butterfield, E. C., Wambold, C., & Belmont, J. M. (1973) "On the theory and practice of improving short-term memory." *American Journal of Mental Deficiency* 77: 654-669.

Camp, B. W., & Zimet, S. G. (1975) "Classroom behavior during reading instruction." *Exceptional Children* 42: 109-110.

Campanelli, P. A. (1970) "Sustained attention in brain damaged children." *Exceptional Children* 36: 317-325.

Cobb, J. A. (1972) "Relationship of discrete classroom behaviors to fourth-grade academic achievement." *Journal of Educational Psychology* 63: 74-80.

Cohen, N. J., & Douglas, V. I. (1972) "Characteristics of the orienting response in hyperactive and normal children." *Psychophysiology*, 9: 238-245.

Crosby, K. G. (1972) "Attention and distractibility in mentally retarded and intellectually average children." *American Journal of Mental Deficiency* 77: 46-53.

————, & Blatt, B. (1968) "Attention and mental retardation." *Journal of Education* 150: 67-81.

Denny, M. R. (1964) "Research in learning and performance." In H. A. Stevens & R. Heber (eds.), *Mental retardation: A review of research*, Chicago: University of Chicago Press, pp. 104-142.

Doleys, D. M. (1976) "Distractibility and distracting stimuli: Inconsistent and contradictory results." *The Psychological Record* 26: 279-287.

Douglas, V. I. (1972) "Stop, look, and listen: The problem of sustained attention and impulse control in hyperactive and normal children." *Canadian Journal of Behavioral Science* 4: 259-282.

Doyle, R. B., Anderson, R. P., & Halcomb, C. G. (1976) "Attention deficits and the effects of visual distraction." *Journal of Learning Disabilities* 9: 48-54.

Dureman, I., & Palshammer, A. (1970) "Differences in tracking skill and psychophysiological activation dynamics in children high or low in persistence in school work." *Psychophysiology* 7: 95-102.

Dweck, C. S. (1977) "Learned helplessness and negative evaluation." *UCLA Educator* 19: 44-49.

Dykman, R. A., Ackerman, P. T., Clements, S. D., & Peters, J. E. III. (1971) "Specific learning disabilities: An attentional deficit syndrome." In H. R. Mykelbust (ed.), *Progress in learning disabilities*, Vol. 2. New York: Grune & Stratton, pp. 56-93.

Ellis, M. J., Witt, P. A., Reynolds, R., & Sprague, R. L. (1974) "Methylphenidate and the activity of hyperactives in the informal setting." *Child Development* 45: 217-220.

Ellis, N. R. (1969) "A behavioral research strategy in mental retardation: Defense and critique." *American Journal of Mental Deficiency* 73: 557-566.

Firestone, P, & Douglas, V. (1975) "The effects of reward and punishment on reaction times and autonomic activity in hyperactive and normal children." *Journal of Abnormal Child Psychology* 3: 201-216.

Forness, S. R. (1975) "Looking: Use of classroom observation in early identification." In R. Rutherford & J. Buckhalt (eds.), *Distinguished lectures in special education*, Los Angeles: University of Southern California Press, pp. 19-41.

————, & Esveldt, K. C. (1975) "Classroom observation of children with learning and behavior problems." *Journal of Learning Disabilities* 8: 382-385.

Gale, A., & Lynn, R. (1972) "A developmental study of attention." *British Journal of Educational Psychology* 42: 260-266.

Gampel, D. H., Gottlieb, J., & Harrison, R. H. (1974) "Comparison of classroom behavior of special-class EMR, integrated EMR, low IQ, and nonretarded children." *American Journal of Mental Deficiency,* 79: 16-21.

Gampel, D. H., Harrison, R. H., & Budoff, M. (1972) *An observational study of segregated and integrated EMR children and their nonretarded peers: Can we tell the difference by looking?* Cambridge, Mass.: Research Institute for Educational Problems. (ERIC Document Reproduction Service No. ED 062 747.)

Gibson, E., & Rader, N. (1979) "Attention: The perceiver as performer." In Gittale & M. Lewis (eds.), *Attention and the development of attentional skills.* New York: Plenum. (In press.)

Gold, M. S., & Gold, J. R. (1975) "Autism and attention: Theoretical considerations and a pilot study using set reaction time." *Child Psychiatry and Human Development* 6: 68-80.

Gosling, H., & Jenness, D. (1974) "Temporal variables in simple reaction times of mentally retarded boys." *American Journal of Mental Deficiency* 79: 214-224.

Graham, F. K., & Clifton, R. K. (1966) "Heart-rate change as a component of the orienting response." *Psychological Bulletin* 65: 305-320.

Grassi, J. R. (1970) "Auditory vigilance performance in brain damaged, behavior disordered, and normal children." *Journal of Learning Disabilities* 3: 302-305.

Hallahan, D. P., & Kauffman, J. M. (1977) "Labels, categories, behaviors: ED, LD, and EMR reconsidered." *The Journal of Special Education* 11: 139-149.

Harper, C. B. J., & Graham, E. N. (1974) "Attending behaviour and reading." *New Zealand Journal of Educational Studies* 9: 122-126.

Harris, L. P. (1976) "Attention and learning disordered children: A review of theory and remediation." *Journal of Learning Disabilities* 9: 100-110.

Hewett, F. M., & Forness, S. R. (1977) *Education of exceptional learners,* 2nd ed. Boston: Allyn & Bacon.

Hudgins, B. B. (1967) "Attending and thinking in the classroom." *Psychology in the Schools* 4: 211-216.

Humphrey, M. M. (1978) "Children's deployment of attention capacities: The nature of distraction and avoidance of distraction." Unpublished doctoral dissertation, University of Illinois.

Humphrey, M., & Kleiman, G. (1978) "An analysis of children's avoidance of distraction within a framework of attention processes." Manuscript submitted for publication.

Jackson, P. W. (1968) *Life in classrooms.* New York: Holt, Rinehart, & Winston.

Jacob, R. G., O'Leary, K. D., & Rosenblad, C. (1978) "Formal and informal classroom settings: Effects on hyperactivity." *Journal of Abnormal Child Psychology* 6: 47-59.

James, W. (1950) *The principles of psychology.* New York: Dover (1890), 402-458.

Kahneman, D. (1973) *Attention and effort.* Englewood Cliffs, N.J.: Prentice-Hall.

Keogh, B. K., & Margolis, J. (1976a) "Learn to labor and to wait: Attentional problems of children with learning disorders." *Journal of Learning Disabilities* 9: 276-286.

———, & ———(1976b) "A component analysis of attentional problems of educationally handicapped boys." *Journal of Abnormal Child Psychology* 4: 349-359.

Kinsbourne, M. (1973) "Minimal brain dysfunction as a neurodevelopmental lag." *Annals of the New York Academy of Sciences* 205: 268-273.

Kirby, N. H., Nettelbeck, T., & Bullock, J. (1978) "Vigilance performance of mildly mentally retarded adults." *American Journal of Mental Deficiency* 82: 394-397.

Kirchner, G. L. (1976) "Differences in the vigilance performance of highly active and normal second-grade males under four experimental conditions." *Journal of Educational Psychology* 68: 696-701.

———, & Knopf, I. J. (1974) "Differences in the vigilance performance of second-grade children as related to sex and achievement." *Child Development* 45: 490-495.

Krupski, A. (1975) "Heart rate changes during a fixed reaction time task in normal and retarded adult males." *Psychophysiology,* 12: 262-2267.

———(1976) "Heart rate changes during reaction time: An approach for understanding deficient attention in retarded individuals." In R. Karrer (ed.), *Developmental psychophysiology of mental retardation*. Springfield, Ill.: Charles C Thomas, pp. 92-118.
———(1977) "Role of attention in the reaction time performance of mentally retarded adolescents." *American Journal of Mental Deficiency*, 82: 79-83.
———(1979) "Are retarded children more distractible? An observational analysis of classroom behaviors in retarded and intellectually average children." *American Journal of Mental Deficiency* 84: 1-10.
———, & Boyle, P. R. (1978) "An observational analysis of children's behavior during a simple reaction-time task: The role of attention." *Child Development* 49: 340-347.
———, Raskin, D. C., & Bakan, P. (1971) "Physiological and personality correlates of commission errors in an auditory vigilance task." *Psychophysiology* 8: 304-311.
Kupietz, S. S. (1976) "Attentiveness in behaviorally deviant and nondeviant children: I. Auditory vigilance performance." *Perceptual and Motor Skills* 43: 1095-1101.
Lahaderne, H. M. (1968) "Attitudinal and intellectual correlates of attention: A study of four sixth-grade classrooms." *Journal of Educational Psychology* 59: 320-324.
Leontiev, A. N. (1932) "The development of voluntary attention in the child." *Journal of Genetic Psychology* 40: 52-83.
Liebert, A. M., & Baumeister, A. A. (1973) "Behavioral variability among retardates, children, and college students." *The Journal of Psychology* 83: 57-65.
Luria, A. R. (1963) "Psychological studies of mental deficiency in the Soviet Union." In N. R. Ellis (ed.), *Handbook of mental deficiency*, New York: McGraw-Hill, pp. 353-387.
Lynn, R. (1966) *Attention, arousal and the orientation reaction*. Elmsford, N.Y.: Pergamon Press.
Mackworth, J. F. (1969) *Vigilance and habituation: A neuropsychological approach*. Baltimore: Penguin.
———(1970) *Vigilance and attention*. Baltimore: Penguin.
Magnusson, D., & Endler, N. S. (eds.) (1977) *Personality at the crossroads: Current issues in interactional psychology*. Hillsdale, N.J.: Erlbaum Associates.
Margolis, J. A. (1972) "Academic correlates of sustained attention." Unpublished doctoral dissertation, University of California, Loss Angeles.
McKinney, J. D., Mason, J., Perkerson, K., & Clifford, M. (1975) "Relationship between classroom behavior and academic achievement." *Journal of Educational Psychology* 67: 198-203.
Meldman, M. J. (1970) *Diseases of attention and perception*. Elmsford, N.Y.: Pergamon Press.
Milgram, N. A. (1969) "The rationale and irrational in Zigler's motivational approach to mental retardation." *American Journal of Mental Deficiency* 73: 527-532.
Mischel, W. (1973) "Toward a cognitive social learning reconceptualization of personality." *Psychological Review* 80: 252-283.
Moray, N. (1969) *Attention: Selective processes in vision and hearing*. London: Hutchinson.
Mulcahy, R. F. (1976) "Vigilance-like performance and SCR in retardates and normals." Paper presented at the Fourth Congress of the International Association for the Scientific Study of Mental Deficiency (IASSMD), Washington, D.C.
Neisser, U. (1976) *Cognition and reality. Principles and implications of cognitive psychology*. San Francisco: W. H. Freeman.
Nelson, C. M. (1971) "Techniques for screening conduct disturbed children." *Exceptional Children* 37: 501-507.
Noland, E. C., & Schuldt, W. J. (1971) "Sustained attention and reading retardation." *The Journal of Experimental Education* 40: 73-76.
Obrist, P. A., Webb, R. A., Sutterer, J. R., & Howard, J. L. (1970) "The cardiac-somatic relationship: Some reformulations." *Psychophysiology* 6: 569-587.
Paris, S. G., & Haywood, H. C. (1973) "Mental retardation as a learning disorder." *Pediatric Clinics of North America* 20: 641-651.

Pavlov, I. P. (1960) *Conditioned reflexes.* New York: Dover.
Pick, A. D., Frankel, D. G., & Hess, V. L. (1975) "Children's attention: The development of selectivity." In F. Mavis Hetherington (ed.), *Review of child development research,* Vol. 5. Chicago: University of Chicago Press, pp. 325-383.
Pope, L. (1970) "Motor activity in brain-injured children." *American Journal of Orthopsychiatry,* 40: 783-794.
Porges, S. W. (1976) "Peripheral and neurochemical parallels of psychopathology: A psychophysiological model relating autonomic imbalance to hyperactivity, psychopathy, and autism." In H. W. Reese (ed.), *Advances in Child Development and Behavior,* Vol. 11, pp. 36-65.
———, Walter, G. F., Korb, R. J., & Sprague, R. L. (1975) "The influences of methylphenidate on heart rate and behavioral measures of attention in hyperactive children." *Child Development* 46: 727-733.
Powazek, M., & Johnson, J. T., Jr. (1973) "Heart rate response to novel and signal stimuli in nonretarded and retarded subjects." *American Journal of Mental Deficiency* 78: 286-291.
Ribot, T. (1903) *The psychology of attention,* Rev. 5th ed. Chicago: The Open Court Publishing Co.
Robertson, D. E. (1979) "The effects of examiner- and self-pacing on the reaction time performance of normal and learning disabled children." Unpublished doctoral dissertation, University of California, Los Angeles,
Rosvold, H. E., Mirsky, A. F., Sarason, I., Bransome, E. D., Jr., & Beck, L. H. (1956) "A continuous performance test of brain damage." *Journal of Consulting Psychology* 20: 343-350.
Rourke, B. P. (1976) "Reading retardation in children: Developmental lag or deficit?" In R. M. Knights & D. J. Bakker (eds.), *The neuropsychology of learning disorders.* Baltimore: University Park Press, pp. 125-137.
Routh, D. K., & Schroeder, C. S. (1976) "Standardized playroom measures as indices of hyperactivity." *Journal of Abnormal Child Psychology* 4: 199-207.
Rugel, R. P., Cheatam, D., & Mitchell, A. (1976) "Body movement and inattention in learning-disabled and normal children." *Journal of Abnormal Child Psychology* 6: 325-337.
———, & Rosenthal, R. (1974) "Skin conductance, reaction time, and observational ratings in learning-disabled children." *Journal of Abnormal Child Psychology* 2: 183-192.
Runcie, D., & O'Bannon, R. M. (1975) "Relationship of reaction time to deceleration and variability of heart rate in nonretarded and retarded persons." *American Journal of Mental Deficiency* 79: 553-558.
Samuels, S. J., & Turnure, J. E. (1974) "Attention and reading achievement in first-grade boys and girls." *Journal of Educational Psychology,* 66: 29-32.
Satz, P., & van Nostrand, G. K. (1973) "Developmental dyslexia: An evaluation of a theory." In P. Satz & J. J. Ross (eds.), *The disabled learner.* The Netherlands: Rotterdam University Press, pp. 121-148.
Schleifer, M., Weiss, G., Cohen, N., Elman, M., Cvejic, H., & Kruger, E. (1975) "Hyperactivity in preschoolers and the effect of methylphenidate." *American Journal of Orthopsychiatry* 45: 38-50.
Semmel, M. I. (1965) "Arousal theory and vigilance behavior of educable mentally retarded and average children." *American Journal of Mental Deficiency* 70: 38-47.
Shaffer, D., McNamara, N., & Pincus, J. H. (1974) "Controlled observations on patterns of activity, attention, and impulsivity in brain-damaged and psychiatrically disturbed boys." *Psychological Medicine* 4: 4-18.
Sokolov, E. N. (1963) *Perception and the conditioned reflex.* New York: Macmillan.
Soli, S. D., & Devine, V. T. (1976) "Behavioral correlates of achievements: A look at high and low achievers." *Journal of Educational Psychology* 68: 335-341.
Spitz, H. H. (1963) "Field theory in mental deficiency." In N. R. Ellis (ed.), *Handbook of mental deficiency.* New York: McGraw-Hill, pp. 11-40.
Spring, C., Greenberg, L. M., Yellin, A. M. (1977) "Agreement of mothers' and teachers' hyperac-

tivity ratings with scores on drug sensitive psychological tests." *Journal of Abnormal Child Psychology* 5: 199-204.

Sroufe, L. A. (1975) "Drug treatment of children with behavior problems." In F. D. Horowitz (ed.)., *Review of Child Development Research,* Vol. 4. University of Chicago Press, pp. 347-407.

——, Sonies, B. C., West, W. D., & Wright, F. S. (1973) "Anticipatory heart rate deceleration and reaction time in children with and without referral for learning disability." *Child Development* 44: 267-273.

Stores, G. (1973) "Studies of attention and seizure disorders." *Developmental Medicine and Child Neurology* 15: 376-382.

Stroh, C. M. (1971) *Vigilance: The problem of sustained attention.* Elmsford, N. Y.: Pergamon Press.

Sykes, D. H., Douglas, V. I., & Morgenstern, G. (1973) "Sustained attention in hyperactive children." *Journal of Child Psychology and Psychiatry,* 14: 213-220.

——, Douglas, V. I., Weiss, G., & Minde, K. K. (1971) "Attention in hyperactive children and the effect of methylphenidate (ritalin)." *Journal of Child Psychology and Psychiatry* 12: 129-139.

Tarver, S. G. & Hallahan, D. P. (1974) "Attention deficits in children with learning disabilities: A review." *Journal of Learning Disabilities* 7: 560-569.

Titchener, E. B. (1908) *Lectures on the elementary psychology of feeling and attention.* New York: Macmillan.

Torgesen, J. (1975) "Problems and prospects in the study of learning disabilities." In E. Mavis Hetherington (ed.), *Review of child development research,* Vol. 5. University of Chicago Press, pp. 385-440.

vanHover, K. I. (1974) "A developmental study of three components of attention." *Developmental Psychology* 10: 330-339.

Vygotsky, L. S. (1962) *Thought and language.* Cambridge, Mass.: MIT Press.

Ware, J. R., Baker, R. A., & Sipowicz, R. R. (1962) "Performance of mental deficients on a simple vigilance task." *American Journal of Mental Deficiency* 66: 647-650.

Weiner, B. (1977) "Psycho-social determinants of achievement evaluation." *UCLA Educator* 19: 5-9.

Werner, C. S., & Simpson, R. L. (1974) "Attention to task and completion of work as a function of level of adjustment and educational environment." *Journal of Educational Research* 68: 56-58.

Werry, J. S., & Quay, H. C. (1969) "Observing the classroom behavior of elementary school children." *Exceptional Children* 35: 461-470.

Wickens, C. D. (1974) "Temporal limits of human information processing: A developmental study." *Psychological Bulletin* 81: 739-755.

Yendovitskaya, T. V. (1971) "Development of attention." In A. V. Zaporozhets, & D. B. Elkonin (eds.), *The psychology of preschool children.* Cambridge, Mass.: MIT Press, pp. 65-88.

Zahn, T. P., Abate, F., Little, B. C., & Wender, P. H. (1975) "Minimal brain dysfunction, stimulant drugs, and autonomic nervous system activity." *Archives of General Psychiatry* 32: 381-387.

——, Little, B. C., & Wender, P. H. (1978) "Pupillary and heart rate reactivity in children with minimal brain dysfunction." *Journal of Abnormal Child Psychology* 6: 135-147.

Zeaman, D., & House, B. J. (1963) "The role of attention in retardate discrimination learning." In N. R. Ellis (ed.), *Handbook of mental deficiency.* New York: McGraw-Hill, pp. 159-223.

Zigler, E. (1967) "Familial retardation: A continuing dilemma." *Science* 155: 292-298.

SELECTIVE ATTENTION AND DISTRACTIBILITY*

Daniel P. Hallahan, UNIVERSITY OF VIRGINIA

Ronald E. Reeve, UNIVERSITY OF VIRGINIA

INTRODUCTION

One of the burgeoning areas of interest in the experimental literature concerned with the learning processes of the mildly handicapped is that of selective attention—the ability to focus on the task at hand while ignoring incidental, irrelevant stimuli. Experimental interest in this area coincides with a tremendous growth in the clinician's concern for children who are described by parents, teachers, and clinicians as inattentive, distractible, and hyperactive. Our review in this chapter will focus on studies investigating the selective attention abilities of children who are at risk for such problems. Because the greatest amount of clinical and research literature dealing with inattention has concentrated on children identified as learning-disabled, the great majority of studies reviewed in this chapter will reflect this bias.

This chapter is divided into three main sections: Selective Attention, Distractibility, and Some Educational Implications. The first section covers literature that investigates the child's ability to attend to relevant features of a stimulus array that contain both relevant and irrelevant stimuli. The section on Distractibility, on the other hand, primarily covers studies wherein the child is asked to perform in the face of peripheral rather than proximal distractors. While both sections, in a sense, deal with distractors, the body of literature that has come to fall under the rubric of "selective attention" usually concerns the child's ability to attend to relevant stimuli in the context of "distractors" that are proximal to the to-be-attended-to stimuli. While such a dichotomy may at first glance appear merely a convenient way of dividing the chapter, previous research (Hallahan, 1975b; Tarver & Hallahan, 1974) suggests conceptual validity for the distinction. Different results have obtained in studies using proximal versus distal distractors. These differences will be noted in the Distractibility section.

SELECTIVE ATTENTION

Since the mid-1960s, information processing as a field of study has grown in popularity among developmental psychologists. Coinciding with this dramatic increase in experimental studies of information processing has come a more specific concern for how the child develops the ability to process relevant information in the face of irrelevant information. The study of such selective processing skills has come to be referred to as the study of selective attention. From this plethora of studies has developed a rather well-documented theory of the development of selective attention abilities. While certainly not all of the pieces of the puzzle are in place, some generalizations that are consistent with the data are that:

1. With age, the normal child develops the ability to attend to relevant stimuli in the face of irrelevant stimuli. In particular, there appears to be a dramatic increase in this ability in the normal child at about 12 to 13 years of age.
2. The processing of relevant and irrelevant information is reciprocal, so that giving up the processing of irrelevant information is accompanied by increased processing of relevant information.
3. Children identified as learning-disabled generally demonstrate about a two- to three-year developmental lag in the ability to attend selectively.
4. One of the primary reasons learning-disabled children do poorly on tasks of selective attention is that they are deficient in the application of strategies to learn. In particular, compared to normal peers, they often do not apply verbal rehearsal strategies to tasks requiring selective attention.
5. The deficiency in the use of verbal rehearsal strategies can be overcome by specific training in these skills. In other words, when instructed to rehearse verbally, the selective attention performance of learning-disabled children equals that of normal controls.

The above conclusions are by no means the only ones that can be drawn from research on the development of selective attention, but they are among the most reliable findings and are pertinent to our general discussion in this chapter. We will now turn to a review of the key studies that have culminated in the above-mentioned generalizations. We will begin with a discussion of the results obtained with normal children. This presentation is necessarily brief because our primary interest in this chapter is in abnormal selective attention processes. For a more detailed review of the development of selective attention in normal children, the reader is referred to reviews by Hagen & Kail (1975); Pick, Frankel, and Hess (1975); and Wright & Vlietstra (1975).

Selective Attention in Normal Children

Although many investigators have studied the development of selective attention, none has been more influential than John W. Hagen. Originally using Broadbent's (1958) stimulus filter theory as a conceptual base, Hagen has generated a corpus of studies that, when considered together, has greatly influenced the field of developmental psychology in its view of the construct of selective attention. Using a task first devised by Maccoby and Hagen (1965) and later modified by Hagen (1967), Hagen and his colleagues have been able to compare children's ability to recall central (relevant) and incidental (irrelevant) stimuli.

While different variants of the task have been used (e.g., group administration instead of individual administration), the basic paradigm consists of a memory task wherein the child is required to remember the serial position of cards, each of which contains the drawing of an animal and the drawing of a household object. In the typical procedure, the experimenter presents the child with a series of these cards. Each one is shown to the child for two seconds and then turned face down in a row before him. Before the experiment starts, the experimenter tells the child to pay attention to the serial position of the animals. In fact, if the child makes any mention of, or points to, the household objects, the experimenter reminds him that he is to pay attention to the animals. Thus, animals are defined by the investigator as relevant or central information, whereas household objects constitute the irrelevant or incidental information. After a series of from about three to seven cards (the length has varied from one experiment to another), the experimenter presents a cue card containing one of the animals and asks the child to point to where in the face-down array that particular animal is to be found. The experimenter presents about 12 to 14 of these trials, and the number of times the child chooses the correct card is referred to as his *central recall* score. After all of the central recall trials are presented, the child is asked to remember the correct pairings of the animals and the household objects (each animal was always paired with the same object). Since during the original instructions the child has been told to pay attention only to the animals, the number of correct pairings the child makes is termed *incidental recall*.

In a number of studies generally covering the range of from about 5 to 15 years of age, investigators have found a developmental increase in central recall

(Druker & Hagen, 1969; Hagen, 1967; Hagen & Sabo, 1967; Hallahan, Kauffman, & Ball, 1974; Hallahan, Stainback, Ball, & Kauffman, 1973; Maccoby & Hagen, 1965). At the same time, these studies have shown that incidental recall increases only slightly, if at all, with age; and, in fact, some investigators report that incidental recall decreases significantly at about 12 to 13 years of age. Furthermore, investigators have consistently found a positive correlation between central and incidental recall at younger ages, with a shift to a negative correlation at about 12 years of age. This shift has been hypothesized as reflecting the older child's ability to adopt a strategy for giving up incidental information in order to recall central material.

Lending credence to the above findings, other researchers using somewhat different tasks have reached essentially the same conclusions (e.g., Crane & Ross, 1967; Hale, Miller, & Stevenson, 1968; Siegel & Stevenson, 1966). Hale et al., for example, showed a film to children in grades three through seven. After the film was shown, children were asked questions related to auditory and visual aspects of the film that were incidental to the central plot. The results indicated a strong curvilinear relationship between ability and age in remembering incidental material. The drop in performance between grades six and seven coincides with the drop in incidental learning at about 12 to 13 years of age found on Hagen's central-incidental task. Hale et al. also hypothesized that at about this age the child has learned to ignore irrelevant information.

Selective Attention in Deviant Children

Research with Retarded Children. While much of the research specifically on the selective attention abilities of deviant populations has been conducted with learning-disabled children, the first applications of Hagen's central-incidental paradigm were with mentally retarded children. Actually, interest in attentional problems in general in retarded children can be traced at least as far back as the 1930s and and 40s. Heinz Werner and Alfred Strauss conducted a series of studies that demonstrated consistent individual differences among mentally retarded children in ability to separate the figure from the background on tasks containing both figural and background components (Werner & Strauss, 1939a, 1939b, 1940, 1941). Although they explored this ability in a variety of modalities, most of their efforts concentrated on the visual domain. In a typical experiment, they tachistoscopically presented the child visual figure-background slides for brief exposure times. After each slide, the experimenter asked the child what he had just seen. Essentially, the results were that children *thought to be* brain-damaged were more likely to respond to the background while the children not diagnosed as brain-damaged were more likely to respond to the figure.

Werner and Strauss's research, however, was aptly criticized by Sarason (1949) because of the questionable diagnostic criteria they used for brain damage (the reader is referred to Hallahan and Cruickshank [1973] for a lengthier discussion of these issues). Even though it can be seriously questioned whether or not brain damage results in figure-background problems, Werner & Strauss did find evidence indicating that some mentally retarded children may exhibit such problems. Because of the methodological problems in diagnosis, the importance of Werner & Strauss's findings regarding two different subgroups of mentally retarded children is often overlooked. At a time (1930s and 40s) when most professionals viewed mental retardation as a homogeneous condition, Werner & Strauss were pioneers in championing for the case of individualization of instruction based on psychological characteristics.

Despite the importance of their findings, there was relatively little study of attentional processes in retarded individuals for a number of years after Werner & Strauss's work. In the 1960s, however, there was a resurgence of interest in the attentional abilities of the retarded. The studies of Zeaman & House (1963) were instrumental in reviving work in this area. They conducted investigations of the discrimination learning of retarded individuals, and found that once the retarded child learns to attend to the relevant dimension (e.g., size, form, color) that differentiates two objects, he learns the discrimination just as quickly as normal controls. Zeaman & House advanced the theory that, at least with regard to simple discrimination tasks, retarded individuals do not have a learning deficit so much as they have an attention deficit.

The provocative results and conclusions of Zeaman & House provided impetus for further studies of attentional processes in the retarded. While the discrimination learning paradigm was not directly analogous to the central-incidental memory paradigm, the two were similar enough to encourage Hagen and his colleagues to explore the selective attention capabilities of the retarded. In 1971 Hagen & Huntsman reported a study of selective attention ability in retarded persons. In response to the criticisms that Werner & Strauss's and Zeaman & House's work was done exclusively with institutionalized populations (Zigler, 1969), Hagen & Huntsman included institutionalized and community-reared retarded children in their study. Consistent with their hypotheses, they found differences in selective attention ability between institutionalized retardates and normal controls matched on mental age, but found no differences between community-reared retarded children and their normal peers. Hallahan et al. (1973) partially replicated these results with noninstitutionalized, cerebral-palsied, mentally retarded children. In addition to finding no selective attention deficit in these community-reared retarded children, Hallahan et al. found that mental age was a more crucial variable than either chronological age or IQ in the determination of selective attention ability.

That institutionalization per se is responsible for poor selective attention performance, however, can be questioned because Hagen et al. (1974) were unable to replicate the results of Hagen & Huntsman. Noting that many of the institutionalized retarded children of Hagen & Huntsman were poor children whose families resided in the inner city of Detroit, Hagen et al. compared an institutionalized sample of retarded children from a more heterogeneous socioeconomic background. In this study, no differences on selective attention performance obtained between the retarded and normal groups equated on mental age. It may be, then, that social class is a more salient determiner of selective attention ability than is institutionalization. This conclusion must be qualified by two points. First, institutionalization is far from being a homogeneous variable. Institutional regimens differ, and evidence has accumulated indicating that the effects of institutionalization on cognitive performance varies from one situation to another (Balla et al., 1974). It is therefore possible that some institutions more than others might create environments more conducive to selective attention performance. Second, Hagen & Huntsman's sample was composed primarily of children in the mildly retarded range whereas the mean IQ of Hagen et al.'s retarded sample was only 54, with none higher than 60. Level of intelligence, thus, cannot be ruled out as a possible critical variable.

Research with Learning Disabled Children. In terms of deviant populations, the learning-disabled child is the one whose selective attention performance has been studied most often. This is probably because an extensive clinically based literature has evolved concerning the distractibility and hyperactivity of the learning-disabled. Attentional problems are probably cited more often by teachers and parents than any other category of problems (except academic failure itself) as a behavioral symptom of learning disabilities. Ross (1976), in fact, has formulated a theory that essentially posits that virtually all learning-disabled children have selective attention deficits. Such a position may seem radical at first, but it is difficult to deny the research documentation of attentional deficits as a characteristic of learning disabilities. While it may be that not all learning-disabled children exhibit attentional problems, data show that attentional problems are more likely to be found in learning-disabled than in normal-achieving children. The work of the senior author and his colleagues as well as other researchers around the country have established a strong case for selective attention deficits in learning-disabled children. We now turn to some of our own studies.

In the first of a series of studies on the selective attention abilities of learning-disabled children we compared the performance of a small group ($N = 10$) of overachievers with a small group ($N = 10$) of underachievers in the sixth grade on the central-incidental task (Hallahan, Kauffman, & Ball, 1973). As was hypothesized, the overachievers recalled more central stimuli than did the underachievers. The two groups did not differ on incidental recall. While it would have been even more convincing for the hypothesis of a selective attention deficit if the low achievers had recalled more incidental information than the high achievers, the results were at least suggestive, particularly when one considers that in his developmental studies Hagen has not *always* found a *decrease* in incidental performance at the older age levels. That low achievers "stayed even" with the high achievers on incidental but not central recall was encouraging to our hypothesis. More supportive to our hypothesis was the finding of drastically different correlations between central and incidental learning for the two groups. For high achievers, the correlation was −.77, but for low achievers it was .53. Thus, replicating the results of Hagen with normal samples, the overachievers were apparently giving up incidental information in order to recall central stimuli; the underachievers, on the other hand, were performing similarly to normal children of a much younger chronological age.

Because the above study was based on a small N, Experiment I of our next study was a replication effort with a larger sample (Tarver et al., 1976). The Hallahan et al. (1973) results were essentially replicated with a group of eight-year-old learning-disabled children ($N = 18$) and a group of normal controls ($N = 15$). In addition, unlike the Hallahan study, this one included school-verified "learning disabled" children and "normal" controls rather than under- and overachievers. Like the Hallahan study, however, the two groups did not differ on CA, IQ, or MA, but the learning-disabled group was an average of 2.23 years below expected reading grade level. Again, the normal sample performed better on central but not on incidental recall. Also, the correlations between central and incidental recall were in the predicted opposite directions for the two groups (−.28 for normals and .36 for learning-disabled).

Even more informative to us than the above replication was a further analysis we performed on the data in Experiment I. This study was based upon developmental research of memory performance that indicated that young children do poorly on serial memory tasks partly because they do not engage in rehearsal strategies (Ellis, 1970; Hagen, 1971; Hagen, Meacham, & Mesibov, 1970: Hagen, Streeter, & Raker, 1974) and on literature indicating that learning-disabled children have language problems (Blank & Bridger, 1966; McGrady & Olson, 1970). We hypothesized, therefore, that learning-disabled children may do poorly in selective attention performance because of the absence of rehearsal strategies. One way researchers have assessed whether an individual is using rehearsal strategies on serial memory tasks is through the analysis of serial position curves. Better recall of positions late in a series (recency effect) (e.g., the 3 and 8 if asked to remember the series—7, 4, 2, 9, 1, 3, 8) than positions intermediate in a series (e.g., 2, 9, and 1) is evident across a wide age span from very young children on up into adulthood. Better recall of the early positions (primacy effect) (e.g., 7 and 4) does not generally occur until about seven or eight years of age. The appearance of a primacy effect for both visual and auditory materials corresponds with the child's use of rehearsal as a learning technique. The rationale for rehearsal increasing primacy recall is that the early items are rehearsed more often and without the interfering effect of having items encoded before them (as is the case for the middle items).

The normal children, as predicted, demonstrated both a recency and a primacy effect, whereas the learning-disabled children, as predicted, exhibited only a recency effect. This lack of a primacy effect suggested to us that the learning-disabled child may have difficulties in selective attention for other than simply the inability to focus his or her visual perception on the task at hand. We need a more complex explanation that takes into account the interaction of verbal rehearsal skills with selective attention.

Experiment II of the Tarver et al. (1976) study further confirmed the hypothesis of a verbal rehearsal deficiency in learning-disabled children. In this portion of the study, 10- and 13-year-old learning-disabled children were tested either under the standard condition or under a condition in which they were instructed to label, chunk, and rehearse items. The findings indicated that the verbal rehearsal condition was effective in increasing selective attention performance. Using a measure of selective attention efficiency, (proportion of central recall minus proportion of incidental recall), the verbal rehearsal group was significantly better than the standard condition group. The fact that the learning-disabled children were able to improve performance under the verbal rehearsal condition is reminiscent of the production deficiency hypothesis forwarded by Flavell (1970). Flavell maintains that young children compared to older children do poorly on memory tasks not because verbal mediators are ineffective for young children but because young children fail to produce mediators at the appropriate time. When given verbal mediation instructions, however, young children do as well as older children. The same appears to be the case for learning-disabled children's performance on selective attention tasks. If given specific verbal rehearsal instructions, learning-disabled children are able to use them to advantage.

Not only did Experiment II provide us with important information concerning the possible existence of a verbal rehearsal deficit, but it also provided insight into the developmental progression of selective attention abilities. The data indicated that learning-disabled children lag about two years or more behind their normal peers in selective attention performance. Data from the 8-year-old learning-disabled children of Experiment I and the 10- and 13-year-old learning-disabled children of Experiment II (who were tested under the standard condition) showed a clear and consistent development increase in selective attention performance. First, there were significant differences favoring the 13-year-olds over the 8- and 10-year-olds, and the 10-year-olds over the 8-year-olds on central recall, but no differences obtained on incidental recall. There was also an age by serial position interaction showing that the two older age groups, particularly the 13-year-olds, demonstrated a primacy as well as a recency effect. In addition, the correlation between central and incidental performance followed the predicted trend from positive at the younger ages to negative at the older ages; that is, .36 for the 8-year-olds, .27 for the 10-year-olds, and $-.16$ for the 13-year-olds.

To summarize, the results of the two experiments in the Tarver et al. (1976)

study support the following notions about selective attention performance of learning disabled children:

1. Learning-disabled children are deficient in selective attention compared to normal peers.
2. Problems with selective attention appear to be developmentally based in that learning-disabled children do not perform qualitatively different than younger normal children. Another way of saying this is that learning disabled lag developmentally behind normal children in selective attention performance.
3. Deficient selective attention performance appears to be linked to deficient verbal rehearsal strategies.
4. Instruction in the use of verbal rehearsal strategies will improve the performance of learning-disabled children.

We will return to the issue of verbal rehearsal, but first it is important to point out that the hypothesis of a developmental lag in selective attention has also been confirmed in at least two other studies, one conducted within our own laboratory and one reported by an independent team of researchers. First, because developmental studies with normal children have sometimes shown a decline in incidental learning at about 12 to 13 years of age, Tarver et al. (1977) tested a group of 15-year-old learning-disabled children. It was reasoned that if, indeed, with these 15-year-olds one could find a decline in incidental recall compared to younger children, this would be further evidence of a developmental lag. This hypothesis was again supported. The 15-year-olds' incidental recall decreased, but their selective attention efficiency (as measured by $\%C \times \%I$) increased relative to the younger children of the previous study. Going against prediction, however, we found a positive rather than a negative correlation (.32) between central and incidental recall. The small N (14) may have been a factor in this failure to find the predicted negative correlation since correlations can fluctuate radically when calculated on small samples, particularly samples of individuals who are as variable as learning-disabled children.

Pelham & Ross (1977), using a slight modification of Hagen's central-incidental task, also found a developmental lag. Comparing first-, third-, and fifth-grade poor readers and normal controls, Pelham & Ross found that at all age levels the poor readers performed better than controls on incidental recall and poorer on central recall. Correlations between central and incidental recall were also consistently higher for the poor readers at all age levels. Failure to find a significant group by age interaction also led the investigators to suggest that selective attention ability is delayed from about two to four years in poor readers. Pelham & Ross's results replicate nicely those of our own and corroborate our suspicion that learning-disabled children tend to follow the same, albeit considerably delayed, developmental pattern as do normal children.

Before moving on to consideration of training in selective attention skills, we emphasize that there are also a number of studies, not specifically using Hagen's central-incidental paradigm, that confirm the hypothesis that learning-disabled children exhibit problems in attending to relevant information in the presence of proximal irrelevant information (Atkinson & Seunath, 1973; Deikel & Friedman, 1976; Elkind et al., 1965; Keogh & Donlon, 1972; Mondani & Tutko, 1969; Sabatino & Ysseldyke, 1972; Silverman et al., 1963; Willows, 1974). Because some of these studies have already been reviewed elsewhere (Hallahan, 1975b), and some will be taken up later in this chapter, we will only briefly discuss the two studies not included in the earlier review. Deikel & Friedman (1976) gave 11- to 13-year-old learning-disabled and normal children the task of sorting IBM punch cards into three separate piles. They were instructed to place cards having at least two holes punched in each of the nine rows into pile 1; to place cards having holes punched only in the even-numbered rows into pile 2; and to place cards having holes punched only in the odd-numbered rows into pile 3. In addition to this "primary" information punched on the cards, there was "incidental" material contained on the cards. For example, three of the cards had the word "SORT" typed in the upper left-hand corner and seven had an "X" drawn in the upper right-hand corner. As predicted, compared to normals, learning-disabled children made more errors on the sorting task. Also, on a posttest questionnaire designed to assess recall of primary and incidental information, the learning-disabled children were poorer on primary recall but significantly *better* on incidental recall.

Willows (1974) compared sixth grade, good and poor readers on an ingeniously designed selective reading task. Half of the subjects read a passage under a standard condition in which the text was typed double-space in black ink and half read a passage typed double-space in black ink with "interfering" words typed in red ink between the lines. Whereas the good readers read equally fast under both conditions, the poor readers took longer to read the stories under the selective than under the control condition. Also, poor but not good readers took longer to answer questions about the story under the selective compared to the control condition. An unexpected finding, however, occurred on an error analysis on multiple-choice questions asked after the reading task. Good readers made more intrusion errors (errors that could be attributed to the "interfering" words in red ink) than did poor readers. Willows notes that the results on the time variables may indicate that poor readers are deficient in selective attention. Given the intrusion error findings, however, Willows states that

> an alternative possibility is that poor readers are more susceptible to interference from any adverse reading conditions because their attention is concentrated on the visual dimensions of the reading task.... Good readers, on the other hand, have automatized the more basic visual skills involved in reading to the extent that they can be handled "preattentively" [Neisser, 1969]. Thus, they are able to concentrate most of their processing capacity on the extraction

of meanings, a process that normally serves them well but which in the present task results in more intrusion errors (pp. 413-415).

The Training of Selective Attention Abilities

There have been surprisingly few studies concerned with attempting to improve selective attention performance on Hagen's (1967) task. This is probably partly because it was not until recently that selective attention was found through systematic study to be deficient in some children. Since most of the investigations showing selective attention ability to be lacking or deficient have been conducted with learning-disabled children, most of the training studies have been carried out with them.

The Use of Verbal Rehearsal. We have already reviewed a study (Tarver et al., 1976) from our laboratory showing that verbal rehearsal facilitates selective attention performance. To summarize briefly, based on data suggesting that learning-disabled children's poor performance on Hagen's selective attention task may be due to lack of, or inefficient use of, verbal rehearsal strategies, we gave half of groups of 10- and 13-year-olds verbal rehearsal instructions and gave half standard instructions. The verbal rehearsal condition actually involved a combination of verbal rehearsal and chunking instructions. In other words, the experimenter instructed the child to rehearse the names of the seven pictures in groups of two, three, and two. The adult said:

> It will help you to remember if you say the name of each animal out loud as you see its picture and rehearse the names in groups like this: Say the name of each of the first two animals as you see them. Then repeat the names of both animals in the order in which you saw them (demonstrate). Then, say the names of each of the next three pictures as you see them and repeat all three of those names in order (demonstrate). Then name the last two animal pictures as you see them (p. 379).

While there were no significant differences between the verbal rehearsal and standard condition on central or incidental recall, the means were in the predicted directions for both age levels. In addition, selective attention efficiency as measured by $\%C = \%I$ *was* significantly facilitated by verbal rehearsal at both age levels.

The Use of Reinforcement. That selective attention performance could be improved through the use of reinforcement was suggested by the results of a study by Hagen & West (1970) using institutionalized retarded children of two different mental age levels—8 and 10½ years. The task used differed from Hagen's original one in that a trial consisted of presenting a slide that was partitioned into four sections, each containing a different geometric shape and a dot of a different color. The adult instructed the child to pay attention to the positions of the geometric shapes and colored dots and gave differential pay-off for the dimension designated as primary (high pay-off- and secondary (low pay-off). The experimenter, for example, gave the child a red and white chip (worth one point) for each correct primary and secondary response. No points were awarded for only a correct secondary response. Hagen & West found better recall of primary over secondary stimuli for both age levels.

There are, however, a couple of difficulties with the paradigm of this study that made it only suggestive that reinforcement facilitates selective attention. First, there was no control condition wherein subjects received no rewards or equal rewards for remembering each dimension. Second, the secondary response was not reinforced except when it was correct along with the primary response; thus, there was no direct measure of response to low pay-off stimuli alone.

Using the Hagen & West study as impetus, we compared learning-disabled children's selective attention performance under reinforcement, response cost, and a standard condition (Hallahan et al., in press). We modified the Hagen task by using cards containing three different classes of stimuli—animals, household objects, and geometric figures (the latter were included as "distractors" only to make the task more difficult). Each trial consisted of five of these cards, each of which contained a picture of an animal, household object, and geometric figure, one above the other in random order. The experimenter told the child that he/she was to pay attention to the positions (in the series, not on the card) of both the animals and the household objects. After each trial, the child was asked to recall the position of one of the animals and one of the household objects. In the reinforcement condition, the child was given three cents for each correct response to one of the categories (e.g., animals) and only one cent for the other category (e.g., household objects). In the response cost condition, all the pennies he could possibly earn after all the trials were placed before the child, and three were taken away for every wrong response to one of the categories (e.g., animals) and only one cent was removed for incorrect responses to the other category (e.g., household objects). In the control condition, the child was rewarded with two cents for each correct response in each of the two categories. Besides allowing one to look at breadth of attention and the effects of reinforcement and response cost, the Hallahan et al. modification of the Hagen task offers a couple of other advantages. First, it allows one to assess selective attention in a repeated measures design. Using the standard Hagen task, one is unable to do this because once the child, to his surprise, is given the incidental task, he/she would be very likely to anticipate it if tested again. Second, the "relevant" and "irrelevant" recall in the modified version are solely defined by the amount of pay-off provided. They are, thus, tested in the same way, i.e., by asking the serial position of the relevant *and* the irrelevant stimuli after each trial. Thus, relevant and irrelevant recall are asessed in the same way, whereas the relevant recall on the Hagen task requires short-term, serial recall but the irrelevant recall requires matching of pairs learned somewhat outside of the parameters time-wise of a short-term memory task.

The results indicate that reinforcement, but not response cost, is effective in increasing learning disabled children's recall of high pay-off relative to low pay-off stimuli. In addition, the dramatically different correlation between recall of the two categories for the reinforcement condition ($-.59$, $p < .05$) compared to the response cost (.34, ns) and control (.42, ns) conditions suggests that reinforcement induces the child to give up attention to the low pay-off stimuli in order to attend to high pay-off material. A somewhat surprising finding occurred when we took recall of irrelevant stimuli and subtracted it from relevant stimuli (in order to obtain an index of selective attention efficiency analogous to %C×%I used with the standard Hagen task), and then plotted serial position curves. We found a pronounced primacy and recency effect within the reinforcement condition, but only a recency effect for the other two conditions. Apparently, the children were induced to use rehearsal strategies under the reinforcement condition even though no instructions to rehearse were given. The results suggest that a high degree of pay-off for attending to one stimulus category over another provides enough impetus to activate a verbal rehearsal strategy appropriately. Questions still remain whether it is a case of the learning-disabled child's learning to use strategies already in his repertoire at the appropriate time or better learning to use strategies that are only minimally developed. Either interpretation, however, is again consistent with a "production deficiency hypothesis."

Comparison of Verbal Rehearsal and Reinforcement. Our next study was a direct comparison of reinforcement and verbal rehearsal, using the standard Hagen task (Dawson et al., 1978). Learning-disabled children of two different ages (9½ and 11½ years) were given the task under one of four conditions: (a) one group received the standard administration with no reinforcement, (b) one group was given verbal rehearsal instructions, (c) one group received reinforcement for correct performance, and (d) one group was given both rehearsal *and* reinforcement. In this direct comparison of verbal rehearsal and reinforcement, three general results obtained:

1. Verbal rehearsal by itself was more effective than reinforcement by itself.
2. Verbal rehearsal combined with reinforcement was the most effective condition.
3. Reinforcement by itself was, in a sense, the least effective in that significantly more incidental learning occurred in this than in the verbal rehearsal condition.

The third result noted above should only be taken with caution. First, the Hallahan et al. (in press) study discussed earlier found contradictory results in that reinforcement was effective. Differences in the nature of the two tasks may explain these inconsistent results. In the Hallahan et al. study the relevant and irrelevant stimuli were well defined by the amount of pay-off received for each. In the absence of such obvious cues in the Dawson et al. study, reinforcement may cause the child to increase attention to *all* cues. Reinforcement, as Kausler, Laughlin, and Trapp (1963) have suggested, may increase the child's breadth of attention to all cues in the learning environment.

Overselectivity of Attention

In general, then, the literature on selective attention indicates that the ability to attend to a few relevant stimuli in the presence of proximal, irrelevant stimuli is a mature and efficient response style. There is, however, a body of literature that, at first blush, appears to run counter to these data. A number of studies on discrimination learning point to the conclusion that the developmentally immature child is overselective in his attention, i.e., he or she attends to only a small portion of the stimuli important for making a discrimination. Although these two bodies of research are seemingly contradictory, we believe a rapprochement between the two can be made. First, let us briefly turn to the overselectivity literature.

Overselectivity in Autistic Children. Interest in the phenomenon of overselectivity has its roots in research with autistic children, in particular, the work of Lovaas, Schreibman, Koegel, and Rehm (1971). In the first of a series of studies on this topic, Lovaas et al. presented autistic, mentally retarded, and normal children with three simultaneous stimuli (a red light, white noise, and an increase in pressure from a blood-pressure cuff wrapped around the leg). The subject was reinforced for pressing a bar in the simultaneous presence of these visual, auditory, and tactile stimuli. When these were not present, the child was not reinforced. During training trials, the three stimuli were either all presented together or not at all. Once the child learned to make the discrimination of when and when not to press the bar, he/she was presented with test trials in which each of the three kinds of stimuli was presented alone. The child was reinforced for responding to the single stimulus. The results indicated that during the test trials the autistic children responded primarily to only one stimulus component, the retardates to two, and normals to all three. In other words, the autistic children during the original training trials had made their discriminations on the basis of only one of the three possible relevant stimuli. Other studies have essentially replicated these results with only two stimuli (Lovaas & Schreibman, 1971) and when the stimuli fall within the same modality (Koegel & Wilhelm, 1973; Reynolds, Newsom, & Lovaas, 1974; Schreibman & Lovaas, 1973).

Based on the consistent findings that autistic children are overselective, Lovaas and his colleagues have hypothesized that overselectivity may be at the root of a variety of behavioral symptoms of autistic children. For example, they have speculated that the extremely retarded speech development of these children may at least in part be due to their attending to only a minute portion of the necessary discriminative elements of speech production. Also, with regard to their bizarre social interactions, Schreibman and Lovaas (1973) state:

> Social situations, of course, require response to a multiplicity of cues. Even the simple recognition of another person necessitates response to many cues. It is the unique arrangement of several separate elements (facial features, hair, clothing, etc.) which comprise the significant stimulus (a particular person). Since a person changes over time and over situations . . . adequate recognition requires response to more than one aspect of that person. Clearly, if one were to form one's knowledge or recognition of a person on the basis of only a small and inconsistent cue (such as a piece of clothing), then one would not be able to maintain a stable or durable response to that person.
> . . . For example, it was informally noted that one autistic child only recognized his father when his father was wearing glasses . . . . Autistic children are known to show major behavioral disorganization with minor changes in their environment (to insist on "maintaining sameness"). If they do form significant associations to minor aspects of their environment, as the findings on stimulus overselectivity suggest, then one may be in a better position to understand this apparently "psychotic" behavior (p. 154).

Another implication of being overselective in attention is the difficulty this poses for the use of prompting. Teachers working with autistic and severely retarded children often use prompts in an effort to help children make discriminations. If a child is overselective, however, he may learn the discrimination only on the basis of the prompt and may not be able to make the discrimination when the prompt is faded. Two studies have shown that this may be a problem for autistic children (Koegel & Rincover, 1976; Schreibman, 1975). Prompting may be a particular problem when the stimulus prompt is extraneous to the to-be-discriminated stimuli. Schreibman, for example, with autistic children found that an "extra-stimulus" prompt (pointing) was detrimental when used as a cue to discriminating between two stick figures. However, the careful sequencing of a "within-stimulus prompt," emphasizing the distinctive features of the two stick figures, was successful.

Overselectivity as a Developmental Phenomenon. The conclusion reached from the early studies of overselectivity was that autistic children are more overselective compared to normal controls. However, at least partly because so many autistic children are untestable, these early studies did not match autistic with normal children on mental age. Later studies have provided data indicating that overselectivity is a characteristic of both normal and retarded children of early developmental levels (Schover & Newsom, 1976; Wilhelm & Lovaas, 1976). The latter study, for example, using retarded subjects of different IQ and mental age levels found a decrease in overselectivity with an increase in IQ and mental age. Because the variables of IQ and mental age were confounded, it is not possible to determine the relative contribution of each. There is evidence from other areas of study, however, that point to developmental level as the crucial variable (Eimas, 1969).

Flexibility of Attention: Evidence for the Development of Appropriate Strategies
At the beginning of this section, we noted that the research on selective attention and the research on overselectivity appear to contradict one another. We believe there are plausible reasons for these differences. First, the tasks used in these two bodies of literature are considerably different. Most of the selective attention research has used short-term memory tasks, whereas the overselectivity investigations have primarily used simple discrimination tasks. It may be hypothesized that performance on the latter kinds of tasks is helped by broadening one's attention, whereas performance on the more complex selective attention tasks is helped by narrowing one's attention. The key to the developmental findings, thus, may be that the developmentally mature child learns to adopt the strategy most appropriate to the particular task with which he/she is faced (Brown, 1974). Hale & Taweel (1974) and Brown, Campione, & Gilliard (1974) have found evidence that fits with this proposed hypothesis. Hale & Taweel tested five- and eight-year-old children with tasks that involved either selective *or* broad-based attention. They found a developmental increase in breadth of attention when that was helpful for learning, but no developmental increase on incidental learning on the tasks where incidental learning was irrelevant or actually misleading. They concluded that, with age, children develop the ability to differentiate between situations when breadth of attention is helpful and when it is not. Brown et al. likewise found that when background information is relevant to performing well, then older children are more likely than younger children to attend to it.

If it is true that normal children develop the ability to be flexible in their distribution of attention, it would be interesting to see how children deficient in selective attention for their age (e.g., learning-disabled children) would do on tasks requiring breadth of attention. Based on our conclusions that learning disabled children are developmentally immature in using appropriate strategies, we would predict that they would be overselective relative to normals.

Conclusions Based Upon Selective Attention Studies with Learning Disabled Children: Evidence for a Task Strategy Deficit. While specific results vary to a certain extent from study to study, the conclusions based on the selective attention abilities of the learning disabled are amazingly consistent. This is all the more promising for theory-building when one considers that most research literature in learning disabilities is fraught with contradictory results (Hallahan, 1975a). At this time, it appears that the most parsimonious explanation for the learning-disabled child's tendency to have problems in attending to relevant cues and ignoring irrelevant cues (when the relevant and irrelevant cues are in close proximity) is his/her inability to bring to the task a specific learning strategy.

This explanation corresponds well with frequent anedoctal reports from teachers describing the learning disabled child as a trial-and-error learner in the sense that for each new situation the child faces the teacher must be very directive in explaining the task and how to attack it. Apparently, then, it is not so much the learning-disabled child's inability to attend selectively that is his/her basic problem so much as it is the inability to analyze the task in terms of the best strategies needed for performing it. If directly instructed, for example, in a verbal rehearsal strategy, she/he is able to employ this strategy and hence attend more selectively.

It should be pointed out that a body of literature not specifically directed at selective attention points to basically the same conclusions noted above. Fritz (1974), looking at the slowness of learning-disabled children to form reversal and intradimensional shifts, and Swanson's (1977) and Torgesen and Goldman's (1977) studies of the memory abilities of learning-disabled children are relevant here. Torgesen's work (*Editor's note:* See the chapter by Torgesen & Kail in this volume) is particularly important, and his conclusions are compatible with ours. Torgesen (1977) sees learning-disabled children as passive rather than active learners. He believes also that even though learning-disabled children exhibit a wide variety of performance problems from child to child, this apparent heterogeneity may be misleading. In his view a more general characteristic of a large number of learning-disabled children is that they may have a problem in actively engaging in learning strategies. Ann Brown (1974), in her studies of the memory processes of the mentally retarded, has also reached similar conclusions. It is her contention, and there is abundant data to back her up, that retarded children, particularly mildly retarded individuals, experience the greatest difficulty on memory tasks requring the use of strategic plans.

Another conceptualization of the development of selective attention ability that fits well with our own formulations has been provided by Wright & Vlietstra (1975). Looking at a slightly different body of literature than what we have reviewed (their review focuses heavily on experiments designed to assess the effects of cue salience), and looking primarily at studies using normal samples, they have reached conclusions pertinent to our discussion. It is their contention that as the normal child matures she/he shifts from a rather random *exploration* of his environment to a more systematic, logical *search* of its various features. The young child's exploration behavior is controlled to a large extent by salient features of his/her environment, but the older child is able to use his/her own strategies for a logical search of the environment. The following statement by Wright & Vlietstra coincides nicely with our own conclusions that the learning-disabled child functions like a younger normal child in that he/she is deficient in the use of task-appropriate strategies:

> In summary, our developmental hypothesis is that exploration is motivated by curiosity and guided by stimulus salience, that it is natural and dominant in young children. With development and growing familiarity of a wider range of situations, exploration becomes less dominant and is more restricted to playful situations and novel environments. With experience and

maturation, there evolves a goal-oriented search mode of attending that is more deliberate and purposeful, more organized and systematic, and more based on relevance and informativeness of cues. Perceptually based information processing as seen in iconic representation [Bruner, Olver, & Greenfield, 1966] and eidetic imagery [Haber & Haber, 1964], both of which occur more frequently in children than in adults and which exemplify the exploratory mode, are replaced by linearly organized, verbally guided, and logically programmed routines [G.A. Miller et al., 1960] (Wright & Vliestra, 1975, p. 202).

DISTRACTIBILITY

While the preceding section on selective attention dealt with children's ability to attend to relevant stimuli in the presence of proximal irrelevant stimuli, this section focuses on research investigating the influence of distal distractors. The rationale for this distinction stems from the fact that learning-disabled children's performance relative to normal peers is different in the two situations.

An assumption made in much of the research discussed thus far is that the ability to attend selectively to stimuli of central importance requires that the subject somehow be able to shut out competing, incidental stimuli. A subject who cannot selectively focus on the relevant stimulus in a situation learns less efficiently, perhaps because his attention is being diverted to nonrelevant stimuli. These nonrelevant stimuli are commonly referred to as "distractors," and a subject who has difficulty selectively focusing is often referred to as "distractible."

Distractibility is among the most common behavioral characteristics attributed to learning-disabled children (and to those in related, overlapping categories, e.g., minimally brain-damaged, reading-disabled, hyperactive). "Disorders of attention" including distractibility was the fifth most frequently cited characteristic of such children (ahead of "specific learning disabilities in reading, arithmetic, writing, and spelling") in a list compiled by Clements (1966). Numerous clinical reports, beginning with those of Strauss & Lehtinen (1947), have tended to corroborate distractibility's assumed role as a major problem among learning-disabled children (Benton, 1962; Cruickshank & Paul, 1971; Strauss & Kephart, 1955; Wender, 1971). For example, talking about the "brain-injured" child, Strauss & Kephart stated that distractibility is ". . . often the most obvious of his difficulties. He finds it impossible to engage in any activity in a concentrated fashion but is always being led aside from the task at hand by stimuli which should remain extraneous but do not" (p. 135). Despite this general acceptance of distractibility as a defining characteristic of learning-disabled children, surprisingly little research-based corroboration exists.

Several different methods have been employed to assess distractibility. One popular approach operates on the assumption that lapses in sustained attention indicate that the subject has been distracted. In other words, attention and distractibility are seen as two sides of the same coin. Thus, any time a subject is not paying attention, she/he is in a state of distraction. It is assumed that something else has diverted the child's attention. Research utilizing the Continuous Performance Test (CPT) (Rosvold et al., 1956), or one of its variants, are examples of this approach. Vigilance tasks such as the CPT typically require the subject to look (or listen) steadily until specified stimuli appear (or are heard). The subject at that point is to respond, then continue to attend until the stimulus reappears, and so on for periods set by the experimenter. Using the CPT in this way, Sykes, Douglas, and Morgenstern (1973), for example, concluded that hyperactives experience significantly greater attentional problems than do normal children. (*Editor's note:* See the chapter by Krupski, in this volume, for detailed review and discussion of sustained attention, including consideration of distractibility.)

Similarly, performance on various standardized tests or parts of tests is assumed to require attentional skills. The most commonly used format requires the subject to repeat a series of spoken words or numbers, forwards and/or backwards. Such tests of attention and concentration have been included in intelligence tests since Binet originated cognitive assessment. A three-subtest factor from the Wechsler Intelligence Scale for Children—Revised (Wechsler, 1974), including such a "Digit Span" measure as well as the Arithmetic and Coding subtests, is in fact commonly called the "Freedom from Distractibility Factor." Some research (Huelsman, 1970; Nicholls & Tavormina, 1978) has indicated that learning-disabled children perform quite poorly on this factor, providing some support for the notion that distractibility (or inability to sustain attention) is a problem for many learning-disabled children.

The assumption that inattention and distractibility are identical, or can be inferred from one another, while perhaps intuitively appealing, is not totally acceptable. A subject who falls asleep while taking a CPT or Digit Span test, under this approach, would be considered distracted. But what would be the distraction? For the purposes of this review, distraction will be assumed to have occurred only when an irrelevant, incidental stimulus (or multiple stimuli of the kind) is identifiable in the experimental setting.

In Hagen's central-incidental task, the incidental stimuli are presumed to be distractors. One central stimulus, visually presented, and one visual distractor are present on each card. As noted in the earlier section of this chapter, this research instrument has generated a wealth of data, and from that point of view obviously has made a significant contribution to understanding attentional processes. Research with the central-incidental task has documented a strong developmental trend in children's ability to focus selectively on one stimulus dimension while ignoring simultaneously present "distractors," the incidental stimuli (Hagen & Hale, 1973). A simple extrapolation from these results would be that, as children get older, they are less influenced by distractions. Despite some necessary qualifications, that one general notion appears to be valid regardless of type of learning task, type of distractor, or type of child. Of course the "real world" in which children function academically, the classroom, offers a much more complex situation. "Central" tasks to which a child must attend may be visual, auditory, tactual, or all three simultaneously, and potential distractors may come through any or all modalities, in changing patterns, with varying intensities and durations. Thus the question of the effect of distraction on learning is a complex one.

Results of distractibility studies, including those utilizing normal subjects, are confusing and often apparently contradictory. A manipulation of task conditions to inject "distractions" has resulted, in various studies, in (a) decreases in performance, (b) increases in performance, (c) no change in performance level, and/or (d) variable changes, in which performance initially shifts in one direction and then changes direction. This situation is more readily understood when one recognizes the many different types of distractions which have been used experimentally. Subjects have been asked to perform under continuous exposure to distracting stimuli or to intermittent bursts of distraction; to distractions which are peripheral to the subject, or to those that are only inches from the child's eyes and ears; to those which are actually integrated into or closely related to the learning task itself or to those where distraction was extraneous "white noise"; to those where the distraction is auditory, visual, tactual, or a combination. Further, distractors have been present during the task or presented after learning but before testing for recall. Other variables which must be considered include such concerns as the intensity and duration of the distracting stimulus, and whether or not the subject is acquainted with and comfortable in the experimental setting. Given these and other possible variations in experimental format, it is little wonder that conclusions must be tenuously propounded at this point. We know only the effects of some types of distractors on a few kinds of learning with certain classifications of children under a narrow set of conditions.

Effect of Visual Distractors on Learning-Disabled Children

Several researchers have sought directly to assess the effects of distraction on learning-disabled children (and on related classifications such as reading-disabled, low-achieving, brain-injured, etc.) compared to normal children. Some have used the Hagen Central-Incidental task (or other highly similar tasks) discussed earlier (Deikel & Friedman, 1976; Hallahan, Kauffman, & Ball, 1973; Hallahan, Gajar, Cohen, & Tarver, in press; Pelham & Ross, 1977; Tarver, Hallahan, Kauffman, & Ball, 1976). These studies, as a group, have shown that learning-disabled children are not as able as normal peers to attend to relevant versus irrelevant stimuli. Another way of stating the findings is to say that low achievers were more distracted by incidental stimuli.

Mondani & Tutko (1969), using a different experimental task, found supporting evidence. They hypothesized that underachievers would be more distracted than normals by incidental information. If true, they reasoned, then underachievers should learn more incidental stimuli than their comparison group. They administered a "social responsibility test" to their junior high school age subjects. On the pages of the test were various pencil markings, such as question marks and flowers. After taking the test, subjects were asked questions about the irrelevant doodles. Underachievers recalled significantly more, suggesting that they do concentrate more on materials not central to the task—that they are more distracted by incidental information.

In another study comparing achievers and underachievers, Silverman, Davids, and Andrews (1963) found similar results. They used the Stroop Color-Word Test (1935), which requires the subject to say the color in which a color name is printed. The word "blue," written in red, would thus call for the response "red." If distracted, a subject should take longer to respond and should make more errors. Underachievers in the Silverman et al. study had significantly more difficulty with the task, leading the authors to the conclusion that their underachievers were more distractible. A major flaw in the study's design, the lack of IQ data on controls and the fact that controls were older, weakens the results somewhat, but the data are suggestive of greater distractibility for the underachievers.

Elkind et al. (1965), using third- through sixth-grade "retarded readers" and normals as subjects, studied performance on a task requiring the differentiation of figures embedded in extraneous backgrounds. The poor readers experienced significantly more problems in differentiating the figures, suggesting that the background distracted the retarded readers to a greater extent than normals.

Sabatino & Ysseldyke (1972) split a sample of learning-disabled children into two groups, one of retarded readers and the other of normal readers. They gave the Bender Gestalt test to both groups under standard conditions, and then repeated the administration with the Bender designs embedded in extraneous backgrounds. No differences were found for the standard condition, but the retarded readers were inferior to the normal readers when the designs were presented within the extraneous background.

Keogh & Donlon (1972) used a portable rod and frame apparatus to assess the field dependence-independence of a group of learning-disabled boys. Witkin et al.'s (1962) construct a field dependence-independence holds that some individuals are not influenced by the perceptual field around them (independents), while others rely extensively on cues from the context, or field (dependents). The rod and frame apparatus assesses the degree to which a subject can position a movable rod at the true vertical even when the rod is placed in a misleading context. In Keogh & Donlon's (1972) study, the learning-disabled boys were found to be highly field-dependent. The learning-disabled children, in other words, were much more influenced or distracted by the irrelevant background than were normal children.

Reasoning that nearby rather than peripheral distractors should have a relatively greater distracting effect, Atkinson & Seunath (1973) compared learning-disordered and normal children using distractions (stimulus changes) contained within the stimulus array itself. Their task required subjects to watch slides with squares of various colors. When a red square with a black dot in it appeared (in about 20 percent of the slides), subjects were to push a button. Two conditions were employed. Half of the children performed with the colored squares in the same position on each slide (constant condition), while for the other half, the squares were randomly assigned to different positions on the slides (stimulus-change condition). The two groups did not differ under the constant condition. However, under changing stimuli, the learning-disordered group made significantly more errors of omission (though not of commission) than the normals. A possible explanation offered by the authors was that, since the changes were associated more with the irrelevant stimuli than with the relevant stimulus, the learning-disordered children were attending more to irrelevant stimuli. This interpretation, which seems reasonable, would further support the hypothesis of differentially greater distractibility among learning-disabled than normal children, at least for this type of task.

The studies reviewed to this point all found learning-disabled children to be less able than normals to focus on a central, relevant stimulus and shut out irrelevant, distracting stimuli. They all had other elements in common as well. Each used visual tasks and visual distractors, and in each study the central tasks were very close to or actually embedded within the distracting stimuli. Only one exception to this trend of results in the literature was found. Using a nonreading version of the Stroop Color Word Test, Alwitt (1966) compared nonreaders and normal controls. Both groups performed more poorly under distraction, but no difference was found between the groups in intensity of the effect.

Though reasonably strong corroboration exists of the distracting effects of irrelevant visual distractors near the child, some evidence suggests that distractors at a distance from the child or target tasks do not have a negative effect. Browning (1967) reported three experiments in which subjects were required to perform a visual discrimination learning task to criterion under standard or distracting conditions. The distraction consisted of batteries of multicolored lights on wall and ceiling panels which flashed at various frequencies. These irrelevant peripheral visual distractions did not interfere with the brain-damaged subjects' learning performance.

Effect of Auditory Distractor on Learning-Disabled Children

Two studies compared learning-disabled and normal children's performance on visual tasks under conditions of auditory distraction. Dykman et al. (1970) asked subjects to press a key when a red light appeared on a panel and to release the key when a white light subsequently appeared. In the distraction phase of the study, intermittent, loud, one-second bursts from a hooter were sounded during the task. An examination of the tables presented by the authors indicates that no differential effect between learning-disabled and normal control children resulted from the distraction.

Likewise, Yekell (1974) played records at low and high volumes while subjects worked arithmetic problems or took a "concentration and attention" test.

Again, no difference between minimally brain-damaged children and normal control children resulted from the auditory distraction. The report of the study did not indicate what type of records were played.

Two other studies investigated the effect of auditory distractions on learning-disabled children's performance, but these used auditory-verbal performance tasks. Lasky & Tobin (1973) asked first-graders questions about verbally presented material. On all four sides of the subject were speakers through which tape-recorded sounds could be played. From the speaker in front came the relevant materials, while side and rear speakers played distractions. The speaker positioning was intended to simulate a classroom with the front speaker the "teacher." Two different kinds of distractions were employed. One was white noise, while the other consisted of voices speaking words. The learning-disabled group's performance was no different from the control group's under the white noise condition, but the linguistic distraction caused them problems. Results suggested that the learning-disabled children had significantly more difficulty than normals in dealing with linguistic material. When the relevant stimuli were not distinctly different from the irrelevant, the learning-disabled children apparently attended to the irrelevant more frequently than did normals. They could not, in other words, separate figure from ground as effectively as normal children when the distracting, incidental stimuli were similar to the central, relevant stimuli.

Nober & Nober's (1975) results do not confirm those of Lasky and Tobin. The Nobers administered the Wepman Auditory Discrimination Test to learning-disabled and control children in a quiet test room and with tape-recorded classroom noise in the same room. Though learning-disabled children made more errors in both conditions, the noise did not differentially affect the two groups.

With regard to auditory distractors, then, results suggest that learning-disabled children are not distracted excessively by formless white noise, by music, or by loud, unusual, intermittent sounds. However, they may have greater difficulty than normals in separating relevant from irrelevant sounds when the two are quite similar, as when both consist of spoken words.

Distractibility and Hyperactivity

Distractibility and hyperactivity frequently have been described as correlates of each other, and both often are considered to occupy central places in the learning-disabilities "syndrome." Evidence for a direct relationship between the two is sparse, clinical wisdom notwithstanding. It is important to bear in mind when comparing research studies using learning-disabled subjects with those having hyperactives as subjects that the two groups often overlap extensively. That is, many learning-disabled children may be hyperactive, and many hyperactives may be learning-disabled. Some authors make a clear distinction between the groups, but most do not. Therefore, studies using one group, in certain cases, may be equally applicable to the other. Sroufe et al. (1973) did report indirect evidence for a relationship between distractibility and hyperactivity. They found that an increase in anticipatory heart-rate deceleration (an indicator of attention) occurred when activity levels of learning-disabled subjects were reduced. Also, Sykes and his colleagues (Sykes, Douglas, & Morgenstern, 1973; Sykes, Douglas, Weiss, & Minde, 1971) have found that hyperactives perform more poorly on a test of sustained attention (the Continuous Performance Test, or CPT). However, distractibility and hyperactivity increasingly are being seen as different problems. This is occurring because direct experimental attempts to distract hyperactive subjects as compared to normal controls typically have not yielded the expected results. Sykes et al. &1971, 1973), for example, introduced a colored background for stimuli appearing on a screen which was discrepant from the color of the background of their target stimuli. This condition was meant to introduce distracting cues, and was expected particularly to bother the hyperactives. However, it disrupted both hyperactives and controls equally. Also, in the earlier study (Sykes et al., 1971), intermittent white noise was piped into the test room at random intervals while subjects were performing on a visual vigilance task. This attempt to introduce distraction again did not influence the hyperactives more than the normals.

Other researchers have reported results similar to those of Sykes et al., questioning the general distractibility of hyperactives. Kirchner (1976), for example, compared visual vigilance task performance of highly active and normal second-graders. Doorbell chimes were rung at various intervals during the testing. No difference between normal and highly active children was found as the result of the distraction.

Worland et al. (1973) compared performance on several cognitive and motor tasks in two settings, nondistracting and highly distracting. The nondistracting room was bare. The highly distracting room, on the other hand, was packed with stimuli. It had colorful pictures on the walls, streamers hanging from the ceiling, toys, comic books, balls, a mirror, a Bobo clown, and a punching bag. In addition, tape-recorded sounds of children playing was piped into the room. Results indicated that the distraction condition was no more detrimental for hyperactives than for controls.

On a color distraction test, Campbell et al. (1971) found no difference between hyperactives and normals. Differences did appear, however, on the Children's Embedded Figures Test. Hyperactives were found to be more "field dependent," suggesting that they may have been distracted by irrelevant cues from the background.

Barkley & Ullman (1975) set up an experimental playroom with a table and chair in each quadrant. On each table were five toys. Hyperactive and both clinic and community control groups were compared on their performance on several tasks, including visual and auditory continuous performance tests as well as toy changes in a free-play situation. They also took a number of measures of activity, including wrist and ankle activity and quadrant changes. No consistent relationship was found between measures of distractibility and of activity. Relative to other subject groups, hyperactives were not more distractible in this situation.

Several studies, on the other hand, have indicated a relationship between hyperactivity and distractibility. Doyle, Anderson, & Halcomb (1976), for example, compared learning-disabled and control groups (though no IQ data were available for controls). Subjects performed a visual vigilance task with distractors in the form of lights and numbers flashing intermittently occuring nine inches away and to the lower left of the relevant stimuli. Group differences were found, with learning-disabled children performing significantly more poorly under distraction. However, Doyle et al. had split their learning-disabled sample into three groups—hyperactive, hypoactive, and normoactive—on the basis of activity level. Further analysis of the data indicated that almost all the difference found between the larger learning-disabled group and the control group was the result of the very poor performance under distraction of the hyperactive group.

Bremer & Stern (1976) compared hyperactives and controls on a silent reading task under two distraction conditions, each of which consisted of both visual and auditory stimuli. In the first condition, a telephone with flashing lights on it rang intermittently. In the second distraction situation, a sinusoidal oscilloscope display was visible to the child. When activated, the oscilloscope display was accompanied by the sound of a Monroe calculator performing multiplication operations. It was unclear from the description of the study how far from the subjects the distractions were. The hyperactive subjects looked at distractors more often, and for longer durations, than the controls. Interestingly, however, no differences were found between the groups on measures of reading speed. The authors believe the lack of difference for reading efficiency was the result of matching groups for reading skill during the selection process.

Adams et al. (1974) had hyperactive and control children complete the Bender Gestalt Test under normal conditions, and then on special paper having "a moderately dense background of randomly placed intersecting curved lines." The task was quite similar to that employed by Sabatino & Ysseldyke (1972) with learning-disabled subjects, reported earlier. Adams et al. found significant decrement scores for their hyperactives under the background interference condition.

For hyperactives, then, as for subjects identified as learning-disabled, distractibility is not an invariably occurring phenomenon. The popular picture of learning-disabled and hyperactive children being totally at the mercy of their irrelevant stimulus-laden environment is clearly overdrawn. Both groups apparently are bothered by irrelevant, incidental distractors in close proximity (Deikel & Friedman, 1976; Doyle et al., 1976; Hallahan et al. (in press); Mondani & Tutko, 1969; Pelham & Ross, 1977; Tarver et al., 1976) and/or similar in form (Lasky & Tobin, 1973) to the relevant, central stimuli in a task situation. When central stimuli are actually embedded in a background of extraneous stimuli, it is clear that both learning-disabled and hyperactive subjects are at a distinct disadvantage compared to normal children (Adams et al., 1974; Elkind et al., 1965; Keogh & Donlon, 1972; Silverman et al., 1963), although Alwitt's (1966) results are contradictory. However, neither learning-disabled nor hyperactive children seem generally distractible in the face of clearly extraneous, peripheral stimuli (Barkley & Ullman, 1975; Browning, 1967; Dykman et al., 1970; Kirchner, 1976; Lasky & Tobin, 1973; Nober & Nober, 1975; Sykes et al., 1971; Worland et al., 1973; Yekell, 1974), despite the apparently discordant results of the Bremer & Stern (1975) study.

In general, evidence for this pattern is clearer with regard to learning-disabled children than for those children labeled "hyperactive." Perhaps this results from the incredible diversity among groups considered to be hyperactive. Though "learning disability" is also something of a catch-all category, even less agreement appears to exist about the identifying criteria for hyperactivity.

Hypothesized Reasons for the Proximal-Distal Dichotomy

The fact that "distal" distractors (those at a distance from the subject) and noises of various sorts have not often been found to distract learning-disabled or hyperactive children has led to at least one interesting hypothesis. Browning (1967), whose multicolored flashing lights failed to distract minimally brain-injured subjects, suggested that a subgroup of these children are actually *hypo*responsive. They have, in other words, a reduced responsiveness to stimuli. They are harder to arouse than normal children, and they are thus at the opposite extreme from hyperresponsive children. With a mixed group of hyporesponsive and hyperresponsive learning-disabled children, under conditions of extraneous stimulation, the effects of the distraction would be washed out. This hypothesis is supported by the Doyle et al. (1976) study. In addition, some physiological evidence does suggest that certain learning-disabled children may be deficient in orienting response (Cohen, in Douglas, 1972; Dykman et al., 1971).

Browning's hypothesis of the arousing nature of extraneous distractors was supported by Stainback, Stainback, & Hallahan (1973). Working with mentally retarded children, Stainback et al. found that performance on Hagen's central-incidental task was best under a condition of background music and taped hall noises. Perhaps the "distractors" operated to arouse the subjects to respond. Turnure (1970) also found that distractors positively influence performance by the age of 7½ years, though not for 5½-year-olds. Turnure's subjects were normals, and his distractor was a mirror placed immediately in front of the subjects.

A somewhat different interpretation also is possible for the failure of distal, extraneous stimuli to distract, and in fact sometimes to aid performance. It may be that, for some children in certain conditions, the extraneous stimuli actually help the child determine what is a relevant stimulus. When confronted by an array of stimuli, a learning-disabled child may have a difficult time deciding which is relevant. A clearly extraneous stimulus might serve to reduce some of the uncertainty, thereby aiding the child to know what *not* to attend to.

"Internal" distractibility. Given that many teachers and parents describe the learning-disabled child as distractible, it is at first puzzling that distal distractors in laboratory situations have generally failed to be more distracting for learning-disabled compared to normal children. However, it may be that distractible behavior as noted by adults is due to sources other than those in the child's external environment. (Before the reader's imagination runs wild, we hasten to point out that we are not referring to spectral phenomena.)

It is interesting to note that virtually all notions of the distractibility of the learning-disabled child conceive of the impetus for the distraction as something occurring outside of the child. The vast majority of clinical and anecdotal literature as well as research conducted thus far has focused on the effects environmental distractors may have on the child's ability to perform. This view of the learning-disabled child's distractibility has, of course, shaped educational approaches provided for him. For example, one of the most popular educational procedures for the distractible child has been that of stimulus reduction (Cruickshank et al., 1961; Strauss & Lehtinen, 1947). This approach stresses shielding the child from extraneous environmental stimulation while making more salient those stimuli in the environment that one wants the child to attend to. While this technique has proved moderately successful in increasing the on-task behavior of some distractible children, it has not automatically led to gains on higher-level cognitive tasks, e.g., academics (Hallahan & Kauffman, 1975).

One possible problem with this emphasis on the importance of *environmental* distractors is that it may have contributed to the neglect of a source of distractibility at least equally likely to interfere with the child's performance—*internal* distraction. Is it not possible that a child whom we describe as inattentive is distracted more by his own thought processes than by events that occur in the environment? Is it not possible that a child may be unable to concentrate because he is too often thinking about such things as what fun it would be to be playing baseball, whom he is going to tease on the way home from school, how painful the last visit to the dentist was, or what a great day it was last spring when the wind blew warm and the snow melted in gushes?

This is not to deny the possibility that some distracting thoughts may be triggered by events occurring in the environment; however, it is highly unlikely that all extraneous thoughts are the result of something that occurs in one's immediate environment. This is also not to deny the possibility that distracting thoughts may be a symptom rather than a cause, i.e., they may be the result of such things as boredom with school work, fear of failure on academic tasks, etc. It is reasonable that some extraneous thought processes are normal, and, indeed, may be necessary for one's mental health. It would be a dull world, certainly, if one were unable to entertain an occasional fantasy or two. What we are proposing here is the *possibility* that some children who appear inattentive and distractible may be engaging in excessive daydreaming that interferes with their ability to concentrate on school work.

While we believe that considering the child's own thought processes as a source of distraction is a relatively new idea with regard to children referred to as distractible, there is a substantial body of literature dealing with obsessional thinking in adults that has some relevance to our discussion here. Unfortunately, few well-controlled investigations have been conducted in this area. As one might guess, the largest problem hindering scientific advancement in this area is that there is yet no reliable or valid way to measure an individual's thoughts, a fact that continues to be a stumbling block for further research. In most cases, the researcher has had to rely on the client's own monitoring of his thoughts. The problems inherent in such an approach are obvious and need not be detailed here.

The treatment technique that has generated the most research support (although much of this research suffers from the same methodological limitations noted above) is that of "thought stopping." In spite of the inherent measurement problems and the uncontrolled nature of some of the research, in the past few years a great deal of interest has been generated among behavior therapists in thought-stopping procedures (Mahoney, 1974; Wolpe, 1969). Although there are variations of the technique, the sequence outlined by Mahoney (1974) is a good summary. The emphasis of Mahoney's sequence is on negative, self-defeating thoughts. The general sequence is also applicable to thoughts that are not specifically negative, however. It should be noted that Mahoney combines thought stopping, steps 1-5, with covert assertion training, steps 6-8.:

1. Irrational self-verbalizations (and images) are established, and the client is persuaded of their self-defeating nature.
2. Client closes eyes and imagines target situation, verbalizing thoughts aloud. Therapist shouts "Stop" at beginning of obsessive thought.
3. Same as above, except the client does not say his/her thoughts aloud but signals when he/she begins to obsess.
4. Client verbalizes to him/herself and shouts "STOP" aloud when he/she begins to obsess.
5. Same as above except client says "Stop" to him or herself.
6. Client provides therapist with appropriate assertive statements.
7. Immediately after saying "Stop" to him/herself client engages in an assertive statement in an emphatic loud voice.
8. Same as above, except the client makes the assertive statement to him or herself (p. 436).

There is not space in this chapter to describe all of the obsessive behaviors and thoughts for which thought stopping has been used; however, it has been reported to be successful for such diverse problems ranging from fear of cancer to uncontrollable thoughts about being brain-damaged, persecuted, and "odd" (Anthony & Edelstein, 1975; Bergin, 1969; Campbell, 1973; Gentry, 1970; Kumar & Wilkinson, 1971; Mahoney, 1971; Rimm, 1973; Rosen & Schnapp, 1974; Shelton, 1973; Stern, 1970; Wisocki, 1973; Wisocki & Rooney, 1974; Yamagami, 1971).

The applicability of the general notion of internal rather than external distraction and the particular value of thought stopping as a training technique await empirical test. As we mentioned earlier, what will undoubtedly impede research efforts in this area will be the problem of reliable measurement. There are at least two general methods, however, that do hold promise in this regard. Horowitz, in a series of investigations (Horowitz & Becker, 1971a, b, c; Horowitz, Becker, & Moskowitz, 1971) used a technique that might be adaptable for use with children suspected of being "internally" distractible. Horowitz and his coworkers showed either a highly stimulating or a neutral film to adults followed by a vigilance (signal detection) task. Subjects were then given questionnaires designed to assess whether instrusive thoughts resulted from having watched the highly stimulating film. These questions plus level of performance on the signal detection task could be used to determine how much each individual's thoughts were disrupted by the content of the films. The paradigm of these studies, of course, does not circumvent the methodological problems connected with self-report data. However, the use of films as an independent variable holds promise for the measurement of one's susceptibility to "carryover" distracting thoughts beyond the time interval during which they are first brought about. Another advantage to this technique is that one can measure the influence of such task-irrelevant thoughts on task performance, although it should be hastily pointed out that Horowitz et al. were not very successful in showing such an effect in their studies.

Given the problems associated with self-report, electro-physiological measurement has also been advanced as a method of assessing covert thought processes. Mahoney (1974), for example, notes that a more straightforward evaluation of covert thought activity might be obtained using such dependent variables (Jacobson, 1973; McGuigan, 1973). Complexities of measurement techniques and interpretation of findings are clear limitations of this technique.

Etiological Considerations

Except for proximal distractors in the environment and the possibility of "internal" distractors, the evidence indicates that learning-disabled children are not distracted by distal stimuli. What is the source of the apparent "distractibility" of learning-disabled children with reference to proximal and embedded irrelevant stimuli? That question is very much open to debate, but at least three major positions are prominent: a) physiological dysfunction, (b) maturational lag, and (c) various personality constructs, including motivation.

The first hypothesis regarding the etiology of distractibility, and attentional disorders generally, is also the first to appear historically. For years it has been assumed that the atypical behaviors of learning-disabled children are the result of brain damage and especially of birth injuries. "Minimal brain damage," "minimal cerebral dysfunction," and numerous similar labels have been synonymous with learning disability for many individuals in the field. Following Strauss & Lehtinen (1947), such labels were selected because of the similarity between these children's behaviors and behaviors exhibited by children known to have suffered brain damage (e.g., hyperactivity, emotional lability, distractibility, perceptual problems). It is true that "soft signs" of neurological difficulties have been documented for many learning-disabled children. However, the status of current technology for assessing the presence or absence of brain damage is so primitive that a definitive evaluation of how pervasive such a condition is with learning-disabled and hyperactive children is, at best, many years away. It seems reasonable at this point to acknowledge that at least a subgroup of children who come to be labeled learning-disabled do have brain damage.

Another form which the physiological dysfunction perspective takes is that learning-disabled and/or hyperactive children may suffer from a biochemical disorder, which may or may not be inherited (Silver, 1971; Stewart, 1970). Norepinephrine is the most frequently cited biochemical agent suspected of causing difficulties (Stein & Wise, 1969). This and other possibilities should provide sufficient research fodder for physiological psychologists for the foreseeable future. Certainly no definitive answers are now available.

Another perspective has grown in popularity in recent years. A "maturational lag" is posited by many to explain the recurring finding that learning-disabled children tend to perform across numerous task much like two- or three-year younger normal children. The lag hypothesis assumes a general cognitive immaturity, or retardation, in information processing style and capabilities.

The third major category of etiological speculation with regard to attentional deficits has to do with personality differences between learning-disabled and normal children, and/or with various cognitively oriented constructs. One interesting line of speculation revolves around the closely related concepts of internal versus external locus of control, inner versus outerdirectedness, field independence-dependence, and task versus social (or investigator) orientation. These have to do with the manner in which a child views his own ability to control what happens to him. Subjects found to have internal locus of control, inner-directedness, field independence, and task orientation rely more on their own resources and trust their own abilities to a relatively greater extent. On the other hand, those with external locus of control, outer-directedness, field dependence, and social or investigator orientation seem to be dependent on cues from their environment in order to function, believe others are responsible for what happens to them, and generally do not trust themselves or consider themselves to be competent. These personality variables may be genetically determined, but it seems more likely that they develop as a result of developmental experiences. Some interaction, of course, between genetics and learning also is possible.

Zigler and his colleagues (Turnure & Zigler, 1964; Zigler & Yando, 1972) found evidence attributing the relatively poorer performance of mentally retarded children compared with MA matched normals to the retardates' greater reliance on external, situational cues. This outer-directedness was thought to result from the retarded child's history of frequent failure and subsequent expectations of failure. Similar differences have been observed with normals (Ruble & Nakamura, 1972; Keogh, 1971).

Perhaps any child can learn to distrust his or her own solutions through continuous early failures and thereby become outer-directed (or field dependent, or whatever similar term is used). Evidence that children who might be called "learning disabled" exhibit external locus of control (or whatever) is accumulating, Shaw & Uhl (1971) found a relationship between low reading ability and external locus of control. McGhee & Crandall (1968) found that internal locus of control and achievement were associated. They cited several other studies (Cellura, 1963; Chance, 1965; Crandall, Katkovsky & Preston, 1962) with similar results. Keogh & Donlon (1972), as discussed earlier, discovered that their samples of learning-disabled children were strongly field-dependent.

Distractibility and outer-directedness have been linked directly. Turnure & Zigler's (1964) retarded subjects, who were highly outer-directed, glanced away from the target task toward the experimenter much more frequently than did normals. Turnure (1973) subsequently found that retarded children glance away more when an experimenter is present than when not present. This has led to the hypothesis that glancing-away behavior occurs because the child feels he/she cannot rely on his/her own problem-solving skills and must therefore look around for external cues. Ruble & Nakamura (1972, 1973) also have used glancing-away behaviors as their only measure of outer-directedness.

Given the results of studies relating locus of control, inner- versus outer-directedness, etc., and achievement, as well as the accumulating evidence that learning-disabled children are more field-dependent (e.g., Keogh & Donlon, 1972), it is reasonable to postulate that at least some of the distractibility of learning-disabled children may occur because they are unsure of themselves and are looking about for external cues. Of course, it is also possible to suggest that outer-directedness or field dependence causes poor academic performance. Whatever the direction of causality, the explanatory significance of these constructs in relation to attentional disorders in general and distractibility in particular seems substantial.

SOME EDUCATIONAL IMPLICATIONS

While the bulk of the literature reviewed in this chapter is basic rather than applied, a few comments regarding educational implications are in order. The fact that there is a great deal of support for the position that many children labeled as inattentive and/or distractible suffer more from an inability to engage in task-appropriate strategies (a production deficiency) rather than from an inherent inability to attend or an inherent susceptibility to distraction points, we believe, to certain educational implications.

First, it is our belief that educators in general, and particularly those who deal with the inattentive child, are prone to view the child as a passive organism—someone to whom you do something, e.g., administer reinforcers, feed drugs, place in a cubicle, give instructions, etc. All of these are important, to be sure, but they simply may not be enough. We mentioned earlier, for example, that investigators who have concentrated on shielding the child from external distractors by placing him/her in a cubicle have shown an increase in on-task behavior, but have not produced increased learning. This could very well be not only because distal distractors are not terribly disruptive to the learning processes of some children, but also because merely shielding them from distractors without providing them with learning strategies is doomed to failure. It is important to note in this context that the original conceptualization of stimulus reduction (Strauss & Lehtinen, 1947; Cruickshank et al., 1961) called for a great deal more actual teaching of the child than just stimulus reduction; yet most tests of these ideas have focused exclusively on the stimulus reduction component. There is some limited evidence indicating that some hyperactive children are not responsive to reinforcement procedures (Douglas, et al., 1976). It may be that simply reinforcing correct answers is not enough, but reinforcement must be provided for appropriate task strategies.

An approach that we believe holds a great deal of promise for children with attentional problems is that of cognitive-behavior modification. [For a thorough theoretical account of cognitive-behavior modification the reader is referred to Mahoney (1974); for a more practical account see Meichenbaum (1977).] Pioneered by Donald Meichenbaum and his colleagues at the University of Waterloo, its promise for children like those described in this chapter is based on the fact that it stresses teaching the child to use self-instructional learning strategies. These strategies range from merely having the child instruct him or herself to slow down, to fairly complex sets of instructions. An important aspect of this strategy-training is that the child him or/herself is required to verbalize, usually overtly at first and later covertly. This overt verbalization is seen by cognitive-behavior modifiers as important in that it helps the child maintain attention. An additional possible advantage is that it aids the adult in following the child's various thought processes step by step and allows him or her to correct errors at specific stages of the problem-solving process.

While the final word on the efficacy of cognitive-behavior modification procedures is far from spoken, research to this point has indicated its promise, particularly for inattentive children. (See Kauffman & Hallahan (in press) for a review of this literature.) The approach has been used with two general areas—behavioral and academic problems. With regard to the former, for example, cognitive-behavior modification or other highly similar procedures have been used in the control of impulse and/or hyperactive behavior (Bem, 1967; Bender, 1976; Blackwood, 1970; Bornstein & Quevillon, 1976; Camp et al., 1977; Douglas et al., 1976; Egeland, 1974; Finch & Kendall (in press); Giebink et al., 1968; Hartig & Kanfer, 1973; MacPherson et al., 1974; Meichenbaum & Goodman, 1969, 1971; Palkes, Stewart, & Freedman, 1972; Palkes, Stewart, & Kahana, 1968; Patterson & Mischel, 1975, 1976; Ridberg, Parke, & Heterington, 1971; Zelnicker & Oppenheimer, 1976). While not as thoroughly researched, similar procedures have provided suggestive evidence for its use with academic responses (Bower, 1975; Camp et al., 1977; Douglas et al., 1976; Egeland, 1974; Epstein, 1975; Grimm, Bijou, & Parsons, 1973; Lovitt & Curtiss, 1968; Parsons, 1972; Robertson & Keeley, 1974; Robin et al., 1975; Wozniak & Neuchterlein, 1973).

One final point should be noted with regard to the use of cognitive-behavior modification or any approach that attempts to foster in the child a more active problem solving orientation. Any educator who works with a child who has experienced a great deal of failure in his past should be aware that the child may have a high expectancy of failure. In addition, his particular causal attributions may be such that when he does succeed or fail he perceives these actions to be the result of forces external to himself (Crandall et al., 1962; McGhee & Crandall, 1968; Shaw & Uhl, 1971). In many ways, an approach like cognitive-behavior modification that stresses the active use of learning strategies is diametrically opposed to an attitude of external attribution. Future research should further determine the particular influence procedures such as cognitive-behavior modification have on attribution and vice versa. One study that has already been done in this area indicates that, indeed, there is a high probability of an interaction between the two. Bugental et al. (1977) found no significant differences on teacher ratings of hyperactivity, but significantly greater error reduction on Porteus Mazes for self-instruction versus contingent social reinforcement for children under self-control intervention who were not taking medication *and* who were high in perceived personal causality. However, social reinforcement resulted in greater error reduction for children who were medicated *and* were low in perceived personal causality. These results suggest not only, as Bugental et al. point out, that a child's attributional status should be matched with the particular intervention; but, to our way of thinking, they also suggest that the *sequence* of the interventions may need to be carefully considered. In the early stages of working with hyperactive and inattentive children it may be necessary to rely solely on tangible and social reinforcers. As the child learns to control his or her behavior and has a chance to succeed, his/her attributions may become flexible enough that self-instructional procedures can be employed.

FOOTNOTE

*Preparation of this chapter was supported by a contract (300-77-0495) from the Bureau of Education for the Handicapped, Office of Education, for the University of Virginia Learning Disabilities Research Institute.

REFERENCES

Adams, J., Hayden, B. S., & Canter, A. (1974) "The relationship between the Canter Background Interference procedure and the hyperkinetic behavior syndrome." *Journal of Learning Disabilities* 7: 110-115.

Alwitt, L. F. (1966) "Attention on a visual task among non-readers and readers." *Perceptual and Motor Skills* 23: 361-362.

Anthony, J., & Edelstein, B. A. (1975) "Thought-stopping treatment of anxiety attacks due to seizure-related obsessive reminations." *Journal of Behavior Therapy and Experimental Psychology* 6: 343-344.

Atkinson, B. R., & Seunath, O. H. M. (1973) "The effect of stimulus change in attending behavior in normal children and children with learning disorders." *Journal of Learning Disabilities,* 1973, 6: 569-573.

Balla, D. A., Butterfield, E. C., & Zigler, E. (1974) "Effects of institutionalization on retarded children: A longitudinal cross-institutional investigation." *American Journal of Mental Deficiency* 78: 530-549.

Barkley, R. A., & Ullman, D. G. (1975) "A comparison of objective measures of activity and distractibility in hyperactive and nonhyperactive children." *Journal of Abnormal Child Psychology* 3: 231-244.

Bem, S.L. (1967) "Verbal self-control: The establishment of effective self-instruction." *Journal of Experimental Psychology* 74: 485-491.

Bender, N.N. (1976) "Self-verbalization versus tutor verbalization in modifying impulsivity." *Journal of Educational Psychology* 68: 347-354.

Benton, A.L. (1962) "Behavioral indices of brain injury in school children." *Child Development* 33: 199-208.

Bergin, A.E. (1969) "A self-regulation technique for impulse control disorders." *Psychology: Theory, research, and practice* 6: 113-118.

Blackwood, R.O. (1970) "The operant conditioning of verbally mediated self-control in the classroom." *Journal of School Psychology* 8: 251-258.

Blank, M., & Bridger, W. (1966) "Deficiencies in verbal labeling in retarded readers." *American Journal of Orthopsychiatry* 36: 840-847.

Bornstein, P.H., & Quevillon, R.P. (1976) "The effects of a self-instructional package on overactive preschool boys. *Journal of Applied Behavior Analysis* 9: 179-188.

Bower, K.B. (1975) "Impulsivity and academic performance in learning and behavior disordered children." Unpublished doctoral dissertation, University of Virginia.

Bremer, D.A., & Stern, J.A. (1976) "Attention and distractibility during reading in hyperactive boys. *Journal of Abnormal Child Psychology* 4: 381-387.

Broadbent, D.E. (1958) *Perception and communication.* New York: Pergamon Press.

Brown, A.L. (1974) "The role of strategic behavior in retardate memory." In N.R. Ellis (ed.), *International review of research in mental retardation,* Vol. 7. New York: Academic Press.

———, Campione, J.C., & Gilliard, D.M. (1974) "Recency judgments in children: A production deficiency in the use of redundant background cues." *Developmental Psychology* 10: 303.

Browning, R.M. (1967) "Effect of irrelevant peripheral visual stimuli on discrimination learning in minimally brain-damaged children." *Journal of Consulting Psychology* 31: 371-376.

Bruner, J.S., Olver, R.R., & Greenfield, P.M. (1966) *Studies in cognitive growth.* New York: Wiley.

Bugental, D.B., Whalen, C.K., & Henker, B. (1977) "Causal attributions of hyperactive children and motivational assumptions of two behavior change approaches: Evidence for an interactionist position." *Child Development* 48: 874-884.

Camp, B.W., Blom, G.E., Hebert, F., & Van Doorninck, W.J. (1977) "'Think Aloud': A program for developing self-control in young aggressive boys." *Journal of Abnormal Child Psychology* 5: 157-169.

Campbell, L.M. (1973) "A variation of thought-stopping in a twelve-year-old boy: A case report." *Journal of Behavior Therapy and Experimental Psychiatry* 4: 69-70.

Campbell, S. B., Douglas, V.I., & Morgenstern, G. (1971) "Cognitive styles in hyperactive children and the effect of methylphenidate." *Journal of Child Psychology and Psychiatry* 12: 53-67.

Cellura, A.R. (1963) "Internality as a determinant of academic achievement in low SES adolescents." Unpublished manuscript, University of Rochester, 1963.

Chance, J.E. (1965) "Internal control of reinforcements and the school learning process." Paper given at Society for Research in Child Development, Minneapolis.

Clements, S. (1966) "Minimal brain dysfunction in children: Terminology and identification." U.S. Public Health Service, Pub. No. 1415. Washington, D.C.: Government Printing Office.

Crandall, V.J., Katkovsky, W., & Preston, A. (1962) "Motivational and ability determinants of young children's intellectual achievement behaviors." *Child Development* 33: 643-661.

Crane, N.L., & Ross, L.E. (1967) "A developmental study of attention to cue redundancy introduced following discrimination learning. *Journal of Experimental Child Psychology* 5: 1-15.

Cruickshank, W.M., Bentzen, F.A., Ratzeburg, F.H., & Tannhauser, M.T. (1961) *A teaching method for brain-injured and hyperactive children.* Syracuse University Press.

———, & Paul, J.L. (1971) "The psychological characteristics of brain-injured children." In W. M. Cruickshank (ed.), *Psychology of exceptional children and youth,* 3rd ed. Englewood Cliffs, N.J.: Prentice-Hall.

Dawson, M. M., Hallahan, D. P., Reeve, R. E., & Ball, D. W. (1978) "The effect of reinforcement and verbal rehearsal on selective attention in learning disabled children." Unpublished manuscript, University of Virginia.

Deikel, S. M., & Friedman, M. P. (1976) "Selective attention in children with learning disabilities." *Perceptual and Motor Skills* 42: 675-678.

Douglas, V. I. (1972) "Stop, look and listen: The problem of sustained attention and impulse control in hyperactive and normal children." *Canadian Journal of Behavioural Science* 4: 259-282.

———, Parry, P., Marton, P., & Garson, C. (1976) "Assessment of a cognitive training program for hyperactive children." *Journal of Abnormal Child Psychology* 4: 389-410.

Doyle, R. B., Anderson, R. P., and Halcomb, C. G. (1976) "Attention deficits and the effects of visual distraction." *Journal of Learning Disabilities* 9: 48-54.

Druker, J. F., & Hagen, J. W. (1969) "Developmental trends in the processing of task relevant and task irrelevant information." *Child Development* 40: 371-382.

Dykman, R. A., Ackerman, P. T., Clements, S. D., & Peters, J. E. (1971) "Specific learning disabilities: An attentional deficit syndrome." In Myklebust, H. R. (ed.), *Progress in learning disabilities,* Vol. II. New York: Grune & Stratton.

———, Walls, R. C., Suzuki, T., Ackerman, P., & Peters, J. E. (1970) "Children with learning disabilities: Conditioning, differentiation, and the effect of distraction." *American Journal of Orthopsychiatry* 40: 766-782.

Egeland, B. (1974) "Training impulsive children in the use of more efficient scanning techniques." *Child Development* 45: 165-171.

Eimas, P. (1969) "Multiple-cue discrimination learning in children." *Psychological Record* 19: 417-424.

Elkind, D., Larson, M., & Van Doorninck, W. (1965) "Perceptual decentration learning and performance in slow and average readers." *Journal of Educational Psychology* 56: 50-56.

Ellis, N.R. (1970) "Memory processes in retardates and normals." In N.R. Ellis (ed.), *International review of research in mental retardation,* Vol. 4. New York: Academic Press,

Epstein, M.H. (1975) "Modification of impulsivity and arithmetic performance in underachieving children." Unpublished doctoral dissertation, University of Virginia,

Finch, A.J., & Kendall, P.C. (1979) "Impulsive behavior: From research to treatment." In A.J. Finch & P.C. Kendall (eds.), *Treatment and research in child psychopathology.* Spectrum. (In press.)

Flavell, J.H. (1970) "Developmental studies of mediated memory." In L.P. Lipsitt & H.W. Reese (eds.), *Advances in child development and behavior.* New York: Academic Press.

Fritz, J.J. (1974) "Reversal-shift behavior in children with specific learning disabilities." *Perceptual and Motor Skills* 38: 431-438.

Gentry, W.D. (1970) "In vivo desensitization of an obsessive cancer fear." *Journal of Behavior Therapy and Experimental Psychiatry* 1: 315-318.

Giebink, J.W., Stover, D.O., & Fahl, M.A. (1968) "Teaching adaptive responses to frustration to emotionally disturbed boys." *Journal of Consulting and Clinical Psychology* 32: 366-368.

Grimm, J.A., Bijou, S.W., & Parsons, J.A. (1973) "A problem-solving model for teaching remedial arithmetic to handicapped young children." *Journal of Abnormal Child Psychology,* 1: 26-39.

Haber, R.N., & Haber, R.B. (1964) "Eidetic imagery: I. Frequency." *Perceptual and Motor Skills* 19: 131-138.

Hagen, J.W. (1967) "The effect of distraction of selective attention." *Child Development* 38: 685-694.

———— (1971) "Some thoughts on how children learn to remember." *Human Development* 14: 262-271.

————, & Hale, G.A. (1973) "The development of attention in children." In Pick, A. (ed.), *Minnesota Symposia on Child Psychology,* Vol. 7. Minneapolis: University of Minnesota Press, pp. 117-140.

————, Hallahan, D.P., & Kauffman, J.M. (1974) "Selective attention in retardates: A validation study." Unpublished paper.

————, & Huntsman, N.J. (1971) "Selective attention in mental retardates." *Developmental Psychology* 5: 151-160.

————, & Kail, R.V. (1975) "The role of attention in perceptual and cognitive development." In W.M. Cruickshank and D.P. Hallahan (eds.), *Perceptual and learning disabilities in children.* Syracuse, N.Y.: Syracuse University Press.

————, Meacham, J.A., & Mesibov, G. (1970) "Verbal labeling, rehearsal, and short-term memory." *Cognitive Psychology,* 1: 47-58.

————, & Sabo, R. (1967) "A developmental study of selective attention." *Merrill-Palmer Quarterly* 13: 159-172.

————, Streeter, L.A., & Raker, R. (1974) "Labeling, rehearsal, and short-term memory in retarded children." *Journal of Experimental Child Psychology* 18: 259-268.

————, & West, R.F. (1970) "The effects of a pay-off matrix on selective attention." *Human Development* 13: 43-52.

Hale, G.A., Miller, L.K., & Stevenson, H.W. (1968) "Incidental learning of film content: A developmental study." *Child Development,* 39: 69-77.

————, & Taweel, S.S. (1974) "Age differences in children's performance in measures of component selection and incidental learning." *Journal of Experimental Child Psychology* 18: 107-116.

Hallahan, D.P. (1975a) "Comparative research studies on the psychological characteristics of learning disabled children." In W.M. Cruickshank & D.P. Hallahan (eds.), *Perceptual and learning disabilities in children,* Vol. 1. *Psychoeducational practices.* Syracuse, N.Y.: Syracuse University Press.

————(1975b) "Distractibility in the learning disabled child." In W.M. Cruickshank & D.P. Hallahan (eds.), *Perceptual and learning disabilities in children.* Vol. 2. *Research and Theory.* Syracuse, N.Y.: Syracuse University Press.

———, & Cruickshank, W.M. (1973) *Psychoeducational foundations of learning disabilities.* Englewood Cliffs, N.J.: Prentice-Hall.

———, Gajar, A.H., Cohen, S.B., & Tarver, S.G. (1979) "Selective attention and locus of control in learning disabled and normal children." *Journal of Learning Disabilities.* (In press.)

———, & Kauffman, J.M. (1975) "Research on the education of distractible and hyperactive children." In W.M. Cruickshank & D.P. Hallahan (eds.), *Perceptual and learning disabilities in children.* Vol. 2. *Research and Theory.* Syracuse, N.Y.: Syracuse University Press.

———, ———, & Ball, D.W. (1973) "Selective attention and cognitive tempo of low achieving and high achieving sixth grade males." *Perceptual and Motor Skills*, 36: 579-583.

———, ———, & ———, (1974) "Developmental trends in recall of central and incidental auditory material." *Journal of Experimental Child Psychology* 17: 409-421.

———, Stainback, S., Ball, D.W., & Kauffman, J.M. (1973) "Selective attention in cerebral palsied and normal children." *Journal of Abnormal Child Psychology* 1: 280-291.

———, Tarver, S.G., Kauffman, J.M., & Graybeal, N.L. (1979) "Selective attention abilities of learning disabled children under reinforcement and response cost." *Journal of Learning Disabilities,* (In press.)

Hartig, M., & Kanfer, F.H. (1973) "The role of verbal self-instructions in children's resistance to temptation." *Journal of Personality and Social Psychology* 25: 259-267.

Horowitz, M.J., & Becker, S.S. (1971a) "Cognitive response to stress and experimental demand." *Journal of Abnormal Psychology* 78: 86-92.

———, & ———(1971b) "Cognitive response to stressful stimuli." *Archives of General Psychiatry* 25: 419-428.

———, & ———(1971c) "The compulsion to repeat trauma." *The Journal of Nervous and Mental Disease* 153: 32-40.

———, ———, & Moskowitz, M.L. (1971) "Intrusive and repetitive thought after stress: A replication study." *Psychological Reports* 29: 763-767.

Huelsman, C.B. (1970) "The WISC subtest syndrome for disabled readers." *Perceptual and Motor Skills* 30: 535-550.

Jacobson, E. (1973) "Electrophysiology of mental activities and introduction to the psychological process of thinking." In F.J. McGuigan & R.A. Schoonover (eds.), *The psychophysiology of thinking.* New York: Academic Press.

Kauffman, J.M., & Hallahan, D.P. (1979) "Learning disability and hyperactivity." In B.B. Lahey & A.E. Kazdin (eds.), *Advances in child clinical psychology,* Vol. 2. New York: Plenum. (In press.)

Kausler, D.J., Laughlin, P.R., & Trapp, E.P. (1963) "Effects of incentive set on relevant and irrelevant (incidental) learning in children." *Child Development* 34: 195-199.

Keogh, B.K. (1971) "Pattern copying under three conditions of an expanded spatial field." *Developmental Psychology* 4: 25-37.

———, & Donlon, G. (1972) "Field independence, impulsivity, and learning disabilities." *Journal of Learning Disabilities* 5: 331-336.

Kirchner, G.L. (1976) "Differences in the vigilance performance of highly active and normal second-grade males under four experimental conditions." *Journal of Educational Psychology* 68: 696-701.

Koegel, R.L., & Rincover, A. (1976) "Some detrimental effects of using extra stimuli to guide learning in normal and autistic children." *Journal of Abnormal Child Psychology* 4: 59-71.

———, & Wilhelm, H. (1973) "Selective responding to the components of multiple visual cues by autistic children." *Journal of Experimental Child Psychology* 15: 442-453.

Kumar, K., & Wilkinson, C.M. (1971) "Thought stopping: A useful treatment in phobias of 'internal stimuli.'" *British Journal of Psychiatry* 119: 305-307.

Lasky, E.Z., & Tobin, H. (1973) "Linguistic and nonlinguistic competing auditory message effects." *Journal of Learning Disabilities,* 1973 6: 243-250.

Lovaas, O.I., & Schreibman, L. (1971) "Stimulus overselectivity of autistic children in a two stimulus situation." *Behavior Research and Therapy* 9: 305-310.

———, Schreibman, L., Koegel, R., & Rehm, R. (1971) "Selective responding by autistic children to multiple sensory input." *Journal of Abnormal Psychology* 77: 211-222.

Lovitt, T.C., & Curtiss, K.A. (1968) "Effects of manipulating an antecedent event on mathematics response rate." *Journal of Applied Behavior Analysis* 1: 329-333.

Maccoby, E.E., & Hagen, J.W. (1965) "Effects of distraction upon central versus incidental recall: Developmental trends." *Journal of Experimental Child Psychology* 2: 280-289.

McGhee, P.E., & Crandall, V.C. (1968) "Beliefs in internal-external control of reinforcements and academic performance." *Child Development* 39: 91-102.

McGrady, H.J., & Olson, D.A. (1970) "Visual and auditory learning processes in normal children and children with specific learning disabilities." *Exceptional Children* 36: 581-589.

McGuigan, F.J. (1973) "Electrical measurement of covert processes as an explication of 'higher mental events.' ". In F.J. McGuigan & R.A. Schoonover (eds.), *The Psychophysiology of thinking*. New York: Academic Press.

MacPherson, E.M., Candee, B.L., & Hohman, R.J. (1974) "A comparison of three methods for eliminating disruptive lunchroom behavior." *Journal of Applied Behavior Analysis* 7: 287-297.

Mahoney, M.J. (1971) "The self-management of covert behavior: A case study." *Behavior Therapy* 2: 575-578.

———(1974) *Cognition and behavior modification*. Cambridge, Mass.: Ballinger.

Meichenbaum, D. (1977) *Cognitive-behavior modification*. New York: Plenum.

———, & Goodman, J. (1969) "Reflection-impulsivity and verbal control of motor behavior." *Child Development* 40: 785-797.

———, & ——— (1971) "Training impulsive children to talk to themselves: A means of developing self-control." *Journal of Abnormal Psychology* 77: 115-126.

Miller, G.A., Galanter, E., & Pribram, K.H. (1960) *Plans and the structure of behavior*. New York: Holt-Dryden.

Mondani, M.S., & Tutko, T.A. (1969) "Relationship of academic underachievement to incidental learning." *Journal of Counseling and Clinical Psychology* 33: 558-560.

Neisser, U. (1969) *Cognitive psychology*. Appleton-Century-Crofts (Prentice-Hall).

Nicholls, C.J., & Tavormina, J.B. (1978) "Learning disabilities: Prediction from the WISC-R." Unpublished manuscript, University of Virginia, Department of Psychology.

Nober, L.W., & Nober, E.H. (1975) "Auditory discrimination of learning disabled children in quiet and classroom noise." *Journal of Learning Disabilities* 8: 656-659.

Palkes, H., Stewart, M., & Freedman, J. (1972) "Improvement in maze performance of hyperactive boys as a function of verbal training procedures." *The Journal of Special Education* 5: 337-342.

———, Stewart, M., & Kahana, B. (1968) "Porteus maze performance of hyperactive boys after training in self-directed verbal commands." *Child Development* 39: 817-826.

Parsons, J.A. (1972) "The reciprocal modification of arithmetic behavior and program development." In G. Semb (ed.), *Behavior analysis and education—1972*. Lawrence: University of Kansas.

Patterson, C.J., & Mischel, W. (1975) "Plans to resist distraction." *Developmental Psychology* 11: 369-378.

Pelham, W.E., & Ross, A.O. (1977) "Selective attention in children with reading problems: A developmental study of incidental learning." *Journal of Abnormal Child Psychology* 5: 1-8.

Pick, A.D., Frankel, D.G., & Hess, V.L. (1975) "Children's attention: The development of selectivity." In E.M. Hetherington (ed.), *Review of child development research*, Vol. 5. Chicago: University of Chicago Press.

Reynolds, B.S., Newsom, C.D., & Lovaas, O.I. (1974) "Auditory overselectivity in autistic children." *Journal of Abnormal Child Psychology* 2: 253-263.

Ridberg, E., Parke, R., & Hetherington, E.M. (1971) "Modification of impulsive and reflective cognitive styles through observation of film mediated models." *Developmental Psychology* 5: 369-377.

Rimm, D.C. (1973) "Thought stopping and covert assertion in the treatment of phobias." *Journal of Consulting and Clinical Psychology* 41: 466-467.

Robertson, D.U., & Keeley, S.M. (1974) "Evaluation of a mediational training program for impulsive children by a multiple case study design." Paper presented at American Psychological Association Convention.

Robin, A.L., Armel, S., & O'Leary, K.D. (1975) "The effects of self-instruction on writing deficiencies." *Behavior Therapy,* 6: 178-187.

Rosen, R.C., & Schnapp, B.J. (1974) "The use of a specific behavioral technique (thought-stopping) in the context of conjoint couples therapy: A case report." *Behavior Therapy* 5: 261-264.

Ross, A.O. (1976) *Psychological aspects of learning disabilities and reading disorders.* New York: McGraw-Hill.

Rosvold, E.H., Mirsky, A.F., Sarason, I., Bransome, E.D., Jr., & Beck, L.H. (1956) "A continuous performance test of brain damage. *Journal of Consulting Psychology* 20: 343-350.

Ruble, D.N., & Nakamura, C.Y. (1972) "Task orientation versus social orientation in young children and their attention to relevant social cues." *Child Development* 43: 471-480.

———, & ——— (1973) "Outerdirectedness as a problem-solving approach in relation to developmental level and selected task variables." *Child Development* 44: 519-528.

Sabatino, D.A., & Ysseldyke, J.E. (1972) "Effect of extraneous 'background' on visual-perceptual performance of readers and non-readers." *Perceptual and Motor Skills* 35: 323-328.

Sarason, S.B. (1949) *Psychological problems in mental deficiency.* New York: Harper.

Schover, L.R., & Newsom, C.D. (1976) "Overselectivity, developmental level, and overtraining in autistic and normal children." *Journal of Abnormal Child Psychology* 4: 289-298.

Schreibman, L. (1975) "Effects of within-stimulus and extra-stimulus prompting on discrimination learning in autistic children." *Journal of Applied Behavior Analysis* 8: 91-112.

———, & Lovaas, O.I.)1973) "Overselective response to social stimuli by autistic children." *Journal of Abnormal Child Psychology* 1: 152-168.

Shaw, R.L., & Uhl, N.P. "Control of reinforcement and academic achievement." *Journal of Educational Research* 64: 226-228.

Shelton, J.L. (1974) "Murder strikes and panic follows—Can behavior modification help?" *Behavior Therapy* 4: 706-708.

Siegel, A.W., & Stevenson, H.W. (1966) "Incidental learning: A developmental study." *Child Development* 37: 811-817.

Silver, L.B. (1971) "A proposed view on the etiology of the neurological learning disability syndrome." *Journal of Learning Disabilities* 4: 123-133.

Silverman, M., Davids, A., & Andrews, J.M. (1963) "Powers of attention and academic achievement." *Perceptual and Motor Skills* 17: 243-249.

Sroufe, L.A., Sonies, B.C., West, W.D., & Wright, F.S. (1973) "Anticipatory heart rate deceleration and reaction time in children with and without referral for learning disability." *Child Development* 44: 267-273.

Stainback, S.B., Stainback, W.C., & Hallahan, D.P. (1973) "Effect of background music on learning." *Exceptional Children* 40: 109-110.

Stein, L., & Wise, C.D. (1969) "Release of norepinephrine from hypothalamus and amygdala by rewarding medial forebrain bundle stimulation and amphetamine." *Journal of Comparative and Physiological Psychology* 67: 189-198.

Stern, R. (1970) "Treatment of a case of obsessional neurosis using thought-stopping technique." *British Journal of Psychiatry* 117: 441-442.

Stewart, M.A. (1970) "Hyperactive children." *Scientific American* 222: 94-98.

Strauss, A., & Kephart, N.C. (1955) *Psychopathology and education of the brain-injured child,* Vol. II. *Progress in theory and clinic.* New York: Grune & Stratton.

Strauss, A.A., & Lehtinen, L.E. (1947) *Psychopathology and education of the brain-injured child.* New York: Grune & Stratton.

Stroop, J.R. (1935) "Studies in interference in serial verbal reactions." *Journal of Experimental Psychology* 18: 643-661.

Swanson, H.L. (1977) "Nonverbal visual short-term memory as a function of age and dimensionality in learning-disabled children." *Child Development* 48: 51-55.

Sykes, D.H., Douglas, V.I., & Morgenstern, G. (1973) "Sustained attention in hyperactive children." *Journal of Child Psychology and Psychiatry* 14: 213-220.

———, Douglas, V.I., Weiss, G., & Minde, K.K. (1971) "Attention in hyperactive children and the effect of methylphenidate (ritalin)." *Journal of Child Psychology and Psychiatry* 12: 129-139.

Tarver, S.G., & Hallahan, D.P. (1974) "Attention deficits in children with learning disabilities: A review." *Journal of Learning Disabilities*, 7: 560-569.

———, ———, Cohen, S. B., & Kauffman, J.. M. (1977) "The development of visual selective attention and verbal rehearsal on learning disabled boys." *Journal of Learning Disabilities* 10: 491-500.

———, ———, Kauffman, J. M., & Ball, D.W. (1976) "Verbal rehearsal and selective attention in children with learning disabilities: A developmental lag." *Journal of Experimental Child Psychology* 22: 375-385.

Torgesen, J.K. (1977) "The role of nonspecific factors in the task performance of learning disabled children: A theoretical assessment." *Journal of Learning Disabilities* 10: 27-34.

———, & Goldman, T. (1977) "Verbal rehearsal and short-term memory in reading-disabled children." *Child Development* 48: 56-60.

Turnure, J.E. (1970) "Children's reactions to distractors in a learning situation." *Developmental Psychology* 2: 115-122.

——— (1973) "Outerdirectedness in EMR boys and girls." *American Journal of Mental Deficiency* 78: 163-170.

———, & Zigler, E. (1964) "Outerdirectedness in the problem solving of normal and retarded children." *Journal of Abnormal and Social Psychology* 69: 427-436.

Wechsler, D. (1974) *Wechsler Intelligence Scale for Children—Revised*. New York: Psychological Corporation,

Wender, P. (1971) *Minimal brain dysfunction in children*. New York: Wiley-Interscience.

Werner, H., & Strauss, A.A. (1939a) "Problems and methods of functional analysis in mentally deficient children." *Journal of Abnormal and Social Psychology* 34: 37-62.

———, & ——— (1939b) "Types of visuo-motor activity in their relation to low and high performance ages. *Proceedings of the American Association on Mental Deficiency* 44: 163-168.

———, & ———, A. A. (1940) "Causal factors in low performance." *American Journal of Mental Deficiency* 45: 213-218.

———, & ——— (1941) "Pathology of figure-background relation in the child." *Journal of Abnormal and Social Psychology* 36: 236-248.

Wilhelm, H., & Lovaas, O.I. (1976) "Stimulus overselectivity: A common feature in autism and mental retardation." *American Journal of Mental Deficiency* 81: 26-31.

Willows, D.M. (1974) "Reading between the lines: Selective attention in good and poor readers." *Child Development* 45: 408-415.

Wisocki, P.A. (1973) "The successful treatment of a heroin addict by covert conditioning techniques." *Journal of Behavior Therapy and Experimental Psychiatry* 4: 55-61.

———, & Rooney, E.J. (1974) "A comparison of thought stopping and covert sensitization techniques in the treatment of smoking: A brief report." *Psychological Record* 24: 191-192.

Witkin, A.A., Dyk, R.E., Faterson, H.F., Goodenough, D.R., & Karp, S.A. (1962) *Psychological differentiation*. New York: Wiley.

Wolpe, J. (1969) *The practice of behavior therapy*. New York: Pergamon.

Worland, J., North-Jones, M., & Stern, J.A. (1973) "Performance and activity of hyperactive and normal boys as a function of distraction and reward." *Journal of Abnormal Child Psychology* 1: 363-377.

Wozniak, R.H., & Nuechterlein, P. (1973) "Reading improvement through verbally self-guided looking and listening, summary report." University of Minnesota Research, Development and Demonstration Center on Education of Handicapped Children.

Wright, J.C. & Vlietstra, A.G. (1975) "The development of selective attention: From perceptual exploration to logical search." In H.W. Reese (ed.), *Advances in child development and behavior*, Vol. 10. New York: Academic Press.

Yamagami, T. (1971) "The treatment of an obsession by thought-stopping" *Journal of Behavior Therapy and Experimental Psychiatry* 2: 133-135.

Yekell, H.S. (1974) "Distractibility and attention in MBD and normal children." *Dissertation Abstracts International* 35: (1-5) 530.

Zeaman, D., & House, B.J. (1963) "The role of attention in retardate discrimination learning." In N.R. Ellis (ed.), *Handbook of mental deficiency*. New York: McGraw-Hill.

Zelnicker, T., & Oppenheimer, L. (1976) "Effect of different training methods on perceptual learning in impulsive children." *Child Development* 47: 492-497.

Zigler, E. (1969) "Developmental versus difference theories of mental retardation and the problem of motivation." *American Journal of Mental Deficiency* 73: 536-556.

―――, & Yando, R. (1972) "Outerdirectedness and imitative behavior of institutionalized and noninstitutionalized younger and older children." *Child Development* 43: 413-425.

OPTIMIZING MOTIVATION IN AN ACHIEVEMENT CONTEXT*

Diane N. Ruble, PRINCETON UNIVERSITY

Ann K. Boggiano, PRINCETON UNIVERSITY

Evaluations of educational practices and student progress usually emphasize factors related to intellectual performance and advancement, often to the extent of excluding more motivationally relevant aspects of a student's development, such as self-confidence or freedom from evaluation anxiety. Yet, such motivational variables are clearly important, not only because of their relevance for children's feelings about themselves but also because they have been shown to influence achievement-related performances as well (Ball, 1977; de Charms, & Muir, 1978). Although most books on teaching, in general, and on special education, in particular, acknowledge the importance of "motivating students" or maintaining "interest" in the subject matter, there is rarely little elaboration of what this involves. Our goal in this chapter is to identify variables in the research literature on achievement motivation that hold potential for realizing the desires of educators to optimize the motivational level of students in an achievement context.

The chapter is divided into three sections. Section I contains a summary of the major theoretical approaches to achievement motivation, after which we attempt to derive a few central variables and principles involved in optimal motivation. In Section II we describe several areas of motivational research. This section is intended to provide a sense of the range of approaches to the issue of motivation, and to demonstrate empirically the operation of the principles identified in Section I as important in influencing levels of motivation. In Section III we propose a developmental perspective to these processes, and suggest that children's motivational orientations may be highly susceptible to social information and influence at particular ages. Although most of the studies reviewed and the conclusions drawn throughout the chapter are not based on special education students, we see no reason to propose that the general *principles* of motivation and motivational change should differ across populations, since individual differences (e.g., self-perceptions of competence) are an integral part of most models and research programs. Motivation is viewed in terms of the extent to which one's abilities are used on a given occasion (Atkinson, 1977), regardless of the individual skills or limitations with which one begins. We do, however, make a point of including studies that have indicated areas of particular concern for educators of these pupils.

Before beginning Section I, a word of caution is in order concerning the relationship between achievement *motivation* and achievement *behavior*. Presumably the reason most educators are interested in enhancing motivation is to optimize performance. However, this relationship may not be as simple and straightforward as it might appear. Recent analyses have questioned the seemingly logical implication from achievement models that performance at a particular task should be linearly related to motivation (Atkinson, 1974, 1977; Sorrentino & Short, 1977). Consistent with the original Yerkes-Dodson law of arousal and performance (which was primarily based on studies of discrimination learning), the relationship between overall strength of motivation and efficiency of performance seems best described as curvilinear, with maximal efficiency occurring at intermediate levels of motivation. "Overmotivation" results in decrements in performance, presumably because of trying too hard to perform well; several possible mediators of this overmotivation effect have been described by Atkinson (1974). While recognizing the importance of this possible motivational effect, the primary thrust of this chapter will be on enhancing motivation; the issue of "overmotivation" is rarely raised as a problem in most of the research areas reviewed below.

I. THEORIES OF ACHIEVEMENT MOTIVATION

The goal of theoretical formulations concerning achievement motivation is to identify the components or determinants of the strength of desire to engage and persist in achievement-related behavior. Theoretical developments of achievement motivation have seen a long and productive history, and have resulted in some of the most systematic and coherent sets of principles and relationships in the prediction of behavior. In addition, the area of achievement has been one of the most flexible in terms of adding or modifying constructs to be consistent with increasing empirically based knowledge; various revisions and extensions of basic models continue to appear in the literature, some of which will be described below.

Theories Based on Individual Motivational States

Contemporary theories of achievement motivation have their origins in the early work on measures of human motivation by McClelland and colleagues during the late 1940s and 1950s (McClelland, Atkinson, Clark, & Lowell, 1953). Their research program represented an attempt to develop and extend existing theories of motivation, based primarily on animal studies, to research on acquired or secondary "drives" in humans. The major barrier to this kind of theoretical advancement appeared to be the lack of an appropriate and standardized measure of strength of individual motivation. The major purpose, then, of their initial work was to discover such a measure so they could proceed in the investigation of the social origins and consequences of variations in achievement motivation.

It is important to understand how achievement motivation was measured by these investigators, because most subsequent research in achievement has either used directly the original operationalization of the measure or has referred to it as a starting point for extensions and modifications. For the purposes of measurement, achievement motivation, as well as other acquired human motives, was assumed to possess characteristics similar to basic or primary drives, such as hunger. Thus, for example, just as a desire for food would be aroused after a period of food deprivation, so too would achievement motivation be aroused after achievement deprivation, such as failure. Guided by psychoanalytic theory, these investigators viewed these variations in motive arousal as unconscious processes, and they were measured by projective tests—individuals' indications of concern with the motive in question as seen in their productions of fantasy on a Thematic Apperception Test (TAT) (Murray, 1936). Specifically, subjects were asked to make up a story in response to pictures portraying ambiguous situations. The strength of an individual's achievement motive was then scored in terms of the number of achievement themes of behaviors, as defined by "Success in competition with some standard of excellence" (McClelland et al., 1953, p. 110). The various studies involved in the development of the measure, and the examination of its psychometric properties and its relationship to behavior are described in the McClelland book, *The Achievement Motive,* and more recently in Atkinson's (1958) *Motives in Fantasy, Action and Society.* In general, these studies helped legitimize the measure and promote wider interest in the study of achievement motivation.

Atkinson's Model

Individual strength of achievement motivation became part of a more general and elaborated theory of achievement orientation by Atkinson in 1957. Atkinson viewed achievement orientation as a kind of approach-avoidance conflict consisting of attraction to the possibility of success versus fear of possible failure. According to the theory, the relative strengths of these two opposing tendencies were jointly determined by three factors: (a) motivational differences across individuals, (b) expectations concerning the likelihood of success or failure in the situation, and (c) the incentive or reward value of succeeding or failing in the situation. The latter two are consistent with expectancy×value theories of behavior in other areas (e.g., Lewin, 1938; Tolman, 1955).

The basics of the theory, as described by Atkinson (1964), consist of specifying a mathematical relationship among the three factors in the prediction of achievement behavior. Each of the factors has components representing both a success and a failure orientation. The first factor is viewed as a relatively stable and enduring characteristic of the individual to be oriented relatively more toward approaching success (high achievement motivation) or toward avoiding failure (low achievement motivation). The motive to succeed (M_s) consists of the TAT operationalized need for achievement, described above, and is viewed as the capacity to experience pride in success. For several years, research on achievement was concerned only with this measure of individual motivation. However, it became clear that the motive to avoid failure (M_{af}), or anxiety about achievement, was equally important in determining achievement behavior (Atkinson, 1974). The latter motive is viewed as the tendency to react with shame following failure, and is usually measured by the Mandler & Sarason (1952) Test Anxiety Questionnaire (TAQ).

The second factor, expectancy, refers to the belief that a particular act will result in a particular consequence—specifically, the probability that one will succeed (P_s) or fail (P_f) at a given task. Approach or avoidance tendency is postulated to increase in direct proportion to the probability of success and of failure, respectively. This variable is usually defined either in terms of subjects rated expectations on a trial or by providing the probability of success at a task by means of social norms. The two probabilities are assumed to total unity, and thus P_f is usually written as $1-P_s$.

Finally, incentive value of success (I_s) or failure (I_f) is defined in terms of an affect—pride or shame in the outcome. Greater anticipated pride increases the approach tendency, and greater anticipated shame increases the avoidance tendency. This factor is typically defined in terms of P_s such that I_s and P_s (and I_f and P_f) are assumed to be inversely related. That is, increasing pride is assumed to result from success at increasingly difficult tasks and increasing shame from failure at increasingly easy tasks. Thus, I_s is often represented as $1 - P_s$; and I_f as P_s [i.e., $I_f = 1 - (P_f) = 1 - (1 - P_s) = P_s$].

According to the theory, the relationship of these three factors in predicting the tendency to approach achievement activities (T_a) is as follows:

$$T_a = (M_s \times P_s \times I_s) - (M_{af} \times P_f \times I_f)$$

This equation represents mathematically the conflict described earlier— that the tendency to engage in achievement behavior is determined by the relative or resultant strength of the dual tendencies to approach success and avoid failure. Including the assumptions described above by arithmetic substitution results in the following simplified equation, in which only three independent variables (M_s, M_{af}, and P_s) need to be measured:

$$T_a = (M_s - M_{af}) [P_s \times (1 - P_s)]$$

There have been numerous reviews of evidence both supporting and questioning the assumptions of the model, the precise mathematical relationship among the elements, and its ability to make accurate predictions of behaviors, such as choosing to engage in an achievement activity, level of aspiration, persistence, risk taking, and quality or quantity of performance (e.g., Atkinson & Feather, 1966; Birney, 1968; Heckhausen, 1977; Klitzner & Anderson, 1977; Weiner, 1972). We do not think it is useful here to review these data. However, there is sufficient empirical support to continue to take seriously many of the features and derivations of the model in evaluating educational policies.

Extensions of the Model

There have been a number of modifications of and questions raised about the model since its initial presentation. We will now briefly describe the changes that most affect theoretical predictions and thus have the greatest implications for educational application.

Extrinsic motivations. One problem with the original model is that it failed to acknowledge the existence of nonachievement-related sources of motivation. That is, even individuals low in achievement needs may engage in achievement activities if external incentives are available, e.g., monetary or social rewards. Thus, a global category called extrinsic motives became an additive factor in the model. Since many education programs often include extrinsic incentives of various types, the specific effect of this factor on motivation is of considerable interest. Although it was assumed in the Atkinson model that extrinsic sources *enhanced* motivation, subsequent research has suggested, instead, that external incentives may *decrease* intrinsic interest in an activity (see review of intrinsic/ extrinsic motivation in Section II).

Inertial Tendencies. A second major weakness of the original model is that it failed to allow for motivation which persists in the absence of the stimulus, such as the desire to resume an interrupted task. Thus, in order to account for the maintenance of goal-seeking, purposive behavior, a new element was added to the model called "inertial tendency" (T_{Gi}). T_{Gi} represents the motive to persist in an achievement task, once the motive is aroused, until the task is successfully completed. The most important implication of this addition to the model is that goal-oriented activity should be greater after failure than after success (Atkinson & Cartwright, 1964; Weiner, 1965).

The concept of inertial tendencies has recently been extended by Revelle & Michaels (1976), who have analyzed the likely effects of the number of trials at a particular task. One question, for example, concerns the effects of a string of failures, assuming that a single failure increases motivation. For multiple trials, the difficulty of the task (P_s) becomes important in examining inertial tendencies, since it determines the number of trials since the last success (i.e., for a very hard task, there are likely to be many intervening trials between successes).

According to the analysis presented by Revelle & Michaels effort should be positively related to the number of trials since the last success because there is a cumulative impact of inertial tendency after several failures. That is, achievement orientation should increase as the number of trials and the difficulty of the task increases—but only up to a point. Once a very low probability of success is reached, motivation level drops rapidly, a prediction consistent with the original Atkinson model. In sum, the concept of inertial tendency in conjunction with variations in the number of trials in a task leads to some significant modifications in the predictions regarding the optimization of achievement approach tendencies. Unfortunately, several elements of the revised model proposed by Revelle & Michaels remain sufficiently vague so that the specific implications are as yet unclear.

Future Orientation. The inertial tendencies concept described above concerns the motivational implications of multiple trials in which the outcome on any given trial is assumed to have little implication for future outcomes—i.e., a series of *noncontingent* trials. It also seems reasonable to expect a series of *contingent* trials to modify the predictions of the basic model. Raynor (1969, 1974) presents a modification to account for the fact that tasks differ in their relevance to future goals— that in many cases the final goal is contingent upon completing a series of tasks. Since a large number of classroom achievement activities involve these kinds of contingent relationships among tasks (e.g., a series of workbook exercises that build on each other in order to teach general concepts), it seems important to understand the implications of future orientation on motivational tendencies.

In Raynor's elaboration of the model, the tendency to achieve success in an immediate activity is a function of the sum of component tendencies for each intermediate step necessary to achieve the final goal. This modification of the model has two main implications. First, since the components summate to yield the total tendency to engage in an immediate activity, the resultant motive increases as the number of steps increase. Thus, for example, the achievement approach tendencies of high achievers should tend to increase as they anticipate more distant goals. Second, resultant achievement tendencies should also be related to increasingly higher probabilities of success as the number of steps along the contingent path increase. That is, when tasks are functionally related to each other, an intermediate failure means a loss of the opportunity to continue and thus a failure to achieve future goals. In some sense then, the definition of intermediate probability of success shifts and necessitates a more conservative approach in order to maintain the opportunity to strive for the final goal. Thus, in terms of educational implications, an achievement-oriented individual will be motivated toward a long-term goal only if the intermediate steps are perceived as easy enough to make the final goal appear attainable.

Other Modifications or Differing Perspectives
Several other limitations of early achievement motivation models should be acknowledged, though it is not possible to treat each in detail. For example, one important point is that such models lack a cross-cultural perspective. Thus, they were based on an ethnocentric conception of achievement motivation in terms of what were defined as desirable goals as well as the appropriate ways to attain them (Maehr & Lysy, in press). A related issue concerns sex differences. Because females did not fit the predictions from the models, achievement motivation in women was ignored for several years (Horner, 1974). Recently, there have been numerous analyses of sex differences in achievement and alternative models for women (e.g., Frieze, et al., 1978; Horner, 1974; Mednick, Tangri, & Hoffman, 1975; Parsons & Goff, 1978). Finally, it should be noted that Atkinson & Birch (1974) and Birch & Atkinson (1970) have turned to a different way of approaching achievement motivation. Based on a more dynamic conception of action, Atkinson & Birth are seeking to determine what causes changes in a "stream of action."

Summary
Several features of the Atkinson model, including the extensions, are particularly relevant to the concern for optimizing motivation. Most noteworthy, perhaps, is the idea that although achievement orientation or behavior is related to the need for achievement of individuals, accurate predictions depend on other factors operating in the situation, such as task difficulty information affecting expectations for success. Futhermore, these external factors are assumed to have differential effects depending on the motive orientation of the individual. For example, the model predicts that the maximal approach tendency is at intermediate levels of task difficulty ($P_s = .5$) for high achievement motivated individuals (i.e., $M_s > M_{af}$), while for individuals low in need for achievement ($M_{af} > M_s$), the approach tendency is predicted to be greatest for extremely easy or difficult tasks. What this means is that responses to challenge vary across individuals, motivating success-approach people and creating anxiety in failure-avoidance people.

Taken at face value, such predictions have interesting implications for several types of educational experiences (Weiner, 1972). For example, the theory suggests that indices of motivation (e.g., speed; persistence) are differentially affected by P_s, depending on individual factors. That is, high achievers should be most persistent and low achievers least persistent at levels of intermediate task difficulty. In addition, it suggests that educational programs to maximize or change motivation must be geared to individual needs. For example, attempts to enhance expectations of success by frequent success feedback, as in programmed instruction, may be less effective with high achievers than with low achievers because it reduces challenge. Similar arguments may be applied to the effectiveness of programs modifying standards of evaluation, as in ability groupings.

Recently, some important questions have been raised about central aspects of the model and its predictions which affect the implications of the model for educational practice. There appear to be two key problem areas. The first concerns the "challenge" aspect of the model. This has been the element of most concern in the extensions of the model described above. In essence, it appears the P_s values of .5 may maximize motivation only under the most limited circumstances (e.g., when an individual undertakes only a single trial at a task). There is even evidence that a different value of P_s than .5 maximizes challenge even under this most simple case (Heckhausen, 1967, 1977).

The second area consists of a growing critique of the individual differences variable (e.g., Heckhausen, 1977; Kukla, 1972), especially concerning the implications of the dual motivational tendencies to approach success or avoid failure. The questions do not concern the importance of incorporating individual differences per se, but rather that these differences identify two sharply differentiated categories of persons. The major difficulty is that the model necessitates opposing predictions for resultant approach versus resultant avoidance tendencies on every variable. $P_s = .5$ is the level assumed to be most motivating for approach individuals and least motivating for avoidance individuals. This feature makes predictions based on the model very awkward. In addition, empirical tests of dual tendency predictions have typically not found two opposite patterns of results, with the major problem occurring in the predictions for the avoidance-oriented subjects (e.g., Kukla, 1972; Meyer, Folkes, & Weiner, 1976; Revelle & Michaels, 1976). Some current approaches to the individual differences issue include (a) identifying multiple parameters of individual differences as opposed to the more global approach of Atkinson (Heckhausen, 1977), and (b) defining the differences along a dimension rather than categorically, allowing consistency of prediction across individuals once their place along the dimensions has been identified (Kukla, 1972).

THEORIES BASED ON INDIVIDUAL COGNITIONS

More recent theories of achievement orientation have increasingly included cognitive constructs as determinants of behavior. The conceptual and empirical justifications of this shift to postulating cognitive mediations have been extensively discussed elsewhere (Heckhausen, 1977; Heckhausen & Weiner, 1974; Weiner, 1972) and need not concern us here. What is of concern is the nature of the cognitions involved and how they are related to achievement-related behaviors. One major construct that has become prominent in the study of achievement, as well as in other areas, is perception of personal control over outcomes. We will first describe this construct and the role it plays in a few major theories and then describe in some detail Weiner's theory of achievement, since Weiner focuses on a broad analysis of perceptions of causality in which perception of control is but one aspect.

Perception of Control Over Outcomes

Several theories or programs of research relevant to achievement include some variant on the concept of perception of control. This distinction refers to whether or not individuals perceive their outcomes or reinforcements as determined by personal control (i.e., by purposive behavior). Such perceptions are thought to be important determinants of the reinforcement value of many experiences, and to influence the extent to which people are likely to modify their behavior in attempts to attain their goals (see Lefcourt, 1976, for an extended discussion on the concept of perceived control).

The concept of personal control is probably most readily identified with Rotter's (1954) "social learning theory," in which perceptions of control over reinforcements produce *expectancies* regarding reinforcement which guide behavior. The mathematical formulation of the theory is similar to Atkinson (1964) in that the potential for behavior is viewed as a function of (1) expectations that behavior will result in reinforcement, and (2) the value of reinforcement. There are, however, two major differences. First, in contrast to Atkinson, expectancy for Rotter consists of two types: (1) a specific expectancy based on knowledge of the particular situation, and (2) a generalized expectancy of the individual based on personal history of reinforcement across situations. Thus, the individual difference construct in Rotter's model consists of a cognitive (expectancy) variable rather than a stable motivational one, as postulated by Atkinson.

One of the major determinants of expectancy is the perception of control of reinforcement. For example, a person may desire a goal but perceive that there is nothing he or she can do to achieve that goal. This belief that reinforcements are noncontingent on an individual's own action represents perceived "external control." In contrast, a belief in a contingent relationship between action and outcome is termed "internal control." Expectations are raised or lowered systematically by outcomes only if the outcomes are seen as caused by one's own actions, not if some external force is seen as the cause. Thus, it is assumed that relatively stable modifications in achievement orientation could occur only after perceptions of internal control were induced.

Locus of control has been examined both as an individual difference measure and as situationally induced. For the latter, situations are manipulated by describing performance on a task as primarily due to luck (external control) or primarily due to skill (internal control). As predicted, results of such studies usually show that shifts in expectations are of greater magnitude and more predictable from the previous outcomes under skill than under chance instructions (Lefcourt, 1966; Rotter, 1966). Studies using the individual differences measure (Rotter's Locus of Control Scale) have been less successful in predicting expectancy shifts. However, research examining correlates of internal versus external (I-E) locus of control, such as need for achievement, has been extremely prolific, and there are numerous suggestions of its importance in understanding educational achievement (Bar-Tal & Bar-Zahar, 1977).

The locus of control variable has been incorporated, with modifications, into other theories or research programs relevant to achievement motivation. For example, one theory incorporating the I-E construct as it applies specifically to achievement situations has been developed by Crandall and her colleagues (Battle, 1965, 1966; Crandall, 1978; Crandall et al., 1965). The personal control variable in Crandall's model is measured by the Intellectual Achievement Responsibility (IAR) questionnaire, which differs from Rotter's Locus of Control scale in that the items refer only to achievement situations and it is aimed at assessing the perceptions of achievement responsibility of *children*. Crandall views perceived internal control as a necessary prerequisite to achievement striving. Her own program of research has been largely concerned with the socialization antecedents of internal achievement responsibility (Crandall, 1967).

In addition to internal responsibility, there are three types of cognition important for behavioral predictions in Crandall's model: (1) Attainment Value (AV), (2) Expectancy (EX), and (3) Minimal Standard (MS). The first two concepts are similar to those described in previous expectancy-value models: AV refers to the importance attached to feedback, though it is defined more broadly than the difficulty of the task; and EX refers to the predicted level of outcome at a task. As for Rotter (1966), AV and EX are assumed to be independent. The main new element in the model is MS, which refers to the point on the continuum which is perceived as distinguishing a success from a failure. For example, for some people a score of 80 per cent constitutes positive feedback, while for others it is quite negative. The concept is central to the theory and implies that expectancy per se is not directly related to achievement orientation but rather that the discrepancy between expectancy and minimal standards is of primary importance.

In sum, the concept of personal control has been an important addition to theories of achievement, in part because it represents a shift from a more psychodynamic or nonconscious view of motivation to a more conscious cognitive approach. The application of this construct to programs aimed at optimizing motivation (e.g., deCharms, 1968) will be discussed in Section II.

Weiner's Attributional Theory of Achievement Motivation

Probably the best known and most influential cognitive approach to achievement is the program developed by Weiner and colleagues (Weiner et al., 1971;

Weiner, 1974). Weiner's theory is based on previous Expectancy × Value models, except that the elements are defined in cognitive rather than motivational terms. Individuals are viewed as actively attempting to interpret the causes of their outcomes; it is the pattern of perceived causes, i.e., attributions, that determines expectancies, level of affect (pride/shame) or incentive, and resulting achievement behaviors.

Guided by the ideas of Heider (1958) and the concept of locus of control in Rotter's and Crandall's work, Weiner has proposed a model which consists of four possible perceived causes of an achievement outcome: ability, effort, task difficulty, and luck. These four causal elements are divided into two dimensions as follows:

	Locus of Control	
Stability	Internal	External
Stable	Ability	Task Difficulty
Unstable	Effort	Luck

Locus of control is the concept described above in the work of Rotter and Crandall, and it is also similar to the person/entity distinction prevalent in attributional theories of social perception (Jones & Davis, 1965; Kelley, 1967). Ability and effort describe personal, internal qualities; task difficulty and luck involve forces external to the person or are properties of the situation. Stability is a dimension central only to the Weiner model; it has not been discussed either in previous theories of achievement or social attribution. Ability and the difficulty of a particular task are seen to have enduring or stable qualities, while effort and luck are more variable. Finally, it should be noted that recent papers have called attention to the importance of attributions about achievement that do not fit within this two-dimensional model, and have thereby emphasized the importance of considering other dimensions along which achievement explanations may vary (Elig & Frieze, 1975; Weiner, 1979). These new analyses are likely to be expecially applicable to educational settings because of the types of additional attributions being examined (e.g., the teacher, cheating, mood, etc.).

Weiner's research program has been concerned with both the implications and antecedents of variations in attributions for success and failure, especially as these investigations promote an integration of the attributional approach with previous expectancy-value theories. With respect to implications, the two dimensions of the model are postulated to influence different types of achievement-related behaviors. The locus of control dimension primarily influences affective reactions (pride and shame), such that greatest pride for success and shame for failure occur when attributions are made to internal factors. Weiner's more recent work, however, has linked many affects (e.g., surprise) to specific attributions (e.g., luck) rather than to dimensions (Weiner, Russell, & Lerman,

1978, 1979). The dimension of stability primarily influences expectancy changes, such that greater "typical" shifts in expectancy (i.e., shifts consistent with previous outcomes) follow attributions to stable factors than to unstable factors.

There is considerable empirical support for both of the above predictions (cf. Weiner, 1974), suggesting that the expectancy and value elements of previous models are, as hypothesized, readily interpretable in terms of causal attributions of success and failure. In addition, in the several cases where different predictions are derivable from the various models, the attributional model generally receives the most support. For example, Rotter and Weiner make differential predictions concerning the determinants of changes in people's expectancy of success. For Rotter, expectancy change is related to the locus of control dimension, whereas for Weiner, expectancy for change is influenced primarily by the stability dimension. A review of studies contrasting the predictions indicates a consistent relationship between expectations and attributions to high versus low stability of causal factors, but not to internal versus external control (Weiner, Nierenberg, & Goldstein, 1976). Indeed, in at least one case, a negative correlation was reported between the locus of control dimension and expectations (McMahan, 1973).

Similarly, support for the attribution model is provided by research contrasting predictions from Weiner versus Atkinson on the reasons for people's preferences for tasks of intermediate difficulty. The results of studies examining the diagnostic value of a task separately from task difficulty suggest that it is the informational value rather than the affective value of outcomes that determine choice among tasks, findings consistent with Weiner's theory (Meyer et al., 1976; Trope, 1975; Trope & Brickman, 1975).

There has also been considerable research on antecedents of differing attributional patterns. Three categories of antecedents seem adequate to represent these studies. The first concerns the *nature of information available,* such as social norms or history of past success. For example, when the outcome on a particular task is consistent with previous outcomes, and consistent with outcomes on similar tasks, the person's ability rather than other factors, such as luck or task difficulty, is seen as a more likely cause of the present outcome (Frieze & Weiner, 1971). In addition, the situational context is an important determinant of attributions, such that a particular attribution (e.g., effort) may be quite common or important in some situations (e.g., academic) but less so elsewhere (Frieze & Snyder, 1978).

The second category of antecedent concerns the *processes of integrating the information.* Variations in causal perceptions may result from the way in which the information is presented, as for example, sequentially versus simultaneously (Frieze, 1976), or from rules based on socially learned beliefs concerning the causes of particular events (Kun & Weiner, 1973). For some tasks, a single cause (e.g., ability) may be perceived as sufficient to produce an outcome (success);

while for other tasks, effort as well as ability may be perceived as necessary for a successful outcome.

The final category of antecedents consists of *individual differences in causal perceptions*. That is, consistent with the approaches of Rotter and Crandall, who argue that there are relatively stable individual differences in perceptions of personal causation, there may be characteristic tendencies to perceive outcomes as, for example, luck or effort-determined. Empirical work on individual attributional tendencies has primarily been directed at explaining the need for achievement variable (in the Atkinson model) in attributional terms. This research has demonstrated that high achievers tend to attribute successes to ability, while low achievers are more likely to attribute their failures to lack of ability. In addition, high achievers are more likely than low achievers to perceive covariation between their effort and outcomes (Kukla, 1972; cf. Weiner, 1974). According to Weiner's theory, the behavioral differences between high and low achievers (e.g., level of persistence at achievement tasks) should be interpreted in terms of different cognitions (e.g., attributions to effort) rather than in terms of different motivational states.

The educational implications of the attributional approach are multifaceted. Most basically, the fact that causal perceptions have been clearly and systematically related to achievement-oriented behaviors suggests that one way to enhance motivation is to modify attributions for performance outcomes. In addition, the theory suggests several possible ways of accomplishing this objective—both in terms of optimizing the way a situation is structured (and thus the information available) and in terms of optimizing personal attributional tendencies. The results of some of these attributional research programs will be discussed in Section II.

SUMMARY AND INTEGRATION

What do the various theoretical formulations, separately or together, tell us about the processes which optimize the motivational aspect of performance in achievement situations? Are there several variables or a constellation of factors that provide guidance for decisions regarding educational programs? On at least a surface level there seems to be considerable agreement across theories about what are the major determinants of achievement orientation. Every model contains, explicitly or implicitly, three factors: (1) individual differences, (2) expectations or probability of success and (3) incentive values of outcomes. Although the specific relationship among these factors varies across models, their universal presence is worth noting. The same sorts of variables appear in different theories, in part for historical reasons; newer theories must be justified in terms of previous formulations. We hope, however, that the level of agreement also indicates something more substantive about the "true" nature of motivation. We will now attempt to integrate the various theories in terms of these three variables, hoping to get directives for action that may allow evaluation of the various motivational research programs discussed in Section II.

Individual Differences

Although every theory acknowledges the predictive importance of individual predispositions, there are considerable differences across theories in what these individual factors mean, how they are measured, and what they imply in attempting to optimize motivation. The Atkinson Model and its extensions are based on an unconscious motive, presumed to be relatively stable and developed in childhood. It is thus not easily incorporated into optimization programs because it is difficult to measure (see Entwistle, 1972; Revelle & Michaels, 1976, for critiques of the TAT measure), and because it is assumed to be fairly resistant to change. From the perspective of this model, the main optimization techniques must consist of relating to individual needs by modifying situational factors, these modifications being limited for the most part to probability of success (P_s) and extrinsic motives.

More cognitively oriented theorists have questioned the usefulness of the global motivation concept as well as the need to make two opposing predictions for two distinct categories of motives—approach versus avoidance (Heckhausen, 1977; Kukla, 1972). These cognitive theories seem to provide a somewhat more flexible account of individual differences from the point of view of modifying achievement orientation. Specifically, individuals are seen to differ in their cognitions or self-perceptions in achievement situations. Thus, optimization can be affected not only by means of modifying situational factors to suit individual perceptions but also by modifying cognitions about the self.

Two interrelated self-perceptions seem to emerge most consistently as critically related to achievement orientation: the perception of competence and the perception of personal control over outcomes. These self-perceptions in Weiner's attributional terminology would involve perceptions of ability and effort-outcome covariation. In other cognitive approaches, these two self-perceptions appear to be represented by a single term, such as de Charm's (1968) construct, "origin-pawn," and the "self-efficacy" notion recently described by Bandura (1977) in his analysis of therapy-related behavioral change. Since these self-perceptions have been shown to be related both to expectations of success and to the affective value of success, changes in these variables seem almost certain to affect motivation. Weiner, de Charms, and Bandura all provide suggestions for enhancing such self-perceptions, to be discussed in Section II.

Expectations or Probability of Success (P_s)

As with the individual differences factor, the specific definition of P_s varies across theories and, in some cases, has multiple meanings within a single theory. For example, in the Atkinson Model, P_s can refer either to subjective probability of success or to task difficulty as defined through social norms. These are two very different meanings and are likely to generate differential predictions (Kukla, 1972, 1975; Moulton, 1974).

In addition, predictions based on P_s may vary considerably depending on other interactive or confounding factors included in the models. As a first example, several investigators have suggested that perceptions of competence or ability level are likely to be an important determinant of P_s, thereby possibly confounding it with the individual difference variable included in the model (Kukla, 1972; Moulton, 1974; Weiner, 1974). To illustrate, individuals who believe they are highly skilled at a particular activity are likely to have a high expectancy of success even if the task clearly is difficult.

A second example concerns the findings that expectations are influenced by level of efforts expended or intended at the task (Kukla, 1972; Revelle & Michaels, 1976). Although this relationship is generally described in terms of the effect of P_s on effort, it is fairly obvious that the relationship is reciprocal and that subjective expectancies will be higher as anticipated effort increases (Kukla, 1972).

A third factor confusing predictions based on P_s is the number of trials involved and the degree of contingency among the trials. As noted earlier, according to Raynor (1974), based on the future orientation extension of Atkinson's model, the highest approach orientation should result from *relatively* easy tasks when there are several intermediate and contingent tasks leading to a final goal. In contrast, according to Revelle & Michaels' (1976) extension of Atkinson's theory based on the concept of inertial tendency, individuals should be most motivated by relatively *difficult* tasks when there are several trials involved. Thus, predictions based on multiple trials become complex, as it becomes necessary to determine the contingency among tasks and presumably among subjects' perceptions of final goal orientation.

Resolution would seem to depend on a conceptual separation of the motivational effects of real task difficulty (e.g., enhancement of effort following failure) and subjective expectations of success or level of confidence, which is multiply determined. The Weiner attributional model provides for this separation in that level of expectancy is defined as a result of a causal analysis in which the difficulty of the task is only one of the possible causes to be considered. Thus, this model allows for the "confounds" between P_s and other factors and, in fact, predicts them. The main limitation of the model for our purposes is that although the antecedents of expectancy are well specified, the results are not; the model fails to make specific predictions for level of motivation and performance based on subjective expectations of success. It is not clear, for example, if subsequent achievement orientation should be a direct linear function of expectancy, as the results of several studies have suggested (e.g., Crandall, 1969; Feather, 1966), or if expectations relate to increased achievement orientation only up to some optimal level, as in the Atkinson model. Nevertheless, the attributional model seems to provide a useful beginning toward a more finely tuned analysis and set of predictions based on P_s.

Incentive or Reinforcement Value of the Outcome

Recommendations based on this construct are also made difficult by vagueness of definition and inconsistencies across theories. For Atkinson, the incentive value of success (I_s) was intended to represent the degree of affect attached to achieving a goal. However, its operational definition was limited in the sense that the only factor assumed to influence incentive was the difficulty of the task in terms of how challenging it was; other intuitively important aspects of incentive, such as the significance of the particular area of achievement for the individual (Crandall & Battle, 1970) and its information value (Weiner, 1974) were not included. The cognitive theories have deviated from the Atkinson model in two respects: (1) partly for empirical reasons, incentive value is assumed to be independent of expectation for success, and (2) incentive value is defined more generally, though more vaguely, as whatever contributes to pride or the value of the task.

Upon closer examination, however, there may be less difference across theories than this analysis implies. For example, aspects of incentive other than challenge may be included in the Atkinson model as part of extrinsic motivation or Raynor's (1974) future goal orientation. In addition, incentive value and expectations of success are not completely independent in cognitive models. For example, attribution of success to high ability produces both higher incentive value (pride) and higher expectations for success (Weiner et. al., 1978a).

Conclusion

The analysis of points of integration across theories suggests that attempts to make specific predictions become extremely complicated because of confounds and interactions across variables. It is clear that we are *not* dealing with three totally separate constructs that make independent contributions to achievement orientation. Nevertheless, one may conclude that motivation can be enhanced in at least the following ways: (1) increasing perceptions of competence and personal control over outcomes; (2) providing challenging tasks, in which the optimal difficulty of the task depends on both individual (e.g., perceptions of competence) and task (e.g., multiple trials) parameters; and (3) providing additional incentives, such as matching the nature of the task to individual interests or providing an orientation to future goals.

II. AREAS OF RESEARCH IN MOTIVATING ACADEMIC ACHIEVEMENT

There have been numerous empirical approaches to the basic issues of how optimally to motivate children in achievement situations and to determine what factors contribute to lack of motivation. Some of these approaches are explicitly based on the theoretical models described above, while in others the necessary mediating variables can only be inferred. In this section, we will describe several of these topic areas in terms of major issues and the tentative conclusions. Obviously, we cannot hope to provide a thorough and in-depth coverage of the research relevant to achievement motivation, given the extensiveness of the field. Rather, the goal in this section is to provide a sense of the range of variables which educators concerned with motivation must consider, and to provide a basis for future integration of theoretical models and application-oriented research.

The structure of this section is roughly intended to move from a focus on variables that are primarily internal to the person being motivated toward more situational or external determinants of motivation. Of course, this distinction is not clear cut, and in most of the sections described below, the two sorts of variables are shown to interact.

First, literature will be presented which has focused on conditions precipitating perceived lack of control of behavior over outcomes (learned helplessness) and its effects on achievement striving; we will also describe various approaches to modifying unrealistic perceptions of lack of control and perceptions of competency. We will then discuss pupils' expectations of success as potential determinants of achievement outcome, including the various processes which may underlie expectancy-performance relationships. Finally, we will present an overview of some areas of research which can be considered related to the effects of various situational aspects of the educational setting on students' perceptions of competency and control; specifically, we examine the effects of teachers' expectancies, rewards, and testing situations on students' attitudes, motivational level, and/or performance.

ATTRIBUTION RESEARCH AND CHANGE PROGRAMS

The importance of self-perception of competence and control as a central factor in models of achievement striving is receiving increasing empirical attention in the motivation literature. The specific question of interest concerns the effects of varying attribution patterns on performance and on other indicators of motivation. Rather than provide a complete survey of the range of relevant studies, we will focus on the findings of studies identified as a sub-area within an attributional approach to achievement motivation: learned helplessness. We will then discuss various possible approaches to modifying attributional tendencies.

Learned Helplessness

Learned helplessness is a recent and highly visible topic in the literature concerning the motivational effects of perceptions of personal control. The basic idea is that prolonged exposure to noncontingent outcomes signals a loss of control and results in an inappropriate generalized debilitation such that the individual fails to exhibit coping responses even when control is restored. The term has its origins in animal conditioning studies showing how dogs became debilitated when they were subjected to a series of shocks while restrained (and thus unable to control the aversive stimulation by any voluntary response). Specifically, the debilitation became evident when these "helpless" dogs were later placed in a two-sided chamber in which they could avoid shock by jumping a barrier. Instead of escaping, they passively accepted the shock by lying down and whining. In contrast, their naive counterparts quickly learned to jump the barrier. Presumably, the dogs exposed to uncontrollable outcomes learned that their responses and reinforcements were independent (Seligman, 1975).

This phenomenon has been extended to humans at both a conceptual and empirical level; its relevance to education and achievement are clear. Seligman makes explicit the application to special education by citing an excerpt from Kozol's *Death at an Early Age* which describes the helplessness of a "special student in a normal, crowded classroom" (Seligman, 1975, p. 153). The implication of the example is that children who are left in situations in which nothing they do is good enough give up trying eventually and fall further behind. We will briefly summarize the helplessness literature for humans in terms of responses to noncontingent events that are both negative and positive.

Effects of Noncontingent Negative Outcomes

Numerous studies have attempted to replicate conceptually the original animal findings with humans by examining people's behaviors when they lose control over aversive outcomes. For example, one investigation, representing a particularly close analog to the animal studies, was reported by Hiroto & Seligman (1975). Subjects were told they could avoid an aversive noise by pushing a button connected to a panel. This statement about control was true in one condition (escapable tone), while in another it was not (inescapable tone). The subjects in the two conditions received the identical number and patterns of aversive noises and differed only in perceived escapability. A control group was instructed to sit passively and listen to the same number of noises. After this pretraining, subjects were tested for helplessness in a "human shuttle box" in which a tone could be avoided by learning to move a knob from one side to the other. Consistent with predictions, the results showed that subjects given the helplessness pretraining (inescapable condition) were significantly poorer in learning to escape than were subjects in the other two groups.

Several recent studies have attempted to induce helplessness in more achievement-related situations, by presenting insoluble problems or providing random feedback for subjects working on problems (Dweck & Goetz, 1978). For example, in one study (Dweck & Reppucci, 1973) fourth-to-sixth graders were given a series of soluble problems by one experimenter and insoluble ones (helplessness training) by another. After several trials, the problems from the "failure" experimenter became soluble, and in fact were essentially identical to ones solved earlier with the "success" experimenter. Yet, when children were subsequently given problems by the failure administrator, they had great difficulty with the same problems they had solved with ease earlier. Evidently the children had learned to be helpless in this situation. This kind of situation-dependent helplessness may be a good model of selective performance deterioration in the classroom. That is, some children may respond poorly only with some teachers, or in some subjects, such as math (Seligman, 1975). A study of children with severe reading problems is illustrative of this point (Rozin et al., 1971). When special tutoring was given in reading English, the children consistently failed, as they had done in the classroom. However, when presented with Chinese characters and told that each one represented an English word, they were quickly able to learn to read entire paragraphs in Chinese.

Although helplessness has been demonstrated in humans in some studies, there are many inconsistencies and interpretive problems. For example, in some studies it is difficult to determine if performance deterioration resulted because of helplessness training (i.e., perceived loss of control) or because the "helpless" subjects received a greater number of negative consequences. Even more problematic are the findings in some studies that helplessness training facilitates performance. For these reasons, in a recent review of this literature, Wortman and Brehm (1975) conclude: "It is clear from an examination of the human helplessness literature that we know very little about what produces helplessness in humans" (p. 306).

On the basis of empirical evidence and conceptual analyses, it appears that examination of two major factors is necessary for understanding helplessness in humans. The first is the amount of helplessness training received. Approached from several different perspectives and based on several different kinds of data, a consistent conclusion emerges: there is a curvilinear relationship between amount of helplessness training and helplessness effects. That is, the initial reaction to failure or loss of control is a redoubling of efforts or active striving to maintain control.

The initial performance increase has been hypothesized to occur for several different reasons: (1) reaction to threatened loss of freedom (Wortman & Brehm, 1975); (2) inertial tendencies (Revelle & Michaels, 1976); (3) initial invigoration response to disengagement from incentives (Klinger, 1975); and (4) attempts to reestablish competency (Wortman et al., 1976). In all models, however, after prolonged failures or noncontingent outcomes, efforts cease and a pattern of helplessness emerges. Thus, studies reporting facilitation effects of helplessness training (e.g., Hanusa & Shulz, 1977; Roth & Bootzin, 1974; Thornton & Jacobs, 1972; Wortman et al., 1976) may have tested subjects at the peak of their active as opposed to passive point on the response cycle. In support of this interpretation, these studies generally presented fewer training trials than did studies where helplessness effects were produced (e.g., Roth & Kubal, 1975; Tennen & Eller, 1977).

A second important factor is the causal attribution made for failure of lack of control. Several recent studies have demonstrated that attributions or situational factors as opposed to personal incompetence result in differential responses to helplessness training. The basic prediction is intuitively obvious—that generalized helplessness effects will be stronger when lack of control is attributed to personal incompetence as opposed to the specific situation. This hypothesis has received some support in studies examining individual differences in attributions (Dweck & Reppucci, 1973) and in studies manipulating attributions experimentally (Roth & Kubal, 1975; Tennen & Eller, 1977). In direct contrast, however, other research has shown that attributing lack of control to ability as opposed to the situation *facilitates* performance (Hanusa & Shulz, 1977; Wortman et al., 1976).

This apparent contradicition may be resolved by considering these two factors—amount of helplessness training and attributions—as interacting to influence helplessness effects. That is, in studies finding facilitating effects of attributions to ability, relatively few trials or weak manipulation of helplessness were used as compared to studies demonstrating debilitating effects. It appears that the curvilinear relationship between helplessness training and helplessness effects may occur only when individuals perceive their failures as due to incompetence. Apparently, individuals' initial reaction to failure is to try to reestablish their competence, although later they give up trying. On the other hand, when subjects are led to attribute their failures to the situation, they apparently continue to increase their efforts, even after numerous failures, presumably because situationally based failures are perceived as unstable. The result is a linear increasing relationship between performance and number of trials of helplessness training. (For recent discussions of an attributional analysis of learned helplessness effects, see Abramson et al., 1978, and Wortman & Dintzer, 1978.)

There are important implications of the learned helplessness analysis for classroom experiences of the special child. That is, there are many children who for various reasons are likely to encounter situations in which they experience lack of personal control (Diener & Dweck, 1978). Learning-disabled children or mildly retarded children in a normal classroom may be faced with instructional materials that are impossible for them to master, given their present skills; thus, they fail regardless of their efforts. If such experiences are prolonged or especially severe, a form of learned helplessness may result, adding to the child's problems. From an attributional analysis of learned helplessness, it is possible that techniques to induce attributions to the situation or to lack of effort as opposed to incompetence, in addition to modifying the frequency of the failure experience, may change the helplessness set (Dweck, 1975).

Effects of Noncontingent Positive Outcomes

Since the major variable responsible for a learned helplessness response is perception of lack of control for outcomes, theoretically, helplessness responses should result from noncontingent successes as well as failures. Seligman (1975) does refer to a "success depression" resulting from the experience of "the good life" when it seems unrelated to one's actions. However, there is little experimental data on this issue, the one directly relevant study reporting no evidence of performance debilitation after noncontingent success feedback (Benson & Kennelly, 1976). It should be noted, however, that the noncontingent success group did perform significantly worse on the test trials than did a group that had experienced contingent success, thereby suggesting some negative effects of perceptions of lack of control for success.

This kind of motivational phenomenon is particularly relevant to one aspect of special education—the education of the gifted. Presumably such children in most classroom situations experience nearly consistent success regardless of their efforts, and thereby experience noncontingent success. In Weiner's terms, they never learn to perceive a correlation between efforts and outcomes. Thus, they may begin to exhibit the low effort pattern defined as characteristic of poor achievers.

A recent, related hypothesis concerning lowered motivation in achievement situations has been termed self-handicapping (Berglas & Jones, 1978; Jones & Berglas, 1978). This analysis pertains to situations in which individuals perceive their past successes as undeserved—i.e., due to something beyond their control or to factors irrelevant to task competence, such as physical attractiveness. In order to maintain the success facade, they must avoid situations in which the truth about their competence might be revealed, since such information may be disappointing. Therefore, such individuals select situations or engage in extraneous activities which make success unlikely, though not impossible. This way, if success occurs, it must be attributed to competency while the cause of a failure is ambiguous.

This characterization of achievement avoidance is similar to the description of low achievers provided by Atkinson in terms of a desire to choose tasks that minimize the negative affective result of possible failure. However, the self-handicapping formulation provides important extensions of Atkinson's hypothesis. Specifically, it shows that the process of avoiding self-information can be productively viewed from a social psychological perspective. For example, individuals may involve themselves in numerous social or other extracurricular activities in order to make it clear to themselves and other that it would be extremely difficult to do well at the task at hand (e.g., grades in school; performance on exams), since so little time is available to prepare. In addition, the self-handicapping hypothesis points to a particular set of antecedent conditions that might lead to such avoidance responses in individuals experiencing success—i.e., when those successes are perceived to be undeserved.

In sum, there are at least two reasons why even highly successful individuals may exhibit signs of learned helplessness; and as with the case for the experience of failure, an attributional analysis appears helpful in understanding these processes. The first is best represented by the case of the gifted child who ascribes outcomes to high ability and fails to learn an effort-outcome relationship. The second type seems best described in terms of attributions of success to luck or similar external or unstable factors, resulting in a fear that one's level of competence may not actually be commensurate with the outcomes received. With regard to special education, this interpretation raises questions about the practice of giving special favors or benefits to handicapped individuals, without consideration that this may at times result in a kind of debilitating self-perception.

Approaches for Modifying Attributional Tendencies

The preceding section suggests that under some conditions, the perception that one's outcomes are independent of one's responses may lead to the cessation of achievement striving, especially after failures. In some cases, of course, this self-perception is realistic; ceasing to strive for an unreachable goal is an adaptive response. In other cases, however, a negative self-perception may be reached prematurely or may be overgeneralized across situations. Major questions of importance to special educators include: Is it possible to change such attributional tendencies once they are formed? Do such changes affect subsequent achievement strivings? Several studies have provided affirmative answers to both questions.

One approach has been to preselect children who show particularly maladaptive attributional patterns of behavioral responses to failure. For example, Dweck (1975) provided attributional retraining to a highly selected group of "helpless" children—those identified as having low expectations of success and unable to cope with failure. The attribution retraining consisted of giving the children a series of problem-solving trials daily over 25 days, in which the success-to-failure ratio was 4:1. After each failure, the experimenter explicitly ascribed the outcome to lack of effort. As predicted, by the end of this training period, the children responded positively to failure information both in terms of their attributional and behavioral responses. In contrast, a control group who received training consisting of 100 per cent success showed no improvement in reactions to failure. Dweck's findings suggest that modifying the instructional environment in terms of matching ability levels may not be sufficient to affect achievement orientation, but rather that it is necessary to provide alternative ways of interpreting achievement outcomes. Similar findings have been reported in other field studies oriented toward inducing effort attributions in children who show debilitating effects of failure (Andrews & Debus, 1978; Weiner, 1977).

A second approach has been to provide a false external basis for attributing the causes of failure (Weiner & Sierad, 1975). This "misattribution" approach is based on several previous studies, not related to achievement, which manipulate the apparent source of an arousal state or overt behavior. For example, subjects have been shown to tolerate higher levels of shock when they mistakenly attribute their arousal to a pill instead of to their fear (Nisbett & Schachter, 1966). Weiner & Sierad demonstrated that a similar effect on achievement strivings can be obtained by inducing subjects to attribute their failure at a task to a pill (actually a placebo) that presumably interferes with hand-eye coordination. Specifically, subjects scoring low on a measure of need for achievement performed better at a digit-symbol substitution task when they had taken a pill than low-achieving subjects who had not taken the pill and, thus, had no basis for an external attribution. Presumably, this effect was obtained because the inhibiting negative affective consequences of failure were lessened by the external attribution to the pill. In contrast, high achievers performed better in the control than in the pill condition because the control high-achieving subjects would attribute failure to effort and therefore try harder, while in the pill condition effort was irrelevant to success.

A third approach to modifying attributional tendencies has been large-scale field projects incorporating several special instructional features hypothesized to be related to perception of personal competence or to achievement striving more generally. We will only exemplify their approach by describing one such program—that of de Charms (1972,1976)—which is heavily based on an attributional perspective. There exist, however, numerous experimental programs which have shown positive effects on motivation and achievement (see, for example, Alschuler et al., 1970; Bloom, 1976; Glaser, 1976; Torshen, 1977). However, since such programs are typically broad in scope, they are difficult to evaluate in terms of specific motivational changes.

De Charms (1972, 1976) argues for a motivation training program which is described in terms of a four-year longitudinal project with children beginning in the fifth grade. Although the training is multifaceted, its primary focus is on developing feelings of personal control—i.e., in his terms, changing pawns into origins. The project attempts to apply laboratory findings regarding the origin-pawn distinction (deCharms, 1976) to teacher and student training in the classroom. Specifically, processes such as initiating activities, setting goals, understanding own motives and limitations were induced or taught to teachers at the beginning of the project and to students in the sixth and seventh grades. Fifth- and eighth-grade pupils provided pretest baseline and follow-up change results on some criterion measures.

The effects of the training program on various measures of achievement and motivation were assessed by comparing scores of students in experimental classrooms with students in control classrooms; the latter pupils were in the same school district but received no training. The findings from the study were mixed. Several motivation measures (e.g., achievement themes in stories) showed no differences or only small, selected differences. However, the results did suggest that the trained children learned to respond more like origins, and that these children did better than control children on the achievement tests. In addition, trained students had better attendance records and better grades in some areas. Thus, the program was quite successful given the enormous difficulties inherent in this kind of large-scale field project, and relative to findings of most compensatory education projects.

A major difficulty with de Charms's study is identifying the specific features of the program that produced the changes. De Charms acknowledges the possibility that general enthusiasm generated by being part of a special program (Hawthorne effect) may in part account for the findings. In order to examine mediating variables more specifically, de Charms provided additional analyses which compared initially low origin children who changed in a positive direction as a function of training ("changers") with those who did not ("resistors"). This analysis indicated that the changers did better on the achievement tests (at the sixth-grade level only) than did the resistors. Thus, according to de Charms, "These data seem to establish the Origin concept as a mediator between the personal causation training and increased academic achievement" (1976, p. 157). Unfortunately, it is still difficult to specify which of the numerous aspects of the training program led to changes in the origin dimension. It still seems possible, for example, that any kind of special attention to achievement may induce students to think of themselves more as "origins," as opposed to the effects being specific to the origin training part of the program. Nevertheless, the results do reinforce and provide suggestive empirical evidence for the conclusion in Section I concerning the centrality of self-perceptions of personal competence and control in achievement orientation.

EXPECTATIONS OF SUCCESS

Expectations concerning success/failure outcomes in achievement situations have been identified as a major theoretical variable for predicting achievement orientation (Section I), and have received considerable empirical attention. A brief and overgeneralized characterization of this literature suggests two primary conclusions. First, a history of previous success and failure has been shown to predict future expectations for success and failure, respectively (Frieze & Weiner, 1971). For example, on a novel task, subjects receiving failure feedback on a series of trials are more likely to have low expectations for subsequent success at that task than subjects receiving success feedback (e.g., Diggory, 1966; Parsons & Ruble, 1977). Second, expectations of success and failure have been related to various indices of performance. Such effects are shown in experimental studies by manipulating previous success or failure (e.g., Feather, 1966, 1968; Latta, 1976), or by providing false expectations (e.g., Zanna et al., 1975), and in correlational studies by demonstrating relationships with previous outcomes in naturalistic settings (e.g., Battle, 1966; Crandall & McGhee, 1968), or through ratings of expectancy of success (Kier et al., 1977). On the whole, this literature suggests that people's achievement outcomes may be partially determined by their expectations, as a kind of self-fulfilling prophecy. (See Archibald, 1974, and Crandall, 1969, for reviews of these effects and why they might occur.)

Despite the appeal of the argument, there are some important limitations or qualifications to any simple relationship between expectations and motivational variables, e.g., that higher expectancies lead to better performance. First, attributional processes underlying expectancy relationships appear to modify the effects

(Weiner, 1974). For example, after receiving failure feedback, subjects' expectancies have been found to be lower when they attributed the outcome to low ability or to a hard task (stable factors) as opposed to attributions to a lack of effort or bad luck (Weiner, Heckhausen, Meyer, & Cook, 1972). Such attributional differences and their concomitant effects on achievement-related expectancies could result either from situational variations or from individual differences in perceptions of competence. This, of course, suggests the need for a more systematic investigation of the differential effects of situationally based expectations versus more stable differences in expectancies—e.g., self-confidence. The literature on sex differences in achievement expectancies provides some interesting examples of the action of the two processes together, in that females tend to report lower average expectations for success than do males. This individual difference has been shown to relate to situationally based outcome information in several ways. For example, females are more likely than males to attribute their successes to luck and their failures to lack of ability (Frieze et al., 1978). In addition, the performance of females appears to be more negatively affected by failure than is that of males (Nicholls, 1975; Parsons & Ruble, 1977). These examples suggest that a more general feeling of self-confidence allows individuals to withstand the otherwise negative influences of situationally based lowered expectancies and to benefit from such temporarily raised expectancies.

A second qualification concerns the relationship between personal standards and performance expectancies. As noted in Section I, Crandall (1978) has suggested that the effects of specific performance expectations depend on individuals' minimal standards for success, such that the same absolute level of performance expectation (e.g., six out of ten puzzles correct) may be positive for one individual but negative for another.

A final qualification to the expectancy literature is that the self-fulfilling prophecy hypothesis implies that motivation increases in direct proportion to expectancies, while expectancy-value theories of motivation tend to assume a more curvilinear relationship, such that when expectations become very high, motivation decreases. It is possible that most studies examining the effects of modifying expectancies involve tasks that are relatively difficult to begin with, such that a lack of challenge problem never arises. In addition, as Wilkins (1977) suggests, the strength of the self-fulfilling prophecy effect may be overrated, in that some studies actually show better performance by subjects receiving low expectations. While it is not within the scope of this review to provide a resolution of such inconsistencies, it is clear that attribution, personal standards, and task challenge variables must be incorporated into the analysis of motivational effects of expectations for success.

Low Expectations of Success by Retarded Children

A number of investigators have suggested that a low expectation of success is a particularly important motivational factor characterizing at least some groups of exceptional children, particularly retarded children. For example, according to

Turnure & Zigler (1974), retarded children must frequently encounter problems appropriate to chronological but not mental age. Thus, they develop a pattern of frequent failure which presumably results in low expectations of success. Similarly, some research has shown that retarded children have more problems in heterogeneous groupings than in special classrooms, presumably because of lower expectations of success (Gruen et al., 1975; Schwarz & Jens, 1969).

Do retarded children have lower performance expectancies than normal children? Results of previous research, focusing specifically on verbal expectancies, have been mixed. In general, expectancies in the form of verbal predictions or betting behavior obtained from retarded subjects are quite positive, predicting good performance, and do *not* differ from normal subjects (Cromwell, 1963; MacMillan, 1975; Schuster & Gruen, 1971).

Other lines of research, however, suggest that retarded children behave *as if* they have lower expectancies. Several different kinds of task-related behaviors have been associated with subjective expectancies or with manipulations of success and failure in both normal and retarded children. One category of such behaviors is an outerdirected versus innerdirected approach to tasks, in which outerdirectedness refers to a style of problem solving which is characterized by an overreliance on external cues rather than utilizing one's own cognitive resources (Yando & Zigler, 1971). This external orientation presumably represents an attempt to cope with perceptions of low probabilities of success. Several studies support the hypothesis that low expectations of success result in outerdirectedness. For example, both normal and retarded children showed more imitative responses following failure experiences than following success experiences (Turnure & Zigler, 1964). Similarily, normal kindergarten children through third-graders glanced away from a task more when it was described as very difficult than when it was described as very easy, even when there was no actual difference in difficulty level (Ruble & Nakamura, 1973). Furthermore, in this study, independent ratings of teachers suggested that the outerdirected children at all four levels were perceived as having lower expectations for success than the children who were task-oriented during the experimental task.

Related research in social psychological literature also supports the proposed failure expectancy-outerdirectedness relationship. Numerous studies have confirmed a negative relationship between self-esteem and influenceability, especially when the influence situation is quite simple, as in an Asch-type conformity situation as opposed to more subtle influence attempts (see McGuire, 1969; Walters & Parke, 1964, for reviews of relevant studies). The self-esteem findings become even more relevant to the failure expectancy hypothesis when it is realized that often self-esteem is defined in terms of a success/failure manipulation (e.g., Gollob & Dittes, 1965).

Consistent with the hypothesis that retarded children have relatively low expectations of success compared to normal children of the same mental age, retardates are consistently found to be more outerdirected, regardless of which measure is used. They are more imitative (Turnure & Zigler, 1964; Yando &

Zigler, 1971), rely more on external cues (Achenbach & Zigler, 1968; Sanders, Zigler, & Butterfield, 1968; Turnure & Zigler), and glance away from a task more than normals (Turnure & Zigler).

Another type of evidence related to the incidence of failure hypothesis is that noninstitutionalized retarded children were found to be more outerdirected than institutionalized retardates. For example, Green & Zigler (1962) found that a higher percentage of noninstitutionalized than institutionalized retardates terminated their performance on a game following a suggestion from an adult experimenter. Similarly, noninstitutionalized retardates were more dependent on specific external cues during a discrimination task than were institutionalized retardates (Achenbach & Zigler, 1968; Yando & Zigler, 1971), although the latter authors found this effect for organic retardates only. The explanation for these findings may be that institutionalized retardates live in an environment better adapted to their intellectual capacities. The noninstitutionalized retardate must continue to face all the complexities of the real world and is, thus, more likely to meet frustration and failure.

Finally, one other line of research supports the idea that retarded children tend to expect failure. Retarded children were found to be more self-blaming than normal children in interpreting task interruption. This effect occurred regardless of whether the experimenter described interruption as indicating success, failure, or as neutral (MacMillan & Keogh, 1971a, 1971b). This self-blaming tendency was attributed to the retardates' history of failure in problem-solving situations. That is, the retardates interpret interruption as a failure because they expect to fail. An additional indication that self-blame was related to history of failure rather than to mental or chronological age per se was given by a study with educationally handicapped children, who are characterized by a history of failure but who have an IQ similar to normal children. As expected, the older educationally handicapped children were similar to retardates in perception of interruption—they were overwhelmingly self-blaming (Keogh, Cahill, & MacMillan, 1972).

Thus, circumstantial evidence suggests that, on the average, at least some groups of exceptional children are more expecting of failure than are normal children. Theoretically, these lower expectations should result in a self-fulfilling prophecy of underachievement. Furthermore, there is considerable evidence that the task approach behaviors presumably reflecting these expectancies represent strategies that are likely to result in poor performance in a traditional classroom. For example, only when external relevant cues are available are outerdirected children likely to perform well (Ruble, 1975).

TEACHER EXPECTANCY

The preceding discussion focused on expectations of success as an important factor influencing motivational level and achievement outcome. A second potent factor hypothesized to affect student motivation and performance is "teacher expectancies'' (Bannatyne, 1971; Hamill & Bartel, 1971). Briefly stated, teacher expectancies are assumed to *produce* behavior on the part of students in line with their teachers' expectations (Rosenthal & Jacobson, 1968). Teacher expectancies, elicited by such factors as IQ and labeling of students (Dunn, 1968), are assumed to operate in the following ways (Cooper & Fazio, 1979): (1) expectations affect how a teacher evaluates a student's performance so that the initial expectancy is perpetuated; (2) attributions can be made regarding the cause of a student's performance level (e.g., ability, effort) so that the expectation is held in spite of disconfirming evidence; (3) teachers' expectations can influence their behavior (verbal and nonverbal) toward different students, these behaviors, in turn, affecting the performance of the students for whom these expectations are held. We will present evidence here relevant to each of these mechanisms which demonstrate how teacher expectancies operate to affect student performance. Our emphasis in this section will be on research examining the effect of expectancies of exceptional children, since these children are likely to be frequently subjected to negative expectancies by virtue of their being labeled "handicapped" (Dunn, 1968).

Evaluation of Performance as a Function of Labeling

Recent research indicates that simply labeling a child as learning-disabled (LD), emotionally disturbed (ED) or as an educable mental retardate (EMR) induces negative expectancies on the part of teachers and distortion of their students' performance levels. Foster & Ysseldyke (1976) have shown that teachers evaluated a child labeled as EMR, LD, ED more negatively than a child labeled as "normal," even though the teachers actually observed the same child on videotape. The same effect was found for elementary schoolteachers who perceived a child labeled as LD as less capable and as exhibiting more personality, attentional, and perceptual problems than the same "normal" child on videotape (Foster, Schmidt, & Sabatino, 1976). Mason, Larimore, & Kifer (1976) report that teachers with three of more years of teaching exhibit less bias than teachers with less experience. Yet, when evaluating a child labeled negatively (e.g., low IQ, negative teacher comments, background), Foster et al. (1976) have reported evaluation bias as a function of labeling a child "handicapped" in teachers who had approximately nine years of teaching experience. Thus, the labels EMR, ED, and LD have been shown to generate negative expectancies in teachers, which influence the evaluation of the personality characteristics and achievement level of the children so labeled, even when there is no actual basis for the negative evaluation.

Attributional Bias as a Function of Labeling

If expectations regarding the performance of another are disconfirmed, do people modify their attitudes toward that individual? That is, when a person assumed to be incapable at a given task performs exceedingly well, do people change their opinion about the person's capability or generate other hypotheses to account for the evidence at hand? The evidence suggests that people use differential attributions to account for the unexpected competent performance of persons for whom low expectations are held (Regan, Strauss, & Fazio, 1974). For example, in one study, failure at a task was more frequently attributed to ability level when a child was believed to be "retarded" than when the subjects thought the child was "normal." Similarly, subjects used ability attributions to explain the successful performance of "normal" children but not of retarded children. Further, success had a positive effect on subjects' expectations of future success for the "normal" child; a similar expectancy of success was not evidenced for the child labeled as retarded, even though the labeled and nonlabeled children exhibited the exact same level of performance (Severance & Gasstrom, 1977). The latter finding conflicts with the findings of Yoshida & Meyers (1975), however, who used experienced special education and regular classroom teachers rather than college students as subjects.

An important generalization from these empirical data is that attributions for the success and failure of another can explain away a performance level that could otherwise disconfirm one's initial expectancies. Attributional bias can enter into the judgment of personality characteristics as well. Hayden & Mischel (1976) demonstrated that an aggressive act was attributed internally if the person had been labeled as aggressive at the outset but was attributed to situational factors if no label had been provided. Other research has shown that when a child labeled as retarded behaves aggressively he or she is more apt to be perceived negatively by nonretarded peers than is a nonlabeled child behaving in an identical manner (Gottlieb, 1975). The label mental retardation, with its connotation of social deviancy, appears to be comparable to labeling a person as aggressive as in the Hayden & Mischel study described above.

The Effect of Expectancies on Teacher Behavior

How are these expectancies communicated to the child to affect performance? Empirical evidence indicates that teachers differ in their verbal and nonverbal *behaviors* toward students due to their perceptions of the students' differential ability levels. Chaikin, Sigler, & Derlega (1974) demonstrated that persons tutoring supposedly "bright" elementary school students were more likely to engage in nonverbal behaviors indicating liking and approval (i.e., smile more, longer eye contact, used more affirmative head nods) than did tutors working with "dull" or control group children. In another study, these investigators found that tutors who were falsely led to believe that some students of elementary school age were intellectually "gifted" while others were "average," praised and called upon their "gifted" students more frequently than upon their average students. Other research has shown similar effects using preschool children (Beez, 1968) and high school students (Rothbart, Dalfen, & Barrett, 1971). These studies provide a clear demonstration of the differential behaviors of teachers toward students as a function of induced expectancies elicited by bogus IQ information.

The Effect of Teacher Behavior on Student Achievement

Differential behavior on the part of teachers would be expected to affect the performance of students. Correlational studies support the proposition that enhanced achievement scores of students relate positively to teacher expectancy and corresponding behavior toward students of differing ability levels. Brophy & Good (1970) provide evidence that teachers discriminate in favor of children for whom they have high rather than low expectations of success by demanding and reinforcing a higher quality of performance from them. Students who were expected to do well were given more praise and less criticism than others who were not expected to perform as well academically. Further, higher average scores on achievement tests were evidenced for the high compared to the low-expectancy groups. Similarly, Rubovits & Maehr (1971) have provided evidence that teachers show greater responsiveness to more capable students and encourage them more than the less capable ones.

Several studies have also shown that simply telling teachers that some students will improve their academic performance over the school year is sufficient to enhance the achievement scores of those children, relative to controls (Rosenthal & Jacobson, 1968; Rosenthal, Baratz, & Hall, 1974; Meichanbaum, Bowers, & Ross, 1969). Other research however, has failed to confirm these findings (e.g., Jose & Cody, 1971; Wilkins & Glork, 1973). Thus, this area of research is still inconclusive and controversial. The original Rosenthal & Jacobson (1968) study has been criticized severely on methodological grounds (Snow, 1969; Thorndike, 1968); yet these critics have not rejected the possibility that teacher bias is a potent variable affecting learning in children. Since children who have had a past history of failure are particularly susceptible to the expectations of high status others (Bridgeman, 1974; Means, 1971), educators of exceptional children in particular need to be aware of the potential negative effects of biases generated from labels which may derive from school reports, IQ scores, former teachers' comments, etc. Guskin (1974) argues that "the label [handicapped] includes a wide range of children—including those who are mislabeled because of instrument inadequacies or language problems." While mislabeling may be an unavoidable part of any categorization process, the well-documented detrimental effects of labeling do not appear to be an inevitable result of the process.

EXTRINSIC INCENTIVES

As noted in Section I, a basic component of models of achievement orientation relates to incentives. Atkinson & Raynor (1974) have proposed that the tendency to undertake an achievement-oriented activity in a given situation should increase when "extrinsic incentives" such as social approval, monetary compensation, intrinsic interest, or other incentives are present. Such incentives may enhance a student's willingness to undertake an achievement-related task at a given point in time. Of critical concern, however, is the question of the effect of such extrinsic incentives on a student's continued willingness to undertake the activity when the incentive is not longer available. We will present research here which has addressed this question and will attempt to delineate the conditions under which extrinsic incentives have been shown to have an important bearing on both motivation and performance.

The Effect of Positive Incentives on Intrinsic Motivation

Studies examining the effect of reward on intrinsic motivation (i.e., interest in a task for its own sake) are of particular concern to educators. On an intuitive basis, it seems likely that intrinsic interest in an activity often determines the amount of time a child spends in discussion, reading, and projects related to that activity, both inside and outside the classroom. In the first study examining the effect of positive incentives on children's intrinsic interest in a task, Lepper, Greene, & Nisbett (1973) hypothesized that subsequent interest in an activity would be undermined when a child was offered an extrinsic incentive to engage in the task. To test this hypothesis, Lepper et al. introduced a drawing activity into a nursery school classroom where children had access to the target materials during their "free play" period. After having established a baseline level of interest in the activity, children who demonstrated a high level of interest in the activity were assigned to one of three groups. Children in the expected award condition were told that they would receive a reward (a "good player" award with a red ribbon) if they merely agreed to play with the drawing material. Children in a second unexpected award group did not anticipate a reward but received a reward unexpectedly after completing the activity. Finally, a control group who neither anticipated nor received a reward was included for comparison purposes. The critical measure of intrinsic interest was the amount of time children played with the target activity relative to alternative attractive toys when the drawing material was reintroduced into the classroom *two* weeks after the experimental session. The results indicated that, as expected, children who had engaged in the task to receive the reward (the expected reward group) showed a significant decrease in interest in the activity from baseline to post-experimental observations. Children assigned to the nonreward and unexpected reward groups did not differ significantly from each other. Thus, the reward by itself was shown to be a nonsignificant factor in undermining interest in a task, since children in the group who did *not* expect but who, in fact, received a reward did not show less interest in the activity than nonrewarded subjects. Interest level was undermined by the reward only for subjects who contracted to engage in the task in order to receive the reward.

Why should intrinsic interest be undermined when one agrees to perform a task for an extrinsic incentive? From an attributional perspective, people infer their internal states (e.g., feelings, motives) by observing their behavior and the context in which it occurs. They then attribute their degree of interest either to intrinsic or extrinsic motivation on the basis of cues in the environment, such as the contingencies apparent when the behavior occurs. It is assumed that people will perceive their behavior as intrinsically motivated when there are no extrinsic rewards expected for performing the behavior. Conversely, when extrinsic rewards are anticipated for performing a task, people will discount intrinsic interest as the sole reason for having performed the task (Bem, 1972; Kelley, 1972). Performing the task is perceived as a means to an end; namely, the reward. Given the absence of cues signifying extrinsically motivated behavior, one is apt to view the task as an end in itself rather than a means to an end.

The undermining effect of extrinsic incentives on continued interest in a task has been documented by an extensive body of additional research. This effect has been demonstrated using a wide variety of incentives, including money (Calder & Staw, 1975; Deci, 1971; 1972; Kruglanski, Ritter, Amitai et al., 1975), symbolic rewards (Greene & Lepper, 1974; Lepper et al., 1973), prizes (Kruglanski, Alon & Lewis, 1972; Ross, 1975), food (Ross, 1975, 1976), and special activities (Kruglanski et al., 1971; Lepper & Greene, 1975). This effect has also been demonstrated with a wide variety of ages, from preschoolers through adults beyond college age.

Taken as a whole, there is considerable evidence that anticipated positive incentives lower subsequent interest in an otherwise highly interesting task. This finding is of particular concern to educators, since diminished interest in pursuing school subjects, both inside and outside of the classroom, would appear to be detrimental to long-range achievement. The findings are particularly important given the heavy commitment of many special educators to reinforcement programs.

Effect of Highly Salient Rewards

It has been shown that a person's interest in an activity is undermined because he or she perceived the reward as the dominant reason for engaging in an activity. Thus, it could be argued that a highly salient reward should increase the person's perception of the reward as the factor controlling the behavior (Deci, 1975) and should provide compelling evidence that the behavior is extrinsically motivated. Research addressing this issue suggests that salience of reward is a highly important variable affecting later interest. For example, Ross (1975) manipulated salience of reward by placing a surprise reward under a box in front of children (high salience), or by hiding the reward (low salience). A third group of children engaged in the same task as the other two and neither expected nor received a reward. The undermining effect of reward was observed for the salient-reward children only. Further, boys in the salient reward condition showed significantly less interest in the target activity relative to boys in the nonrewarded or nonsalient conditions *four* weeks after the initial session.

Level of Interest and Positive Incentives

The above studies have shown that continued interest in an activity decreases when a subject anticipates and receives a reward for engaging in an interesting task. Of particular note is the effect of rewards on interest level when the task is a boring, monotonous one or when the task is not perceived as interesting to a given subject. The few studies examining the effect of rewards on both interesting and uninteresting tasks suggest that rewards do not have the same effect on tasks varying in interest level. For example, research using attitudinal measures of interest demonstrated the expected undermining of later interest when reward was offered for engaging in an interesting task, but showed that reward actually increased interest when the task was boring (Calder & Staw, 1975). Comparable results were found in an experiment using a behavioral measure of interest and special education students as subjects (Lee, Syrnyk, & Hallschmid, 1976).

The evidence that rewards may enhance intrinsic motivation to engage in a task otherwise considered uninteresting is of particular interest to educators who often find children unwilling to persist in doing a boring or repetitious task. However, the results of only one or two studies should be interpreted on a cautionary note. Furthermore, not all children in a given classroom may find an activity uninteresting. Thus reliance on overly sufficient rewards requires careful monitoring in any classroom.

Effect of Negative Incentives on Intrinsic Interest

Tests and monitoring of children's performance are techniques that are often used in the classroom to increase a child's motivation to learn. While negative incentives may facilitate performance, it is important to consider the effect of such incentives on a child's interest in further pursuing the given subject matter tested.

Researchers investigating the effect of different negative incentives on subsequent interest have found that negative incentives do not affect either performance or continued interest in the manner intended by educators. For example, Maehr & Stallings (1972) conducted two investigations of the effect of a test context on performance and motivation. Subjects were told either that the experimental task was a "test" of the child's ability and would be shown to teachers, or that the task was not an evaluational tool and that the child's teachers would not have access to the child's score. In addition, children were given a booklet containing either difficult or easy discrimination items. The results indicated that the children who had completed the booklet in the test context showed continued interest for easier items. Conversely, children who had performed the task under the nonevaluative context indicated their preference for completing the more difficult task on a subsequent occasion. There was also a slight but nonsignificant tendency for children in the evaluation condition to show higher level of performance. Other research using nursery school children suggests that the very knowlege that performance is being evaluated by an adult is sufficient to produce a decrement in subsequent intrinsic interest, but does not necessarily influence the performance (Lepper & Greene, 1975). A conceptually similar study by Smith (1974) with adults also demonstrated the negative effect of evaluation. There is also evidence demonstrating that imposing a deadline for completion of a task undermines later interest without affecting performance quality (Amabile, De Jong, & Lepper, 1976). In this study, change in interest was evidenced in both unobtrusive behavioral and attitudinal measures.

It seems a reasonable generalization that negative as well as positive incentives appear to lower intrinsic interest, while not significantly affecting performance. Since the studies examining the effect of *negative* incentives on continued interest have all used tasks which pretesting had found to be highly interesting for the given populations, one can only speculate whether the same effect would hold for tasks of low interest. Clearly, more research is needed to clarify under what conditions evaluation may hinder or enhance intrinsic interest as well as performance.

Effect of Extrinsic Incentives Signifying Competence

The evidence cited here raises serious questions about the use of extrinsic incentives to motivate special education students. Many educators, upon considering this body of data, may feel that under certain conditions, such incentives will not produce a decrement in interest. For example, a child who wins an award for an excellent project may enthusiastically begin working on similar projects, even when awards are no longer offered for doing so. Empirical research addressing the issue of the effect of rewards signifying *competence* on intrinsic interest have, in fact, indicated that there are several boundary conditions under which rewards are not detrimental to continued interest (Arkes, 1978; Lepper & Greene, 1978).

A number of investigators using a social reward paradigm have demonstrated that task-related praise averts the undermining of later interest (e.g., Deci, 1971; Swann & Pittmann, 1977). The sustaining effect of social reward on intrinsic interest is assumed to result from feedback regarding competence from which feelings of efficacy can be derived. But is this effect limited only to information provided through *verbal* feedback? Recent evidence suggests that making receipt of a tangible reward contingent on successfully meeting a given standard of performance also mitigates the typically produced "hidden costs" of rewards (Karniol & Ross, 1977). The concept of competence can, then, account for the second condition under which rewards do not decrease subsequent interest. Additional relevant research, however, suggests that the type of information regarding competence conveyed through rewards which will effectively sustain intrinsic interest depends on the developmental level of the child (Boggiano & Ruble, 1979). Developmental changes in children's concepts of competence will be discussed in greater detail in Section III.

Effect of Extrinsic Incentives on Performance

While positive incentives may adversely affect intrinsic interest in otherwise enjoyable tasks, what is their effect on academic performance? Levine & Fasnacht (1974) have argued that token economies lead to "token" learning. Studies examining the effect of rewards on performance when the incentive is not made contingent on performance quality have, in fact, shown "token learning" to have negative effects on noncontingently rewarded subjects. Noncontingently rewarded subjects have shown inferior performance in discrimination learning tasks (Masters & Mokros, 1973), a lower quality of drawing (Lepper et al., 1973), and have demonstrated less creativity in writing (Kruglanski et al., 1971) than their nonrewarded counterparts. Noncontingent rewards are also more detrimental to performance level than contingent rewards (Terrell, Durkin & Wiesley, 1959; Holcomb, 1969).

But is a reward made contingent on performance level more beneficial to learning than no reward at all? Evidence examining this question is far from conclusive. A number of studies suggest that subjects whose "reward" is accuracy feedback (either through a verbal or symbolic medium) perform better than others who expect to receive a material reward. This has been demonstrated based on performance level in discrimination learning tasks (Marshall, 1969; Miller & Estes, 1961) and in probability learning tasks (McGraw & McCullers, 1974). Other research, on the other hand, suggests that performance contingent rewards facilitate performance on spelling tests (Berowitz & Busse, 1970; 1975), programmed mathematical materials (McMillan, 1973) and probability learning tasks (Brackbill, Kappy, & Starr, 1962; Offenbach, 1964), when performance of contingently rewarded subjects is compared with nonrewarded controls.

We can only speculate as to the reasons for these discrepant results. For tasks that require rote memorization or are simple drill activities, or are uninteresting to a given child, rewards based on performance accuracy may enhance motivation and subsequent learning. Other activities necessitating more complex problem-solving skills or creative abilities may be adversely affected by extrinsic factors (Koch, 1956). Atkinson (1977) has postulated that "overmotivation," resulting from the desire to procure the positive incentive made contingent on performance level, may be detrimental to performance efficiency in complex tasks. Further work is clearly needed to specify the conditions under which rewards facilitate academic achievement in tasks of varying complexity.

The conditions under which rewards enhance or are inimical to intrinsic motivation and performance require specification. (*Editor's Note:* See the chapter by Faust & Faust in this volume.) A major task for education and psychology researchers is to understand how we can instill in children the intrinsic motivation to learn and think about a topic area, while at the same time maximizing their academic achievement in that area. How can work be converted into productive play (Maehr, 1976)?

TEST ANXIETY

Anxiety is assumed to be an important determinant of achievement behavior in Atkinson's theory (see Section I). Because of the extensive amount of research devoted to the relationship between anxiety and achievement, we will treat this topic separately here rather than include the conclusions from these studies in the theoretical section. Since performance in testing situations is of primary concern to educators, we will emphasize in this section the relationship between individual differences in test anxiety and level of achievement in evaluative and nonevaluative settings. We will also consider the potential mediating factors accounting for these differences.

Test Anxiety and Performance

Test anxiety is not meant necessarily to imply a high overall general anxiety level which has been measured by instruments such as the Taylor Manifest Anxiety Scale (Taylor, 1953). While test anxiety may relate in some extent to general anxiety level, correlations between measures of general anxiety level and performance in a testing setting are weak and not significantly related to level of performance (Sarason, 1960, 1961). Our focus, then, will be research using scales which have been constructed specifically to examine the effect of anxiety on performance: the Test Anxiety Questionnaire (TAQ) (Mandler & Sarason, 1952), Test Anxiety Scale (TAS) (Sarason, 1958), or Test Anxiety Scale for Children (TASC) (Sarason, Davidson, Lighthall, Waite, & Ruebush, 1960). Other useful scales constructed for similar purposes which provide evidence generally consistent with that obtained using the scales devised by Sarason include Alpert & Haber's (1960) Achievement Anxiety Test (AAT) and Liebert and Morris's (1967) analysis of test anxiety into the components of worry (W) and emotionality (E).

The test anxiety scales devised by Sarason and his colleagues were constructed to measure the recalled intensity of negative affect of behaviors experienced immediately before and during testing situations and in other evaluative contexts. Research examining the relationship between test anxiety (as measured through the TAS, TAQ, or TASC) and academic performance indicates that highly test-anxious students typically perform worse than low test-anxious students in evaluative testing conditions, particularly when the task involved is a complex problem-solving task. For example, Sarason & Paola (1960) reported that highly test-anxious undergraduates performed at a higher level than low test-anxious students on a relatively *easy* task, regardless of whether the instructions stressed the importance of the task as an evaluative tool (i.e., reflecting IQ and predicted subsequent course grades). They also performed better than low test anxious students on a difficult task in a non-evaluative context, but performed worse than low anxious students given both the highly evaluative setting and difficult task.

Conceptually similar studies demonstrating the same effect have been reported by Sarason (1958, 1972).

More recent research investigating the effects of test anxiety on elementary school children using the Test Anxiety Scale for Children (TASC) has shown similar findings in elementary school children. For example, highly test-anxious children performed worse and more slowly than low anxious others when the task was a difficult one and completion of individual math problems was interrupted intermittently throughout the testing session. The highly anxious children's quality and rate of performance was comparable to that of low anxious children, however, when the task was administered without interruption or time constraints, and included problems that were easier (Hill & Eaton, 1977). It should be noted, however, that the correlation between test anxiety and test performance is close to zero during the early school years, gradually increasing up to the fifth- or sixth-grade levels (Hill & Sarason, 1966).

The differential level of performance of students exhibiting different levels of test anxiety in evaluative and nonevaluative settings may be interpreted as providing evidence that maximal performance results from an intermediate or moderate level of anxiety. That is, performance in low anxious students is enhanced when an evaluative context increases their anxiety level to an intermediate level. Highly test-anxious students whose anxiety level is assumed to be close to this intermediate level, on the other hand, show marked performance decrements when confronted with a difficult task in a highly evaluative testing situation, since this combination of factors presumably further increases their anxiety above the optimal intermediate level. Maximal efficiency of performance, then, may occur at an intermediate level of anxiety (Yerkes & Dodson, 1908; Eysenck, 1966) or motivational level (Atkinson & Raynor, 1974).[1]

Factors Mediating Test and Performance Level

While it could be argued that low ability is the cause of the high level of test anxiety and impaired performance evidenced in test-anxious students in evaluative settings, Sarason (1960) has argued that test-anxious students do less well than matched low anxious students of like grade, sex, and intelligence. While Sarason (1960) acknowledges that these results are not conclusive, he proposes that this evidence makes less plausible the argument that ability level is necessarily the causative factor in the negative correlation between scores on TASC and performance.

If cognitive-motivational factors rather than ability per se are the important determinants of the test performance of test anxious students, their performance level would be expected to vary as a function of situationally based outcome information. Research demonstrates that the quality of performance of test-anxious students can be modified by altering their perceptions of their expectations of success, or of the complexity of the task. This, of course, suggests a cognitive-motivational interpretation of performance differences.

For example, when students were given bogus information that they were performing poorly relative to others at an *easy* task, the test-anxious students learned the easy task more slowly than did students low in test anxiety. The highly anxious students learned a difficult task more rapidly than the low anxious students, however, when they were falsely led to believe that they were doing well relative to others (Weiner & Schneider, 1971). Similar results were obtained in a study manipulating perceptions of task difficulty level in students with varying levels of test anxiety (Sarason, 1971). Evidence provided by Liebert and Morris is consistent with the cognitive-motivational interpretation of performance differences evidenced in students differing in level of test anxiety. Using a measure of anxiety based on TAQ items, these researchers found that "worry" or cognitive concern about one's performance level was negatively related to test performance and to expectations of success (Liebert & Morris, 1967; Morris & Liebert, 1970). Other research has shown lower expectations of success in highly test-anxious students relative to low anxious others even when differences in preformance level between the groups were negligible (Trapp & Kausler, 1958).

Finally, some recent studies have suggested that the performance differences between low and high test-anxious students result from cognitive-motivational factors such as differences in the attentional foci of these students during task performance (Sarason, 1972; Wine, 1971). Low anxious individuals focus on task relevant variables in an evaluative context, while highly test-anxious persons direct their attention internally i.e., engage in self-deprecatory thoughts, or are concerned with the consequences of failure in an evaluative setting, or engage in excessive off-task behaviors (Nottelman & Hill, 1977). In addition, Sarason and his colleagues have reported that test-anxious students are more likely to describe themselves in more negative, self-devaluing ways than do low anxious others (Sarason & Ganzer, 1962, 1963; Sarason & Koenig, 1965), and are likely to blame themselves for their failures (Doris & Sarason, 1955). In a review of the relevant literature, Wine (1971) cites evidence suggesting that highly anxious students are particularly susceptible to focus on self-deprecatory thoughts which interfere with efficiency of performance when confronted with the pressures of the highly evaluative setting (Ganzer, 1968; Mandler & Watson, 1966; Marlett & Watson, 1968; Neale & Katahn, 1968; Stanford, Dember, & Stanford, 1963). The link between anxiety and attentional functions is a particularly interesting one given the frequency with which "attentional" distractions are reported as characteristic of exceptional children. (*Editor's Note:* See the chapters by Hallahan and Reeve and Krupski, in this volume.)

Approaches to Modifying the Negative Effects of Test Anxiety

This body of research suggests that situational factors such as the perceived complexity of a test, the setting in which a test is taken (evaluative versus nonevaluative), and imposed time limits affect the performance of students differing in anxiety level. Based on such research, Hill (1977) proposes modifying test instructions to minimize the adverse effects of the "test-like" character of school tasks on test-anxious children's school performance (e.g., let the child know that the problems are difficult and mistakes are to be expected). In addition, he argues that grading procedures such as the traditional letter-grade report card, which may induce excessive competition, should be substituted by individual progress reports which would reduce concern over the potential consequences of failure, thereby enhancing attention to relevant task variables during testing sessions. The removal of time pressure during testing sessions is an additional technique suggested by Hill to attenuate the interfering and debilitating effects of anxiety on test performance.

Modifying various aspects of the testing situation in the classroom to maximize test performance in highly anxious students, however, may inadvertently negatively affect the performance of low anxious children who generally perform more efficiently in an evaluative setting or under time pressure. Alternative techniques proposed to modify test-anxious students' responses to the testing situation rather than alter the situation itself have, thus, been proposed. These include attention-retraining programs (Wine, 1971), systematic desensitization (Wolpe, 1958), and attributional retraining programs concerned with stressing the importance of effort-outcome covariation (Hill, 1977). Since test-anxious children have been found to have lower expectations of success than low anxious children, and causal attributions presumably underlie such expectancies which are related to performance outcome (see Section I), attributional retraining programs may be a particularly effective means of changing test anxious children's perception of and response to the testing situation.

III. A DEVELOPMENTAL PERSPECTIVE ON ACHIEVEMENT MOTIVATION

In this review to this point we have adopted a generalistic perspective regarding achievement striving—essentially implying that a particular set of principles is operative from the moment a child begins achievement-related activities. Indirectly in support of this assumption are arguments concerning a mastery or effective motive that characterizes a child's approach to achievement from infancy onward (e.g., Harter, 1975; 1978; White, 1959). At the same time, however, there are various reasons to suspect that the nature of achievement striving may change substantially across the course of childhood, and that these changes may have important implications for subsequent achievement-related behaviors.

There are numerous indications of important developmental shifts in aspects of achievement motivation. For example, studies examining task preferences consistently find that children younger than six–seven years prefer easy tasks (e.g., Halperin, 1977; Veroff, 1969). As a second example, there are several reports of age-related decreases in positive evaluations of the self, such as self-perceptions of ability and expectations for success (Heckhausen, 1967; Nicholls,

1978; Parsons & Ruble, 1977; Ruble, Parsons, & Ross, 1976). Although such trends may represent, in part, response biases associated with age differences, they can also be interpreted in terms of more significant developmental changes.

What might account for such developmental changes? On the one hand, a series of age-related structural cognitive changes or information-processing shifts are probably involved. For example, Piaget suggests that it is not until the stage of concrete operations (after about seven years of age) that children de-center and can integrate information in making judgments. In addition, there is clear evidence of major developmental changes in children's attention and memory processes (cf. Flavell, 1977). (*Editor's Note:* See the chapters by Faust and Faust; Torgesen and Kail; and Krupski, this volume.) Another possible source of developmental differences in achievement motivation is social-experiential in nature. Children probably become more familiar with making evaluative judgments, with success and failure outcomes, and with comparing their performance with others, once they enter school. Thus, major changes in the meaning and use of achievement-related information in the early grades of school would be expected.

Until very recently, the study of the development of achievement motivation implied a focus on socialization factors, such as parental characteristics or child-rearing practices related to individual differences in achievement striving and behavior. Since this approach has been reviewed extensively elsewhere (e.g., Crandall, 1967; Smith, 1969), in this chapter we will discuss a cognitive-developmental perspective which focuses on age-related changes that are more universal rather than being oriented toward individual differences.

Investigators are just beginning to examine the specific impact of such global cognitive and social developmental changes on variables related to achievement motivation, and thus it is not possible to provide conclusions or generalizations. Instead, we will present a possible framework for describing the specific developmental changes most likely to affect children's achievement-related evaluation and behaviors. Two categories of shifts will be analyzed: (1) changes in children's concepts of the central constructs of achievement, and (2) changes in the way the constructs are integrated. (See Ruble, 1978, for a more extensive description of the rationale for this framework and for other types of developmental shifts.)

CHANGES IN CHILDREN'S CONCEPTS OF ACHIEVEMENT

The Concept of Ability

Throughout the literature reviewed so far, inferences concerning ability have emerged as a major determinant of achievement orientation, both in influencing responses to previous outcomes and in goal orientation and expectations for the future. Yet, the concept of ability is complex, involving inferences concerning abstract internal states and perceptions of some degree of stability over time and situation. To what extent do young school-age children think of themselves and others as possessing relatively stable abilities?

A number of studies examining children's perceptions of other people suggest that fairly dramatic changes in this process occur during the early years of school. In general, with increasing age, descriptions of other people become more abstract and complex, involve more inferential concepts, focus less on overt characteristics (e.g., appearance), and tend to indicate perceptions of greater consistency or stability of other people's qualities (Livesley & Bromley, 1973; Peevers & Secord, 1973; Shantz, 1975). Similar trends have also been reported regarding conceptions of the self (Montemayor & Eisen, 1977).

As Shantz (1975) notes, one of the more interesting aspects of these findings is that the developmental changes do not appear to be gradual, but rather show quite radical shifts at a particular age level—sometime between seven and eight years of age. For example, Livesley & Bromley (1973) found that the differences between seven- and eight-year-olds were often greater than differences between eight- and 15-year-olds. These findings suggest that the first two or three years of school may be critical times in the development of children's conceptions of themselves and others, and that research focusing on processes underlying the development of dispositional concepts may find this age group particularly productive.

Some recent research has focused specifically on developmental changes in children's concepts of abilities. For example, Nicholls (1978) has suggested that five- to 13-year-olds' concepts of ability and effort can be described in terms of four developmental levels: at level 1 (five-six-year-olds), effort, ability and outcome are not distinguished from each other; only by level 4 (after age 10-11) is ability used systematically as a capacity which may be clearly differentiated from effort in predicting outcomes. These levels, however, are based on children's conceptions of ability in only a limited sense—i.e., perceptions of the abilities of a pair of children working on math problems in which levels of effort and outcome were varied. Additional analyses in this study revealed that a different aspect of the concept of ability (i.e., recognizing that more difficult tasks require more ability) showed the major developmental shifts between six- and eight-years of age. Clearly, additional work is needed on developmental changes in this very basic aspect of achievement orientation.

The Concept of Success and Failure

Children's standards of success or concepts of attainment appear to shift developmentally in two different, though interrelated ways. The first concerns the perception of control or personal responsibility for outcomes. Several investigators have suggested that an important change occurs in young children's achievement orientation once they become aware of their role in producing goal-oriented outcomes (Bialer, 1961; Crandall et al., 1965; Heckhausen, 1967; Veroff, 1969). For example, according to Bialer (1961), very young children respond to all goal attainment with pleasure and to nonattainments with displeasure, but there is no real evaluation of success and failure because the child does not associate the outcome with his/her own behavior. The exact nature of this shift, the approximate age levels at which it occurs, and its causes have not been made explicit, partly because the concept must be inferred from diverse behaviors. However, these questions deserve systematic empirical attention since the ability to perceive personal causation is central to cognitive theories of achievement motivation; and, in fact, "true" achievement motivation may not develop until this point (Heckhausen, 1967).

Second, standards of success appear to shift developmentally in the extent to which they are based on normative (social comparison) versus absolute standards. According to one theory of developmental changes in achievement (Veroff, 1969), there are two kinds of achievement motivation: (1) autonomous, which is based on *internalized* standards or comparisons of the self with the self, and (2) social, which concerns standards based on *social comparison*. According to the theory, the second type does not develop until the early school years, after "considerable reinforcement, usually from siblings or parents" (Veroff, p. 50). Recent empirical research generally supports these ideas: (1) There seems to be little use made of social comparison information for self-evaluation until at least second grade (e.g., Ruble et al., 1976; Ruble, Boggiano, Feldman, & Loebl, in press); (2) children's appraisals of their class standing, as compared to their teachers' ratings, were found to be dramatically more realistic after age eight (Nicholls, in press); (3) there appears to be an increase in interest in comparing one's performance with others during the early school years (Dinner, 1976; Ruble, Feldman, & Boggiano, 1976); and (4) social comparison information appears to have little impact on behaviors based on judgments of competence until after seven-eight years of age (Boggiano & Rubble, 1979; Spear & Armstrong, 1978).

The Concepts of Challenge

Central to the idea of achievement striving is the concept of challenge—selecting activities that involve some uncertainty about success in order to maximize the affective value of succeeding or to increase self-knowledge concerning competence. Numerous findings have suggested, however, that an orientation toward challenge does not seem to characterize the achievement behavior of preschool or kindergarten-aged children. For example, several studies have indicated that younger children tend to prefer to repeat tasks at which they have experienced previous success, while older children prefer to repeat tasks at which they failed (cf. Van Bergen, 1968). Similarly, young children tend to prefer to work on easy tasks, while older children prefer tasks of moderate or high levels of difficulty (Halperin, 1977; Veroff, 1969). Finally, older children have been found to spend a longer time at insoluble than soluble tasks, while younger children do not seem to differentiate among the tasks (Harter, 1975).

Thus, there appears to be an important change during the early school years in children's orientation toward, or awareness of, the value of challenge in the tasks. Although the specific mental age at which such shifts occur are difficult to designate, given the numerous differences across studies in ages of subjects and tasks used, the major changes seem to appear between the ages of six to nine years (cf. Veroff, 1969). There is, thus, a correspondence in developmental changes among concepts of challenge and the concepts of ability and attainment. This correspondence may indicate that the changes in behavioral response to challenge reflect an increasing awareness of the incentive value of difficult tasks, as the concept of ability and its relationship to outcomes on difficult tasks emerges (Nicholls, 1978).

A few limitations should be noted. First, the developmental differences in children's task preferences may reflect something other than an increased desire for mastery or challenge. In one recent study, for example, no developmental trend was found in the number of children choosing to repeat an interrupted task when the difficulty level of the task was matched to the child's grade level (Young & Egeland, 1976). Thus, previously reported developmental differences using the same task may have been partly due to differential perceptions of the task by children at varying age levels. Second, findings that young children prefer easy tasks or continue to work on a task already solved does not necessarily imply an absence of mastery motivation. Harter (1975, 1978) suggests that the young children's continued interest in an already solved task may reflect a different kind of mastery motivation. That is, the task itself may represent an interesting sensory event that they can control on their own; and, as such, correctness as a goal may be relatively unimportant.

CHANGES IN WAYS OF RELATING THE CONCEPTS

According to cognitive models, achievement striving is related to perceptions of achievement situations, such as the causes of success and failure or the determinants of positive evaluations and rewards. Such perceptions often involve quite complex inferential processes and are thus, not surprisingly, age-related. A few examples of apparent changes in achievement-related information integration and their possible implications will serve to illustrate the importance of this developmental factor in the study of achievement motivation.

Evaluative Judgments of Others

One line of research has examined children's evaluations of others as a function of information about effort, ability, and outcome. Consistent with most findings in the moral judgment literature, the youngest age groups (four-six years) primarily distribute rewards received on the basis of outcome, while the impact of the explicitly volitional variable (in this case, effort) increases with age, at least until about 10-12 years of age (Salili, Maehr, & Gilmore, 1976; Weiner & Peter, 1973). As in moral judgment research the magnitude and timing of the shift may be partly dependent on artifactual aspects of the task, such as a recency effect of the outcome information (e.g., Feldman et al., 1976). Nevertheless, recognizing the importance of effort in the evaluation process is a developmental change of major interest to motivation theorists, and further study of its emergence is clearly needed.

Inferences Concerning an Achievement Outcome or its Possible Causes

A second line of research has been concerned with developmental changes in the perception of the interdependent relationship among effort, ability, difficulty of the task, and outcome. It is reasonably well established that even first-grade children can integrate different elements of achievement information in making judgments and that they have some idea of the compensatory relationships between possible causes of outcomes—e.g., that a child with low ability will have to try harder than a child with high ability to achieve the same outcome (Karabenick & Heller, 1976; Kun, Parsons, & Ruble, 1974; Shaklee, 1976). However, it is also the case that the ability to make finer discriminations and more complex judgments increases with age (Karabenick & Heller, 1976; Nicholls, 1979; Shaklee, 1976). More interesting perhaps is that there also seem to be shifts in the perception of the logic underlying relationships among elements. For example, Kun (1977) presents findings from five-year-olds showing an asymmetry in the judgments of inferring ability from effort information as opposed to inferring effort from ability information. She describes the findings in terms of a "halo schema" for ability inferences and suggests that young children may perceive themselves as competent only if they try very hard, not if they succeed with little effort. Similar finding are reported by Nicholls (1978).

Integrating Sequential Information

A third example of the developmental changes in integrating information about achievement concerns inferences made on the basis of events separated in time. Children's abilities to relate information about a series of success and failure outcomes increase with age both in terms of inferences about the difficulty of the task and the abilty required (Shaklee, 1976), and in terms of changing expectations about their own successes (Parsons & Ruble, 1977). Furthermore, for both types of inferences, consistent significant effects of success/failure outcome information were shown only after the preschool age level.

SUMMARY

In spite of the scarcity of work in this area and the diversity of the issues addressed, a pattern seems to emerge from the converging lines of research described above. Perceptions of the nature of the factors involved in achievement and of achievement striving more generally appear to shift dramatically during the early school years. Indeed, most of the findings suggest the appearance of major changes around the second-grade level. Perhaps the most important point derived from this conclusion is the possible long-term implications of changes occurring at this time. For example, once a more stable self-perception of competence is established, an attributional pattern may develop which results in a kind of self-fulfilling prophecy, as discussed in Section II. That is, for highly competent children, failures would be unexpected and attributed to something unstable, such as effort, leading to increased vigor at future tasks. On the other hand, for children who perceive themselves as incompetent, failures are expected and attributed to something stable, such as ability, making future effort appear futile.

Thus, as children begin to form more stable concepts of their own qualities, the context in which this process takes place and, in turn, the specific conclusions drawn may be of more than immediate significance. The emergence of social comparison standards takes on added importance when viewed from this more long-term perspective. As the use of social comparison feedback increases, most children can no longer see themselves as good at everything, particularly if the feedback received is only in relative terms. Educators may want to consider the possibility of introducing such information more gradually or providing strategies for using it so that the utility of social comparison feedback for realistic assessment is optimized and the negative effects minimized.

FOOTNOTE

*We would like to express our appreciation to Virginia C. Crandall, Irene H. Frieze, Kennedy T. Hill, Edward E. Jones, Martin L. Maehr, John Nicholls, and Bernard Weiner for many helpful suggestions on an earlier draft.

1. While the position taken here regarding performance efficiency and optimal level of motivation appears consistent with the achievement model proposed by Atkinson (1974), the present position differs from Atkinson's in that it is assumed here that high test anxiety adversely affects performance at difficult tasks. Atkinson (1974), on the other hand, proposes that high test anxiety in persons "overmotivated" *increases* the performance level of those students relative to others who are also overmotivated but *less* anxious since, he proposes, anxiety can decrease the absolute level of motivation or arousal (see Atkinson, 1974, 1977). The evidence which Atkinson (1974) provides in support of this argument (excluding studies where need for affiliation may account for the findings) demonstrates that college students high in test anxiety perform better than low test-anxious students in an evaluative setting where an extrinsic incentive was anticipated for superior performance in a simple arithmetic task (Smith, 1966). An alternative and perhaps more parsimonious explanation for these results is that highly test-anxious students perform better than low anxious students in an evaluative context when the task is an easy one (see Sarason & Paola, 1960). As Atkinson (1974) has noted, the argument that high anxiety will paradoxically enhance achievement level in highly motivated persons performing complex or difficult tasks is a hypothesis in search of more definitive evidence.

REFERENCES

Abramson, L.Y. Seligman, M.E.P., & Teasdale, J.D. (1978) "Learned helplessness in humans: Critique and reformulation." *Journal of Abnormal Psychology* 87: 49-74.

Achenbach, J.M., & Zigler, E. (1968) "Cue-learning and problem-learning strategies in normal and retarded children." *Child Development* 39: 827- 848

Alpert, R., & Haber, R.M. (1960) "Anxiety in academic achievement situations." *Journal of Abnormal and Social Psychology* 61: 207-215.

Alschuler, A.S., Tabor, D., & McIntyre, J. (1970) *Teaching achievement motivation.* Middletown, Conn.: Educational Ventures.

Amabile, T.M., DeJong, W., & Lepper, M. (1976) "Effects of externally imposed deadlines on subsequent intrinsic motivation." *Journal of Personality and Social Psychology* 34: 92-98.

Andrews, G.R., & Debus, R.L. (1978) "Persistence and the causal perception of failure: Modifying cognitive attributions." *Journal of Educational Psychology* 70: 154-166.

Archibald, W.P. (1974) "Alternative explanations for self-fulfilling prophecy." *Psychological Bulletin* 81: 74-84.

Arkes, H.R. (1978) "Competence and the maintenance of behavior." *Motivation and Emotion* 2: 201-211.

Atkinson, J.W. (1957) "Motivational determinants of risk-taking behavior." *Psychological Review* 64: 359-372.

——— (1958) *Motives in fantasy, action and society.* Princeton, N.J.: Van Nostrand.

——— (1964) *An introduction to motivation.* Princeton, N.J.: Van Nostrand.

——— (1974) "Strength of motivation and efficiency of performance." In J.W. Atkinson & J.O. Raynor (eds.), *Motivation and achievement.* Washington, D.C.: Winston.

——— (1977) "Determinants of intellective performances that are evaluated." *Educator* 19 (2): 37-43.

———, & Birch, D. (1974) "The dynamics of achievement-oriented activity." In J.W. Atkinson, & J.O. Raynor (eds.), *Motivation and achievement.* Washington, D.C.: Winston.

———, & Cartwright, D. (1964) "Some neglected variables in contemporary conceptions of decision and performance." *Psychological Reports* 14: 575-590.

———, & Feather, N.T. (eds.) (1966) *A theory of achievement motivation.* New York: Wiley.

———, & Raynor, J.O. (eds.) (1974) *Motivation and achievement.* Washington, D.C.: Winston.

Ball, S. (1977) *Motivation in education.* New York: Academic Press.

Bandura, A. (1977) "Self-efficacy: Toward a unifying theory of behavior change." *Psychological Reveiw* 84: 191-215.

Bannatyne, A. (1971) *Language, reading and learning disabilities.* Springfield, Ill.: C. C Thomas.

Bar-Tal, D., & Bar-Zahar, Y. (1977) "The relationship between perception of locus of control and academic achievement." *Contemporary Educational Psychology* 2: 181-199.

Battle, E.S. (1965) "Motivational determinants of academic task persistence." *Journal of Personality and Social Psychology* 2: 209-218.

——— (1966) "Motivational determinants of academic competance." *Journal of Personality and Social Psychology* 4: 634-642.

Beez, W.V. (1968) "Influence of biased psychological reports on teacher behavior and pupil performance." *Proceedings of the 76th Annual Convention of the American Psychological Association* 3: 605-606.

Bem, D.J. (1972) "Self-perception theory." In L. Berkowitz (ed.), *Advances in Experimental Social Psychology,* Vol. 6, New York: Academic Press, pp. 2-57.

Benowitz, M.L., & Busse, T.V. (1970) "Material incentives and the learning of spelling words in a typical school situation." *Journal of Educational Psychology* 61: 24-26.

——— & Busse, T.V. (1975) "Effects of material incentives on classroom learning over a four-week period." *Journal of Educational Psychology* 67: 57-62.

Benson, J.S. & Kennelly, K.J. (1976) "Learned helplessness: The result of uncontrollable reinforcements or uncontrollable aversive stimuli." *Journal of Personality and Social Psychology* 34: 138-145.

Berglas, S., & Jones, E.E. (1978) "Drug choice as a self-handicapping strategy in response to noncontingent success." *Journal of Personality and Social Psychology* 36: 405-417.

Bialer, I. (1961) "Conceptualization of success and failure in mentally retarded and normal children." *Journal of Personality* 29: 303-320.

Birch, D., & Atkinson, J.W. (1970) *The dynamics of action.* New York: Wiley.

Birney, R.C. (1968) "Research on the achievement motive." In E.F. Borgatta & W.W. Lambert (eds.) *Handbook of personality theory and research.* Chicago: Rand McNally.

Bloom, B.S. (1976) *Human characteristics and school learning.* New York: McGraw-Hill.

Boggiano, A.K., & Ruble, D.N. (1979) "Competence and the overjustification effect: A developmental study." *Journal of Personality and Social Psychology* 37: 1462-1468.

Brackbill, Y., Kappy, M.S. & Starr, R.H. (1962) "Magnitude of reward and probability learning." *Journal of Experimental Psychology* 63: 32-35.

Bridgeman, B. (1974) "Effects of test score feedback on immediately subsequent test performance." *Journal of Educational Psychology* 66: 62-66.

Brophy, J.E., & Good, T.L. (1970) "Teacher's communication of differential expectations for children's classroom performance." *Journal of Educational Psychology* 61: 365-374.

Calder, B.J. & Staw, B.M. (1975) "Self-perception of intrinsic and extrinsic motivation." *Journal of Personality and Social Psychology* 31: 599-605.

Chaikin, A.L., Sigler, E., & Derlega, V.J. (1974) "Nonverbal mediators of teacher expectancy effects." *Journal of Personality and Social Psychology* 30 (1): 144-149.

Cooper, J., & Fazio, R.H. (1979) "The formation and persistence of attitudes that support intergroup conflict." in W.G. Austin, & S. Worchel (eds.), *The Psychology of Intergroup Relations.* Monterey, Calif.: Brooks/Cole.

Crandall, V.C. (1967) "Achievement behavior in the young child." In W.W. Hartup (ed.), *The young child: Reviews of research.* Washington, D.C.: National Association for the Education of Young Children.

―――― (1969) "Sex differences in expectancy of intellectual and academic reinforcement." In C. P. Smith (ed.), *Achievement-related motivation in children.* New York: Russell Sage Foundation.

―――― (October, 1978) "A cognitive learning model of achievement behavior and development." Paper presented at Conference on Motivation and Education, Ann Arbor, Mich.

――――, & Battle, E.S. (1970) "The antecedents and adult correlates of academic and intellectual Fyans (ed.), *Recent trends in achievement motivation; Theory and Research.* Englewood Cliffs, N.J. (In press.)

――――, & Battle, E.X. (1970) "The antecedents and adult correlates of academic and intellectual achievement effort." In J.P. Hill (ed.) *Minnesota Symposia on Child Psychology,* Vol IX., Minneapolis: University of Minnesota Minnesota Press.

――――, Katkovsky, W., & Crandall, V.J. (1965) "Childrens' beliefs in their own control of reinforcements in intellectual-academic situations." *Child Development* 36: 91-109.

――――, & McGhee, P.E. (1968) "Expectancy of reinforcement in academic competence." *Journal of Personality* 36: 635-648.

Cromwell, R. L. (1963) "A social learning approach to mental retardation." In N. R. Ellis (ed.), *Handbook of mental deficiency.* New York: McGraw-Hill.

deCharms, R. (1968) *Personal causation: The internal affective determinants of behavior.* New York: Academic Press.

―――― (1972) "Personal causation training in the schools." *Journal of Applied Social Psychology* 2: 95-113.

―――― (1976) Enhancing motivation. New York: Irvington Publishers.

――――, & Muir, M.S. (1978) "Motivation. Social approaches." *Annual Review of Psychology* 29: 91-113.

Deci, E.L. (1971) "The effects of externally mediated rewards on intrinsic motivation." *Journal of Personality and Social Psychology* 18: 105-115.

―――― (1972) "The effects of contingent and noncontingent rewards and controls on intrinsic motivation." *Organizational Behavior and Human Performance* 8: 217-229.

―――― (1975) *Intrinsic motivation.* New York: Plenum.

Diener, C.I., & Dweck, C.S. (1978) "An analysis of learned helplessness: Continuous changes in performance, strategy, and achievement cognitions following failure." *Journal of Personality and Social Psychology* 36: 451–462.

Diggory, J. (1966) *Self-evaluation: Concepts and Studies.* New York: Wiley.

Dinner, S.H. (1976) "Social comparison and self-evaluation in children." Unpublished doctoral dissertation.

Doris, J. & Sarason, S.B. (1955) "Test anxiety and blame assignment in a failure situation." *Journal of Abnormal and Social Psychology* 50: 335–338.

Dunn, L.M. (1968) "Special Education for the mildly retarded—Is much of it justifiable?" *Exceptional Children* 34: 5–22.

Dweck, C.S. (1975) "The role of expectations and attributions in the alleviation of learned helplessness." *Journal of Personality and Social Psychology* 31: 674–685.

———, & Goetz, T.E. (1978) "Attributions and learned helplessness." In J.H. Harvey, W. Ickes, & R.F. Kidd (eds.), *New directions in attribution research.* Vol. 2, Hillsdale, N.J.: Erlbaum Associates.

———, & Reppucci, N.D. (1973) "Learned helplessness and reinforcement responsibility in children." *Journal of Personality and Social Psychology* 25: 109–116.

Elig, T.W., & Frieze, I.H. (1975) "A multi-dimensional scheme for coding and interpreting perceived causality for success and failure events: The coding scheme of perceived causality (CSPC)." *JSAS: Catalog of Selected Documents in Psychology* 5: 313.

Entwistle, D.R. (1972) "To dispel fantisies about fantasy-based measures of achievement motivation." *Psychological Bulletin* 77: 377–391.

Eysenck, H.J. (1966) "Personality and experimental psychology." *British Psychological Society Bulletin* 19: 1–28.

Feather, N.T. (1966) "Effects of prior success and failure on expectations of success and subsequent performance." *Journal of Personality and Social Psychology* 3: 287–298.

——— (1968) "Change in confidence following success or failure, as a predictor of subsequent performances." *Journal of Personality and Social Psychology* 9: 38–46.

Feldman, N.S., Klosson E., Parsons, J.E., Rholes, W.S., & Ruble, D.N. (1976) "Order of information presentation and children's moral judgments." *Child Development* 47: 556–559.

Flavell, J.H. (1977) *Cognitive development.* Englewood Cliffs, N.J.: Prentice-Hall.

Foster, G.G., Schmidt, C.R., & Sabatino, D. (1976) "Teacher expectancies and the label 'learning disabilities,'" *Journal of Learning Disabilities* 9: 58–66.

———, & Ysseldyke, J. (1976) "Expectancy and halo effects as a result of artificially induced teacher bias." *Contemporary Educational Psychology* 1: 37–45.

Frieze, I.H. (1976) "The role of information processing in making causal attributions for success and failure." In J.S. Carroll & J.W. Payne (eds.), *Cognition and Social Behavior,* Hillsdale, N.J.: Erlbaum.

———, Fisher, J., Hanusa, B., McHugh, M., & Valle, V.A. (1978) "Attributions of success and failure in internal and external barriers to achievement in women." In J. Sherman & F. Denmark (eds.), *Psychology of women: Future directions of research.* New York: Psychological Dimensions.

———, & Snyder, H.N. (1978) "Children's beliefs about the causes of success and failure in school settings." Unpublished Paper, Learning Research & Development Center, University of Pittsburgh.

———, & Weiner, B. (1971) "Cue utilization and attributional judgments for success and failure." *Journal of Personality* 39: 591–606.

Ganzer, V.J. (1968) "Effects of audience presence and test anxiety on learning and retention in a serial learning situation." *Journal of Personality and Social Psychology* 8: 194–199.

Glaser, R. (1976) *Adaptive instruction: Individual diversity and learning.* New York: Holt, Rinehart, and Winston.

Gollub, H.F., & Dittes, J.E. (1965) "Different effects of manipulated self-esteem on persuasibility depending on the threat and complexity of the communications." *Journal of Personality and Social Psychology* 2: 195-201.

Gottlieb, J. (1975) "Attitudes toward retarded children: Effects of labeling." *Journal of Educational Psychology* 67: 581-585.

Green, C., & Zigler, E. (1962) "Social deprivation and the performance of retarded and normal children on a satiation type task." *Child Development* 33: 499-508.

Greene, D., & Lepper, M.R. (1974) "Effects of extrinsic rewards on children's subsequent intrinsic interest." *Child Development* 45: 1141-1145.

Gruen, G., Ottinger, D.R., & Ollendick, T.H. (1975) "Probability learning in retarded children with differing histories of success and failure in school." *American Journal of Mental Deficiency* 79: 417-423.

Guskin, S.L. (1974) "Research on labeling retarded persons: Where do we go from here? (A reaction to MacMillan, Jones, and Alsia.)" *American Journal of Mental Deficiency* 79: 262-264.

Halperin, M.S. (1977) "Sex differences in children's responses to adult pressure for achievement." *Journal of Educational Psychology* 69: 96-100.

Hammill, D.D., & Bartel, N.R. (eds.) (1971) *Educational perspectives in learning disabilities*. New York: Wiley.

Hanusa, B.H., & Shulz, R. (1977) "Attributional mediators of learned helplessness." *Journal of Personality and Social Psychology* 35: 602-611.

Harter, S. (1975) "Developmental differences in the manifestation of mastery motivation on problem-solving tasks." *Child Development* 46; 370-378.

———, (1978) "Effectance motivation reconsidered. Toward a developmental model," *Human Development* 21: 34-64.

Hayden, T & Mischel, W. (1976) "Maintaining trait consistency in the resolution of behavioral inconsistency: The wolf in sheep's clothing." *Journal of Personality* 44: 109-132.

Heckhausen, H. (1967) *The anatomy of achievement motivation*. New York: Academic Press.

——— (1977) "Achievement motivation and its construction: A cognitive model." *Motivation and Emotion* 1: 283-329.

———, & Weiner, B. (1974) "The emergence of a cognitive psychology of motivation." In B. Weiner (ed.), *Achievement motivation and attribution theory*. Morristown, N.J.: General Learning Corporation (Silver Burdett).

Heider, F. (1958) *The psychology of interpersonal relations*. New York: Wiley.

Hill, K.T. (1977) "The relation of evaluative practices to test anxiety and achievement motivation." *Educator* 19: 15-22.

———, & Eaton, M.O. (1977) "The interaction of test anxiety and success/ failure experiences in determining children's arithmetic performance." *Developmental Psychology* 13: 205-211.

———, & Sarason, S.B. (1966) "The relation of test anxiety and defensiveness to test and school performance over the elementary-school years: A further longitudinal study." *Monographs of the Society for Research in Child Development* 31: (2).

Hiroto, D.S., & Seligman, M.E.P. (1975) "Generality of learned helplessness in man." *Journal of Personality and Social Psychology* 31: 311-327.

Halcombe, C.G., & Blackwell, P. (1969) "Motivation and the human monitor: The effect of contingent credit." *Perceptual and Motor Skills* 28: 623-629.

Horner, M.S. (1974) "The measurement and behavioral implications of fear of success in women." In J.W. Atkinson & J.O. Raynor (eds.), *Motivation and achievement*. Washington, D.C.: Winston.

Jones, E.E., & Davis, K.E. (1965) "From acts to dispositions: The attribution process in person perception." In L. Berkowitz (ed.), *Advances in Experimental Social Psychology*, Vol. 2, New York: Academic Press.

———, & Berglas, S. (1978) "Control of attributions about the self through self-handicapping

strategies: The appeal of alcohol and the role of under achievement." *Personality and Social Psychology Bulletin* 4: 200-206.
Jose, J. & Cody, J.J. (1971) "Teacher-pupil interaction as it relates to attempted changes in teacher expectancy of academic ability and achievement." *American Educational Research Journal* 8: 49-59.
Karabenick, J.D. & Heller, K.G. (1976) "A developmental study of effort and ability attributions." *Development Psychology* 12: 559-560.
Karniol, R. & Ross, M. (1977) "The effect of performance-relevant and performance irrelevant rewards on children's intrinsic motivation." *Child Development* 48: 482-487.
Kelley, H.H. (1967) "Attribution theory in social psychology." In D. Levine (ed.), *Nebraska Symposium on Motivation*. Lincoln: University of Nebraska Press.
———— (1972) "Attribution in social interaction." In E.E. Jones et al. (eds.), *Attribution: Perceiving the causes of behavior*. Morristown, N.J.: General Learning Corporation (Silver Burdett).
Keogh, B.H., Cahill, C.W., & MacMillan, D.L. (1972) "Perception of interruption by educationally handicapped children." *American Journal of Mental Deficiency* 77: 107-118.
Kier, R.J., Styfco, S.J., & Zigler, E. (1977) "Success expectancies and the probability learning of children of low and middle socioeconomic status." *Developmental Psychology* 13: 444-449.
Klinger, E. (1975) "Consequences of commitment to and disengagment from incentives." *Psychological Review* (1977) 82: 1-25.
Klitzner, M.D., & Anderson, N.H. (1977) "Motivation × expectancy × value: A functional measurement approach." *Motivation and Emotion* 1: 347-365.
Koch, S. (1956) "Behavior as 'intrinsically regulated: Worknotes toward a pretheory of phenomenon called Motivational.'" In M.R. Jones (ed.), *Nebraska Symposium on Motivation* (vol. 4). Lincoln: University of Nebraska Press.
Kruglanski, A.W., Alon, S., & Lewis, I. (1972) "Retrospective misattribution and task enjoyment." *Journal of Experimental Social Psychology* 8: 493-501.
————, Friedman, I. & Zeevi, G. (1971) "The effects of extrinsic incentives on some qualitative aspects of task performance." *Journal of Personality* 39: 606-617.
————, Ritter, A., Amitai, A., Margolin, B.H., Shabtai L., & Zakah, D. (1975) "Can money enhance intrinsic motivation? A test of the content-consequence hypothesis." *Journal of Personality and Social Psychology* 31: 744-750.
Kukla, A. (1972) "Foundations of an attributional theory of performance." *Psychological Review* 79: 454-470.
———— (1975) "Preferences among impossibly difficult and trivially easy tasks: A revision of Atkinson's theory of choice." *Journal of Personality and Social Psychology* 32: 338-345.
Kun, A. (1977) "Development of the magnitude - covariation and compensation schemata in ability and effort attributions of performance." *Child Development* 48: 862-873.
————, Parsons, J.E., Ruble, D.N. (1974) "Development of integration processes using ability and effort information to predict outcome." *Developmental Psychology* 10 (5): 721-732.
————, & Weiner, B. (1973) "Necessary vs. sufficient causal schemata for success and failure." *Journal of Research in Personality* 7: 197-207.
Latta, R.M. (1976) "Differential tests of two cognitive theories of performance: Weiner vs. Kukla." *Journal of Personality and Social Psychology* 34: 295-304.
Lee, D.Y., Syrnyk, R. & Hallschmid, C. (1976) "Self-perception of intrinsic and extrinsic motivation: Effects on institutionalized mentally retarded adolescents." *American Journal of Mental Deficiency* 81: 331-337.
Lefcourt, H.M. (1976) *Locus of control. Current trends in theory and research*. Hillsdale, N.J.: Erlbaum.
Lepper, M.R., & Greene, D. (1976) "Turning play into work: Effects of adult surveillance and extrinsic rewards on children's intrinsic motivation." *Journal of Personality and Social Psychology* 31: 479-486.
————, & Greene, D. (1978) *The hidden costs of rewards*. Hillsdale, N.J.: Erlbaum.
————, Greene, D., & Nisbett, R.E. (1973) "Undermining children's intrinsic interest with extrin-

sic reward: A test of the 'overjustification' hypothesis." *Journal of Personality and Social Psychology* 28: 129-137.
Levine, F.W., & Fasnacht, G. (1974) "Token rewards may lead to token learning." *American Psychologist* 29: 816-820.
Lewin, K. (1938) *The conceptual representation and the measurement of psychological forces.* Durham, N.C: Duke University Press.
Liebert, R.M., & Morris, L.W. (1967) "Cognitive and emotional components of test anxiety: A distinction and some initial data." *Psychological Reports* 20: 975-978.
Livesley, W.J., & Bromley, D.B. (1973) *Person perception in childhood and adolescence.* New York: Wiley.
MacMillan, D.L. (1975) "Effect of experimental success and failure on the situational expectancy of EMR and nonretarded children." *American Journal of Mental Deficiency* 80: 90-95.
———, & Keogh, B.K. (1971a) "Normal and retarded children's expectancy for failure." *Developmental Psychology* 4: 343-348.
———, & Keogh, B.K. (1971b) "Effect of instructional set on twelve-year-old children's perception of interruption." *Developmental Psychology* 4: 106.
Maehr, M.L. (1976) "Continuing motivation: An analysis of a seldom considered educational outcome." *Review of Educational Research* 46: 443-462.
———, & Lysy, A. (in press) "Motivating students of diverse sociocultural backgrounds to achieve." *International Journal of Intercultural Relations.*
———, & Stalling, W.M. (1972) "Freedom from external evaluation." *Child Development* 43: 177-185.
Mandler, G., & Sarason, S.B. (1952) "A study of anxiety and learning." *Journal of Abnormal and Social Psychology* 47: 166-173.
——— & Watson, D.L. (1966) "Anxiety and the interruption of behavior." In C.D. Spielberger (ed.), *Anxiety and behavior.* New York: Academic Press.
Marlett, N.J., & Watson, D. (1968) "Test anxiety and immediate or delayed feedback in a test-like avoidance task.' *Journal of Personality and Social Psychology* 8: 200-203.
Marshall, H.H. (1969) "Learning as a function of task interest, reinforcement and social class variables." *Journal of Educational Psychology* 60: 133-137.
Mason, E.J., Larimore, D.L., & Kifer, E. (1976) "Teaching experience and teacher expectancy for grades in academic subject areas." *Contemporary Educational Psychology* 1: 369-375.
Masters, J.C., & Mokras, J.R. (1973) "Effects of incentive magnitude on discrimination learning and choice preference in young children." *Child Development* 44: 225-231.
McClelland, D.C., Atkinson, J.W., Clark, R.A., & Lowell, E.L. (1953) *The Achievement motive.* New York: Appleton-Century-Crofts.
McGraw, J., & McCullers, J. (1974) "The distracting effect of material reward: An alternative explanation for the superior performance of reward groups in probability learning." *Journal of Experimental Child Psychology* 18: 149-158.
McGuire, W.J. (1969) "The nature of attitudes and attitude change." In G. Lindzey & E. Aronson (eds.), *The Handbook of Social Psychology.* Reading, Mass.: Addison-Wesley.
McMahan, I.D. (1973) "Relationships between causal attributions and expectancies of success." *Journal of Personality and Social Psychology* 28: 108-114.
McMillan, W.B. (1973) "The effectiveness of tangible reward systems with sixth-grade ghetto children in a regular classroom situation: An experimental investigation." *Psychology in the Schools* 10: 373-378.
Means, R.S. & Means, G.H. (1971) "Achievement as a function of the presence of prior information concerning aptitude." *Journal of Educational Psychology* 62: 185-187.
Mednick, M.T.S., Tangri, S.S., & Hoffman, L.W. (eds.), (1975) *Women and achievement: Social and motivational analyses.* Washington, D.C.: Hemisphire.
Meichenbaum, D.H., Bowers,K.S., & Ross, R.R.S. (1969) "Behavioral analysis of teacher expectancy effect." *Journal of Personality and Social Psychology* 13: 306-316.

Meyer, W-U., Folkes,V., Weiner, B. (1976) "The perceived informational value and affective consequences of choice behavior and intermediate difficulty task selection." *Journal of Research in Personality* 10: 410- 423.

Miller, L.B., & Estes, B.W. (1961) "Monetary reward and motivation in discrimination learning." *Journal of Experimental Psychology* 61: 501-504.

Montemayor, R., & Eisen, M. (1977) "The development of self-conceptions from childhood to adolescence." *Developmental Psychology* 13: 314-319.

Morris, L.W., & Liebert, R.M. (1970) "Relationship of cognitive and emotional components of test anxiety to physiological arousal and academic performance." *Journal of Consulting and Clinical Psychology* 35: 332-337.

Moulton, R.W. (1974) "Motivational implications of individual differences in competence." In J.W. Atkinson & J.O. Raynor (eds.), *Motivation and Achievement*. Washington, D.C.: Winston.

Murray, H.A. (1936) "Techniques for a systematic investigation of fantasy." *Journal of Psychology* 3: 115-143.

Neale, J.M. & Katahn, M. (1968) "Anxiety choice and stimulus uncertainty." *Journal of Personality* 36: 235-245.

Nicholls, J.G. (1975) "Causal attributions and other achievement-related cognitions: Effects of task outcome, attainment value, and sex." *Journal of Personality and Social Psychology* 31: 379-389.

―――― (1978) "The development of the concepts of effort and ability, perception of academic attainment and the understanding that difficult tasks require more ability." *Child Development* 49: 800-814.

―――― (1979) "The development of perception of own attainment and causal attributions for success and failure in reading." *Journal of Educational Psychology* 71: 94-99.

Nisbett, R.E., & Schachter, S. (1966) "Cognitive manipulation of pain." *Journal of Experimental Social Psychology* 2: 227-236.

Nottelmann, E.D., & Hill, K.T. (1977) "Test anxiety and off-task behavior in evaluative situations." *Child Development* 48 (1): 225-231.

Offenbach, L.I. (1964) "Studies of children's probability learning behavior: Effect of reward and punishment at two age levels." *Child Development* 35: 709-715.

Parsons, J.E., & Goff, S.B. (October, 1978) "Achievement motivation: A dual modality." Paper presented at the Second Annual Conference on Motivation and Education, Ann Arbor, Mich.

――――, & Ruble, D.N. (1977) "The development of achievement-related expectancies." *Child Development* 48: 1075-1079.

Peevers, B.H., & Secord, P.F. (1973) "Developmental changes in attributions of descriptive concepts to persons." *Journal of Personality and Social Psychology* 27: 120-128.

Raynor, J.O. (1969) "Future orientation and motivation of immediate activity: An elaboration of the theory of achievement motivation." *Psychological Review* 76: 606-610.

――――, (1974) "Future orientation in the study of achievement motivation." In J.W. Atkinson & J.O. Raynor (eds.), *Motivation and achievement*. Washington, D.C.: Winston.

Regan, D.T., Strauss, E., & Fazio, R.H. (1974) "Liking and the attribution process." *Journal of Experimental Social Psychology* 10: 385-397.

Revelle, W., & Michaels, E.J. (1976) 'The theory of achievement motivation revisited: The implications of inertial tendencies." *Psychological Review* 83: 394-404.

Rosenthal, R. Baratz, S.S., & Hall, C.M. (1974) "Teacher behavior, teacher expectations, and gains in pupils' rated creativity." *The Journal of Genetic Psychology* 124: 115-121.

――――, & Jacobson, L. (1968) *Pygmalion in the classroom: Teacher expectation and pupils' intellectual development*. New York: Holt, Rinehart & Winston.

Ross, M. (1975) "Salience of reward and intrinsic motivation." *Journal of Personality and Social Psychology* 33: 245-254.

―――― (1976) "The self-perception of intrinsic motivation." In J.H. Harvey, W.J. Ickes, & R.F. Kidd (eds.), *New directions in attribution research*. Hillsdale, N.J.: Erlbaum.

Roth, S., & Bootzin, R.R. (1974) "Effects of experimentally induced expectancies of external control: An investigation of learned helplessness." *Journal of Personality and Social Psychology* 29: 253-264.
――――, & Kubal, L. (1975) "Effects of noncontingent reinforcement on tasks of differing importance: Facilitation and learned helplessness." *Journal of Personality and Social Psychology* 32: 680-691.
Rothbart, M., Dalfen, S., & Barrett, R. (1971) "Effects of teacher's expectancy on student-teacher interaction." *Journal of Educational Psychology* 62: 49-54.
Rotter, J.B. (1954) *Social learning and clinical psychology*. Englewood Cliffs, N.J.: Prentice-Hall.
―――― (1966) "Generalized expectancies for internal vs. external control of reinforcement." *Psychological Monographs* 80: 1-28.
Rozin, P., Poritsky, S., & Sotsky, R. (1971) "American children with reading problems can easily learn to read English by Chinese characters." *Science* 171: 1264-1267.
Ruble, D.N. (1975) "Visual orientation and self-perceptions of children on an external-cue-relevant or cue-irrelevant task situation." *Child Development* 46: 669-676.
―――― (October, 1978) "A developmental perspective of theories of achievement motivation." Paper presented at the Second Annual Conference on Motivation and Education, University of Michigan, Ann Arbor.
――――, Boggiano, A.K., Feldman, N.S., & Loebl, J.H. (in press) "A developmental analysis of the role of social comparison in self-evaluation." *Developmental Psychology*.
――――, Feldman, N.S., & Boggiano, A.K. (1976) "Social comparison between young children in achievement situations." *Developmental Psychology* 12 (3): 192-197.
――――, & Nakamura, C.Y. (1973) "Outerdirectedness as a problem-solving approach in relation to developmental level and selected task variables." *Child Development* 44: 519-528.
――――, Parsons, J.E., & Ross, J. (1976) "Self-evaluative responses of children in an achievement setting." *Child Development* 47: 990-997.
Rubovits, P.C., & Maehr, M.L. (1971) "Pygmalion analyzed: Toward an explanation of the Rosenthal & Jacobson findings." *Journal of Personality and Social Psychology* 19: 197-204.
Salili, F., Maehr, M.l., & Gillmore, G. (1976) "Achievement and morality: A cross-cultural analysis of causal attribution and evaluation." *Journal of Personality and Social Psychology* 33: 327-337.
Sanders, B., Zigler, E., & Butterfield, E.C. (1968) "Outer-directedness in the discrimination learning of normal and retarded children." *Journal of Abnormal Psychology* 27: 368-375.
Sarason, I.G. (1958) "The effects of anxiety, reassurance, and meaningfulness of material to be learned in verbal learning." *Journal of Experimental Psychology* 56: 472-477.
―――― (1960) "Empirical findings and theoretical problems in the use of anxiety scales." *Psychological Bulletin* 57: 403-415.
―――― (1961) "The effects of anxiety and threat on solution of a difficult task." *Journal of Abnormal and Social Psychology* 62: 165-168.
―――― (1972) "Experimental approaches to test anxiety: Attention and the uses of information." In C.D. Spielberger (ed.), *Anxiety: Current trends in theory and research,* Vol.2. New York: Academic Press, pp. 381-403.
――――, & Ganzer, V.J. (1962) "Anxiety, reinforcement and experimental instructions in a free verbalization situation." *Journal of Abnormal and Social Psychology* 65: 301-307.
――――, ―――― (1963) "Effects of test anxiety and reinforcement history on verbal behavior." *Journal of Abnormal and Social Psychology* 67: 513-579.
――――, & Koenig, K.P. (1965) "The relationship of test anxiety and hostility to description of self and parents." *Journal of Personality and Social Psychology* 2: 617-621.
――――, & Paola, E.G. (1960) "The relationship of test and general anxiety, difficulty of task, and experimental instructions to performance." *Journal of Experimental Psychology* 59: 185-191.
Sarason, S.B., Davidson, K.S., Lighthall, F.F., Waite, R.R., & Ruebush, B.K. (1960) *Anxiety in elementary school children*. New York: Wiley.
Schuster, S.O., & Gruen, G.E. (1971) "Success and failure as determinants of the performance of

mentally retarded and nonretarded children." *American Journal of Mental Deficiency* 76: 190-196.

Schwarz, R.H., & Jens, K.G. (1969) "The expectation of success as it modifies the achievement of mentally retarded adolescents." *American Journal of Mental Deficiency* 73: 946-949.

Severance, L.J., & Gasstrom, L.L. (1977) "Effects of the label 'mentally retarded' on causal explanations for success and failure outcomes." *American Journal of Mental Deficiency* 81: 547-555.

Seligman, M.E.P. (1975) *Helplessness: On depression, development, and death.* San Francisco: Freeman.

Shaklee, H. (1976) "Development in inferences of ability and task difficulty." *Child Development* 47: 1051-1057.

Shantz, C.N. (1975) "The development of social cognition." In E.M. Hetherington (ed.), *Review of child development research, Vol. 5.* Chicago: University of Chicago Press.

Smith, C.P. (1966) "The influence of testing conditions on need for achievement scores." In J.W. Atkinson & N.T. Feather (eds.), *A theory of achievement motivation.* New York: John Wiley.

——— (1969) *Achievement-related motives in children.* New York: Russell Sage Foundation.

Smith, W.E. (1974) "The effects of social and monetary rewards on intrinsic motivation." Doctoral dissertation, Cornell University.

Snow, R.E. (1969) "Unfinished Pygmalion." *Contemporary Psychology* 14: 197-200.

Sorrentino, R.M., & Short, J.C. (1977) "The case of the mysterious moderates: Why motives sometimes fail to predict behavior." *Journal of Personality and Social Psychology* 35: 478-484.

Spear, P.S. & Armstrong, S. (1978) "Effects of performance expectancies created by peer comparison as related to social reinforcement, task difficulty, and age of child." *Journal of Experimental Child Psychology* 25: 254-266.

Standford, D., Dember, W., & Stanford, F. (1968) "A children's form of the Alpert-Haber achievement anxiety scale." *Child Development* 34: 1027-1032.

Swann, W.B., & Pittman, J.S. (1977) "Initiating play activity of children: The moderating influence of verbal cues on intrinsic motivation." *Child Development* 48: 1128-1132.

Taylor, J.A. (1953) "A personality scale of manifest anxiety." *Journal of Abnormal and Social Psychology* 48: 285-290.

Tennen, H., & Eller, S.J. (1977) "Attributional components of learned helplessness and facilitation." *Journal of Personality and Social Psychology* 35: 265-271.

Terrell, G., Jr., Durkin, K., & Wiesley, M. (1959) "Social class and the nature of incentives in discrimination learning." *Journal of Abnormal and Social Psychology* 59: 270-272.

Thorndike, R.L. (1968) "Review of Pygmalion in the classroom by R. Rosenthal and L. Jacobson." *American Educational Research Journal* 5: 508-711.

Thornton, J.W., & Jacobs, P.D. (1972) "The facilitating effects of prior inescapable/unavoidable stress on intellectual performance." *Psychonomic Science* 25: 185-187.

Tolman, E.C. (1955) "Principles of performance." *Psychological Review* 62: 315-326.

Torshen, K.P. (1977) *The mastery approach to competency-based education.* New York: Academic Press.

Trapp, E.P. & Kausler, P.H. (1958) "Test anxiety level and goal-setting behavior." *Journal of Consulting Psychology* 22: 31-34.

Trope, Y. (1975) "Seeking information about one's own ability as a determinant of choice among tasks." *Journal of Personality and Social Psychology* 32: 1004-1013.

———, & Brickman, P. (1975) "Difficulty and diagnosticity determinants of choice among tasks." *Journal of Personality and Social Psychology* 31: 918-925.

Turnure, J.E. & Zigler, E. (1964) "Outer-directedness in the problem solving of normal and retarded children." *Journal of Abnormal and Social Psychology* 69: 427-436.

Van Bergen, A. (1968) *Task interruption.* Amsterdam: North-Holland Publishing Co.

Veroff, J. (1969) "Social comparison and the development of achievement motivation." In C.P. Smith (ed.), *Achievement-related motives in children.* New York: Russell Sage Foundation.

Walters, R.H., & Parke, R.D. (1964) "Social motivation, dependency, and susceptibility to social influence." In L. Berkowitz (ed.), *Advances in experimental social psychology,* Vol. 1. New York: Academic Press.

Weiner, B. (1965) "The effects of unsatisfied achievement motivation on persistence and subsequent performance." *Journal of Personality* 33: 428–442.

────── (1972) *Theories of motivation: From mechanism to cognition.* Chicago: Rand McNally.

────── (ed.), (1974) *Achievement motivation and attribution theory.* Morristown, N.J.: General Learning Corporation (Silver Burdett).

────── (1977) "An attributional approach for educational psychology." In L. Shulman (ed.), *Review of Research in Education,* Vol, 4. Itasca, Ill.: Peacock.

────── (1979) "A theory of motivation for some classroom experiences." *Journal of Educational Psychology* 71: 3-25.

──────, Frieze, I., Kukla, A., Reed, L., Rest, S., & Rosenbaum, R.M. (1971) *Perceiving the causes of success and failure.* New York: General Learning Corporation (Silver Burdett).

──────, Heckhausen, H., Meyer, W., & Cook, R.E. (1972) "Causal ascriptions and achievement behavior: A conceptual analysis of locus of control." *Journal of Personality and Social Psychology* 21: 239-248.

──────, Nierenburg, R., & Goldstein, M. (1976) "Social learning (locus of control) versus attributional (causal stability) interpretations of expectancy of success." *Journal of Personality* 44: 52-68.

──────, & Peter, N.V. (1973) "A cognitive-developmental analysis of achievement and moral judgments." *Developmental Psychology* 9: 290-309.

Weiner, B., Russell, D., & Lerman, D. (1978) "Affective consequences of causal ascriptions." In J.H. Harvey, W.J. Ickes, & R.F. Kidd (eds.), *New directions in attribution research,* Vol. 2, Hillsdale, N.J.: Erlbaum.

────── (1979) "The cognition-emotion process in achievement-related contexts." *Journal of Personality and Social Psychology* 37: 1211-1220.

Weiner, B., & Schneider, K. (1971) "Drive versus cognitive theory: A reply to Boor and Harmon." *Journal of Personality and Social Psychology* 18: 258-262.

Weiner, B., & Sierad, J. (1975) "Misattribution for failure and enhancement and achievement strivings." *Journal of Personality and Social Psychology* 31: 415-421.

White, R.W. (1959) "Motivation reconsidered: The concept of competence." *Psychological Review* 66: 297-333.

Wilkins, W. (1977) "Self-fulfilling prophecy: Is there a phenomenon to explain?" *Psychological Bulletin* 84: 55-56.

Wilkins, W.E., & Glork, M.D. (1973) "Teacher expectations and student achievement: A replication and extension." Ithaca, N.Y.: Cornell University (ERIC Document Reproduction Service No. 080-567).

Wine, J. (1971) "Test anxiety and direction of attention." *Psychological Bulletin* 76: 92-104.

Wolpe, J. (1958) *Psychotherapy by reciprocal inhibition.* Stanford, Calif.: Stanford University Press.

Wortman, C.B., & Brehm, J.W. (1975) "Responses to uncontrollable outcomes: An integration of reactance theory and the learned helplessness model." In L. Berkowitz (ed.), *Advances in experimental Social Psychology,* Vol. 8. New York: Academic Press.

──────, & Dintzer, L. (1978) "Is an attributional analysis on the learned helplessness phenomenon viable?: A critique of the Abramson-Seligman-Teasdale Reformulation." *Journal of Abnormal Psychology* 87: 75-90.

──────, Panciera, L., Shusterman, L., & Hibscher, J. (1976) "Attributions of causality and reactions to uncontrollable outcomes." *Journal of Experimental Social Psychology* 12: 301-316.

Yando, R., & Zigler, E. (1971) "Outerdirectedness in the problem-solving of institutionalized and noninstitutionalized normal and retarded children." *Developmental Psychology* 4: 277-288.

Yerkes, R.M., & Dodson, J.D. (1908) "The relation of strength of stimulus to rapidity of habit formation." *Journal of Comparative and Neurological Psychology* 18: 459-482.

Yoshida, R.K., & Meyers, C.E. (1975) "Effects of labeling as educable mentally retarded on teachers' expectancies for change in a student's performance." *Journal of Educational Psychology* 67: 521-527.

Young, E., & Egeland, B. (1976) "Repetition choice behavior as a function of chronological age, task difficulty, and expectancy of success." *Child Development* 47: 682-689.

Zanna, M.P., Sheras, P.L., Cooper, J., & Shaw, C. (1975) "Pygamlion and Galatea: The interactive effect of teacher and student expectancies." *Journal of Experimental Social Psychology* 11: 279-287.

TEMPERAMENT INFLUENCES ON THE DEVELOPMENT OF EXCEPTIONAL CHILDREN*

Barbara K. Keogh, UNIVERSITY OF CALIFORNIA, LOS ANGELES

Michael E. Pullis, UNIVERSITY OF TEXAS AT DALLAS

INTRODUCTION

The historical preoccupation with cognition, so typical of American educational psychology, has lead to conceptualizations of individual differences which are framed primarily by psychometrically defined intellectual constructs. While of obvious importance to the understanding of the development of individual children, emphasis upon the study of cognitive variables may well have resulted in less vigorous investigation of other potential sources of developmental variation. A voluminous and rich clinical literature supports the importance of a number of noncognitive influences on personal and social adequacy, and there is increasing evidence to document the mediating effect of affective and motivational influences on intellectual competence. (*Editor's Note:* See the chapter by Ruble and Boggiano in this volume for a discussion of motivational considerations.) Noncognitive influences may be particularly important in the development of young handicapped children, who by definition have limitations or disturbances of physical and/or intellectual abilities. Often the cognitive characteristics of handicapped children are inadequate to predict or explain the course of development or the ultimate consequences of a handicapping condition. It is possible, too, that individual differences in cognitive dimensions become increasingly important as intellectual or physical limitations or handicaps become severe.

This chapter is focused on the dimension of individual differences subsumed under the rubric "temperament." In a broad sense temperament refers to those within-child stylistic characteristics which affect the relationships of the child and his family, and which determine, in part, his responses to the environmental and experiential demands of socialization. Thomas & Chess (1977), major investigators of temperament, suggest that:

> Temperament may best be viewed as a general term referring to the *how* of behavior. It differs from ability, which is concerned with the *what* and *how well* of behaving, and from motivation which accounts for the *why* a person does what he is doing. Temperament, by contrast, concerns the way in which an individual behaves (1977, p. 9).

Recognizing that temperament is difficult to define precisely or to quantify, it is nevertheless interesting to note that descriptions of individuals are regularly couched in terms of temperament. From a clinical point of view, we are struck with the importance of temperamental characteristics of handicapped children who "make it" or who "fail" in their larger social and educational worlds. It is reasonable to speculate that temperament mediates the interaction of the child and his/her personal and social environment: thus, a good deal of the within-group variance among handicapped children may well relate to individual differences in temperament.

PARENT-CHILD INTERACTIONS

Before beginning a more detailed discussion of temperament and selected empirical and theoretical literatures which address it, it is important to place this construct within the broader context of parent-child interactions. Examination of the parent-child interaction literature of two decades ago reveals that developmental theorists emphasized the influence of the parent *on* the infant or child. Parental rearing practices were presumed to affect children's development in a global and primarily unidirectional way. The unidirectional effect point of view received support from behaviorists who provided a popular conception of the child as a passive recipient of acculturating or socializing processes, and who emphasized the role of environmental influences in shaping development. That the human infant goes through a prolonged period of relative helplessness also fit the picture of the malleable organism, developing according to the teaching and influence of the caregiver.

More contemporary developmental theorists, however, have focused their attention on the ways in which infants affect parents, on the bidirectional interaction of infant and caregiver. This is a more active view, as the child is seen as a social organism with powerful reinforcing and directing capabilities.

Bell (1968) was among the first to call for a reconceptualization of parent-child interactions. Emphasizing that correlations do not specify direction of influence, he maintained that parent-child interactions represent a social system in which each participant's responses are stimuli for the other (Bell, 1971). In this model parents have caregiving repertoires which change as a function of cultural demands and as a result of stimulation and reinforcement from the child. A bidirectional model forces the conclusion that the child is stimulating as well as being stimulated. Bell (1974) suggests that particular infant behaviors initiate, maintain, and terminate interaction with caregivers. The constitutional character of these infant behaviors deserves note, as many are subsumed by the temperamental dimensions hypothesized as mediators of parent-child interactions.

Support for the bidirectional model is found, too, in the work of Rheingold (1969), who suggests that the child modulates, regulates, and refines the caregiver's activities, while at the same time having its own behavior modified. Empirical evidence demonstrating the effects of infants on caregivers is reported by Etzel & Gewirtz (1967), Levy (1953), Moss (1967), Yarrow (1963), and Stern (1974). Their findings support the important observations of Brazelton et al. (1974), who provide ethological descriptions of early mother-infant interactions which illustrate the origins of reciprocity. Brazelton et al. point out the need for each member of the dyad to be able to recognize the nuances of the other's behavior in order for the interaction to be maintained. This perspective is, of course, consistent with the transactional model of development proposed by Sameroff (1975). Commenting upon the importance of individual differences in infants' temperament as documented in the Thomas, Chess, & Birch (1968) longitudinal work, Sameroff noted that behavioral outcomes occurred not simply because of the parents unidirectional influence on the infant or child, but because of the reciprocal influences of child and parent.

> Knowing *only* the temperament of the child or knowing *only* the child- rearing attitudes and practices of the parents would not allow one to predict the developmental outcome for the child... rather,... it is the character of the *specific transactions* that occurred between a given child and parents which determined the course of his subsequent development (Sameroff, 1975, pp. 277-278).

It is reasonable then, to assume that individual differences in the character of infant reactivity and responsiveness are important influences on caregiver activities. Where these infant characteristics are extreme or discrepant, they may be overlooked or misread; they may also elicit inappropriate, even noxious, caregiver response. Studies of battered and abused children, for example (Gil, 1970), suggest that children's characteristics may differentially induce abuse. In sum, from the interactive view of parent-child relationships it is clear that individual differences in infants and children may influence, even mediate, the interaction between parent and child. We propose that many of the important dimensions of individual differences are temperamental in character.

TEMPERAMENT

Despite some difficulties in finding precise definitions of temperament and temperamental dimensions, considerable empirical evidence as well as common sense argue for the importance of individual differences in temperament domains. As noted earlier in this paper, Thomas & Chess (1977) define temperament in terms of behavioral style. Consistent with this emphasis, Buss & Plomin (1975) consider temperament as describing stylistic aspects rather than the content of behavior. Buss & Plomin are concerned more with expressive than with instrumental behavior. Theirs is not a social-cultural approach which emphasizes roles and content of behavior so much as it is an individual difference approach which seeks to identify unique individual contributions to performance. Buss & Plomin and Thomas & Chess and their colleagues view temperament as representing the constitutional or biologic contribution to the socialization process. In their opinion individual differences in temperament are presumed to be at least partly constitutional in basis and to be present at or shortly after birth.

Buss & Plomin, for example, view temperaments as "broad inherited tendencies" which differentiate during development but which affect and are affected by the social environment. Although influenced and modified through the socialization process, temperamental characteristics are considered to have relative stability over time. Buss & Plomin summarize:

> Our model starts with inborn dispositions. The subsequent course of these dispositions is determined by a complex interaction with the environment, but the environment in turn, is also affected by the dispositions. The social environment may be *shaped* by temperament initially or through feedback. Temperament may determine which environments are *selected*. There are limits to the *impact* of the environment, and temperament-environment mismatches can lead to strain (p. 5).

Recalling the definition of temperament proposed by Thomas & Chess (1977), it is clear that both sets of investigators are concerned with behavioral individuality which characterizes infants and young children. Both interpret individual differences in reaction patterns as evidence of temperament variability early on.

More detailed review of the models of temperament proposed by the Thomas & Chess group and by Buss & Plomin provides a basis for considering at least some aspects of the diverse literature relevant to noncognitive functioning of handicapped young children.

Thomas, Chess, & Birch (1968)

Among the best known investigators of temperament, these researchers have amassed considerable clinical evidence in support of their views. In reviewing their work, Thomas & Chess (1977) identify three major considerations or reasons for initiating their studies of temperament. Like many other parents, they were struck by the clear individual differences in their own children early on. As clinicians they were often unable to correlate directly the child's psychological development with specific environmental influences. And finally, they sought to remove the exclusive responsibility for deviant development from parents, a point of view typifying the *Zeitgeist* of the time. In addition to clinical inferences, their views on temperament were derived primarily from the New York Longitudinal Study (NYLS) conducted over a 15-year period beginning in the mid-1950's. Further elaborating studies have continued to emerge from this active clinical group (see Thomas & Chess, 1977, for a recent synthesis) and a number of independent investigators have added to their work on temperament.

The NYLS, a longitudinal effort utilizing an anterospective data collection design, provided the basic data identifying within-child differences in temperament or behavioral styles. Thomas et al. (1968) asked parents to report, via interview and questionnaire, on specific dimensions of their child's development, eliciting description of the "how" of behavior, not necessarily the "what." The interviews were designed to garner both background information and behavioral descriptions. Background categories included information about siblings, obstetrical history, neonatal information, responsibility for the care of the child, and a parental description of the child's personality. Behavioral information focused on the details of daily living, including sleeping, feeding, bathing, responses to people, responses to illness, and the like.

Initial data in the NYLS were collected through interviews with parents of 80 children when the children were approximately three to five months old. Interview information from the first 22 parents was submitted to a content analysis which yielded nine dimensions of temperament. These were: Activity Level, Rhythmicity, Approach/Withdrawal, Adaptability, Intensity of Reaction, Threshold of Responsiveness, Quality of Mood, Distractibility, and Attention Span and Persistence. Although it was recognized that the dimensions were probably not fully independent, neither halo effects nor category intercorrelations contributed significantly to rater reliability, and interrater agreement was high. The nine dimensions and the interview scales provided the framework and methodology for subsequent work. The nine categories of temperament as defined by the investigators are found in Table 1.

Table 1 Temperament Categories and Definitions*

1. Activity Level: the motor component present in a given child's functioning and the diurnal proportion of active and inactive periods. Protocol data on motility during bathing, eating, playing, dressing and handling, as well as information concerning the sleep-wake cycle, reaching, crawling and walking, are used in scoring this category.

2. Rhythmicity (Regularity): the predictability and/or unpredictability in time of any function. It can be analyzed in relation to the sleep-wake cycle, hunger, feeding pattern and elimination schedule.

3. Approach or Withdrawal: The nature of the initial response to a new stimulus, be it a new food, new toy or new person. Approach responses are positive, whether displayed by mood expression (smiling, verbalizations, etc.) or motor activity (swallowing a new food, reaching for a new toy, active play, etc.). Withdrawal reactions are negative, whether displayed by mood expression (crying, fussing, grimacing, verbalizations, etc.) or motor activity (moving away, spitting new food out, pushing new toy away, etc.).

4. Adaptability: responses to new or altered situations. One is not concerned with the nature of the initial responses, but with the ease with which they are modified in desired directions.

5. Threshold of Responsiveness: the intensity level of stimulation that is necessary to evoke a discernible response, irrespective of the specific form that the response may take, or the sensory modality affected. The behaviors utilized are those concerning reactions to sensory stimuli, environmental objects, and social contacts.

6. Intensity of Reaction: the energy level of response, irrespective of its quality or direction.

7. Quality of Mood: the amount of pleasant, joyful and friendly behavior, as contrasted with unpleasant, crying and unfriendly behavior.

8. Distractibility: the effectiveness of extraneous environmental stimuli in interfering with or in altering the direction of the ongoing behavior.

9. Attention Span and Persistence: two categories which are related. Attention span concerns the length of time a particular activity is pursued by the child. Persistence refers to the continuation of an activity in the face of obstacles to the maintenance of the activity direction.

*Thomas & Chess (1977, pp. 21-22).

In the early years of their work, Thomas et al. (1963) were concerned only with descriptions of children in the first two years of life. Using three methods of data analysis—preponderance, rank, and percent-rank index—they concluded that "initially identifiable characteristics of reactivity are persistent features of the child's behavior throughout the first two years of life" (p. 71). Consistent with their clinical stance, Thomas et al. emphasized the reactive and interactive effects of those dimensions of temperament on the socialization process. As an example, they noted that the data were most helpful for parental guidance. Parents came to realize that their children had a variety of individual differences which could not be totally controlled by them; thus, parents felt less guilty and anxious about the behavioral problems of their children. A number of separate but related studies based on the nine-dimensional approach demonstrated the utility of the system and extended the work across age levels.

One of the most important of the continuing studies was the follow-up of children in the original NYLS samples (Thomas, Chess, & Birch, 1968). Details of this study deserve note, as the primary data for interpreting the relationship between temperament and behavior disorders come from this research. Eighty-five families contributing 141 children comprised the longitudinal sample. Over the twelve-year period 136 children were followed, and further follow-up is currently in progress (Chess, 1978). The SES level of the parents was consistently middle to upper class, with both parents often having postgraduate degrees. Sources of data included interviews with parents and teachers, direct observation of the child in the home and the school, psychometric tests, neurological studies, and clinical psychiatric evaluations. Scores from the Parental Attitude Research Instrument (PARI) indicated that there was remarkable homogeneity of attitudes in the parent sample, these attitudes generally reflecting the permissive and child-centered ambiance of the day. Intelligence of the children was assessed at ages three and six. The sample children had a mean IQ of 127, standard deviation of 12.1.

In the follow-up of sample children and their families over a twelve-year period the investigators found that 42 (39 percent) evidenced problem behaviors of sufficient intensity and chronicity to warrant psychiatric evaluation and subsequent intervention. Comparison of the clinical group with active symptoms (N=34) and the nonclinical group (N=94) on the nine temperament dimensions indicated that activity level distinguished the two groups in the first year of life, but that no significant differences were found in the second year; only intensity of reaction was differentiating during the third year. However, differences became apparent later, six of the nine dimensions yielding significant differences at ages four and five. When children with passive clinical symptoms (N=8) were compared with the nonproblem members of the sample, differences were found only in years four and five. Finally, when comparisons among the entire sample were conducted with an analysis of variance procedure, main effects by groups were found for four of the temperamental dimensions: activity level, intensity, mood, and persistence.

To this point Thomas et al. had treated each of the nine temperament dimensions as independent variables. Preliminary correlational studies suggested some clustering of variables, however, leading the researchers to a factor analytic approach. Of the three factors extracted from the NYLS data, factor A seemed to be most meaningful—loading on mood, intensity, approach/withdrawal, and adaptability. When the clinical and normal groups were compared it was found that differences in these variables increased with age. That is, all of the groups had a similar distribution of scores during the first two years; but with age, the groups became more differentiated on factor A characteristics.

Based primarily on their factor analytic findings, Thomas et al. (1968) identified three distinct groups in their sample. The "Easy Child" (40 percent of the longitudinal sample) was characterized by regularity of biological functions, positive approach to new stimuli, high adaptability, and preponderantly favorable mood. The "Difficult Child" (10 percent of the sample) was typically irregular in biological functions, negative in response to normal stimuli, slow to adapt to change, and intense, often negative in mood. The "Slow to Warm Up Child"

(15 percent of sample), while often negative in response to new stimuli or situations, could adapt over time. These children were characterized by mild intensity of response and by reasonable biological regularity. It should be noted that slightly over one-third of the sample children could not be placed within these three categories. These descriptive categories appeared particularly interesting in analyzing the development of children evidencing behavior problems.

Those children who comprised the clinical sample with passive symptoms were generally characterized as the "Slow to Warm Up" children. They were found "to show low activity level, initial withdrawal responses, slow adaptability, low intensity of reactions, and a relatively high frequency of negative mood responses than did the nonclinical cases" (p. 92). Qualitative analysis of anecdotal information indicated that these children developed behavior disorders when demands to adapt quickly and often were placed on them. Children with the constellation of temperamental characteristics of the "Difficult Child" accounted for 4 percent of the nonclinical group as compared to 23 percent of the behavior problem group. Approximately 70 percent of the difficult children developed behavior problems. Case study findings revealed that most of the reported behavior problems of "Difficult Children" were associated with conformity to either family or school constraints, and adjustment to socialization demands in general.

It is important to note that in all cases of behavior disorders, Thomas et al. contended that the problems were the result of temperament-parenting (environmental) interactions, a point of view consistent with the transactional model of development (Sameroff, 1975; Sameroff & Chandler, 1975). The presence of a certain constellation of temperamental characteristics in the child was not in itself sufficient to cause behavior problems, although the Thomas & Chess group did suggest that certain temperament characteristics might be predisposing to behavioral problems given usual parenting practices. As an example, difficulties in shifting from one activity to another were most often reported by parents and teachers. Distractibility was also cited as being problematic because the child seldom was able to complete chores or activities, causing "nagging" by the parent or teacher; interestingly, this trait was the most difficult to manage. Children who had low activity levels were sometimes viewed as lazy or unmotivated by their high-achieving parents.

Consistent with the interactional interpretation of parent-child effects, the Thomas group conceptualized the processes related to the development of behavior problems within a "goodness of fit" model. That is, in their view children may develop behavior disturbances when there is a stressful relationship between parents and the child. Temperamental factors may contribute to this process when there is a certain amount of dissonance between the characteristics of the child and the resources and attitudes of the parents. They propose six types of interactional patterns which in their view may result in disturbed functioning:

(1) Dissonance between the parental practices or demands and the child's temperament or capacities; (2) dissonance between values and behaviors developed in the home, and behavioral expectancies at school and in peer groups; (3) inconsistencies in the patterning of parental practices and attitudes resulting in excessive stress for the child; (4) interparental dissonance and the use of the child's characteristics as a weapon in interparental conflict; (5) dissonance between the child's expectations of acceptance and affection and parental feelings and behavior; and (6) dissonance between the mode of functioning of the teacher or other person in loco parentis and the characteristics of the child (Thomas, Chess, & Birch, 1968, p. 139).

Clearly, in the view of Thomas & Chess, temperament is one contributor to the interaction of the child and the socializing environment.

The temperament frame of reference proposed by Thomas & Chess and their colleagues was developed from their clinical, personal point of view, and provided valuable insights for work with their sample families. The subjective flavor of the clinical approach, however, was recognized, and continuing efforts by the New York group were directed at providing adequate assessment tools. Subsequent to their initial interview techniques, Thomas et al. developed a temperament questionnaire which they viewed as appropriate for assessing temperament of children across the age range three to seven years. The survey has gone through several revisions and the findings validated against interview and other clinical data. The latest revision of the parent questionnaire (Thomas & Chess, 1977) consists of 72 items, eight items tapping each of the nine temperament dimensions. Parents are asked to rate each item on a one-to-seven scale, judging whether the behavior occurs "hardly ever" to "almost always." Items for the most part describe particular behaviors rather than generalized personality characteristics. Examples of items tapping dimensions of activity, approach/withdrawal, and adaptability are, respectively: "When my child moves about in the house or outdoors, he/she runs rather than walks." "My child likes to try new foods." "If my child is shy with a strange adult he/she quickly (within a half hour or so) gets over this." The responses are weighted and averaged to provide a score for each category or dimension of temperament.

A similar questionnaire was developed for use by teachers in order that the interactions of temperament and school performance might be assessed. The teacher survey contains 64 items covering all temperament dimensions except rhythmicity. This aspect of temperament was viewed as tied so closely to biological functions that it was not directly translatable into school relevant descriptions; thus, the teacher form of the temperament survey is comparable to the parent form on eight of the nine categories. The teacher is asked to respond to each item in terms of frequency, that is, "hardly ever" to "almost always." Examples of items in the activity, withdrawal, and adaptability categories are, respectively: "Child seems to have difficulty sitting still, may wriggle a lot or get out of seat." "Child will initially avoid new games and activities, preferring to sit on the side and watch." "Child will adjust quickly to a game if others want to play in a different way." Responses are weighted and averaged, then yield a total score for each dimension.

A third questionnaire for assessment of temperament was developed by Carey (1970) and revised by Carey and McDevitt (1978) for use with infants and very young children. The 1970 scale contains 70 items which could be completed in approximately 20 minutes by the mother in the pediatrician's office. Cary initially standardized his instrument on 101 mothers who had babies between four and eight months of age, later validating his findings on a sample of 200 mothers. The Carey items tapped the nine temperament dimensions proposed by Thomas, Chess, & Birch (1968). In each case the parent's version of the baby's behavior in various situations is assessed. Areas include sleeping, feeding, bathing, visits to the doctor, playing, and the like. The parent is offered three choices for each item. Each item or behavioral dimension is weighted and averaged to give a category score. Carey's findings have been compared with the NYLS data for children of similar age. Both sets of data yielded the same modal results. "Inasmuch as the differences between the Carey questionnaire and NYLS ratings were quantitative and not qualitative the practical usefulness of this short questionnaire and its comparability to the more elaborate NYLS protocol may not be seriously impaired" (Thomas & Chess, 1977, p. 121). Both procedures yielded similar signs for the difficult child category on age matched samples. The Behavioral Styles Questionnaire, developed by McDevitt and Carey (1975) for assessing temperament of children ages 3-7 provides further refinement of a parent rating scale utilizing the Thomas, Chess, and Birch framework.

In summary, the nine temperament dimensions as proposed by Thomas, Chess, and their colleagues have been cast in questionnaire form which are feasible for use by parents and teachers. While the scaling properties of these instruments are not yet certain, they appear promising for temperament research. Work in progress by McDevitt (1976) and by UCLA investigators (Keogh, Pullis, Cadwell, & Burstein, 1978) may clarify and tighten the temperament scales. Work to date has yielded data generally compatible with the Thomas et al. findings, but behavioral correlates require documentation.

The Chess & Thomas approach to the study of temperament has been extended and elaborated within their own research group and by others. Before reviewing the content of that research, however, it is important to consider other approaches to the formulation of temperament and to assess the temperament constructs in light of other evidence.

Buss & Plomin (1975)

Consistent with the approach taken by Thomas, Chess, & Birch (1968), Buss & Plomin view temperament within an interactional framework. They assume that temperament can affect the individual's social environment in three primary ways. First, individual differences in restlessness and composure help set the tone of interactions. That is, constitutionally based characteristics of the individual impinge on others, affecting the way that others behave. Second, temperament affects initiating behavior, and thus influences the ways in which individuals structure their social and nonsocial environments. Finally, temperament influences the nature of the feedback or reinforcement given to others in social interactions.

Buss & Plomin propose five criteria to determine which of many personality dispositions should be considered as "temperaments." Examination of the criteria make clear two basic differences in the approach of Buss & Plomin and that of Thomas and his colleagues. Buss & Plomin are firmly committed to a genetically determined etiology, and they are more precise in their definition of temperament. Their five criteria are: Genetic component; Stability during development; Presence in adults; Adaptiveness; Presence in animals. In Buss & Plomin's view, evidence of these dispostions in animals lends credance to the genetic and biologic basis for the characteristic—necessary requirements in their framework.

Four broadly defined dimensions meet the criteria for temperament variables according to Buss & Plomin. These are Emotionality, Activity, Sociability, and Impulsivity. Emotionality refers to intensity of reaction or level of arousal, including both autonomic nervous system arousal as well as the expressive aspects of emotional arousal. Activity generally refers to total energy output. Sociability consists basically of affiliativeness—a strong desire to be with others. Impulsivity refers to response latency. There are two bipolar components to the last temperament: resisting versus giving in to drives and impulses; responding immediately to stimuli versus holding back and planning before acting. Buss & Plomin acknowledge that there is an inevitable overlap among their four temperaments, but they do not consider this a major problem due to the very broad nature of their definitions.

As with most investigators of temperament, Buss & Plomin have modified and refined their measurement and scaling techniques over the course of their research. Utilizing the acronym EASI (Emotionality, Activity, Sociability, and Impulsivity), they developed a series of EASI Temperament Surveys. The initial scale, EASI-I, consisted of 20 items, five tapping each of the four temperaments. Using a 1–5 Likert type rating scale, mothers were asked to assess their children on each of the 20 items. Examples of items from the four major categories are: "upset easily," "always on the go," "tends to be shy," and "hops from interest to interest." Factor analytic procedures applied to the 139 subject sample revealed that the items generally loaded within the four temperament dimensions as hypothesized. There was, however, some overlap among items, especially in Activity and Impulsivity domains. Revising the statements to be first rather than third person, the EASI-I was administered to a large sample of college students, yielding similar results as with the child sample. Test-retest reliabilities were around .80.

Subsequent work on EASI-II was carried out to reduce the overlap among items and to purify the factor loadings. EASI-III (Buss & Plomin, 1975), the current form of the survey, was expanded from the two earlier versions, and consists of 54 items. It was validated on 137 middle-class families of young twins, both parents responding. In this version the rating scales were expanded to include statements aimed at more differentiated subcomponents of the four basic temperament dimensions. As example, Emotionality was broken into three subcategories: general, fear, and anger. Activity items were concerned with tempo and vigor. Impulsivity included items which dealt with inhibitory control, decision time, sensation seeking, and persistence.

The bulk of the empirical work on temperament by Buss & Plomin utilized twin studies, a research strategy consistent with their strong view as to the importance of a genetic component in temperament variability. Through a series of correlational computations they demonstrated more similarity of temperament between identical than fraternal twins. Values of r ranged from .65 to .84 and .50 to .71 for samples of identical boy and girl twins, respectively. Comparable ranges for samples of fraternal twins were .00 to .20 and .00 to .59; with the exception of the .59 value, no r was greater than .20 for the fraternal twin samples. While factor analysis of the first form of EASI scales did not demonstrate factorial unity, subsequent modifications of the EASI scales lead to more consistent findings, essentially confirming the relative independence of the four temperament dimensions.

Consistent with other biologically based theories (Claridge, Canter, & Hume, 1973), Buss & Plomin suggest that temperament has important physiological substrates. Level of arousal, as an example, is seen as a function of the central and autonomic nervous systems with important consequences for overt behavior. Buss & Plomin propose a connection between Impulsivity and cortical arousal, as well as a connection between level of arousal and the Emotionality and Activity traits. In their view, thus, temperament has strong physiological and neurological underpinnings.

Buss & Plomin assume further that various temperamental combinations provide some explanation for the individual variation in personality development. It seems reasonable, too, that variants of pathology might also be related to temperament extremes and combinations. Buss & Plomin suggest that high Activity and high Impulsivity characterize the hyperactive individual. While derived from their theoretical view, the combination is certainly consistent with empirically determined descriptions of hyperactivity. They propose, too, that a combination of high Impulsivity, low Sociability, and low Emotionality are predisposing to psychopathy, and that aggressiveness is based on temperaments of high Activity, high Emotionality, and high Impulsivity. Buss & Plomin acknowledge that there is no direct causal relationship between temperament and personality and/or psychopathology. Rather, they stress the influence or contribution of temperamental variance to the interaction of children and persons in their enviornment. They urge consideration of factors other than exclusively environmental ones to help delineate the development of personality.

Although they argue for the four temperaments as essential foundations of individuality, Buss & Plomin suggest further that the original range of each temperament dimension may be broad, but that it becomes more narrow with development. Temperaments are not static, but are modified and developed over time and experience, through interaction with the environment. The complexity of personality organization is a function of both constitutional and socializing factors, a point of view compatible with that of Thomas & Chess (1977). Buss & Plomin suggest, too, that parent-child interactions are bidirectional. The determinants of child-rearing practices are the parents' previous learning and their temperamental makeup, as well as the temperament of the child. "The parent-child interaction has three components: parental child-rearing practices, the impact of which is in part determined by the child's temperament; the eliciting effects of the child's temperament, which are in part determined by parental temperament; and modeling, the extent of which is partly determined by parent-child similarity in temperament" (Buss & Plomin, 1975, p. 219).

In summary, Buss & Plomin, and Thomas, Chess, & Birch (1968), primary investigators of temperament, hold a number of points of view in common. Yet, their approaches differ in several important ways. The definitions of temperament constructs, their breadth, pervasiveness, and interrelationships are not entirely consistent, and deserve comment. Thomas, Chess, & Birch identify nine dimensions of temperament, Buss & Plomin, four. Although there is considerable overlap between the two schemes, it appears that some of the nine Thomas et al. temperamental constructs may be subsumed by the broader ones of Buss & Plomin. As an example, Thomas et al. identify "mood" as one of their nine temperament characteristics. In the Buss & Plomin view, mood is a global construct, encompassing and incorporating their four more basic temperamental dimensions. They suggest that mood is positively associated with Activity and Sociability, but is negatively related to Emotionality and Impulsivity. Empirical data from studies of adults lend some statistical support to the Buss & Plomin interpretation. It may well be that the Buss & Plomin "temperaments" are broad dimensions which give rise to the observed behavioral variables which define Thomas, Chess, & Birch's nine categories of temperament. Both sets of researchers argue for the biological predispositions of the temperament variations, and both stress the affects of these individual variations on the interactions of child and persons in his environment. Differences in number and definition of temperament dimensions may in part be related to the level of analysis and the measurement systems employed.

Despite some differences in definitions and measurement, Thomas, Chess, &

Birch and Buss & Plomin lay the groundwork for consideration of biological or physiological variations as influences on personality development and social competence. These investigators are not alone in their interest in constitutional underpinnings of individual differences (see Eysenck, 1967; Claridge et al., 1973). Indeed, the possible contribution of constitutional factors to personality and behavior has been of interest since early Greek philosophers proposed body-personality typologies. Consideration of alternative approaches to the study of temperament is appropriate before reviewing efforts to apply temperament constructs to the study of children and risk groups.

RELATED THEORY AND EVIDENCE

The somatotyping efforts of Sheldon (1942) provide a backdrop for the discussion of constitutional factors in personality. Sheldon described three basic physical prototypes, each with characteristic personality or temperamental attributes. Endomorphs (soft, round, high fat to muscle ratio) were described as viscerotonic, i.e., slow reactors, relaxed in posture and movement, even-tempered, indiscriminately amiable. Mesomorphs (muscular, hard and rectangular in body build), were viewed as characteristically energetic, aggressive, active, and callous. The ectomorph in Sheldon's scheme was inhibited, fast-reacting, hypersensitive to pain—the so-called cerebrotonic personality. Physically the ectomorph was thin and light-muscled, linear and fragile in body build. In addition to claiming high correlations between specific somatotypes and specific temperaments, Sheldon suggested that certain pathological conditions were related to body build, viz., extreme withdrawal, as in schizophrenia, characterizing the ectomorphic somatotype. Sheldon's work has been widely criticized but is conceptually related to other theories of temperament and personality, especially to Eysenck's (1967) work on introversion-extroversion. In Eysenck's view personality differences are due, in part at least, to individual variations in the organization of central nervous system processes. Differences in nervous typology are thought to be mediated by genetic and biological variables, thus for Eysenck the phenotypic or descriptive personality dimensions of introversion-extroversion and neuroticism can be partly explained by these underlying genotypic factors. He suggests specifically that variations in arousal and activation form the basis of personality dimensions. Early work emphasizing initial patterns of reactivity by the Thomas et al. (1963) group are compatible with these ideas.

It should be noted that current investigators of temperament place less weight on the direct contribution of constitutional factor to temperament than did earlier theorists, as the powerful effects of socialization and the bidirectional, interactive relationship of child and caregiver are emphasized. Nevertheless, there is acknowledgement of the reality of individual differences in reactivity, in biologic make-up, and in the contribution of constitutional variance to the interactive equation. For example, in recent work Schalling (1977) notes that impulsivity and "anxiety proneness" are "associated with coherent patterns of individual differences concerning (1) the modulation of sensory input and level of vigilance, and (2) the modulation of emotion" (p. 131).

Infancy Studies

The recognition of definable differences among infants and children in terms of behavioral reactivity is of course not limited to formal temperament research. A number of investigators have described individual differences on temperament-like dimensions. Korner (1971), as an example, reports significantly different infant characteristics (frequency and length of cry, soothability, level of arousal, restlessness) which affect caregivers and which mediate the amount of attention and stimulation provided the child. Her observations are reminiscent of the findings from the longitudinal study conducted by Mary Shirley and her associates many years ago (1933). Their goal was to delineate the expanding repertoire of infant behaviors during the first two years; they were interested particularly in the time of onset and the sequencing of emerging behaviors. Several of Shirley's observations identify stylistic components. For example, fine motor coordination dealt with infants' reactivity; early social development was examined through analysis of approach-withdrawal in novel situation. Included in a number of observational areas were assessment of temperament-like characteristics such as body activity, rhythmicity, persistence and distractibility, activity level, irritability, and attention span. Although Shirley's work centered around biological determinants of specific behaviors and the increasingly greater specificity and complexity of behavioral organization, she inadvertently provided interesting data relevant to the onset, expression, and persistence of temperamental characteristics.

Findings from other studies also relate to temperament considerations. In their study of maternal behaviors and children's intelligence, Bayley & Schaefer (1964) included observations of children's behaviors and subsequent intelligence. While in general the realtionships between single behavioral dimensions and measures of intelligence were low, these investigators noted that for the 10–36 months age range "high mental scores go with extraverted adjusted ratings; that is active babies who are responsive to persons, and perhaps also those who tend to be calm" (p. 44). It is of interest to note that the 27 and 36 month ratings of children on happiness, positive behavior, and calmness were positively correlated to later ratings of friendliness, cooperativeness, attentiveness, and facility. Bayley & Schaefer also identified differences in stability and persistence of characteristics according to the sex of the infant or child. Such sex-related differences were noted more recently by Korner (1971) and Moss (1967). The point to be made is that individual differences among normal infants are identifiable in the neonatal and early infancy period—some of these individual characteristics likely serving as mediating influences in parent-child interactions.

This interpretation has received support from the insightful work of Escalona (1972), who argued that while a single characteristic of an infant is not linked to a particular response to environmental variables, "each infant organism has a whole set of separate reaction tendencies, and it is the combination of these organismic characteristics that determine the child's responsiveness to environmental influence" (p.10). She suggests that individual differences among infants are predispostions which shape the "infant's responsiveness and adaptation" in the early months of life. These early attributes become differentiated and integrated through experience, leading to the emergence of more stable characteristics. For purposes of this review, it is important to note that Escalona & Heider (1959) found more self-consistency of attributes for children evidencing developmental deviations or maladjustments than for those with normal development.

Birns, Barten, & Bridger (1969) also provide some interesting data on temperamental characteristic of 24 babies assessed at birth and at one, three, and four month, respectively. The similarity in the behavioral dimensions assessed and the demonstration of stability of stylistic differences over the first four months provide support for the interpretations of the Chess group. In addition to specific response measures, global ratings of infants were made by observers and testers on eight behavioral dimensions: irritability, soothability, activity level, alertness, vigor of response, sensitivity, tension, and maturity level. Irritability, tension, and sensitivity were found to be stable over the four measurement sessions. Soothability approached statistical significance, and activity level was stable when the neonatal assessment was excluded. Alertness, vigor, and maturity level did not prove to be statistically stable. Measures of pleasurable affect and social responsiveness were highly correlated from three to four months, while a measure of persistence on tracking tasks failed to show stability. These investigators were especially concerned with irritability as they considered it important in personality development as well as in social interactions. They found that at three and four months irritability was "positively correlated with sensitivity, soothability, and tension, and negatively correlated with positive affect and sociability" (p. 1080).

The Birns et al. (1969) demonstration of consistency on some temperament-like dimensions, taken in conjunction with the Thomas et al. work, provides tentative support for the hypothesis that early patterns of reactivity may be related to basic substrates of autonomic arousal and sensory responsiveness. This may be even more true for handicapped than for normal infants, especially for those at risk for some central nervous system disturbance. In this regard the studies of early schizophrenia by Fish and her colleagues are relevant (Fish, 1959; Fish & Alpert, 1963; Fish, Wile, Shapiro, & Halpern, 1966). Fish supports the notion that there are primary constitutional factors which are predisposing to schizophrenia, particularly disorders of "timing and integration of neurological maturation . . . reflected in disturbances of alertness, activity, muscle tonus, autonomic stability, physical growth and the sequence of postural development" (Fish & Alpert, 1963, p. 24). While extreme in degree, a number of the descriptors identified by Fish are reminiscent of the temperament dimensions proposed by the Thomas & Chess group, and provide some further support for the contribution of constitutional factors to the infant-parent interaction. As noted by Birns et al. (1969, p. 1081), "whether one is easily distressed, recovers quickly from stress, has low thresholds for incoming sensory stimuli, and responds with muscular tension may reflect one or more intrinsic qualities of the infant." Consistent with the *Zeitgeist* of the times, Birns et al. contend that these data should be considered in looking at direction of effects in mother-infant interactions. Like Thomas, Chess, & Birch, they want to take some of the onus off parents and suggest that "whether a four-month old is happy and sociable or cranky and irritable is more likely due to response tendencies of the baby than to specific characteristics of the mother" (p. 1081).

A note on Baron's (1972) findings are relevant to this point. Baron used the Carey scale to assess temperament of 18 Down's Syndrome infants 6-18 months of age with mental ages (MA) ranging from four-eight months. While comparable to Carey's standardization infants of similar MA, there was greater variability within the Down's infants. Baron questioned the common impression that Down's infants are especially "easy" to care for, speculating instead that early recognition may, in effect, lower parents' expectations for development, so that they interpret the Down's children's characteristic hypotonia as indicative of adaptability. Finally, since Down's children are not functioning at their chronological level, age-related problems may not occur when they are expected. Baron's work is at least consistent with that of Chess & Korn (1970) who found that temperamental characteristics were similar for normal and retarded children when mental age was taken into account.

It is clear from findings to this point that infants differ on a broad array of response capabilities which have a temperament-like flavor. The significance of these differences is for the most part speculative, however, as the relative weights of infant and-or environmental influences on development of a given child are unknown. Importantly, too, the bulk of evidence in support of temperament variations has come from clinical or quasi-clinical sources, often utilizing parent or teacher reports. The validity and accuracy of these reports, and the robustness and stability of the perceived characteristics is uncertain. A more rigorous test of the continuity and stability of temperament characteristics requires consideration of longitudinal evidence. Several important longitudinal studies, although not planned within a temperament framework, provide data of relevance to temperament questions. These studies deserve more detailed reviews as they are a rich source of information about stability, variability, and influence of temperament attributes.

Longitudinal Studies

As part of ongoing psychoanalytically referenced work at the Menninger clinic, Grace Heider (1966) studied "vulnerability" in young children by following the same subjects from infancy through the preschool years. Her data were derived from psychological testing, observations, interviews, and ratings made by parents and staff psychologists. Vulnerability was loosely defined as a sort of fragility or susceptability toward disorganization by children when confronting relatively normal levels of stress in the environment. Heider suggested at the outset that vulnerability was a function of the individual child's physical and emotional assets or disabilities in interaction with a variety of environmental variables.

Heider collected information on: equipment variables (body build, general health, sensory reactivity, and autonomic stability); management processes (coping and defensive behavior); and environment variables relating to the quality of social relationships. Some of the specific variables deserve mention as they are similar to the dimensions that temperament researchers employ. In Heider's study equipment variables included: Physique (build, energy of movement, fatigability); Vegetative Functioning (sleep, digestion, elimination); Sensory Reactivity (threshold, markedly high reactivity in various modalities, especially tactile); Functional Stability (across changing conditions, noting areas where there is loss of stability, and tempo arousal and decline); and Tendency of Delay Response. Even cursory review suggests that these variables are remarkably similar to the components of temperament portrayed by the Chess group. In essence Heider examined the equipment or resources that the child brings to interactions, characterizing the style with which the child handled stress under various conditions. She tried also to delineate those factors that the caregiver contributes to the ongoing interactions, factors which presumably play important roles in the development of efficient or inappropriate coping strategies.

When her sample children were about two years of age Heider rank-ordered them on a five-level scale of vulnerability—a second ranking occurring at about age four. Although there was significant stability of ranks over time ($r = .53$), a number of children gave evidence of increased vulnerability as they grew older. On the basis of case history analyses Heider suggested that increased vulnerability was due to the presence of organic defect that was unrecognized at the earlier age; to severe illness or increased stress; or to problems in measurement—inadequate weighting of some of the variables for some of the children. Only a few children were rated as less vulnerable; this was attributed to a positive response to stress, reflecting a higher level of functional integration. At the infant level extreme reactivity and high drive, coupled with low frequency of vocalization and intensity of oral behavior, were associated most strongly with ratings of vulnerability.

In a final interpretive summary, Heider proposed some general observations about the development of vulnerability which have direct relevance to the consideration of temperament in young children. She suggested that: vulnerability is inversely related to physiological factors such as robust physique, good energy resources, and easy vegetative functioning; vulnerability show an inverse relationship to good mother-child interaction; extremes of drive level, whether manifested in avoidance or conflict at the management level, may be related to vulnerability; there is a relationship between consistency of relative activity level during sleep and waking behavior and the ability to resist stress effects; narrowness of range of drive or interest may be a source of vulnerability; extreme variability in physiological factors and in maternal environment may affect the development of trust and identity and result in vulnerability. Finally, discomfort related to special qualities of stimuli, rather than to their intensity, may also be related to vulnerability.

It must be remembered that Heider studied a group of normal children. Although the case-study method is not presently in vogue and there is a conspicuous absence of statistical analyses, Heider presents an incredibly rich corpus of data and provides many cogent insights. She has amassed longitudinal data which are organized in such a way as to characterize both the child's and parent's contribution to development. She implicates many of the same variables that have been proposed by special educators as important for handicapped children. Heider's notions concerning energy resources, narrowness of range of drive and interest, and responsivity to special qualities of stimuli capture qualitatively important sources of information about children.

Two other studies from the Menninger group deserve mention. In *Prediction and Outcome,* Escalona & Heider (1959) studied children, infancy through age five. In Escalona's words, the "track record" for prediction over that age range was only "fair." Of particular interest to the present chapter was the observation that infantile patterns of behavior were most likely to persist into later childhood in overtly identical or similar forms among children who experienced significant developmental irregularity or maladaptation. From this point of view it might be argued that phenotypic continuity is indicative of less than optimal development; as according to Escalona & Heider, development involves the dissolving and reintegration of old patterns into new ones. A second point of particular interest was the seeming influence of sex role variables on continuity of development. The possible interactions of temperament and sex role is to be noted.

In separate but related work Murphy & Moriarity (1976) considered several sets of longitudinal data; a number of their findings relate to temperament considerations. Of particular importance was their observation that the "fit" between temperaments of mother and child was a crucial determinant of the viability of that relationship. It is to be emphasized that "fit" did not imply sameness or similarity of temperament of mother and child. It referred rather to the sensitivity and appropriateness of maternal responses to the infant's expressions of temperament. Said differently, it is not so much the match between temperaments as it is the match between the style of the child and the values and expectations of the parent that is the critical factor for congruence. The similarity to the Thomas, Chess, & Birch interpretations is apparent.

Findings from other longitudinal studies bear tangentially upon temperament questions, and deserve mention. Werner, Bierman, & French (1971) reported the findings of their ten-year follow-up study of an entire cohort of 1,000 babies on the island of Kauii, Hawaii. Their goal was to identify maternal prenatal conditions and to document intellectual and emotional development of sample children, noting especially the subsequent variations in growth that were related to problems experienced during the course of pregnancy, labor, and delivery. Follow-up of sample children at age ten did not provide confirming data regarding temperamental variables identified in infancy or in early childhood. Although the earlier measures were consistent with the notion of constitutionally based contributions to individual variation, overall there was little direct evidence of continuity with respect to temperament related problems. It is possible that by age ten stylistic characteristics had been attenuated and modified through the socialization process, especially through educational interventions. It is possible too that the ten-year measures of emotional problems in this study were too broad to identify or differentiate stylistic or temperamental differences. The initial stress might constitute a group that was temperamentally at risk—an interpretation consistent with the Stella Chess (1974) findings with rubella children. Because of the nature of the data collected in the Kauii study, however, it is not possible to test definitively the questions of continuity of temperament or to assess the strength of temperamental influences on problem development.

Findings from the Isle of Wight study (Rutter, Tizard, & Whitmore, 1970) provide some indirect evidence relevant to temperamental influences on problem development. The Isle of Wight study, like the Kauii effort, was a large-scale venture—the entire population of the island within a certain age range studied over time. Screening data about children were obtained from parents and teachers as well as from psychiatric assessments of children. Compared to the nonproblem children, children within the psychiatric group were described as restless, fidgety, irritable, and solitary, and as having poor concentration. Descriptors were similar for boys and girls, and overall suggested that the disordered children were characterized by negative behavioral styles reminiscent of temperament characteristics of "Difficult Children." The behavioral descriptions were also reminiscent of findings from the California Guidance Study (MacFarlane, Allen, & Honzig, 1954) in which characteristics of irritability, excessive dependence, mood swings, negativism, and somberness were found associated with problem development. Rutter et al. noted the similarity of child characteristics between the Isle of Wight study and the Thomas, Chess, & Birch New York Longitudinal Study, interpreting many of the behavioral indicators within a temperament frame of reference. Because the Isle of Wight measures were taken only at one point in time, it is not possible to determine whether the stylistic differences added to the determination of these children's psychiatric status or whether they were expressions of the condition. Nevertheless, the temperament-like variables seemed important when comparing psychiatrically identified children to matched peers in the general population.

Investigators at the Fels Institute have also provided extensive longitudinal data which have at least tentative implications for the study of temperament. Two major publications are of particular relevance. In 1958 Sontag, Baker, & Nelson published a longitudinal study of 140 children followed from preschool to early adolescence. Of particular concern was consideration of personality variables which were related to changes in intelligence (IQ). The Fels investigators attempted to characterize the personality styles of their children relative to the children's approaches to academic, intellectual, and problem solving activities. While lacking direct ties to temperament, the descriptions of the personality correlates of IQ change were somewhat similar to temperament dimensions. The ties between personality and intellectual variables, and the emergence of relatively stable personality clusters early in the child's life are at least consistent with the notion of temperamental predispostions. Examination of hypothesized temperamental dimensions in the development of personality characteristics as defined by the Fels workers may have important implications for the development of young handicapped children. It is tempting to apply the temperament-personality-abilities hypothesis to interpret the finding by Chess (1977) that some of the children in her rubella study were characterized by accelerating IQ changes.

A second major publication utilizing longitudinal data from the Fels Institute also deserves note. Kagan & Moss (1962), in their book *Birth to Maturity*, summarized results from a number of Fels studies of mental and social development conducted within a longitudinal framework. Child variables studied included motive related behaviors, sources of anxiety and conflict, defensive responses to anxiety-arousing situations, and modes of interpersonal interaction. Children were observed in interactive experiences to determine their tendency to approach or avoid social objects, their degree of spontaneity or tension in social interactions, and their tendency to dominate or submit. Maternal behaviors were systematically recorded while maternal and child behaviors were examined in various combinations over different periods in an effort to determine whether certain aspects of personality and achievement orientation demonstrated any continuity over the life-span of the subjects. Investigators also wanted to identify how possible patterns of child variables interacted with maternal behaviors.

As in the other Fels data cited above, there is no direct relationship between the specifics of their project and the study of temperament. However, a number of aspects of this longitudinal work are tangentially relevant. As example, the characteristic of passive approach tendencies in novel situations was found to be relatively stable over the first two years. Citing Gottesman's (1960) twin study on passivity in which he found higher concordance for MZ than DZ twins as consistent with their own data, Kagan & Moss concluded that the propensity to passivity or its derivations in late childhood, adolescence, and adulthood are established during the first six years of life. This interpretation is consistent with a linkage between personality and temperament.

Recent longitudinal studies focusing specifically on temperament have yielded equivocal results concerning continuity and stability, however, As example, Wilson & Lewis (1974) argued that the nine dimensions of temperament proposed by Thomas et al. are not independent and therefore should not be treated as separate facets of individuality. They studied selected aspects of temperament, including intensity of response (vigor), persistence, and activity. Instead of relying on checklists or ratings, they used direct observational techniques on a longitudinal sample of children across the age range 13 months through four years. Both boys and girls were observed at 13, 25, and 44 months of age—data collected in both a structured playroom setting and in a nursery school. A variety of measures were taken, a toy play score, for example, derived from the number of activity changes and the longest time spent in a single activity. At 44 months children's performance on a peg board was used to measure rate and persistence; vigor measures were taken at all ages across the study period through time sampled observations.

Overall Wilson & Lewis (1974) found little evidence to support continuity of temperamental characteristics within their sample. There were few sex differences of significance, and while there was some change with age, they interpreted their findings to suggest that there was little "developmental consistency" demonstrated. Where cross age correlations were high, they tended to be with age weighted variables. Attempting to relate possible temperamental characteristics to other aspects of children's performance, Wilson & Lewis gave the Matching Familiar Figures Test (MFFT) at 44 months. They could demonstrate no clear relationships between the play variables and the MFFT time or error scores. On the basis of their data as a whole, Wilson & Lewis concluded that

> there may be little individual stability in these dimensions. At this point in the research effort it must be concluded that temperament may not be a terribly useful notion.... For one, there may be no individual stability in those behaviors we consider under this construct.... Alternatively, the failure to find stability may be due to the fact that temperamental variables are extremely susceptable to learning and are easily modified.... Finally, the lack of stability may be due to the differential rates of development which could mask consistency (p. 22).

While Wilson & Lewis raise a number of important points which need consideration by investigators of temperament, their data do no warrant dismissal of the topic per se. Their measures were limited, were not always scaled for interage analysis, and most importantly, were sometimes of questionable validity relative to the temperament constructs. Their negative findings, nevertheless, underscore the tentative state of temperament findings and methodology, especially when applied to infants and young children.

In an effort to address specifically the stability and continuity questions, McDevitt (1976) utilized a longitudinal design to assess the Chess et al. temperament dimensions from infancy to early childhood. Temperament was rated by mothers using the Carey questionnaire when the children were between four and eight months of age. The Behavioral Style Questionnaire (McDevitt & Carey, 1975) was used to measure temperament when the children were between three and seven years of age. Dimensions of activity level, adaptability, threshold, and intensity were found to be stable for both sexes up to five years. At five to seven years of age only activity level and mood were stable, and only for boys. The temperament clusters (Easy, Difficult, Slow to Warm Up) showed a significant degree of consistency from infancy to five years, but little stability from infancy to age seven. Overall McDevitt concluded that

> Temperamental characteristics are influential in personality and behavior throughout development, and periods of instability are reflective of concurrent developmental changes in behavioral competence or major changes in social environment.... It is the theoretical definition of the constructs which remains stable (p. 162).

Taken as a whole, then, there is considerable and diverse evidence which argues for the influence of individual differences in temperament on other aspects of development and adjustment. Although a number of theoretical approaches to the study of temperament are available, from an applied point of view the Thomas & Chess approach is particularly promising as these investigators have already demonstrated the utility of their constructs in work with children and families. Their ideas have stimulated considerable research by members of the New York group as well as by others in the United States and Britain. A number of these studies have relevance for consideration of temperament in young children and in handicapped children, and provide a background for further research utilizing their temperament framework.

RESEARCH WITH CHILDREN AND RISK POPULATIONS

Studies of Handicapped and Risk Children

Thomas, Chess, and their colleagues utilized data from the NYLS to demonstrate the influence of temperament on development of children within a middle-class, primarily Anglo sample (Thomas, Chess, Birch, Hertzig, & Korn, 1963; Thomas, Chess, & Birch, 1968). They have also studied temperament variations in a nonmajority culture group—a sample of 95 children from working-class Puerto Rican families (Hertzig, Birch, Thomas, & Mendez, 1968; Thomas, Chess, Sillen, & Mendez, 1974). Children with developmental problems have also been followed longitudinally—one study involving 68 premature children (Hertzig, 1974), another 52 mildly retarded children (Chess & Hassibi, 1970). Additional case history studies on individual children (Birch, Thomas, & Chess, 1964; Thomas & Chess, 1975) and a systematic follow-up of 243 children with congenital rubella have also been reported (Chess, Korn, & Fernandez, 1971). Taken as a whole, the New York research group has amassed considerable data which provide the basis for both clinical and theoretical inferences regarding development of normal and handicapped children. The reader is referred to the volumes by Thomas, Chess, & Birch (1968) and Thomas & Chess (1977) for comprehensive overviews of their work. Several studies deserve more detailed review as they relate specifically to handicapped or risk children.

In an analysis of the development of 52 mildly retarded children ages five-eleven, Chess & Korn (1970) reported that 31 (60 percent) were judged to have signs of psychiatric problems. Parents of mentally retarded children expressed more concerns about children's motor activity, speech and language, mood, and tantrums than did parents of nonretarded but behaviorally disordered children. The latter parents had more complaints in the area of somatic problems, sleep and bedtime difficulties, school behavior problems, and peer relationships. At age five, the mentally retarded children were not appreciably different on temperament ratings from children of normal ability. Using the Easy, Difficult, and Slow to Warm Up clusters, however, the various subgroups did differ—more of the retarded than comparison children evidenced signs of the Difficult Child pattern (problems in rhythmicity, adaptability, approach/withdrawal, intensity, and mood). Chess & Korn concluded that the presence of three signs or extreme scores in three critical temperaments was indicative of risk. Emphasizing, however, that there were a number of instances in which children were inaccurately identified as risk or nonrisk, they warned of overinterpreting possible false negative or false positive information. Of major significance for this review was the generalization that temperament assessment is potentially useful in identifying children at risk for behavior disorders *within* a mentally retarded group. A reasonable generalization is that temperament characteristics become particularly powerful influences in children who are at risk or vulnerable from other conditions.

A follow-up study of 243 children with congenital rubella (Chess, Korn, & Fernandez, 1971) also yielded data of importance in regard to temperament. It is of incidental interest to note that approximately 21 percent of the sample of rubella children were considered well babies with no signs of defect, an important finding in terms of risk predictions. Temperament data on the 243 children were gathered through interviews and questionnaires. One hundred ten of the sample children were judged to have behavior disorders—with three or more signs of the Difficult Child pattern constituting an accurate predictor of the development of problem behavior. A four-year follow-up of 189 of the rubella children indicated that 92 of them had behavior disturbances. These findings closely parallel those of the study of the mentally retarded group already described. Chess (1974) notes in this regard: "Both groups show a high incidence of behavior disorder, and in both there is a significant correlation between the temperamental signs of the Difficult Child and the occurrence of behavioral disturbance. The Difficult Child is more vulnerable to behavior disorder development even without intellectual or physical handicap, as seen in the NYLS findings, but the presence of handicap increases this vulnerability'' (p. 62). These studies are important in that within category differences in temperament variables were recognized, and this variability related, at least tentatively, to behavioral and social competencies.

Another study of risk children provides information relevant to this review. As the findings from this major research effort are of interest both substantively and methodologically, the study is reported in some detail. Graham, Rutter, & George (1973) attempted to replicate the NYLS of Thomas et al. on a different population of children considered at risk for developing behavior disorders. Sixty children, all of whom had a mentally ill parent, comprised the sample. The children's age at study entrance ranged from three to eight years. A behavior questionnaire was completed by the mothers, and a temperamental characteristics interview was independently rated. The following year the mothers again completed the behavior questionnaire and teachers also rated the behavior of the children who had reached school age.

The temperament interview consisted of three parts. First, the mothers were asked to describe their child's behavior over a variety of situations. Second, the mothers commented on the child's regularity of functions in a number of different areas over the previous two weeks. Finally, the mothers commented on the child's behavior in various nonroutine situations, noting especially the child's behavior when asked to change his activity. Each of the children was then rated independently on seven categories of temperament: mood, intensity of emotional expression, activity, regularity, malleability, fastidiousness, and approach/withdrawal to new people. Inter-rater reliability was uniformly high, ranging from 64 percent to 98 percent. Rate-rerate reliability was somewhat disappointing; the investigators' interpretation was that variation in child behavior was the major source of difference on these measures. Age effects on expression of the temperament characteristics yielded only differences in intensity. Some sex differences were found, with boys being less fastidious and more intense in emotional responsiveness than girls.

At the time of the initial assessment, 18 of 44 children, or 41 percent, were judged to be abnormal; comparable figures a year later were 26 of 60, or 43 percent. During the first study year the only temperament factors of apparent importance were intensity and fastidiousness. A year later the disturbed children were those who, at the initial assessment, were more negative in mood and less regular in biological functions. Teachers rated 15 of 43 children as deviant. Nine were described as antisocial and six had neurotic difficulties. Consistent with the interactional view proposed by Thomas & Chess, Graham et al. (1973) concluded that "No simple unidirectional model can adequately explain the relationship between adverse temperamental characteristics (ATC) and psychiatric disorders. Rather, it appears that particular ATC render the child more vulnerable to the adverse effects of family discord and other stress factors" (p. 337). These investigators emphasize the need for further research to elucidate the effects of ATC on parent-child interactions and attitude development, cautioning too that the direct influences of assumed causative factors as well as the stability of temperamental characteristics is uncertain. Overall, Graham and his colleagues interpret their results as supporting the findings of the Thomas, Chess, & Birch NYLS on their different (and at risk) population. Importantly, too, they emphasize the notions of individual differences and interactional models in their attempt to relate qualitative measures of family relationships to the dimensions of temperament in risk children.

Finally, recent work by Cameron (1977) is relevant to the interaction of temperament of child and parent. Cameron reanalyzed data from the New York Longitudinal Study in an effort to delineate possible links between characteristics of parents and children which appeared predisposing to behavioral problems. Basing his work upon data gathered by Thomas et al. (1968) during the third-year parental interview, Cameron utilized a cluster analysis technique, extracting eight oblique parental clusters from the 70-item correlational matrix. These clusters had to do with parental disapproval, conflict, strictness/ permissiveness, protectiveness, inconsistent discipline, depressed living standards, limitations on material supports for the child, and a large family orientation. When children's temperamental characteristics were related to parental dimensions, two temperamental traits, adaptability and intensity, emerged as most powerful. Rhythmicity was related to parental styles only during the first two years of the child's life; activity level was nonsignificantly related across all age levels. Cameron interpreted his findings as supporting the interactional view of development, but stressed that it is necessary to consider the interaction of specific temperaments and particular parental responses or attitudes in describing the development of problems.

School Related Research

In further work by the New York group, Gordon & Thomas (1967) examined kindergarten children's behavioral styles and related them to teacher's appraisals of the children's intellectual abilities. Utilizing a teacher's rating scale called Quality of Participation, the sample of children was divided into four subgroups: "Plungers," "Go-Alongers," "Sideliners," and "Non-Participators." Thomas & Gordon viewed the rating scale information as providing a concurrent measure of the temperament dimensions of approach-withdrawal and adaptability, reflecting the child's initial response to a novel situation and the ease with which an initially negative response was modified. Teachers also estimated the general level of intelligence of each of the children, and the children were given the Kuhlmann-Anderson IQ test. The relationship between teachers' estimates of intelligence and IQ scores was positive and significant, as were the correlations between the Quality of Participation ratings and both IQ scores and the teachers' estimates of intelligence. However, partial correlations holding IQ constant also yielded significant relationships, suggesting that the teachers were influenced in their estimates of ability by nonintellective behavioral characteristics of the children—approach/withdrawal and adaptability in school situations. The direction of the inaccurate estimations is the key finding in this study. Five of the six children who were over-estimated were in the Plunger group. Fifty children were underestimated—11 Plungers, 28 Go-Alongers, and 11 Sideliners. However, the underestimations for the Sideliners were significantly larger than for the other two groups, suggesting that the teachers were more likely to be inaccurate in a negative direction in estimating ability of those children who did not readily approach new situations and who were somewhat slow in adapting.

Gordon & Thomas propose that teachers' judgments are distorted by perceptions of specific aspects of children's temperament or behavioral styles. In their opinion two important implications may be derived from this finding. First, if children's self-concepts are developed, in part at least, from judgments of significant adults, estimations by teachers may influence the quality of interaction between students and teachers and thus be potentially limiting in the development of the child's self-concept. Second, inaccuracies in teachers' estimations may influence the instructional process, as the teacher's expectations for a given child's progress might not match the capabilities of the child. Thus, both quantity and quality of work designed for the student might be affected. This observation received empirical support from the attribution work by Weiner & Kukla (1970) and in recent studies by Lavelle (1977) and Palmer (1977). Gordon & Thomas suggest that individual differences may be accommodated more precisely if teachers are aware of how these stylistic differences affect their perceptions of a child.

Chess, Thomas, & Cameron (1976) provide another illustration of the relationship between temperament and school performance. In a paper that examines the influence of temperament on approach to tasks and adaptation to school activities, Chess et al. cite data collected on a subsample of the NYLS. Temperament ratings for 116 children obtained at age five were compared to seven academic achievement scores. Achievement measures included mean percentile scores in reading and arithmetic obtained for grades one–three and grades four–six, and WRAT scores for reading, spelling, and arithmetic.

For three of the temperament dimensions there were no relationships with the achievement scores. There were scattered significant correlations for four other temperament dimensions. The most substantial relationships were between the temperamental dimensions of adaptability and approach/withdrawal and academic achievement. That is, lower achievement scores were associated with nonadaptability and withdrawal. It is interesting that these are characteristics of the Slow to Warm Up child, findings consistent with the results of the Gordon & Thomas (1967) study. More specifically, the temperament dimensions of adaptability and approach/withdrawal may have influenced teacher expectations and instructional activities, resulting in lowered academic performance. How variation in children's temperament characteristics influence teachers' expectations is currently under investigation by Pullis utilizing a decision-making model.

In work reported in 1975, Garside et al. conducted a research project aimed at defining the dimensions of temperament for British infant school children. They developed a technique to measure those dimensions, a standard, semistructured interview consisting of 48 items relating to 17 themes concerning temperament. The interview was conducted with parents of 209 British children. Inter-rater reliabilities had a median value of .82. Test-retest reliability was somewhat less but still higher than most other reported studies—50 percent of the items were above .8 and 80 percent were above .6. On the basis of two principle-component analyses, Garside et al. concluded that infant school children could be described along the following main dimensions: withdrawal and poor adaptability; assertiveness; high activity and intensity; mood; distractibility and attention span; and irregularity. These components accounted for approximately 42 percent of the variance, leading the investigators to observe, "It seems reasonable to suggest that components deriving from this type of data constitute more fundamental and homogeneous phenomena than components deriving from analysis of behavioral content data" (p. 224).

Garside and his colleagues identified and weighted the 30 most important variables derived through their interview format, finding that they clustered as four main and relatively imdependent components. Analysis of sex-related differences in temperament of infant school children five years of age indicated generally that girls tended to be more withdrawn than boys (not statistically significant) and were significantly more irregular. Boys were more moody. This study confirmed many of the temperamental variables that Thomas, Chess, & Birch posited—seven of the nine dimensions found to be relevant in the description of a normal child at age five.

Further evidence linking temperament with subsequent adjustment is found in a recent study by Carey, Fox, & McDevitt (1977). These researchers were interested in the power of temperamental measures obtained during infancy for prediction of behavior during the early school years. Fifty infants were rated by their parents and assigned to four groups (easy, intermediate low, intermediate high, difficult) based on the temperament scores. Focussing on cognitive styles and school adjustment rather than on achievement scores, Carey et al. collected MFFT scores and teacher ratings concerning socialization when the children were 5½ to 7 years of age. Parents also provided temperament ratings about this time.

Results indicated that the children rated as intermediate high and difficult were significantly more impulsive (reflected by MFFT response latency scores) than those receiving intermediate ratings, but not more than those rated easy during infancy. Response accuracy was not significantly different among the groups. Examination of the school adjustment measures showed that "children rated as easy in infancy were significantly more poorly adjusted compared with other groups. Next came the difficult ones, and the intermediate had the best adjustment scores" (p. 622). Thus, infants with temperament ratings that were extreme were found to have adjusted less readily to early schooling demands. When subsequent temperament data were correlated with the MFFT scores and teachers' ratings, only adaptability was significantly related to school adjustment. Errors on the MFFT were associated with nonadaptability and nonpersistence.

Carey, Fox, & McDevitt (1977) point out that their findings concerning infant temperament and school behavior are inconclusive and therefore of questionable clinical and predictive value. Similarly, there was no clear-cut relationships between infant temperament and impulsivity. However, comparisons of current temperament ratings with problem-solving style and school adjustment provided more reliable information. That is, lower adaptability was associated with difficulties in problem solving situations and was also correlated with school adjustment. Nonpersistence was also related to lower scores on the MFFT, suggesting possible problems in ability to sustain attention. In their 1977 publication Carey et al. pinpointed some of the methodological problems related to sampling and to limited differentiation on their measure of school adjustment. They concluded, however, that although infant temperament data were not found to be highly reliable predictors, concurrent temperament assessments provided information useful in evaluating and understanding children's adjustment in school.

Studies of Preschool Children

A number of investigators have used concurrent assessment rather than predictive strategies in attempting to relate temperament characteristics to young children's performance in social and educational settings. J. Lewis (1977) examined the relationship between individual differences in temperament and social behavior of preschoolers. Using maternal reports to assess temperament on the Thomas & Chess dimensions, and a time sampling observation technique to look at behavior, she focused on three types of social behavior: (1) visual (looking and watching), (2) physical behaviors (approach and action toward other children), (3) verbal behavior (talking and play noises). She also included a measure of social distance. She concluded that the temperament dimensions of activity level, approach/withdrawal, and sensory threshold were highly related to social behavior. In general, the Easy Child characteristics were associated with high social proximity. Activity and approach tendency were correlated across home and school settings. Distractibility as reported by mothers was associated with generally erratic social behavior at school while regularity and persistence at home were related to constructive activity and a high amount of verbal communication with peers. Although Lewis found no direct significant relationships between the factors of adaptability, intensity, or mood and the child's social behavior, she suggested that information about children's temperamental characteristics would be useful for instructional personnel and parents as they could anticipate a child's reaction and modify the nature of the social interaction to facilitate rather than impede the child's adjustment and progress.

A similar argument is made by Klein (1977) based on her study of the relationships of temperament characteristics and adjustment to day care of 43 young children. Using a general ability estimate and a standard behavior questionnaire, Klein asked day care staff to rate children's adjustment to the day care facility after approximately one week and again after three months. She assessed temperament through parent interviews utilizing the Thomas et al. Parent Questionnaire. She found that the nine temperament dimensions were not entirely independent, but rather that there were several clusters of temperament measures: activity, intensity, and distractibility; mood and intensity; and persistence. In general there were few sex or age linked relationships to the temperament findings, but ratings of adjustment improved with age. The temperament variable with the most powerful relationship to adjustment was activity. This finding held for both short-term and long-term adjustment ratings. Klein noted too that distractibility and persistence were significantly correlated with several measures of adjustment, while rhythmicity, adaptability, threshold, and intensity were more modestly related. Her findings were overall consistent with that of J. Lewis (1977) with children of similar age. Klein, too, argues for the importance of temperamental variation in influencing adjustment to group care, noting particularly that increased sensitivity of day care staff to children's temperament might facilitate adjustment of high risk children.

Studies of School-Age Children at Risk

A number of investigators have attempted to delineate the nature of a possible relationship between children's temperament characteristics and their performance and adjustment in school. These findings are somewhat fragmented but nonetheless of interest.

In recent work Lambert & Windmiller (1977) report an exploratory study of temperament in a population of children at risk—a subsample of 327 children from the Stress of School Project carried out in Berkeley, California. The sample included hyperactive children, low-achieving children, and children nominated by teachers as having chronic behavior adjustment problems in school. The study goals were to see if responses to an interview could be used to define temperamental traits; and, if so, would the traits be present in some differential way in the three experimental and control groups. The investigators were particularly interested in discovering early identifiable personality characteristics in the hyperactive group. A multifaceted interview with parents of second-, fourth-, and sixth-grade children provided the primary data. As part of the interview, parents responded to 17 questions designed to yield a temperament profile for each child. Each of the nine dimensions had one question for infancy and one for early childhood. Factor analytic treatment of the ratings yielded six independent dimensions: attention span, threshold level, activity level, distractibility, approach/ withdrawal, and rhythmicity/adaptability.

To see if the temperament characteristics of the various populations differed from each other, the factor scores were subjected to an analysis of variance. Two dimensions, distractibility and rhythmicity/adaptability, differed for the problem and nonproblem samples. Further comparisons demonstrated that the hyperactive group differed significantly from the nonhyperactive group only on the distractibility dimension. Examination of mean scores indicated that the hyperactive group had the most extreme scores on all of the dimensions, but apart from the distractibility factor there were no significant differences between that group and the control and other problem groups. It should be noted that the findings may have been limited by the measurement techniques, as only two questions were directed at each temperament dimension.

In another set of studies with school age children, Seegars (1977) assessed temperament through parents' and teachers' ratings. In his early work with elementary school teachers he consistently identified five rather than three clusters of temperament characteristics which described his sample children. In addition to the Thomas et al. categories of the Difficult, Easy, and Slow to Warm Up child, Seegars identified a cluster he labeled the "Environmentalist" and another he called the "Emotionally Fragile." The latter label described a child who was insecure, hesitant, susceptiable to stress—the former a child who was characterized as "evidencing . . . early sociopathic or conscienceless behavior" (1978). One product of Seegars' work is a Behavior Checklist which can be used by teachers and parents to assess a child's characteristic temperament and his school performance. The Checklist consists of 25 statement, five getting at each of the five temperament groups identified by Seegars. The checklist yields a pattern or profile of weighted scores for each temperament cluster. By relating scores on the Checklist to other measures of behavior, Seegars was able to demonstrate that the clusters were relatively independent and that the temperament types had different behavioral correlates. In subsequent work Seegars related temperament as measured by the Behavior Checklist to various school achievement indices, finding that mean scores for grades were higher for Easy Children than for the Environmentalist group. In current work Seegars is investigating other aspects of possible temperament-personality-behavior patterns which influence school achievement. The stated goal of his research is to match intervention techniques with temperament styles. Preliminary intervention recommendations for each type of child have already been formulated and tested in a clinical-education setting. The Seegars work is particularly interesting as it is aimed at linking intervention strategies to temperament characteristics.

Support for the Seegars approach is provided by data from a series of studies of early identification of educationally high-risk children (Keogh, Hall, & Becker, 1974). As part of a larger research project, Hall & Keogh (1979) attempted to relate children's temperament to their educational competence. These investigators followed progress of the same children from kindergarten through grade three. On the basis of behavioral observations and teachers' ratings in kindergarten, children were identified as risk or nonrisk, their achievement and social-behavioral characteristics monitored over the subsequent years. Temperament information about 15 risk children was collected at the end of the third grade—this information gathered through individual interviews with each child's teacher. No single pattern or profile characterized the children identified as educational risk, although some tentative patterns emerged. Girls were perceived by teachers as moderate in activity level, mild in intensity of response, high in response threshold, positive in mood, initially withdrawing and irregular in self-pacing; their problems were primarily in academic achievement. Risk boys tended to fall into one of two patterns—one characterized by high activity, intense reactions, low thresholds, and negative and uneven mood. These boys were described as low in adaptability, distractible, and lacking in persistence and in self-regulation. A second cluster of temperament-like descriptors characterized another set of risk boys at third grade. These boys were perceived by teachers as slow to adapt to change, distractible, and withdrawing, but relative to the pattern already described, milder in response, more positive in mood, and less extreme in activity level. While the findings from this study must be interpreted with caution because of the small number of children still in the third grade follow-up sample, the variations among children in the risk group were striking. Case study interviews with teachers revealed clearly the importance of temperament-like characteristics of children as influencing a child's success or failure in the classroom. The potential impact of temperamental variations within problem groups was underscored.

GENERALIZATION AND SPECULATION

Taken as a whole, there is considerable evidence that infants and young children show wide individual differences in behavioral styles, in the "how" of behavior subsumed under the rubric of temperament. There is also evidence that affective-social relationships between infants and parents are bidirectional—the interaction a function of both child and caregiver variables. From this perspective variations in temperament may influence, even mediate, socialization, and may directly and indirectly affect broad aspects of the developing child's cognitive and affective competence. It seems reasonable that temperamental characteristics may be particularly important for handicapped children who by definition have some disabling or limiting cognitive or motoric condition. Information contained in this review, together with subjective reports of teachers and clinicians who work with young children, suggest that individual variations in temperament are important influences on a given child's success or failure in a social group, be it family or preschool. Personal competence and social acceptance for exceptional children may be especially influenced by stylistic, temperamental characteristics, suggesting that at least some of the variance in competence within special education groups is a function of temperament. Said directly, temperament may be an especially powerful mediator of social interaction when children have serious cognitive or motoric limitations. The study of temperament by special educators, thus deserves systematic attention.

While there is an intuitive appeal and in some cases supporting evidence for this line of argument, the study of temperament and its influence is limited by serious conceptual and methodological ambiguities reflected in much of the research reviewed in this chapter. On a conceptual level it is necessary to confront such issues as consistency-stability and the recurring trait-setting argument well articulated in personality work (Block, 1977; Bowers, 1977; Emmerich,

1968; Mischel, 1969, 1977). Of particular concern for temperament research are further questions of the number and independence of proposed dimensions, the nature of the organization of dimensions, and the changes in patterns of organization with time and development or in relation to particular formal or informal experiences. Of real concern for those who work with handicapped young children are questions of modifiability of temperament characteristics, especially in terms of educational interventions. The issue of biological contributions or underpinnings to temperament variations is a critical but unsettled one, with clear implications for intervention questions.

On a methodological level the study of temperament is also complex. The psychometric properties of most temperament scales have received only limited attention; there is little evidence to demonstrate the comparability of items across age levels; and validity criteria tend to be subjective and incomplete. Where temperament of infants and young children is studied, assessment of the child's characteristics is made by an adult in the child's life—a parent or teacher. Thus, the variables associated with person perception become important. Bem & Allen (1974) note that individuals "hold implicit personality theories... (which) lead us... to generalize beyond our observations and fill in missing data which are, in fact, not there" (p. 511). Attribution research suggests too, that observers overestimate the degree to which behavior is caused by stable person characteristics and underestimate the effects of setting variables (Jones & Nisbett, 1972). Additionally, raters see only limited, possibly situationally specific, aspects of a given child's tempermental repertoire, thus make generalizations from limited samples of a child characteristics.

Finally, the normative model widely used in assessing many aspects of children's development is clearly not appropriate for the study of temperament, especially for the study of temperament in handicapped or risk children. It is not possible to make assumptions as to distributional characteristics of temperament dimensions, nor do temperament data have specific age-norm referents. It seems reasonable that an ipsative approach (Emmerich, 1968) involving study of "intraindividual organization of behavioral attributes" may be a productive one for studying particular children or groups of children. The real goal of an ipsative approach is to document behavioral attributes in an idiographic, nonnormative fashion. The ipsative approach is important from a developmental standpoint in that structural changes in temperament may be viewed over time, yielding information about integration of structures or differentiation of components. It seems reasonable that there may be precursors, even "core" temperament dimensions, which become more developed and differentiated with time and social experience. An ipsative approach would yield information about this kind of structural reorganization, at the same time providing data which might lead to insights about a given child's functioning at the time the data were gathered.

Keeping in mind the problems of measurement and the somewhat fragile construct validity of many hypothesized temperament dimensions, there is, nevertheless, sufficient evidence to document the importance of temperamental variations on socialization and personal competence. It is our view that there are some consistencies of temperament which characterize individuals early on; these characteristics have some stability over time and situation; and, while modifiable by setting influences, they are not primarily situation specific. Thomas, Chess, & Birch talk of temperament as the "how" of behavior, and Bowers (1977) noted recently that

> the way a person performs a common behavior is sometimes quite revealing.... The more idiosyncratically expressive a common behavior is, the less one can attribute its performance solely to the context and/or to role demand; it is precisely the expressive aspects of a person's behavior that often seems most characteristic... and most attributable to a relatively stable personality and behavioral organization" (p. 75).

Study of the role of temperament in the development of personal and social competence of handicapped young children appears a logical and legitimate extension of the earlier work of Thomas, Chess, Birch and their colleagues. The validity of temperament research is supported too by current personality research demonstrating consistencies of personality and providing reasonable and useful measurement models (Block, 1977). Magnusson's (1977) analysis of behavioral consistency in terms of absolute consistency, relative consistency, and coherence seems especially promising for temperament work (see Magnusson & Endler, 1977).

Several questions derived from the research reviewed here deserve consideration. Can we reliably assess temperament of preschool children taking into account effects of setting, age, culture, and disability? Are there temperamental variations which characterize or are associated with particular handicapping conditions? Do individual differences in temperament affect a child's progress and adjustment in an intervention program by influencing teachers' expectations and attributions, peer interactions and relationships, or the nature of the intervention experience? While data in response to these questions will not settle the trait-setting issue, such data may add substantially to intervention planning and implementation for individual children.*

FOOTNOTES

*Preparation of this chapter was supported in part by Project REACH, under Contract # 300-77-0306 between the University of California and the Bureau for the Education of the Handicapped.

†This chapter contains excerpts from *Temperament and Behavior Disorders in Children* by Alexander Thomas et al., copyright © 1968 by New York University. Published by New York University Press. Reprinted with permission.

‡This chapter contains quotes from pages 21 and 22 of *Temperament and Development* by Alexander Thomas and Stella Chase, copyright © 1977, published by Brunner/Mazel Publishing Company, Inc. Reprinted with permission.

[1] Renewed interest in temperament in the first two years of life is reflected in topics discussed at the International Conference on Infant Studies (1978) and the Louisville Conference on Temperament

(1978). While based mostly on unpublished or inprogress data, common problems considered included measurement, instrumentation, validity, and stability.

REFERENCES

Baron, J. (1972) "Temperament profile of children with Down's Syndrome." *Developmental Medicine and Child Neurology* 14: 640-645.

Bayley, N., & Schaefer, E. (1964) "Correlations of maternal and child behaviors with the development of mental abilities." *Monographs of the Society for Research in Child Development* 29 (6): 97.

Bell, R.Q. (1968) "A reinterpretation of the direction of effects in studies of socialization." *Psychological Review* 75 (2): 81-95.

——— (1971) "Stimulus control of parent or caretaker behavior by offspring." *Developmental Psychology* 4: 63-72.

——— (1974) "Contributions of human infants to caregiving and social interaction." In M. Lewis and L. Rosenblum (eds.), *The effect of the infant on its caregiver.* New York: Wiley.

Bem, D.J., & Allen, A. (1974) "On predicting some people some of the time." *Psychological Review* 81: 506-520.

Birch, H.G., Thomas, A., & Chess, S. (1964) "Behavioral development in brain-damaged children." *Archives of General Psychiatry* 11: 596.

Birns, B., Barten, S., & Bridger, W.H. (1969) "Individual differences in temperamental characteristics of infants." *Transactions of the New York Academy of Science* 31 (8): 1071-1082.

Block, J. (1977) "Advancing the psychology of personality: Paradigmatic shift or improving the quality of research." In D. Magnusson and N. Endler (eds.), *Personality at the crossroads: current issues in interactional psychology,* Hillsdale, N.J.: Erlbaum.

Bowers, K.S. (1977) "There's more to Iago than meets the eye: A clinical account of personal consistency." In D. Magnusson & N. Endler (eds.), *Personality at the crossroads: Current issues in interactional psychology,* Hillsdale, N.H.: Erlbaum.

Brazelton, T.B., Koslowski, B., & Main, M. (1974) "The origins of reciprocity; the early mother-infant interaction." In M. Lewis & L. Rosenblum (eds.), *The effect of the infant on its caregiver,* New York: Wiley.

Buss, A.H., & Plomin, R. (1975) *A temperament theory of personality development,* New York: Wiley.

Cameron, J. (1977) "Parental treatment, children's temperament, and the risk of childhood behavioral problems: relationships between parental characteristics and changes in children's temperament over time." *American Journal of Orthopsychiatry* 47 (4): 568-576.

Carey, W.B., (1970) "A simplified method for measuring infant temperament." *Journal of Pediatrics* 77 (2): 188-194.

———, Fox, M., & McDevitt, S. (1977) "Temperament as a factor in early school adjustment." *Pediatrics* 60: 621-624.

———, & McDevitt, S. C. (1978) "A revision of the Infant Temperament Questionnaire." *Pediatrics* 61:735.

Chess, S. (1974) "The influence of defect on development in children with cogenital rubella." *Merrill-Palmer Quarterly* 201: 255-274.

——— (1978) "Temperament and the handicapped child." Paper presented at UCLA (January).

———, & Hassibi, M. (1970) "Behavior deviations in mentally retarded children." *American Academy of Child Psychiatry* 9: 282-297.

———, & Korn, S. (1970) "Temperament and behavior disorders in mentally retarded children." *Archives of General Psychiatry* 23: 122-130.

———, Korn, & Fernandez, P. (1971) *Psychiatric disorders of children with congenital rubella.* New York: Brunner/Mazel.

———, Thomas, A., & Cameron, M. (1976) "Temperament: Its significance for early schooling." *New York University Education Quarterly* 7 (3): 24-29.

Claridge, G., Canter, S., & Hume, W. (1973) *Personality differences and biological variations; a study of twins.* Elmsford, N.Y.: Pergamon Press.

Emmerich, W. (1968) "Personality development and concepts of structure." *Child Development* 23: 671-690.

Escalona, S. (1972) "The differential impact of environmental conidtions as a function of different reaction patterns in infancy." In J. Westman (ed.), *Individual differences in children.* New York: Wiley.

———, & Heider, G.M. (1959) *Prediction and outcome.* New York: Basic Books.

Etzel, B., & Gewirtz, J. (1967) "Experimental modification of caretaker- maintained high-rate operant crying in a 6- and a 20-week old infant: Extinction of crying with reinforcement of eye contact and smiling." *Journal of Experimental Child Psychology* 5: 303-317.

Eysenck, H. (1967) *The biological basis of personality.* Springfield, Ill.: Charles C Thomas.

Fish, B. (1959) "Longitudinal observations of biological deviations in a schizophrenic infant." *American Journal of Psychiatry* 116 (1): 25-31.

———, & Alpert, M. (1963) "Patterns of neurological development in infants born to schizophrenic mothers." *Recent advances in biological psychiatry.* Vol. 5. New York: Plenum Press.

———, Wile, R., Shapiro, T., & Halpern, F. (1966) "The prediction of schizophrenia in infancy: A ten-year follow-up report of predictions made at one month of age." In *Psychopathology of Schizophrenia.* New York: Grune & Stratton.

Garside, R.F., Birch, H., Scott, D., Chambers, S., Kolvin, E., Tweddle, E., & Barber, L.M. (1975) "Dimensions of temperament in infant school children." *Journal of Child Psychology and Psychiatry and Applied Disciplines* 16: 219-231.

Gil, D.G. (1970) *Violence against children,* Cambridge, Mass.: Harvard University Press.

Gorden, E.M., & Thomas, A. (1967) "Children's behavioral style and the teacher's appraisal of their intelligence." *Journal of School Psychology* 5 (4): 292-300.

Gottesman, I.I. (1960) "The psychogenetics of personality." Unpublished doctoral dissertation, University of Minnesota.

Graham, P., Rutter, M., & George, S. (1973) "Temperamental characteristics as predictors of behavior disorders in children." *American Journal of Orthopsychiatry* 43 (3): 328-339.

Hall, R.J., & Keogh, B.K. (1978) "Qualitative characteristics of educationally high-risk children." *Learning Disabilities Quarterly* 1 (2): 62-68.

Heider, G.M. (1966) "Vulnerability in infants and young children: A pilot study." *Genetic Psychology Monographs* 73: 1-216.

Hertzig, M.E. (1974) "Neurologic findings in prematurely born children at school age." In D. Ricks, A. Thomas, and M. Roff (eds.), *Life history research in psychopathology,* Vol, III. Minneapolis: University of Minnesota.

———, Birch, H., Thomas, A., & Mendez, O. (1968) "Class and ethnic differences in the responsiveness of preschool children to cognitive demands." *Monograph of the Society for Research in Child Development* 33 (1): 1-69.

Jones, E.E., & Nisbett, R.E. (1972) "The actor and the observer: Divergent perceptions of the causes of behavior." In Jones et al. (eds.), *Attribution: Perceiving the causes of behavior,* New York: General Learning Press.

Kagan, J., & Moss, H. (1962) *Birth to maturity, a study in psychological development.* New York: Wiley.

Klein, H.A. (1977) "Early childhood group care: Predicting adjustment from individual temperament." Paper presented at Wright State University.

Keogh, B., Hall, R., & Becker, L. (1974) "Early identification of exceptional children for educational programming." Technical report, UCLA.

———, Pullis, M., Cadwell, J., Burstein, N. (1978) "Studies of temperament in young children: Measurement considerations." Project REACH paper, UCLA.

Korner, A.F. (1971) "Individual differences at birth: Implications for early experience and later development." *American Journal of Orthopsychiatry* 41: 608-619.

Lambert, N.M., & Windmiller, M. (1977) "An exploratory study of temperament traits in a population of children at risk." *Journal of Special Education* 11 (1): 37-47.

Lavelle, N.H. (1977) "Parents' expectations and causal attributions." Doctoral dissertation, UCLA.

Levy, D.M. (1953) "The early development of independent and oppositional behavior." In *Midcentury Psychiatry*, Springfield, Ill.: Charles C Thomas.

Lewis, J.L. (1977) "The relation of individual temperament to initial social behavior. In R.D. Smart and M.S. Smart (eds.), *Readings in child development and relationships*, 2nd edition, New York: Macmillan.

Macfarlane, J.W., Allen, L., & Honzig, M. (1954) *A developmental study of the behavior problems of normal children between twenty-one months and fourteen years*. Berkeley: University of California Press.

Magnusson, D., & Endler, N. (1977) "Interactional psychology: Present status and future prospects." In D. Magnusson and N. Endler (eds.), *Personality at the crossroads: Current issues in interactional psychology*, Hillsdale, N.J.: Erlbaum.

McDevitt, S.C. (1976) "A longitudinal assessment of continuity and stability in temperamental characteristics from infancy to early childhood." Doctoral dissertation, Temple University.

McDevitt, S.C., & A.A. Carey, W. B. (1975) Behavioral Style Questionnaire. Philadelphia.

Mischel, W. (1969) "Continuity and changes in personality." *American Psychologist* 24: 1012-1018. 1018.

——— (1977) "The interaction of person and situation." In D. Magnusson and N. Endler (eds.), *Personality at crossroads: Current issues in interactional psychology*, Hillsdale, N.J.: Erlbaum.

Moss, H.A. (1967) "Sex, age, and state as determinants of mother-infant interaction." *Merrill-Palmer Quarterly* 13: 19-36.

Murphy, L.B., & Moriarity, A.F. (1976) *Vulnerability, coping, and growth*, New Haven: Yale University Press.

Palmer, D.J. (1977) "An attributional investigation of teachers' instructional prescriptions." Doctoral dissertation, UCLA.

Pullis, M. (1979) "The influence of temperament information on teachers' instructional decisions." (Doctoral dissertation, UCLA.

Rheingold, H.L. (1969) "Maintaining the positive behavior of infants by increased stimulation." *Developmental Psychology* 43: 520-527.

Rutter, M., Tizard, J., & Whitmore, K. (1970) *Education, health, and behavior—psychological and medical study of childhood development*, New York: Wiley.

Sameroff, A. (1975) "Early influences on development: Fact or fancy?" *Merrill-Palmer Quarterly* 20: 275-301.

———, & Chandler, M. (1975) "Reproductive risk and the continuum of care-taking causality." In F. Horowitz (ed.), *Review of Child Development Research*, Vol. 4. Chicago: University of Chicago Press.

Seegars, J.E. (1977) "Identification and intervention in child personality temperament." Wofford College, Spartenbring, S.C.

——— (1978) Personal communication.

Schalling, D. (1977) "The trait-situation interaction and the physiological correlates of behavior." In D. Magnusson and N. Endler (eds.), *Personality at the crossroads: Current issues in interactional psychology*, Hillsdale, N.H.: Erlbaum.

Sheldon, W.H. (1942) *The varieties of temperament: a psychology of constitutional differences*, New York: Harper.

Shirley, M. (1933) *The first two years; a study of twenty-five babies*, Minneapolis: University of Minnesota Press.

Sontag, L.W., Baker, C.T., & Nelson, V.L. (1958) "Mental growth and personality development: a longitudinal study" *Monograph of the Society for Research in Child Development*, 23: 2.

Stern, D.N. (1974) "Mother and infant at play: the dyadic interaction involving facial, vocal, and gaze behaviors." In M. Lewis and L. Rosenblum (eds.), *The effect of the infant on its caregiver*. New York: Wiley.

Thomas, A., & Chess, S. (1975) "A longitudinal study of three brain damaged children." *Archives of General Psychiatry* 32: 457–465.

———, & ——— (1977) *Temperament and development,* New York: Brunner/ Mazel.

———, ———, & Birch, H. (1968) *Temperament and behavior disorders in children,* New York: New York University Press.

———, ———, ———, Hertzig, M., & Korn, S. (1963) *Behavioral individuality in early childhood.* New York: New York University Press.

———, ———, Sillen, J., & Mendez, O. (1974) "Cross-cultural study of behavior in children with special vulnerabilities to stress." *Life History Research in Psychotherapy* 3: 53–67.

Weiner, B., & Kukla, A. (1970) "An attributional analysis of achievement motivation." *Journal of Personality and Social Psychology* 15 (1): 1–7.

Werner, E., Bierman, J., & French, F. (1971) *The children of Kauii—a longitudinal study from the prenatal period to age ten,* Honolulu: University of Hawaii.

Wilson, C., & Lewis, M. (1974) "Temperament: A developmental study in stability and change during the first four years of life." Unpublished research bulletin, Educational Testing Service, Princeton, N.J.

Yarrow, J. (1963) "Research in dimensions of early maternal care." *Merrill-Palmer Quarterly* 9: 101–114.

Overview

Barbara K. Keogh, UNIVERSITY OF CALIFORNIA, LOS ANGELES

The scope and richness of content provided by the authors in this volume make a neat and succinct summary or synthesis impossible. Exceptional children and Special Education have been approached from a variety of perspectives, and powerful theoretical constructs have been brought to bear on the particular problems of the education of handicapped children. It is not feasible to review, even to identify, all of the insightful and important observations contained in the preceeding chapters. Yet, after a number of careful readings and after considerable contemplation, four major generalizations stand out. These are worthy of attention, as there is substantial agreement among authors as to their importance.

First, it is clear that the historical and traditional global approach to the conceptualization of atypical development is no longer tenable. To describe children as having cognitive deficits, attentional problems, or emotional or behavioral disturbance does not do justice to the refined constructs and concepts which may be applied to understanding atypical development. As noted by Hobbs (1975), labeling and categorization may serve an important role in identifying problems, may provide a focus for funding, and may serve to marshal support. Broad band global descriptions do not, however, provide direction for appropriate and powerful interventions, nor do such global constructs lead to insightful research. Consider, as example, the many component functions discussed under the rubrics of memory or cognition, or the various attentional or motivational processes delineated by contributors to this volume. Whether from clinical or experimental backgrounds, authors have applied differentiated analyses to Special Education content, and in so doing have identified useful and specific components for special educators to pursue in research and practice. The move from global to differentiated approaches, and the need to develop interventions and educational programs directed at component functions, are clearly implied.

A second and closely related generalization from the content of this volume is that special educators must focus on the development and enhancement of the processing strategies a child uses in interacting with his world. Whether in cognitive, motivational, or affective domains, authors were concerned with the functional aspects of children's performace and behavior, particularly with their integrative or organizing strategies. Individual differences on a variety of dimensions were discussed in terms of the nature and utilization of processing strategies, rather than in terms of presumed deficits or defects. Markedly different perspectives had in common an emphasis upon interactive strategies. Recognition of the importance of a processing approach, taken together with the generalization as to the need for more differentiated analyses of ability domains, argues for changes in both assessment and remediation practices. The practical questions of "can" and "do" become paramount, as special education interventions may in large part be a process of helping an exceptional child in the appropriate utilization of his strategic repertoire.

Third, authors were almost unanimous in stressing the importance of contextual influences on children's behavior. Variability related to cross-cultural, laboratory-natural environment, and within task characteristics were all noted as possible influences on the behavior and performance of exceptional children. Special educators regularly give lip service to this generalization, yet often overlook it when making decisions about individual children in school settings. One needs only to review the history of psychological testing to make the point. We have for many years focused our diagnostic procedures on child characteristics to the exclusion of situational or setting variables; we have interpreted a given child's behavior or performance within a normative frame of reference presumed to be charteristic of all age-similar children. Our research is characterized by artificial tasks administered within a laboratory or test setting which is different from the child's "real world." The results all too often have been inaccurate or at least incomplete information and inefficient practices. This is not to question the importance of experimental research in controlled settings. It does argue, however, for consideration of a broad range of influences in drawing generalizations about the effects of handicap on children's abilities and competence.

Finally, although this volume contains chapters which synthesize theory and evidence, it is clear that the spirit of William James prevails. His writings of almost a century ago have obviously influenced many authors in this volume, a number of them making explicit reference to his work. While we might interpret the references to James to suggest that the state of the art has not advanced to any significant degree, a more likely view and certainly a more generous one is that we are still in the process of recognizing his genius. It may be appropriate, therefore, to end Volume 1 in this series with a brief quote from James, one which has a particular message for special educators.

> Most people live, whether physically, intellectually, or morally, in a very restricted circle of their potential being. They make use of a very small portion of their soul's resources in general, much like a man who, out of his whole bodily organism, should get into a habit of using and moving only his little finger. Great emergencies and crises show us how much greater our vital resources are than we had supposed (James, 1906).

REFERENCES

Hobbs, N. (1975) *Issues in the classification of children,* Vol. 2. San Francisco: Jossey-Bass.

James, W. (1906) *The letters of William James.* In R. C. LeClaire (ed.) The letters of William James and Theodore Flournay. Madison, Wisconsin. University of Wisconsin Press, 1966.

Author Index

Italic numbers represent text pages on which authors are quoted.

Abate, F., 119
Abramson, L.Y., 202
Achenbach, J.M., 209
Ackerman, P.T., 104, 162
Adams, J., 165
Alabiso, F., 104
Allen, A., *271*
Allen L., 258
Alpert, M., 254
Alpert, R., 218
Alwitt, L.F., 162
Amabile, T.M., 216
Anderson, R.P., 113, 165
Andrews, G.R., 204
Andrews, J.M., 161
Appelle, S., 30
Arkes, H.R., 216
Atkinson, B.R., 161-162
Atkinson, J.W., 184, *185-189*, 212-213, 217
Atkinson, R.C., 75
Attneave, F., 17
Atwood, G., 32

Baker, C.T., 258-259
Baldwin, A.L., 41

Ball, D.W., 145, 146-149, 151, 153-154
Balla, D.A., 146
Bandura, A., 196
Bannatyne, A., 210
Barber, L.M., 265-266
Barkley, R.A., 114, 122, 164-165
Baron, J., 255
Barrett, R., 211-212
Bartel, N.R., 210
Barten, S., *254-255*
Bartlett, F.C., 72
Battle E.S., 192, 198
Baumeister, A.A., 119
Bayley, N., 253
Beach, D.R., 87
Beck, L.H., 159
Becker, L., 269
Becker, S.S., 169
Bee, H.L., 23
Beez, W.V., 211-212
Bell, R.Q., 241
Belmont, J.M., 76-80
Bem, D.J., 214, *271*
Benson, J.S., 203
Bentzen, F. A., 167

AUTHOR INDEX

Berglas, S., 203
Berkson, G., 131
Bialer, I., 224
Bierman, J., 257-258
Birch, D., 189
Birch, H., 241, *243-248,* 261, 265-266
Birns, B., *254-255*
Bisanz, G.L., 74
Bisanz, J.H., 71
Block, J., 270, 272
Boggiano, A.K., 216
Bower, A.A., 118
Bowers, K.S., 270, *272*
Boyle, Patricia R., 116, 117, 122
Braine, L.G., 15
Bransome, E.D., Jr., 159
Brazelton, T.B., 241
Brehm, J.W., *201*
Bremer, D.A., 165
Bridgeman, B., 212
Bridger, W.H., *254-255*
Broadbent, D.E., 107, 143
Bromley, D.B., 223
Brooks, L.R., 31-32, 39
Brophy, J.E., 212
Brown, A.L., 76, *79,* 80, 134, 156, 157
Browning, R.M., 162, 166
Bryan, T.S., 126, 127
Bugental, D.B., 173
Burstein, N., 248
Buss, A.H., *242, 248-252*
Butterfield, E.C., 76-80, 134, 146

Cadwell, J., 248
Cahill, C.W., 209
Calder, B.J., 215
Cameron, J., 263-264, 265
Camp, B.W., 125, 130
Campbell, D.T., 84
Campbell, S.B., 164
Campione, J.C., *79,* 80, 156

Canter, A., 165
Canter, S., 250
Capps, C., 89, 90
Carey, W.B., 248, 266-267
Chaikin, A.L., 211
Chalfant, J.C., 91
Chambers, S., 265-266
Chandler, M., 246
Cheatam, D., 113
Chess, S., *240,* 241, *243-248,* 255, *261-262,* 265
Chi, M.T.H., 89
Chinsky, J.M., 87
Church, J., 48
Claridge, G., 250
Clark, E.V., 71-72
Clark, R.A., 185
Clements, S.D., 104, 158, 162
Cofer, C.N., 56
Cohen, L.B., *61*
Cohen, N.J., 108, 119
Cole, M., *67*
Condry, J., *44-45*
Cook, R.E., 207
Cooper, J., 210
Cooper, L.A., 21
Cosgrove, J.M., 19
Craik, F.I.M., 11-12
Crandall, V.C., 171, 192, 195, 197, 198, 207
Cruickshank, W.M., 85, 167

Dalfen, S., 211-212
Danner, F.W., 89
Davids, A., 161
Davidson, K.S., 218-219
Davis, K.E., 193
Dawson, M.M., 153-154
Debus, R.L., 204
de Charms, R., 196, *205-206*
Deci, E.L., 214, 216
Deikel, S.M., 150
DeJong, W., 216

Author Index

Dempster, F.N., 91
Denckla, M., 89
Derlega, V.J., 211
Devine, V.T., 125
Diener, C.I., 202
Diggory, J., 206
Dintzer, L., 202
Dittes, J.E., 208
Doehring, D.G., 83
Donlon, G., 161, 171
Doris, J., 220
Douglas, V.I., 108, 111, 112–113, 114, 119, 130, 159, 164, 172
Doyle, R.B., 113, 165
Dugas, J.L., 81
Dunn, L.M., 210
Dureman, I., 113
Dweck, C.S., 200, 202, 204
Dyk, R.E., 161
Dykman, R.A., 104, 162

Easterbrook, J.A., 28, 41
Eaton, M.O., 219
Egan, D.E., 34
Egeland, B., 225
Eimas, P., 156
Einstein, A., 16, *25*
Elig, T.W., 193
Elkind, D., 161
Ellis, M.J., 122
Ellis, N.R., 76, 129
Emmerich, W., 270, 271
Endler, N., 272
Epstein, S., *47*
Escalona, S., *253–254*, 257
Esrov, L.V., 71
Esveldt, K.C., 125–126
Eysenck, H., 252

Fasnacht, G., 43–44, 217
Faterson, H.F., 161
Faust, M.S., 23, 33
Faust, W.L., 23, 33

Fazio, R.H., 210, 211
Feather, N.T., 197
Feldman, N.S., 226
Fernandez, P., 262
Firestone, P., 119, 130
Fish, B., 254
Fisher, J., 207
Fisher, M.A., 82
Fiske, D.W., 84
Fitzgerald, J.M., 32
Flavell, J.H., 41–42, 59, 62, 63, 64–65, *66, 68, 84,* 87, 148
Fleer, R.E., 81
Forness, S.R., 122, 125–126, 131
Foster, G.G., 210
Fox, M., 266
Frankel, D.G., 109, 110
French, F., 257–258
Friederichs, A.G., 65
Friedman, M.P., 150
Frieze, I.H., 192–195, 193, 194, 206, 207
Fritz, J.J., 157
Frost, N., 82

Galanter, E., 11
Gale, A., 112
Galton, F., 57, 76
Gampel, D.H., 127
Ganzer, V.J., 220
Garside, R.F., *265–266*
Garson, C., 172
Gasstrom, L.L., 211
Gelber, E.R., *61*
George, S., 262–263
Geyer, J.J., 56
Gibson, E.J., 17
Gil, D.G., 242
Gilliard, D.M., 156
Gilmore, G., 226
Goetz, T.E., 200
Golding, S.L., 34
Goldman, S.R., 88–89, 90

Goldman, T., 86-87, 157
Goldstein, D.M., 30-31
Goldstein, M., 194
Gollob, H.F., 208
Good, T.L., 212
Goodenough, D.R., 161
Gordon, E.M., 264-265
Gottesman, I.I., 259
Gottlieb, J., 127, 211
Gough, P.B., 56-57
Graham, E.N., 125
Graham, P., 262-263
Green, C., 209
Green, J.G., 34
Greenberg, L.M., 123
Greene, D., 213, 216
Greenfield, D.B., 82
Guskin, S.L., 212

Haber, R.M., 218
Hagen, J.W., 63, 70, 87, 143-144, 151-152, 159
Halcomb, C.G., 113, 165
Hale, G.A., 144, 156, 159
Hall, J.W., 71
Hall, R., 269
Hallahan, D.P., 85, 131, 142, 146-148, 153-154, 156, 166
Hallschmid, C., 215
Halperin, M.S., 224
Halpern, F., 254
Hamill, D.D., 210
Hanusa, B.H., 202, 207
Harding, C., 89
Harper, C.B.J., 125
Harris, G.J., 81
Harrison, R.H., 127
Harter, S., 44, 221, 225
Hawkins, C.J., 57
Hayden, B.S., 165
Hayden, T., 211
Heckhausen, H., 190, 207, 224
Heider, F., 193

Heider, G.M., 254, 255-257
Henker, B., 173
Hess, V.L., 109, 110
Hewett, F.M., 131
Hibscher, J., 202
Hill, K.T., 219, 220-221
Hiroto, D.S., 200
Hobbs, N., 32-33, *35*
Honzig, M., 258
Horner, M.S., 189
Horowitz, M.J., 169
House, B.J., 82, 145
Hoving, K.L., 62
Hoyt, J.D., 65
Hudgins, B.B., 124
Huelsman, C.B., 58, 159
Hume, W., 250
Humphrey, M., 115-116, 134
Hunt, E., 82
Hunt, J.McV., 44
Huntsman, N.J., 145

Ingram, A.L., 89
Inhelder, B., *23-24,* 27, 36, 68-69, 222

Jackson, P.W., 124
Jacob, R.G., 121-122
Jacobson, L., 210, 212
James, W., *105, 133*
Jenkins, J.J., *10,* 28, 92
Johnson, J.T., Jr., 118
Jones, E.E., 193, 203, 271
Jongeward, R.H., 70, 87

Kagan, J., 259
Kahneman, D., 102, 109
Kail, R.V., 70-71, 87, 89, 90
Karniol, R., 216
Karp, S.A., 161
Kastner, S.B., 86-87
Katkovsky, W., 192

Author Index

Kauffman, J.M., 131, 145, 146-149, 151
Kausler, D.J., 154
Kausler, P.H., 220
Kellas, G., 81, 119
Kelley, H.H., 193, 214
Kelly, G.A., 27, 44, *45*
Kennelly, K.J., 203
Keogh, B.K., 28, 104, 161, 171, 209, 248, 269
Keogh, J.F., 28
Kephart, N.C., 36
Kifer, E., 210
Kimble, G.A., *29*
Kirchner, G.L., 164
Kleiman, G., 115-116, 134
Klein, H.A., 267
Klosson, E., 226
Koch, S., 217
Koegel, R., 154-155
Koenig, K.P., 220
Kohler, W., *14*
Kolers, P.A., *13*, 15, 16, *17-18*
Kolvin, E., 265-266
Konick, D.S., 62
Korb, R.J., 132
Korn, S., 255, 262
Korner, A.F., 253
Koslowski, B., 241
Krauss, R., *18-19*
Kreutzer, M.A., 65-66
Krupski, A., 116, 117, 118, 127, 131-132
Kukla, A., 190, 192-195, 197, 265
Kun, A., 194, 226

LaBerge, D., 57, 90
LaFever, D.K., 71
Lambert, N.M., 268
Larimore, D.L., 210
Larson, M., 161
Lasky, E.Z., 163
Laughlin, P.R., 153-154

Lavelle, N.H., 265
Lee, D.Y., 215
Leeper, R.W., *45*
Lehtinen, L.E., *158,* 167, 170
Leonard, C., 65-66
Leontiev, A.N., 106, 134
Lepper, M.R., 213, 216
Lerman, D., 193-194
Levine, F.M., 43-44
Levine, F.W., 217
Levine, L.E., 70-71
Levy, V.M., 65
Lewin, K., 6, 186
Lewis, J., 82, 267-268
Lewis, M., *259-260*
Liberty, C., 63
Liebert, R.M., 218, 220
Lightall, F.F., 218-219
Lindauer, B.K., 72, *73-74*
Little, B.C., 118, 119
Livesley, W.J., 223
Lockhart, R.S., 11-12
Lovaas, O.I., *154-155*
Lowell, E.L., 185
Lunneborg, C., 82
Luria, A.R., 1-6, 134
Lynn, R., 112
Lysy, A., 189

McCall, R.B., 12
McClelland, D.C., 185
Maccoby, E.E., 23, 143
McDevitt, S.C., 248, *260-261,* 266
MacFarlane, J.W., 258
McGhee, P.E., 12, 171
McGuire, W.J., 208
McHugh, M., 207
Mackworth, J.F., 103, 107, 111
McMahan, I.D., 194
MacMillan, D.L., 209
Maehr, M.L., 189, 212, 215, 217, 226
Magnusson, D., 272
Mahoney, M.J., 168, 169

AUTHOR INDEX

Main, M., 241
Margolis, J.A., 104, 111-112, 115
Marshall, C.V., 90
Marton, P., 172
Mason, E.J., 210
Means, R.S., 212
Meichenbaum, D., 172
Meldman, M.J., 102, *104*
Meyer, W., 207
Meyers, C.E., 211
Michaels, E.J., 188, 197
Miller, G.A., 11
Miller, L.K., 144
Minde, K.K., 164
Mirsky, A.F., 159
Mischel, W., 132-133, 211, 271
Mitchell, A., 113
Mondani, M.S., 160
Moray, N., 103, 104
Morgenstern, G., 111, 112-113, 114, 159, 164
Moriarity, A.F., 257
Morin, R.E., 62
Morris, L.W., 218, 220
Moskowitz, M.L., 169
Moss, H.A., 253, 259
Moulton, R.W., 197
Moynahan, E.D., 66
Mulcahy, R.F., 113
Murphy, L.B., 257
Murray, H.A., 185

Nakamura, C.Y., 171, 208
Naus, M.J., 63
Neisser, U., 103
Nelson, C.M., 125-126
Nelson, K.E., 61
Nelson, V.L., 258-259
Nicholls, C.J., 159
Nicholls, J.G., 207, 223, 225, 226
Nierenberg, R., 194
Nisbett, R. E., 204, 213, 271
Nober, E.H., 163
Nober, L.W., 163

Noland, E.C., 112
North-Jones, M., 164
Nottelmann, E.D., 220

Odom, R.D., 46
O'Leary, K.D., 121-122
Olson, D.R., 23, 31
Ornstein, P.A., 63
Over, J., 31
Over, R., 31

Palmer, D.J., 265
Palshammar, A., 113
Panciera, L., 202
Paola, E.G., 218
Paris, S.G., 72, *73-74*
Parke, R.D., 208
Parry, P., 172
Parsons, J.E., 206, 207, 226
Patterson, C.J., 19
Pelham, W.E., 149
Pellegrino, J.W., 71
Perfetti, C.A., 88-89, 90
Perkins, D.N., *13, 16, 17-18*
Perlmuter, L.C., *29*
Peter, N.V., 226
Peters, J.E., III, 104, 162
Phillips, F., 89
Piaget, J., 12, *20, 21, 23-24,* 27, 36, 68-69, 222
Pick, A.D., 109, 110
Pittmann, J.S., 216
Plomin, R., *242, 248-252*
Porges, S.W., 118, 132
Portisky, S., 201
Powazek, M., 118
Pribram, K.H., 11
Pullis, M., 248, 265

Quay, H.C., 124, 125-126, 127

Ratzeburg, F.H., 167
Raynor, J.O., 188-189, 197, 198, 212-213

Author Index

Reed, L., 192-195
Reeve, R.E., 153-154
Regan, D.T., 211
Rehm, R., 154-155
Reppucci, N.D., 200, 202
Rest, S., 192-195
Revelle, W., 188, 197
Reynolds, R., 122
Rheingold, H.L., 241
Rholes, W.S., 226
Ribot, T., 105
Rickards, C., 86-87
Ritter, K., 63, 66
Robertson, D.E., 119-120, 130
Rohwer, W.D., 91
Rosenbaum, R.M., 192-195
Rosenblad, C., 121-122
Rosenthal, R., 119, 210, 212
Ross, A.O., 146, 149
Ross, M., 214, 216
Rosvold, E.H., 159
Rothbart, M., 211-212
Rotter, J.B., 191-195
Routh, D.K., 121, 130
Rozin, P., 201
Ruble, D.N., 171, 206, 207, 208, 209, 216, 222, 226
Rubovits, P.C., 212
Rudel, R., 89
Ruebush, B.K., 218-219
Rugel, R.P., 58, 113, 119
Russell, D., 193-194
Rutter, M., 258, 262-263

Sabatino, D.A., 161, 165, 210
Salili, F., 226
Sameroff, A., *241*, 246
Samuels, S.J., 57, 90
Sarason, I., 159, 218-219, 220
Sarason, S.B., 144-145, 218-219, 220
Schachter, S., 204
Schaefer, E., 253
Schalling, D., 252

Schlosberg, H., *13*, 31
Schmidt, C.R., 210
Schneider, K., 220
Schreibman, L., *154-155*
Schroeder, C.S., 121, 130
Schuldt, W.J., 112
Scott, D., 265-266
Scribner, S., 67
Seegars, J.E., 269
Seligman, M.E.P., 42, 200, 201, 202-203
Senf, G.M., 83, 84
Seunath, O.H.M., 161-162
Severance, L.J., 211
Shaklee, H., 226
Shantz, C.N., 223
Shapiro, T., 254
Shaw, R.L., 171
Sheldon, W.H., 252
Shepard, R.N., 21
Shiffrin, R.M., 75
Shirley, M., 253
Shulz, R., 202
Shusterman, L., 202
Siegel, A.W., 70-71
Sierad, J., 204
Sigler, E., 211
Silverman, M., 161
Silverman, W.P., 81-82
Simpson, R.L., 125-126
Skinner, B.F., 4, 41
Smith, W.E., 216
Snow, R.E., 212
Snyder, H.N., 194
Soli, S.D., 125
Sonies, B.C., 118, 163-164
Sontag, L.W., 258-259
Sotsky, R., 201
Spence, J.T., 44
Sperber, R.D., 82
Sperling, G., 13-14
Spielman, K.S., 15
Spitz, H.H., 78, 129
Sprague, R.L., 122, 132

Spring, C., 89, 90, 123
Sroufe, L.A., 114, 118, 122, 163-164
Stainback, S.B., 145, 166
Stainback, W.C., 166
Stallings, W.M., 215
Stanovich, K.E., 63
Staw, B.M., 215
Steger, J., 89
Stern, J.A., 164, 165
Sternberg, S., 61-62, 81
Stevenson, H.W., 40, 46, 144
Stone, L.J., 48
Strauss, A., 85, 144-145, *158*, 167, 170
Strauss, E., 211
Stroh, C.M., 107, 111
Swann, W.B., 216
Swanson, H.L., 157
Sykes, D.H., 111, 112-113, 114, 159, 164
Syrnyk, R., 215

Tannhauser, M.T., 167
Tarver, S.G., 142, 147-149, 151
Tate, D.L., 118
Tavormina, J.B., 159
Taweel, S.S., 156
Taylor, J.A., 218
Teasdale, J.D., 202
Thomas, A., *240*, 241, *243-248*, 261, 264-265
Thorndike, R.L., 212
Tizard, J., 258
Tobin, H., 163
Tolman, E.C., 186
Torgeson, J.K., 85-88, 104, 157
Trapp, E.P., 154, 220
Turnure, J.E., 166, 171, 208
Tutko, T.A., 160
Tweddle, E., 265-266

Uhl, N.P., 171
Ullman, D.G., 164-165
Upton, L.R., *73-74*

Valle, V.A., 207
Van Bergen, A., 224
Van Doorninck, W., 161
van Hover, K. I., 118
Vellutino, F., 89
Veroff, J., 224-225
Vlietstra, A.G., *157-158*
Vygotsky, L.S., 106

Wagner, D.A., 67
Waite, R.R., 218-219
Waller, G.T., 90
Walter, G.F., 132
Walters, R.H., 208
Watson, John B., 13, 41
Weiner, B., 190, *192-195*, 204, 206-207, 220, 226, 265
Weiss, G., 164
Wellman, H., 63, 64-65, *66, 68*
Wender, P.H., 118, 119
Werner, C.S., 125-126
Werner, E., 257-258
Werner, H., 59, 85, 144-145
Werry, J.S., 124, 125-126, 127
West, R.F., 151-152
West, W.D., 118, 163-164
Whalen, C.K., 173
White, R.W., 221
Whitmore, K., 258
Wickens, C.D., 116
Wickens, D.D., 14
Wicklund, D.A., 30-31
Wile, R., 254
Wilkins, W.E., 207
Willows, D.M., *150-151*
Wilson, C., *259-260*
Windmiller, M., 268
Wine, J., 220-221
Witkin, A.A., 161
Witt, P.A., 122
Wolf, T.H., 57-58
Wolpe, J., 168, 221
Woodworth, R.S., *13*, 31
Worland, J., 164

Wortman, C.B., *201*, 202
Wright, F.S., 118, 163–164
Wright, J.C., *157–158*

Yando, R., 171, 208–209
Yekell, H.S., 162–163
Yellin, A.M., 123
Yendovitskaya, T.V., 106, 134
Yoshida, R.K., 211

Young, E., 225
Ysseldyke, J.E., 161, 165, 210
Yussen, S.R., 65

Zahn, T.P., 118, 119
Zeaman, D., 82, 145
Zigler, E., 80, 129, 145, 146, 171, 208–209
Zimet, S.G., 125, 130

Subject Index

Ability, change in children's concept of, 222-223
"Accumulative fragmentalism," 27
Achievement Anxiety Test, 218
Achievement avoidance, 203-204
Achievement motivation, optimizing, 183-227 (*see also* "Motivation in achievement context...")
Achievement Motive, The (D. C. McClelland et al.), 185
Achievement of student, effect of teacher behavior on, 212
Affection, 9
Anxiety, 45-48
Apparent movement, perception of, 15-16
Aptitude, theories concerning, 33
Atkinson's model for achievement behavior, 186-187
  extensions of model, 187-189
Attainment, change in children's concept of, 223-224
Attention, establishing, 12
Attention processes, 101-135
  conclusion, 133-135
  interactionist view, 129-133
    child characteristics, 130-133
    task characteristics, 130
  introduction, 101-105
    Behaviorist attack on introspectionist methodology, 102-103
    definitions, 103-105
    and psychopathology, 102
    research, history of, 102-103
  problems, assumptions about, 128-129
    deficit assumption, 128-129
    developmental lag, 128-129
  studies, experimental, in atypical children, 110-128
    classroom observations, 124-128
    distraction, 115-116
    observational research in multiple settings, 120-124
    reaction time, 116-120 (*see also* "Reaction time...")
    vigilance, 111-16 (*see also* "Vigilance...")
  two-dimensional view, 105-110
    orienting responses, 109-110
    short-term, 109-110

Attention processes (cont.)
  sustained, 107–109
  temporal, 106–107
  voluntary/involuntary, 105–106
Attributional retraining, 204–206
Attributional Theory of Achievement Motivation, 192–195
Auditory distractors and learning-disabled children, 162–163

Behavioral Styles Questionnaire, 248, 260
Behaviorist attack on introspectionist methodology, 102–103
Behaviorist position on volitional striving, 40–41
Bender Gestalt test, 161
Binet Intelligence Test, memory test in, 57–58
Birth to Maturity (J. Kagan & H. Moss), 259
Buss and Plomin temperament framework, 248–252 (*see also* "Temperament influences...")

Categorical processing, 22–23
"Ceiling of achievement" theory of aptitude, 33
Cerebrotonic personality, 252
Challenge, change in children's concept of, 224–225
Children's Embedded Figures Test, 164
Classroom observational research, 124–128
Cognitive-behavior modification, 172–173
Cognitive constructing, 1–48
  boundaries, 39–48
    anxiety, 45–48
    information vs. reward, 43–45

intentionality, 40–43 (*see also* "Intentionality...")
summary statement, 48
concept, 9–11
  distinctions between functions, 9–10
  perception, 9–10
  sequential processing model, 10–11
  TOTE (Test-Operate-Test-Exit) process, 11
development, concept of, 2–4
  biological vs. environmental factors, 3–4
  structure, cognitive, 2–3
exceptional children, identifying, 4–6
implications, other, 38–39
  Montessori method, 38
  word recognition, differing methods of, 38
interrelations among processing levels, 31–32
laws and individual differences, 6–9
outcomes, assessment of, 37
processing, Level 1, 11–18
  attention and stimulus change, 12
  cognitive representation, nature of, 15–18
  "distinctive feature" theory of recognition, 17–18
  images, 12–14
  Necker Cube design, 15–16
  perception, constructive nature of, 14–15
  verbal mediation, 13
processing, Level 2, 18–28
  contextual-categorical processing, 22–23
  invention, 27–28
  language, role of, 21
  Level 1 recognition and Level 2 copying, 23–24

Subject Index

mental rotations, 21-22
metacognitions, 19
operations and structures, 24-27
processing, Level 3, 28-31
ear wiggling, 29-30
oblique orientation, 31
processing levels and match, 35-37
processing levels related to teaching methods, 32-35
aptitude, theories about, 33
optimal learning and optimal match, 33-35
Cognitive constructs in theories of achievement orientation, 190-195
antecedents of attributional patterns, 194-195
perception of controls over outcomes, 191-192
locus of control variable, 192-193
"social learning theory" of Rotter, 191
summary and integration, 195-198
Weiner's Attributional Theory of Achievement Motivation, 192-195
Cognitive psychology as spur to attention research, 103
"Cognitive structures," meaning of, 25-26
Conation, 9
Conceptual space, 24
Constitutional factor in temperament, 252
Contextual processing, 22-23
Continuous Performance Test, 111, 114
and distractibility, 159
Critique of Pure Reasoning (I. Kant), 9

Daydreaming as possible explanation of distractibility, 167-168

Death at an Early Age (Kozol), 200
Deficit assumption, 128-129
Determinants of Free Will, The (J. A. Easterbrook), 28
Development, concept of, 2-4 (*see also* "Cognitive constructing")
Developmental lag assumption, 128-129
Devereaux Child Behavior Rating Scale, 126
"Distinctive feature" theory of recognition, 17-18
Distractibility, 158-173
auditory distractor and learning-disabled children, 162-163
educational implications, 171-173
cognitive-behavior modification, 172-173
"Freedom from Distractibility Factor," 159
and hyperactivity, 163-166
proximal-distal dichotomy, hypothesized reasons for, 166-169
daydreaming, 167-168
etiological considerations, 169-171
"internal" distractibility, 167-169
"maturational lag," 170
norepinephrine, role of, 170
obsessional thinking in adults, 168-169
personality variables, 170-171
"thought stopping," 168-169
studies, results of, 160
visual distractors and learning-disabled children, 160-162
Distraction, experimental studies in, with atypical children, 115-116

Ear wiggling, 29-30
EASI (Emotionality, Activity, Sociability, and Impulsivity) Temperament Surveys, 249-250 (*see also* "Temperament influences...")
Ectomorph, 252
Encoding, development of, 70-71
 as "applied semantics," 71-72
 and semantic knowledge, 69-70
Endomorphs, 252
Exceptional children, identification of, 4-6
Extrinsic incentives, achievement orientation and, 212-217
 interest, level of, and positive incentives, 215
 intrinsic motivation, effect of positive incentives on, 213-214
 negative, effect of, 215-216
 performance, effect on, 217
 rewards, effect of, 214
 signifying competence, 216

Failure, change in children's concept of, 223-224
Fels Institute, longitudinal data relevant to study of temperament, 258-259
"Freedom from Distractibility Factor," 159

Grading procedures, altering to reduce test anxiety, 220-221

Hagen Central-Incidental Task, 159, 160, 166
Hawthorne effect, 206
Heart-rate changes and reaction time in handicapped children, 118
Helplessness, research into, 199-206
 with successful individuals, 203-204
Hyperactivity, distractibility and, 163-166

Iconic image, 56
Images, 12-14
 verbal mediation, 13
Incentives, effect of, on intrinsic motivation, 213-214
 negative, effect of, 215-216
Individual differences, recognition of, 6-9
"Inertial tendency" as part of achievement model, 187-188
Infant memory development, 60-61
Intellectual Achievement Responsibility questionnaire, 192
Intentionality, concept of, 40-43
 Behaviorist position, 40-41
 "laziness," 40-41
Interactionist view of attention problems, 129-133 (*see also* "Attention processes")
"Internal" distractibility, 167-169
 daydreaming, 167-168
 "thought stopping," 168-169
International Review of Research on Mental Retardation, 76
Invention, 27-28
Involuntary attention processes, 105-106
Isle of Wight study, 258

Kuhlmann-Anderson IQ Test, 264

Labeling, performance evaluation as function of, 210
 attributional bias, 210-211
Language, role of, in Level 2 processing, 21

Subject Index

Language-specific memory problems, 88-90
"Laziness," concept of, 40-41
Learned helplessness, perceptions of personal control and, 199-200
  with successful individuals, 203-204
Learning disabled children, memory research with, 82-90
  definition, problem of, 83
  historical and conceptual issues, 85
  interpretation, problems of, 83-85
  memory performance and reading skill, 85-90
  linguistic subskills, 88-90
    memory strategies, use of, by poor readers, 86-88
  methodological and conceptual issues, 82-83
  summary, 90
Locus of control concept, Rotter's, 192-193
Longitudinal studies, temperament influences and, 255-261
  Heider's study, 255-257
  miscellaneous, 257-261
  Murphy and Moriarity study, 257
  Prediction and Outcome (S. Escacalona & G. M. Heider), 257
  and interaction with sex roles, 257

Matching Familiar Figures Test, 260
McCarthy Scales of Children's Abilities, 58
Mandler & Sarason Test Anxiety Questionnaire, 186
Memory processes in exceptional children, 55-94
  conclusions and implications, 91-94
    concepts offered as guides, 94

  "working memory," short-term memory as, 93-94
  and differences, individual, 57-59
    McCarthy Scales of Children's Abilities, 58
    psychometric instruments, use of, 58-59
  introduction, 55-57
    processes, different kinds of, 56-57
    and "rote" activities, 56
  knowledge and conceptual development, 68-75
    encoding, development of, 70-71 (see also "Encoding...")
    Piagetian approach, 69
    semantic knowledge and encoding, 69-70
    sentences and stories, recall of, 72-74
  with learning-disabled children, 82-90
    definition, problem of, 83
    historical and conceptual issues, 85
    interpretation, problems of, 83-85
    memory performance and reading skill, 85-90 (see also "Learning disabled...")
    methodological and conceptual issues, 82-83
    summary, 90
  mentally retarded, research with, 75-82
    processing capacity, deficiencies in, 80-82
    stimulus trace theory, 76
    strategies, use of, 77-78
    summary, 82
    training to use strategies, 78-80
  principles of development, 59-68

Memory processes in exceptional children (cont.)
  memory search, 61-62
    mnemonic strategies, changes in use of, 62-68 (*see also* "Mnemonic strategies...")
    processes, basic, 60
    recognition memory, 60-61
  structural and control features, 75
Menninger Clinic, studies of vulnerability, 255
Mental rotations, 21-22
Mesomorphs, 252
Metacognitions, 19
Metamemory, 63-66 (*see also* "Mnemonic strategies...")
Methylphenidate treatment, 122-123
Mnemonic strategies, developmental changes in use of, 62-68
  metamemory, 63-66
  rehearsal skills, 62-63
    serial position recall task, 63
  schooling, effect of, 67-68
Montessori method of teaching, 38
Motivation in achievement context, optimizing, 183-227
  and achievement behavior, relationship between, 184
  developmental perspective, 221-226
    ability, change in children's concept of, 222-223
    challenge, concept of, 224-225
    relating concepts, changes in, 225-226
    success and failure, changes in concept of, 223-224
  "overmotivation," issue of, 184
  research, areas of, 198-221
    achievement avoidance, 203-204
    attributional tendencies, modifying, 204-206

extrinsic incentives, 212-217 (*see also* "Extrinsic incentives...")
learned helplessness, 199-206
noncontingent negative outcomes, effects of, 200-202
noncontingent positive outcomes, effect of, 202-204
sex differences in expectancies, 207
success, expectations of, 206-209 (*see also* "Success...")
teacher expectancy, 209-212 (*see also* "Teacher expectancy...")
test anxiety, 218-221 (*see also* "Test anxiety")
summary, 226-227
theories, 184-198
  Atkinson's model, 186-187
  "challenge" of model extension, 190
  extensions of Atkinson's model, 187-189
  extrinsic motivations, 187
  future orientation, 188-189
  based on individual cognitions, 190-195 (*see also* "Cognitive constructs...")
  and individual motivational states, 185
  inertial tendencies, 187-188
  summary and integration, 195-198
Motives in Fantasy, Action and Society (J. W. Atkinson), 185

Necker Cube design, 15-16
New York Longitudinal Study, 243
Norepinephrine, role of, 170

Subject Index

Oblique orientation, 31
Obsessional thinking in adults, 168–169
Orienting responses, 109–110
Overselectivity of attention, 154–156
  in autistic children, 154–155
  as developmental phenomenon, 155–156

Parent-child interactions, 240–242 (see also "Temperament influences...")
Parental Attitude Research Instrument, 245
Perception, 9–10
  of apparent movement, 15–16
  constructive nature of, 14–15
Perceptual space, 23–24
Performance, effect of extrinsic incentives on, 217
Personality variables, attention deficits and, 170–171
Piagetian approach to memory, 69
Prediction and Outcome (S. Escalona and G. Heider), 257
Preparatory interval (PI) of reaction time, 116
Processing, cognitive, 11–32 (see also "Cognitive constructing")
Psychometric instruments, use of, in memory measurement, 58–59
Psychotropic drugs, use of, 122–123

Reaction time, experimental studies in, with atypical children, 116–120
  in handicapped children, 116–120
  and heart-rate changes, 118
  preparatory interval, 116
  skin conductance responses, 118–119
  and stimulant drug treatment, 120

Reaction-time tasks, voluntary sustained attention and, 107–108
Recognition memory, 60–61
Rehearsal skills, 62–63 (see also "Mnemonic strategies...")
Reinforcement, selective attention performance and, 151–153
Retarded, mentally, memory research with, 75–77
  processing capacity, deficiencies in, 80–82
  stimulus trace theory, 76
  strategies, use of, 77–78
  summary, 82
  training to use strategies, 78–80
Rewards, effect of on intrinsic motivation, 213–214
  signifying competence, 216
  interest, level of, 215
Rotating mental image, 21–22

Schooling, effect of, on memory development, 67–68
Science of Learning and the Art of Teaching, The (B. F. Skinner), 4
Selective attention, 141–158
  in deviant children, 144–151
    flexibility of attention, 156
    learning-disabled children, 146–151
    overselectivity of attention, 154–156 (see also "Overselectivity...")
    reinforcement, use of, 151–153
    retarded children, 144–146
    task strategy deficit, evidence for, 156–158
    training of abilities, 151
    verbal rehearsal, use of, 151
    verbal rehearsal and reinforcement compared, 153–154

Selective attention (cont.)
  educational implications, 171-173
  generalizations, 142
  introduction, 141-142
  in normal children, 143-144
Semantic knowledge, relationship of, to encoding, 69-70
Sensory visual trace, 56
Serial position recall task, 63 (*see also* "Mnemonic strategies...")
Sex differences in achievement expectancies, 207
Short-term attention, 109-110
Short-term memory as "working memory," 93-94
Skin conductance responses, reaction time and, 118-119
Slow Learner in the Classroom, The (N. C. Kephart), 36
Social learning theory of J. B. Rotter, 191
Somatotyping, 252
Stimulant drug treatment for vigilance performance, 114
  and reaction time, 120
Stimulus change theory, 12
Stimulus filter theory, 143
Stimulus trace theory, 76
Stroop Color-Word Test, 161, 162
Structure, cognitive, 2-3
Success, expectations of, 206-209
  in retarded children, 209
  sex differences, 207
Success, change in children's concept of, 223-224
Sustained attention, 107-109
  active and passive tasks, 108

Tasks with active/passive demands, 130
Taylor Manifest Anxiety Scale, 218
Teacher behavior, effect of, on student achievement, 212
Teacher expectancy, motivational level and, 209-212
  labeling, performance evaluation as function of, 210
  attributional bias, 210-211
  student achievement, effect of teacher behavior on, 212
  teacher behavior, effect on, 211-212
Temperament influences on development of exceptional children, 239-272
  Buss and Plomin model, 248-252
    criteria, five, 249
    EASI Temperament Surveys, 249-250
  generalization and speculation, 270-272
  individual differences in, 242-243
  introduction, 239-240
    definition, 240
  parent-child interactions, 240-242
  related theory and evidence, 252-261
    infancy studies, 253-255
    longitudinal studies, 255-261 (*see also* "Longitudinal studies...")
  somatotyping, 252
  research with children and risk populations, 261-270
    handicapped and risk, 261-264
    preschool children, 267-268
    school-age children at risk, 268-270
    school-related, 264-267
  Thomas, Chess, and Birch model, 243-248
    Carey questionnaire, 248
    categories, nine, 243-245
    "goodness of fit" model, 246-247

Subject Index

and New York Longitudinal Study (NYLS), 243
Test anxiety, 218-221
　factors mediating test and performance level, 219-220
　negative effects, approaches to modifying, 220-221
　　grading procedures, altering, 220-221
　　time pressure, removing, 221
　and performance, 218-219
Test Anxiety Questionnaire (TAQ), 218
Test Anxiety Scale (TAS), 218-219
Thematic Apperception Test (TAT), 185
Thomas, Chess, and Birch temperament model, 243-248
　(see also "Temperament influences...")
"Thought-stopping" procedures, 168-169
Time pressure of testing, removing to reduce anxiety, 221
TOTE (Test-Operate-Test-Exit) process, 11

Verbal mediation, 13
Verbal rehearsal in learning-disabled children, 147-149
Vigilance, experimental studies:
　with atypical children 111-116
　Continuous Performance Test, 111, 114
　distraction, 115-116
　in handicapped children, 112-114
　in normal achieving children, 111-112
　voluntary sustained attention and, 107-108
Visual distractors, effect of, on learning-disabled children, 160-162
Voluntary attention processes, 105-106
Vulnerability in children, study of, 255-257

Wechsler Intelligence Scale for Children, (WISC), 58
　Revised, 159
Wepman Auditory Discrimination Test, 163
Word recognition, differing methods of, 38
"Working memory," short-term memory as, 93-94

Yerkes-Dodson law of arousal and performance, 184